THEORIZING

SCRIPTURES

Signifying (on) Scriptures

Vincent L. Wimbush, series editor

Advisory Board:

This publication series aims to foster multi-field, multidisciplinary, comparative and sociopolitically engaged thinking, research, and writing about "scriptures"—what they are, why and how they were invented, what we make them do for us, how they are represented, and what effects they have (had) in society and culture. Proposals are invited from scholars of any field, discipline, or area of inquiry. The books published in this series all revolve around issues of interpretation—not of the content-meaning of texts (narrowly defined), but having to do with how *peoples* make "texts" "signify" / "signify on" "scriptures" as vectors for understanding, establishing, communicating, sometimes undermining, sometimes securing their identities, positions, agency, and power in the world.

THEORIZING SCRIPTURES

New Critical Orientations

to a Cultural Phenomenon

EDITED BY

VINCENT L. WIMBUSH

RUTGERS UNIVERSITY PRESS

New Brunswick, New Jersey, and London

Library of Congress Cataloging-in-Publication Data

Theorizing Scriptures : new critical orientations to a cultural phenomenon / edited by
Vincent L. Wimbush.

     p.   cm. — (Signifying (on) Scriptures)
  Includes bibliographical references and index.
  ISBN 978-0-8135-4203-4 (hardcover : alk. paper) — ISBN 978-0-8135-4204-1 (pbk : alk.
paper)
  1. Sacred books—History and criticism.   I. Wimbush, Vincent L.
  BL71.T49   2008
  208'.2—dc22

                                    2007008421

A British Cataloging-in-Publication record for this book is available from the British Library.

Visit our Web site: http://rutgerspress.rutgers.edu

Manufactured in the United States of America

Contents

Part V   Signifying on the Questions

Foreword

CHARLES H. LONG

Alberto Manguel, the distinguished Argentinean translator, editor, and novelist, tells us that as a young man he was asked by Jorge Luis Borges to read to him, the elderly Borges' sight having failed him in old age. He relates Borges' experience of hearing a text read to him rather than reading it for himself. Borges in his blindness was now "reading" the text through hearing and listening. In another part of his book, he relates the familiar story of Augustine's great surprise when on his first visit to Ambrose in Milan he found the holy man "reading silently" (see Alberto Manguel, *A History of Reading* [New York: Penguin, 1996]). Manguel, by introducing us to several "scenes" of reading, throughout various cultures and histories, allows us to rethink several other issues about the books, texts, exchanges, and communications.

In an analogous manner, Vincent Wimbush has invited us through the Institute for Signifying Scriptures (ISS) to undertake a similar investigation and interrogation. He makes it clear who he is and where he has begun—as an African American male scholar of a prestigious text of the Christian tradition, the New Testament. In some cases, in spite of, and, in other cases, because of who he is, he finds it necessary to raise new and different questions regarding that genre of authority that goes by the name of "scripture." He wants to question how and why certain writings became authoritative. To be sure, we already know that some conception of power is involved, but is that power always the same? And from where does that power originate? Underlying the meaning of scripture is writing itself and its authority. As a student of religion, he is sensitive to the fact that F. Max Müller, a great nineteenth-century Sanskritist more or less invented the "Great World Religions" around what he referred to as sacred texts (scriptures)—writings of various social and institutional constellations in various cultures over time.

Scriptures as the normative expression of the "Great World Religions" all but ignored those cultural traditions that did not possess a tradition of writing. It is very clear that the Institute for Signifying Scriptures is not imputing some kind of romantic, unearned prestige to so-called oral cultures. As a matter of fact, the very process of "signifying" undercuts every binary as a valid statement of an authentic human situation. There is, however, the recognition that writing and scriptures have, especially during the modern period, been used to dominate and oppress. All too often those cultures that did not impute to writing a normative prestige were not respectfully read to; more often than not, writing took on the role of command and law or "words were placed in their mouths" involuntarily. Their silence was forced and not predicated on or expressive of silence as a sign of inner comprehension of self, world, and text. The project of Signifying Scriptures seeks to find the styles and modes of authority and power that sustained these peoples as coherent social and cultural bodies and in so doing create a reciprocity between writing and orality.

The essays gathered here were presented at a conference at the institute in Claremont, California. They explore the wide ranges of issues of this kind from several perspectives and orientations. It is clear that the agenda of the institute represents one of the most comprehensive and radical modes of cultural hermeneutics in the academic world today.

Preface

This book contains revised essays that were originally read as papers for the inaugural conference of the Institute for Signifying Scriptures. Convened February 27–28, 2004, at the Claremont Graduate University, the conference was international, in terms of the mix of participants and attendees, and comparative and multidisciplinary, in terms of intellectual focus and orientation. The conference papers were responses to the conference-opening paper that I had written and distributed ahead of time to participants. My paper was intended to serve as springboard for thinking and discussion. Participants were asked to use my paper "to think with"—about "scriptures" in particular, about the aim of the ISS to model a different research and academic-intellectual programmatic orientation to scriptures. They were not charged to respond necessarily and directly to my paper, but to find a place or opening to join and extend the thinking and the conversation.

Conference participants were divided into one of several conceptual-organizing categories that had been identified on the program with basic or fundamental questions and issues to be raised. These categories as questions or issues and the placement of participants as book contributors have been for the most part retained. But for the sake of greater clarity and in response to some suggestions, some categories have been collapsed or slightly renamed. And because of some changes in the focus of their revised papers, a few participants have been shifted from one category to another. My original conference paper has been revised, corrected, and elaborated upon. But the basic orientation—including the challenge to enter into conversation about "scriptures" on the terms suggested by the organizing questions and issues—remains.

This book represents a complex project that has required the assistance and commitment of a number of persons. I express my gratitude to:

The conference participants and essay writers, many of whom continue to be conversation partners who teach me much.

ISS research assistants—John Adams, Melody Cruz, Kenzie Grubitz, Jacqueline Hidalgo, Simon Joseph, Lalruatkima, Velma Love, Wendell Miller, Quynh-hoa Nguyen, Sana Tayyen, Katrina Van Heest, and Fontella White. They have assisted me in every aspect of the project, often suggesting creative and constructive ideas and proposals.

Anonymous readers for Rutgers University Press, for their careful and sensitive reading of the manuscript. I accepted many of their suggestions and proposals. That I did not take up all their suggestions and proposals will be clear to them, but I hope they will know that I took their readings very seriously.

Friends and colleagues who have challenged, encouraged, even emboldened me regarding this book project and the larger project that is the ISS.

Former editor Kristi Long and her successor editor, Adi Hovav, and the staff at Rutgers University Press for commitment to this book (and book series) and the different type of scholarly work that it inaugurates.

A special expression of gratitude to Jacqueline M. Hidalgo, Lalruatkima, and Katrina Van Heest for the disciplined attention and care they gave the project at every stage, especially the final ones.

Lastly, although clearly not all the arguments in this collection of essays are mine, the overall conceptualization and structure of the book and its meaning is my responsibility. For the inspiration for such work I should like to thank my teachers—Eloise Penn, Anibal Bueno, Ida Rousseau Mukenge, Melvin Watson (deceased), Nils Dahl (deceased), George MacRae (deceased), and Dieter Georgi (deceased)—who challenged me to take that second and odd look at everything.

Vincent L. Wimbush
Institute for Signifying Scriptures
Claremont, California

THEORIZING
SCRIPTURES

Introduction

TEXTureS, GESTURES, POWER:
ORIENTATION TO RADICAL EXCAVATION

VINCENT L. WIMBUSH

I aim in this essay to press the case for our reconsideration of a complex phenom-enon—what in freighted, masking English shorthand is often called "scriptures." It is a call for a re-consideration if not rejection of the conventional academic-intellectual-political and socio-religious-political orientations and practices long associated with "scriptures." It is a challenge to take up "scriptures" and with such to engage in a different type of social-cultural-critical-interpretive practice—a fath-oming, an "excavation." This differently oriented interpretive practice has as its focus not the exegesis of texts but the fathoming of human striving and behaviors and orientations, with their fears, aspirations, low points and high marks, as they are represented in relationships to "scriptures."[1] It has to do with excavating the work—and the consequences of such—that we make "scriptures" do for us.

Not merely as a courtesy to the reader, but as a necessary part of my pressing of the case for the excavation of (the phenomenon of) "scriptures" (far beyond but also in relationship to texts), I should like to introduce myself: I am now a mid-career professional working in a small college town located in one of the world's largest and most diverse population centers. I am a male, but further and more poignantly defined by being called (in this era, at any rate) an "African American"/"black" male. I am a teacher-scholar of religion, more particularly, a teacher-scholar of (a particular representation of) "scriptures."[2] The last two listed aspects of my identity—African American male, scholar of the "New Testament" as representation of "scriptures"—are rather highly charged. The latter category has to do with a phenomenon that has over the centuries clearly been *overde*-termined in terms of a type of investigation (exegesis), but oddly and curiously rather *under*-determined in terms of phenomenology, anthropology, and political and psycho-social criticism of origins, ongoing usages, functions, and effects. The former category—"African American/black male"—has been frighteningly *overde*-termined as a particular symbol in U.S. and Western culture, but barely recognized as that in which one can encounter the authentically complex, free, singular (even if flawed) thinking-speaking-acting subject.

The persistent freightedness of my identity reminds me of the black male character Big Jim Todd in the poem "Pondy Woods" written by Tennessee-native-

1

turned–New Critic Robert Penn Warren. Written in the 1940s, the entire poem was constructed around Jim Todd's frantic run through the woods outside a small Southern town, for reasons that on the surface of the letters of the poem remain unclear. As Warren's Jim Todd runs, he is hovered over and tortured by a clacking, talking buzzard. Jim Todd was, shall we say, very well-defined by the talking buzzard as the Western cultural standard bearer—". . . nigger your breed ain't metaphysical . . ."[3] Jim Todd was silent and on the run—the way most of U.S. society, certainly the way Robert Penn Warren's small-town Tennessee of the early twentieth century, assumed or wanted him to be. How is it that the buzzard could speak—using that violent epithet that haunts us even today!—as though it knew Jim Todd? Knew who he was, what he was about? How could the silent Jim Todd in any significant sense be said or be assumed to be known? How was it possible for him to know himself?

How can it be that certain things and peoples are assumed to be so clearly defined and located in the cultural imaginary and discourse, so much talked about, so much gazed upon, engaged, scripted, exegeted, yet remain unknown? The confusion of the two major categories that are pressed into (significant parts of, even if surely not the totality of) my identity can hardly be without relevance to the agenda that I should like to advance in this essay: I think I am beginning to understand more clearly what are my interests and their stakes: I want and need to know how certain things—a collection of texts here, a particular social demographic there—are invented, are made to work, come to be authorized, come to be determined. And being associated with some of those peoples who have been hyper-determined, hyper-textualized, and hyper-exegeted, I seem now to need to *excavate* in directions and to depths that would afford me the opportunity to think critically back upon textualization and the exegetical and come to a point of unweaving the too-tightly woven, un-determining the overdetermined, including authorized and authorizing texts, gestures, institutions, programs, persons, and myself.

I want to answer Warren's cultural-guardian buzzard not so much in belated distant defense of—but *as*—Jim Todd. And I should like to do so by first invoking a contemporary of Warren—African American poet and essayist Sterling Brown. In response to Warren, Brown reportedly retorted many years ago, "Cracker, your breed ain't *exegetical!*" Brown was right to answer Warren's buzzard's claim about Jim Todd's tribe's supposed lack—in this case, regarding the (dark person's) lack of capacity for conceptualization and theorizing. But it seems to me that Brown may have succumbed to what Henry Louis Gates Jr. called the "tragic lure" of some black critics, the "mistake of accepting the empowering language of white critical theory as 'universal' or as our own language, the mistake of confusing the enabling mask of theory with our own black faces."[4]

The arrogance of the buzzard is clear. (Might it be associated with the ways of a senior [white male] member of a Western academic guild?) Actually, the interest of the buzzard is not so much metaphysics but exegesis—*mere* exegesis. The clacking pedantic practice of exegesis is seen in the parsing of parts of texts (the Bible, among other Western canonical texts). But it is no longer enough to answer

Warren's buzzard (and its contemporary counterparts) in the manner of Sterling Brown. Jim Todd's "breed" must today stop running, must now face the buzzard and talk back, but not by trying to prove that we can get metaphysical—the metaphysical alone would merely take us off the ground, that is, in the wrong direction! All "breeds" practice exegesis, but exegesis is not enough for any breed. The path dug by exegesis is neither deep nor wide enough. Exegesis tends to address only that which has been transmitted or received. We need more than this. Nothing short of excavation—of everything experienced—is required. As peoples who have had to learn to negotiate the darkness or the depths, those of us of Jim Todd's tribe must lead the way, even as we must warn that excavation is most demanding and fraught with danger. Taken to a radical level, the work of excavation is, as Foucault warned, irritating, unpleasant, unbearable; it often provokes painful admissions, anxieties, and fears.[5] It requires all the senses, all the emotions, different types of memory, the disciplined creative coordination of mind and body, the engagement of the whole inquiring interpreting self.[6]

I call now for such work—in relationship to "scriptures." Why "scriptures"? First, regarding the term. This English term is not without problems—in intra- and cross-cultural translation and power issues. Just to begin with, it flashes warning signals regarding the continuing privileging of Christian and Jewish traditions. This I readily acknowledge. There is no term for the phenomenon we need to address that is not problematic. But I think the problematics of the term and the phenomenon is an opportunity and a necessary spur for creative excavation. The problematics of the term must no longer be the excuse for us not to venture forward in collaborative cross-cultural conversation and fathoming. Second, in our time, with the intensifications of religion-inflected ideological, civil, and geopolitical wars and their brutalities and genocide, nothing short of an orientation to *radical excavation* of the phenomenon of "scriptures" is now required. We must collect ourselves as a larger, more complexly constituted group and orient ourselves so as to begin (in some cases, perhaps, begin *again*) to fathom how "scriptures" developed, what work we make them do within and across the societies and cultures, and with what historical and perduring political consequences. Such fathoming should be carried out across the scholarly guilds, across the academic departments and programs, across school types, across social situations and settings. We must together engage in the sociology, anthropology, the cultural history, the psychosocial logics, the performance-expressive, the material and political criticism of "scriptures." With this different orientation or agenda, the primary focus should be placed *not upon texts* per se (that is, upon their content-meanings), but upon textures, gestures, and power—namely the signs, material products, ritual practices and performances, expressivities, orientations, ethics, and politics associated with the phenomenon of the invention and uses of "scriptures."

Of the three focal issues—textures, gestures, and power—the first, "textures," requires immediate additional comment. What I mean by "textures" has to do with much more than the work of historical criticism, with its primary focus upon the establishment of the content-meaning or the artful design of "texts," or the reconstruction of ancient worlds behind the "texts."[7] Some of the practices that have for some time marked historical criticism may very well be taken into the project that I advance here, but they must not define or exhaust it. This "excavation" project is different from historical criticism in the sense that it regards "text" in more layered and expansive terms and positions the narrowly construed "text" in the complicated middle point or middle layer, so to speak, of the investigation; it does not make the "text"—or explication of it—the endgame. In making the endgame of the excavation textures, gestures, power, I seek to turn traditional "historical criticism" into what Pierre Nora called "critical history."[8] Warren's buzzard (and its breed) "ain't" *historical* in this sense.

The orientation that I call for here has been inspired and made compelling by a shift in focus that I make from European–North American or "white" religio-cultural histories and experiences as the unacknowledged[9] default template for critical analysis to some of the histories and forms of expressiveness of *dark, historically subaltern or subordinated peoples* around the world. It should not surprise that the circumstances and experiences of those represented as (nonwhite, dark) "others" can lead to expansiveness in questioning or critical awareness such that a re-consideration of some of the normally taken for granted issues and phenomena associated with dominance, including even the issue or phenomenon of the Western naming and cooptation of the phenomenon of the making and using of "scriptures," is made possible. The new interpretive practice and agenda reflective of this different orientation I term *signifying (on) scriptures.* The new vehicle intended to facilitate ongoing collaborative research in this different direction has been recently established in Claremont and is called the Institute for Signifying Scriptures (ISS).

"Signifying" represents both a different critical mode of investigation and a characteristic of the phenomena to be investigated. It captures the critical mode of investigation that is more encompassing than, and therefore different from, the various assumptions, methods, and approaches—whether popular or academic, traditional or postmodernist—usually associated with conventional textual interpretation and communication of meaning. Through its use of indirect, deflecting, sometimes ironic, exaggerated speech—riffing, woofing, scoring, getting loud on something or someone—it brings into focus the power relations and dynamics involved in but often masked in communication and interpretation. Such practices have been called "signifying on"—something or someone, "signifyin(g)" with a ("Black") difference,[10] "signifying with a vengeance,"[11] or in general, "playing" with discourse on or around the margins by the less powerful, the socially and politically marginalized (as with the play of the monkey with the lion or elephant). Signifying in this sense includes the practices discovered among peoples off the stage, away from the center—in the dark.

"Scriptures" in the title of the new institute and its research agenda becomes shorthand for those symbols or material objects or gestures-practices that are associated with the "vectoring"[12] of meaning creation and meaning translation. What it may mean for "scriptures"—whether as texts or as other objects or performances—to have, or to have been made to have, qualities such that they come to be seen as metonymic of social-cultural centering[13] and social-cultural de-centering, de-formation, and de-construction, invites ongoing criticism.

Through its emphasis on the performative, signifying, as it is understood in the context of this discussion, riffs on the whole phenomenon of the quest for the fixed (generally text-ed) interpretation and the claims for the textual mediation of transcendence or truth as being too politically overdetermined for anyone's good. It leaves no object, no practice or practitioner in the whole phenomenon, without critical attention. It pursues the issue not so much of *what* "scriptures" mean (in terms of content), but *how* "scriptures" mean (in terms of psycho-social-cultural performances and politics). This project, then, involves the agenda not only of *re*capturing the fullest range of possibilities for the registration of the phenomenon in societies and cultures—namely how scriptures signify—but naming loudly (or critically analyzing) the nature and consequences of interpretative practices, their strategies, and play, especially in terms of power relations—namely signifying *on* scriptures.

Note the following situations that can be the focus of the excavation of "scriptures." Note how at such depths "scriptures" are (or have the potential to be) complexly signified and signified upon:

Consider the traditional Zulu village with its orientation toward the center, a reflection of the social-cultural functions of "scriptures."

Note in the following photos, including a Torah scribe and Japanese women reading holy books and praying at popular temple site, how "scriptures" are signified as part of the textures of the social-cultural:

And note on a billboard in Pasadena, California, the wave of signifying as one group provocatively signifies on another group's *sign*-ification of "scriptures."

We can see again how "scriptures" in history dramatically and poignantly signified as cultural cargo in the depiction of John Eliot as "apostle to the Indians," wielding what would become known as the Eliot Indian Bible (*Mamusse wunneetupanatamwe Up-Biblum God naneeswe Nukkone Testament kah wonk Wusku Testament*).[14]

And, of course, "scriptures" can be and are often performed, as can be seen in the Ifa divination ceremony conducted by a *babalawo*.

The very notion and representation of "scriptures" is exploded or is radically expanded as one takes note of some of the dynamics involved in performances normally thought to be far from the domain that is religion. For example, jazz virtuoso John Coltrane's haunting rendition of the standard, "canonical" version of Rodgers's "My Favorite Things" has enormous implications for the idea of the standard, of "the text"—of scripts and "scriptures." Coltrane's signifying on Rodgers's musical script-ures

> suggested that unchecked expressive inquiry—the articulation of the moment's disposition, desire, and intuition—was the "favorite thing" of Coltrane's New Thang . . . Interpretation thus serves not as either assassination or acknowledgment of the prior but as an agitative intervention that propels a dazzling

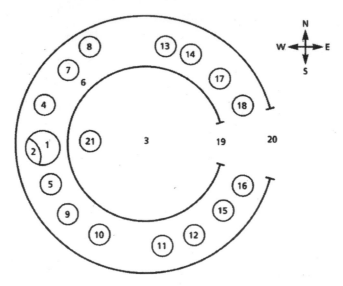

1. Chief Hut (Headman/Priest)
2. *Umsamo*
3. Cattle Enclosure
4, 5. Huts of Great Wife
6. Fence Around Cattle Enclosure
7, 8. Huts of Chief Wife of the Left Section
9, 10. Huts of Chief Wife of the Right Section

11, 12. Huts of the Sons
13, 14. Huts of the Daughters
15, 16, 17, 18. Huts for Guests and Visitors
19. Entrance to Cattle Enclosure
20. Entrance to Village
21. Site for Ritual Ceremonies for Ancestors

Figure 1.1   Layout of a traditional Zulu village. Courtesy of HarperCollins Publishers.

movement of substitutions . . . By . . . exploring a tune in order to thematize the plurivocality of its enunciation, Coltrane signaled that his project was not just that of producing new meanings but of reopening the question of meaning's production.[15]

Beginning of This Orientation and the Framing of Larger Critical Perspectives

What these examples make clear and compelling is that the study of "scriptures" is and ought to be the study of textures, of gestures and power relations. My interest in the sort of work to which the above examples point began with the African Americans and the Bible Research Project that I established in 1995 at Union Theological Seminary in New York and directed there for seven years. This project provided case-study evidence[16] for the theoretical and analytical gains that can be made in research on religion in relationship to signifying cultural practices. Henry Louis. Gates, Jr.,[17] Charles Long,[18] Geneva Smitherman,[19] Claudia Mitchell-Kernan,[20] Roger D. Abrahams,[21] and recently, Mustapha Marrouchi,[22] among a few others, have argued that because dark peoples around the world in relationship to dominant discursive and social formations and as a part of their own ongoing internal life experiences are persistent signifiers, a turn toward signifying practices in the study of such peoples is very much needed. What the African Americans and the Bible project represented was an attempt to begin to excavate rather than

Figure 1.2 A Torah scribe. Photograph by Bill Aron.

Figure 1.3 Japanese women reading holy books and praying at popular temple site. Courtesy of HarperCollins Publishers.

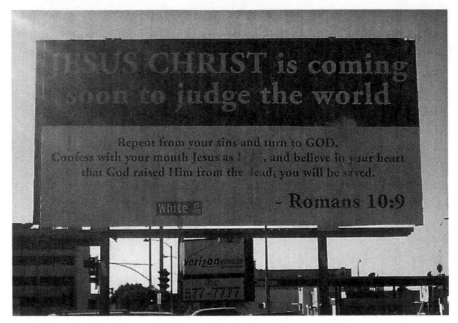

Figure 1.4 Billboard in Pasadena, California. Photograph by Jacqueline M. Hidalgo.

Figure 1.5 John Eliot as "apostle to the Indians" in a nineteenth-century engraving by J. A. Oertel. Courtesy of Mary Evans Picture Library.

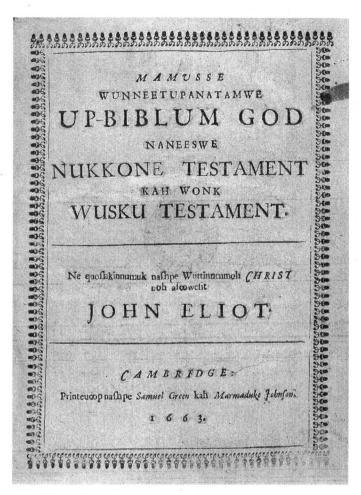

Figure 1.6 The Eliot Indian Bible, *Mamusse wunneetupanatamwe Up-Biblum God naneeswe Nukkone Testament kah wonk Wusku Testament.* Courtesy of the Bodleian Library, Oxford University.

merely exegete; it was an effort to understand *some*[23] of the folk—*some* African Americans—in terms of "scriptures" and signifying practices. Given my disciplinary location—in a field that has as its traditional agenda the exegesis of a particular set of scriptures—this project and its orientation represented a step with serious academic-intellectual political implications.

To be sure, focus upon the phenomenology of "scriptures" has not been altogether ignored in scholarship. The late historian of religion (and former president of the American Academy of Religion) Wilfred Cantwell Smith was for many years the most provocative and trenchant scholar in the area of the phenomenology of "scriptures." He could be said to have revived, modeled, and made compelling this area of research for students of religion of North America of the last three decades or more. Among his many publications, his major book, *What Is Scripture?*,[24] the

Figure 1.7 Ifa divination ceremony conducted by a *babalawo*. Courtesy of Phoebe Apperson Hearst Museum of Anthropology, University of California, Berkeley.

culmination of many decades of work on the topic, became for academics in North America the focal point of thinking and conversation about the phenomenon.[25] So it was (in a certain respect) for me.

In addition to the investigations into the ancient historical contexts for the texts, beyond the philological and formalist-literary studies of the ancient texts, why, Smith pressed the question, should it not be reasonable and compelling to ask what it means for peoples to persist in investing in "scriptures"?

Smith's writings were for me confirmation that my early undeclared orientation and thinking were not totally unique in the world, that I was, as one thinking about the importance of asking questions about *what* scriptures are, *whence* scriptures developed, *how* scriptures functioned, grappling with important scholarly issues that had resonated with others.

But what was most decisive for the turn I took in scholarly orientation was my persistence in thinking about "scriptures" through the prisms of the experiences and practices and politics that defined the world into which I was born. As I freely signed up in the late 1970s for graduate work in a highly regarded program in the study of religion with focus upon the Bible, I was forced to study the Bible on terms that were decidedly and arrogantly culturally and intellectually monochromatic. This constraining experience inspired my thoughts to turn again and again to that world that for good and ill had shaped me, that colorful world, a world that had historically sought, only sometimes with success, to color-code the Bible, to make it, in the words of folklorist and novelist Zora Neale Hurston, "suit our imagination."[26] But it was also the dramatic evidence of differentiation and development in the engagement of the Bible in this world that inspired anxious questioning. In many places, forms of black-inflected "scriptural fundamentalism"[27] were in dramatic evidence as a part of modern-day, intensive, worldwide fundamentalisms. Among black folks, such participation had resulted in the phenomenon of what I term the re-"bleaching" of the Bible. By this term I mean the naïve and sometimes even disingenuous assumption—squaring with and to the continued advantage of the default dominant ideology—that the Bible is mystifyingly culture-neutral in origins, meanings, and import. With this phenomenon all around me, everywhere in evidence, and even as I had nevertheless in my early years of earnest (liberal scholarly!) training and teaching and research participated in the continued cultural fetishization of the Bible as an unproblematized ancient collection of texts mirroring an unproblematized ancient world, I would persist even more in asking (myself and some select others): Why do the folks I know, and other nondominant folks, read and use the Bible? Why do they, why do we, engage it in particular ways, on particular terms, and under particular circumstances? How did we come originally to engage it? Why do we continue to engage it? What is at stake in such engagements?

In light of Smith's trenchant challenge to the field of biblical studies, it can be thought quite ironic that I thought I should pursue the highest academic degree possible in *biblical studies*. Naïve and ironic as it was of me to think that I could pursue my questions in a biblical studies program—it kept me busy exegeting instead of excavating—such training did position me to push further certain recurring questions and issues and to help secure for some who would later join me a safe academic-discursive environment. This environment for the different questioning was created *within* the field of biblical studies—something Smith did not and could not do!

As provocative as it was for me, Smith's work proved to be too delimited by and focused upon the dominant "world" religions and the dominant groups within them. Most important, in relationship to or as a direct result of this delimitation and focus, his work—and that of many of his students—seemed little or inconsistently concerned about political issues and power dynamics, especially as they intersected with racial and ethnic identities. In the end, Smith's answer to the provocative question he raised was that "scriptures" had to do with "human activity" and that it was "relational."[28] This answer can hardly be wrong; but it is not enough. Left vague, this issue of the "relational" with respect to "scriptures" remained apolitical and intellectually mystifying. Smith's legacy is not in any clarity he brought to the issues, in any answers he provided, but in his raising of the question—the simple, pressing, pointed, haunting question, "what is scripture?" Such a question must not be given up.

I threaded the question not through the dominant world religions and the investigative and rhetorical categories and arguments they provoke, but through some of the experiences of the historically and persistently subaltern, usually the darker peoples of the world. These folk, as literary critic Homi K. Bhabha has reminded us, are generally on a different clock: they tend to represent the (psycho-social-cultural) "lag."[29] As subjects who (have been forced to) "lag" behind in terms of certain experiences and the registration of such experiences they are, as the driver is warned about the things viewed in the rearview mirror on the car, "closer than they appear." Such lagging peoples and their relationships to "scriptures" may also be resonant of the argument Freud tried to make about excavation in the analogy he set up between the city of Rome and the mental world of the human adult. Both the city and the psychic structure that is the adult human are layered; that is, they have long complex pasts. The older layers exist along with the newer layers.[30] Might the peoples who are perceived to "lag behind" represent the darker and deeper levels of some widely shared practices and forms of human consciousness such as can be found in relationship to the phenomenon of "scriptures"? Not better, purer, and so forth, should they be claimed to be, but might they afford us deeper access (to ourselves)? And might the greater depth reveal much about all layers (of ourselves)?

My focus upon black peoples—still widely recognized as the metonymic chronic, persistent "other"—meant that "scriptures," like almost all other social-cultural phenomena, had to be approached differently. Here is where signifying practices come into view. Turning not around the supposed stable "transcendent signified," involving not "information giving," but the "technique of indirect argument or persuasion," "the language of implication,"[31] the practices of many of these folk should be understood in association with a more expansive and complex understanding of languages, codes, self-representations, forms of expressiveness.[32]

Obviously, all of the phenomena we continue to refer to with the freighted abbreviation "religion" can be studied in terms of signifying practices—as encoded meanings registered in the wide range of vernacular sociocultural signs, textures, practices, orientations. But few—whether students of religion or not—can fail to get the point of the power and poignancy of scrutinizing as psycho-social-cultural phenomenon what we in English call "scriptures." The latter term[33] has for millennia now been special shorthand for particular powerful social-cultural phenomena and practices historically radically resistant to, even subversive and obfuscating of, critical theorizing, especially theorizing of the sort that includes political criticism. Historically seen as being within the purview and portfolio of elite clerics and certain types of scholars for the sake of attaining and maintaining the correct and orthodox content-interpretation, "scriptures" have not generally been open to the type of questioning and scrutiny that I call for here. Such scrutiny, according to Pierre Bourdieu, falls in the realm of "doxa," the normally taken for granted, the "undiscussed."[34] What I am calling for here is excavation of the normally undiscussable and taken for granted—e.g., "race" and "scriptures."

Using the historical and contemporary experiences of subordinated peoples—especially peoples of color—as the primary although not exclusive conceptual springboard, heuristic lens, analytical cultural wedge, the type of research I am calling for here might focus upon signifying practices not for arguments about the unique and the exotic, or about the sentimental, romantic, or pornographic gaze, but as grounds for *general critical theorizing* about the little understood, seldom problematized, mystifying and occluding signs, practices, orientations, textures, and power dynamics of society and culture that represent the phenomenon of "scriptures."

The Call to a Different Orientation

What I call for is consistent focus upon how societies and cultures continue to be formed and de-formed and re-formed and—on account of the power invested in them—how *texts* in particular are created and pressed into service to effect such things. With such focus, the new Institute for Signifying Scriptures bases critical comparative theorizing about the phenomenon of "scriptures" on the experiences of historically dominated (usually dark) peoples of the world.

This initiative is based upon certain underlying critical theories and assumptions:

With few exceptions, Western theology and critical interpretation of religion have generally participated in an epistemic system in which meanings are located in a conventional semantic order that is mostly reflected in relationship to authoritative texts. The intellectual and power dynamics associated with such interpretation are now clearer than ever before. The tightly controlled almost obsessive focus upon texts and the system of signification upon which texts are constructed severely limit representation and expressions of meaning. It has the effect of rendering invisible or inauthentic vernacular orientations and traditions, whether oral or conventionally and unconventionally scripted and communicated.

The study of "scriptures" in relationship to subordinated peoples is important because such peoples teach us that there is much more to expressiveness and representation than conventional literacy would indicate; they teach us that "scriptures" are about more than the study of texts as conventional scripts, more than the study of interpretation of texts communicated in conventional scripts, with conventional scripts chasing conventional scripts.[35] The issue here is not at all a matter of merely drawing upon the old polar opposites, literacy versus orality; rather it is about the need to come to critical terms with the reality of the wide range of types of communication and expressiveness through which people communicate about themselves.

Nevertheless it is clear that conventional literacy and "texts" and the practices associated with such define the dominant structurings of the world; texts and literacy mark where power is in the world. Conventional scripts or texts, then, are necessarily always a major issue, even or especially for the illiterate. Conventional scripts and texts must always be engaged in some manner by nondominants. Signifying is one of the modes of engagements of such scripts and texts. In their signifying on "scriptures," nondominants have long reflected not only their views and stances but also what seems to be at issue in "scripturalizing" itself. The social power associated with conventional scripts[36] suggests the need for critical orientations and frameworks that problematize representation and meaning seeking, especially in relationship to texts, and, most especially, those texts accorded special status in text-obsessed cultures. This emphasis is needed so that a more

self-reflexive criticism regarding social-cultural practices and their politics in relationship to the texts called "scriptures" can be made possible. The historically
enslaved and conquered peoples of the world represent powerful epistemic, theoretical, and analytical alternatives and challenges. Such folk generally do not stay
within the lines; often they go undetected, uncounted, and unaccounted for. They
almost always scramble the generalities by which dominance defines itself and the
world. Their more clearly delineated, sometimes overdetermined, hard-to-hide
social construction efforts, their thicker lines of "social identity" and social positionality can be thought of as having, in the terms suggested by literature scholar
Satya P. Mohanty, a particular "epistemic status."[37] This means that subordinated
peoples can and should properly be the subject of honest and free critical inquiry,
with a view not only to understanding more about how they represent themselves,
but as examples of how certain peoples in particular, and then by critical extension
human beings in general, come to know, create, and shape their reality and thereby
shape the world around them.

Wider Significance of the Orientation

A different orientation to interpretation is here evident in the call to make the shift
in primary focus of critical inquiry from the texts as the signified (or as the most
reliable or authoritative medium for the signified) to the signifiers, to those who
from below or from the peripheries engage in various verbal strategies of indirection and deflection. In accordance with the shift that is proposed here, texts will be
repositioned so that they become not merely the deposit of content-meaning, but
sites—powerful, controversial, sometimes ironic—for cultural signifying toward
many different ends.[38]

   The shift as proposed here in connection with the different scholarly orientation may have direct and significant impact upon our understanding of several matters: how what we term "religion" may be differently conceptualized—in terms of
a broad range of sociocultural signifying practices; how different practices associated with interpretation may effect social and cultural formation; how "scriptures,"
their invention and engagements, may be seen in terms of signifying practices;
and how through such signifying practices not only the boundaries and frames
and categories of social identity and social relations, but also the orientations and
infra-politics—especially of nondominant peoples, who necessarily communicate
"in other terms" if not always in "hidden transcripts"[39]—may be reconsidered.

   Such a shift requires that serious attention be given to certain basic but difficult
questions, issues, and problematics.[40] Ultimately, these questions, issues, and problematics are interconnected and overlapping; but a division of labor bears its own
compelling logic. What is aimed for here in this volume is the opening up of conversation—wide-ranging, passionate, interested, disciplined conversation, across
schools, programs, fields, disciplines, religious commitments, racial-ethnic and religious group membership, gender, social statuses, even scholarly guild associations/
societies, with all the risks and vulnerabilities that are involved in the effort.

The conversation I suggest should begin in response to five broad, clearly overlapping, but nonetheless isolable categories of questions and issues.[41]

The Phenomenon Itself—and its Origins. If "scriptures" should not simply be equated with or collapsed into texts, in what other terms, categories, might we think and talk about it? What social-cultural phenomena—practices, performances, ideologies—are named in connection with the invention and uses of "scriptures"? How and under what circumstances did such phenomena begin in history? What general meanings or functions can be associated with such beginnings?

Settings, Situations, Practices. What are some of the typical settings and situations—past and present—in which the phenomena, the actions, the practices, take place? What do these settings suggest about the phenomena? How do the settings qualify, delimit, expand, manipulate the contours and boundaries and meanings of the phenomena? What is seen, heard, touched, responded to, represented, performed in connection with the phenomena? How have the practices or performances changed over time? How do the practices and performances and representations differ across cultures. Who's doing it? Who are the performers in the various settings and situations? Are some elites created in such circles? What training or skills are assumed or needed in order to perform or engage in expected practices?

Material and Expressive Representations. What are some of the material/physical objects and forms of expressiveness—past and present—through which, in relationship to which, the practices are carried out? What are their forms, shapes, sounds, colors, textures?

Psycho-Social-Cultural/Power Needs and Dynamics. Why do people persist in relating to them? Why do people (seem to) need them? What are some specific psycho-social and social-cultural needs reflected in connection with the phenomena? Explain how these needs and the terms of the engagement or the practices change in relationship to the individual's psycho-social development? In relationship to a group's development? What are the psycho-social effects of such engagements? Who's up and who's down? If so, under what circumstances? With what difference(s)? How are these differences to be explained? What are some implications and ramifications of these differences? Have poor and illiterate peoples always been associated with it? Have peoples of color, especially unconventionally scripted peoples, always been associated with it? If not, why? When did they begin to be associated with it? With what difference(s) in terms of social power? What sorts of games do we play with one another in relationship to the phenomena?

Signifying on the Questions. What might it mean to flip all the questions above? What is the import of the questions, of the focus of the signifying on scriptures project, the agenda, and orientation of the ISS?

Conclusion

The different critical orientation and framework for the study of "scriptures" advanced here cannot possibly come from a single field. The attitude among scholars of particular scriptural traditions and among some scholars in too many of the other subfields of theological and religious studies that the study of "scriptures" should be left only to a certain group of scholars is troubling. It is far too intellectually and politically narrow, naïve, anachronistic, and sheepish. It is to avoid going deep. The study of "scriptures" cannot be defined by or limited to one type of discourse or one discussant or authority figure or expert. The phenomenon must not even be limited to the purview of scholars of religion! It must not be seen to be simply about religion or only for the religiously committed. For the fathoming of "scriptures" we must have wide-ranging, free, safe debate and conversation entered into by as many thoughtful persons as would show willingness to practice an ethics of listening to and learning from others, in order to try to excavate how we are psychosocially and sociopolitically and textually constituted. For what we are confronted with in "scriptures" is about nothing less than how some human beings are woven, how they shape and reshape themselves, in relationship to whatever they decide should function as vectoring, centering, or canonical forces, *lieux de memoire*.[42]

The study of "scriptures," therefore, must be open to all those who would try to understand human beings—their languages, rhythms, rituals, performances, orientations, their collective psyches, power relations, their fears, pain, ecstasies, and aspirations.

The essays that follow invite you from your different academic-intellectual corners and general social locations at this turn-of-century moment so full of possibilities for conversation, collaboration, and rethinking to join this excavation, to be guided by some of those folk whom Warren's buzzard called metaphysically challenged, those who historically have had little choice but to negotiate the "disrupting darkness,"[43] those who teach us that in the darkness of serious excavation there can be little room or time for academic guild dissimulation and the obfuscating chatter of subfields or the usual cannibalistic religious politics. Those folk forewarn us that because in the darkness the danger of falling is ever real and that the final forms and definitions are ever elusive, listening to each other, holding onto each other, is imperative. In spite of the danger, and notwithstanding their fears, limitations, and foibles, they beckon us down, down, downward, challenging us to see that only in the darkness will we come to learn about the richness and layeredness and luminescence of human existence; only there will we come to terms with the (text-ed and un-text-ed) *textures*, the (performative and ludic) *gestures*, the (dynamics and relations of) *power* that mark our small and larger selves.

NOTES

1. This pressing of the case or challenge to the reader was earlier, as a part of the tone-setting and conceptual opening of the February 2004 "Theorizing Scriptures" international conference held in Claremont, California, a challenge to those whose essays follow.

2. Sometimes, as a concession to the shape of the politics in some places, called "The Second Testament of the Christian Bible," mostly still called "The Bible," or "The New Testament." It should not surprise that I prefer the term "scriptures." It is not without its problems, but it at least keeps us open to the opportunities as well as challenges of comparison. What does it mean for a scholar of a particular example of "scriptures" to engage such with raised consciousness about the fact of other "scriptures"?

3. See Robert Penn Warren, "Pondy Woods," in *New and Selected Poems: 1923–1985* (New York: Random House, 1985), 319–321.

4. Henry Louis Gates Jr., "Canon-Formation, Literary History, and the Afro-American Tradition: From the Seen to the Told," in *Afro-American Literary Study in the 1990s*, ed. Houston A. Baker Jr. and Patricia Redmond (Chicago: University of Chicago Press, 1989), 14–38.

5. Michel Foucault, *Archaeology of Knowledge*, trans. A. M. Sheridan Smith (1969; repr., New York: Pantheon Books, 1972).

6. Greg Dening, *Performances* (Chicago: University of Chicago Press, 1996).

7. See Mark Golden and Peter Toohey, eds., *Inventing Ancient Culture: Historicism, Periodization, and the Ancient World* (New York: Routledge,1997), for discussion of cultural-intellectual politics often involved in such work.

8. Pierre Nora, "Between Memory and History: Les Lieux des Memoire," *Representations* 26 (1989): 7–25.

9. This lack of acknowledgment or blindness feeds into a view of "scriptures" that has had and continues to have serious and tragic consequences. See John Thornton's treatment of the history of the Christian West's understanding of "discontinuous revelation" in relationship to the Bible: *Africa and Africans in the Making of the Atlantic World, 1400–1680* (New York: Cambridge University Press), 239–249. His focus upon the experiences and sentiments of sixteenth-century Lutheran pastor and missionary Wilhelm Mueller is compelling.

10. As Henry Louis Gates Jr. would have it rendered. See *The Signifying Monkey: A Theory of African-American Literary Criticism* (New York: Oxford University Press, 1988).

11. According to Mustapha Marrouchi, *Signifying with a Vengeance: Theories, Literatures, Storytellers* (Albany: State University of New York Press, 2002).

12. Kendall W. Folkert, "The 'Canons' of 'Scripture,'" in *Rethinking Scripture: Essays from a Comparative Perspective*, ed. M. Levering (Albany: State University of New York Press, 1989), 170–179.

13. Regarding the center in social symbolization, see Mircea Eliade, *Images and Symbols: Studies in Religious Symbolism*, trans. Philip Mairet (1952; repr., Princeton: Princeton University Press, 1991); and Rudolf Arnheim, *The Power of the Center: A Study of Composition in the Visual Arts* (Berkeley: University of California Press, 1988).

14. This was the first complete Bible printed in the Western Hemisphere—on the site of what is now Harvard University. It was translated from English into Natick, the dialect of the Algonquins.

15. Kimberley W. Benston, *Performing Blackness: Enactments of African-American Modernism* (New York: Routledge, 2000), 131, 133, 134.

16. See the publication of most of the presentations from the 1999 international conference in Vincent L. Wimbush, ed., with the assistance of Rosamond C. Rodman, *African Americans and the Bible: Sacred Texts and Social Textures* (2000; repr., New York: Continuum, 2001).

17. Gates, *The Signifying Monkey*.

18. Charles Long, *Significations: Signs, Symbols, and Images in the Interpretation of Religion* (Minneapolis: Fortress Press,1986).

19. Geneva Smitherman, *Talkin' That Talk: Language, Culture, and Education in African America* (New York: Routledge, 2001).

20. Claudia Mitchell-Kernan, "Signifying as a Form of Verbal Art," now found in several collections, including *Mother Wit from the Laughing Barrel: Readings in the Interpretation of Afro-American Folklore*, ed. Alan Dundes (Englewood Cliffs, NJ: Prentice Hall, 1973), 310–328.

21. Roger D. Abrahams, *Talking Black* (Rowley, MA: Newbury House Publishers, 1976).

22. Marrouchi, *Signifying with a Vengeance*.

23. The claim need never be that all persons who may in some way belong to a group represent or embody any specific characteristics or orientations. It is enough for my purposes to establish that over a long period of time and in different settings a significant segment of persons squares with the arguments proffered.

24. W. C. Smith, *What Is Scripture? A Comparative Approach* (Minneapolis: Fortress Press, 1993).

25. To be sure, there have been and continue to be other emphases, interests, and tendencies: see Gerhard Maier, ed., *Der Kanon der Bibel*, (Giessen: Brunnen Verlag; Wuppertal: R. Brockhaus, 1990); Guy G. Stroumsa, ed., *Kanon und Kultur: Zwei Studien zur Hemeneutik des antiken Christentums*, (Han-Lietzmann-Vorlesungen; Heft 4; Berlin: De Gruyter, 1999); and A. van der Kooij and K. van der Toorn, eds., with an annotated bibliography compiled by J.A.M. Snoek, *Canonization and Decanonization: Papers Presented to the International Conference of the Leiden Institute for the Study of Religions (Lisor), held at Leiden 9–10 January 1997* (Leiden: Brill, 1998), for some indications of the thinking, orientation, and interests of a segment of European scholars about the phenomenon of canon. And the reader should take note of the works of U.S. biblical scholar James Sanders on canonical criticism, among them see especially *Canon and Community: A Guide to Canonical Criticism* (Minneapolis: Fortress Press, 1984). Canon remains of interest but does not always touch upon the basic question pressed by W. C. Smith.

The basic pressing question or problematic was kept alive in some respects by many of the students Smith inspired, among them Miriam Levering, ed., *Rethinking Scripture: Essays from a Comparative Perspective* (Albany: State University of New York Press, 1989); Barbara Holdrege, *Veda and Torah: Transcending the Textuality of Scripture* (Albany: State University of New York Press,1996); and William Graham, *Beyond the Written Word: Oral Aspects of Scripture in the History of Religion* (New York: Cambridge University Press, 1987). And of course there are other scholars from other school traditions, including panelists of this session. But these scholars have not focused consistently upon differences that emerge along racial-ethnic lines.

Biblical scholars who are also members of racial-ethnic minority communities have not been altogether silent about issues that are related to the phenomenon of "scriptures" and the subordinated. Some of them have been articulate about issues of power (about which more is to be said in later sections). But with few exceptions their concerns have had to do with the different emphases in interpretation of content or in interpretive approaches to the content-meanings and in some cases the formal-rhetorical shaping of texts engaged by different communities of color. Cf. Brian K. Blount, *Cultural Interpretation: Reorienting New Testament Criticism* (Minneapolis: Fortress Press, 1995); Cain H. Felder, ed., *Stony the Road We Trod: African American Biblical Interpretation* (Minneapolis: Fortress Press, 1991); Fernando Segovia, *Decolonizing Biblical Studies* (Maryknoll, NY: Orbis Books, 2000); Randall Bailey, ed., *Yet with a Steady Beat: Contemporary U.S. Afrocentric Biblical Interpretation* (Atlanta: Society of Biblical Literature, 2003); Musa Dube, ed., *Other Ways of Reading: African Women and the Bible* (Atlanta: Society of Biblical Literature, 2001); Tat-siong Benny Liew, ed., *The Bible in Asian America* (Atlanta: Society of Biblical Literature 2002); and R. S. Sugirtharajah, ed., *Asian Biblical Hermeneutics and Postcolonialism* (Maryknoll, NY: Orbis Books 1999); *The Bible and The Third World: Precolonial, Colonial, and Postcolonial Encounters* (New York: Cambridge University Press, 2001). Although there are in their works implications aplenty for the type of research I am calling for here, few of these scholars have taken up consistent theorizing about and analysis of "scriptures" as a social-cultural-political problematic and phenomenon within and across particular social-cultural groups. The well-received major work of theologian Theophus Smith, *Conjuring Culture: Biblical Formations of African America* (New York: Oxford University Press, 1994), contributes much to our understanding of how the Bible has functioned within African American culture. But on the whole and where it counts, Smith writes and argues more as African American–inflected Christian theologian than as historian of religion. He does not put into perspective "the Bible" as example of the phenomenon of "scriptures" or African American culture as complex example of a "scriptures"-creating, "scriptures"-engaging culture.

In his now famous essay "Perspectives for a Study of Afro-American Religion in the United States," having originally appeared in *History of Religions* 11 (1971): 54–66, and included in his collection of essays entitled *Significations*, historian of religion Charles H. Long offers the outline of an interpretive schema for the study of African American religion in the United States. The schema argues that the following "symbolic images" and "meanings" lie behind "black religion"—Africa as historical reality and as religious image; the involuntary presence of the black community in America; and the experience and symbol of God in the religious experiences of black folks. In elaborating upon the last image and its meaning, Long indicated that the "imagery" of the Bible certainly played a "large role" in the "symbolic presentations" of black peoples, but that its influence should not be assumed to be extraordinary or explained in mystifying terms: "The biblical imagery was used because it was at hand; it was adapted to and invested with the experience of the slave." In such an argument I find a pointed challenge to probe more deeply—namely with some of the questions and approaches of the history of religions into African Americans' engagement of the Bible. I consider myself to have taken up part of the challenge Long laid down. But this it seems to me has to be done in relationship to W. C. Smith's haunting question, "What is scripture?" So I begin by dealing with Smith's basic, simple, pressing question.

26. Zora Neale Hurston, *Mules and Men* (Philadelphia: J. B. Lippincott Co., 1935).

27. With this term I am in conversation with Wilson Jeremiah Moses regarding the history of the uses of the Bible in African American popular history. He uses the term "fundamentalist" in ways that blanket almost all African American popular uses of the Bible. My preference is to reserve such a term for the more recent orientation toward the acceptance of the most conservative and race-blind white religious communities. See Wilson's *Afrotopia: The Roots of African American Popular History* (New York: Cambridge University Press, 1998).

28. See Smith, *What Is Scripture?*, 17, and chapter 10.

29. See Homi K. Bhabha, *The Location of Culture* (New York: Routledge, 1994), 191–192, 198, 199, 237, 246–256.

30. Sigmund Freud, *Civilization and Its Discontents*, trans. and ed. James Strachey (1930; repr., New York: W. W. Norton, 1961).

31. Henry. L. Gates Jr. "Blackness of Blackness: A Critique of the Sign and the Signifying Monkey," *Figures in Black: Words, Signs, and the "Racial" Self* (New York: Oxford University Press, 1987), 238–239.

32. Cf. Gates, *The Signifying Monkey*; Benston, *Performing Blackness*; and Norman K. Denzin, *Performance Ethnography: Critical Pedagogy and the Politics of Culture* (Thousand Oaks, CA: Sage, 2003).

33. Note cognates: *scriptura*; *scrittura*; *l'Ecriture*; *die Schrift*; *he graphe/hai graphai*; *ketab/ketuvim*. The assumption that these terms refer to what is written nevertheless does not contradict the long established recognition that what is signified was also oral/aural in engagement. Note especially the *sruti* and Qur'an. Cf. W. C. Smith, *What Is Scripture?*, 7–8.

34. See Pierre Bourdieu, *Outline of a Theory of Practice*, trans. Richard Nice (New York: Cambridge University Press, 1977), chap. 4, in which he has provided provocative analysis of politics of discourse, perspective, and knowledge. The relevance of his arguments to the phenomenon of "scriptures" is powerful and begs elaboration.

35. Cf. Grey Gundaker, *Signs of Diaspora/Diaspora of Signs: Literacies, Creolization, and Vernacular Practice in African America* (New York: Oxford University Press, 1998).

36. Cf. Jack Goody, *The Logic of Writing and the Organization of Society* (New York: Cambridge University Press, 1986); *The Interface Between the Written and the Oral* (New York: Cambridge University Press, 1987); Walter J. Ong, *Orality and Literacy: The Technologizing of the Word* (New

York: Methuen, 1982); Brian Stock, *Listening for the Text: On the Uses of the Past* (Baltimore: Johns Hopkins University Press, 1990); Brian V. Street, *Literacy in Theory and Practice* (New York: Cambridge University Press, 1984); and Jonathan Boyarin, ed., *The Ethnography of Reading* (Berkeley: University of California Press, 1993).

37. Satya P. Mohanty, *Literary Theory and the Claims of History: Postmodernism, Objectivity, Multicultural Politics* (Ithaca, NY: Cornell University Press, 1997).

38. Cf. James N. Baker, "The Presence of the Name: Reading Scripture in a Indonesian Village," in *The Ethnography of Reading,* ed. Jonathan Boyarin (Berkeley: University of California Press, 1993), 98–138.

39. James C. Scott, *Weapons of the Weak: Everyday Forms of Peasant Resistance* (New Haven, CT: Yale University Press, 1985); and *Domination and the Arts of Resistance: Hidden Transcripts* (New Haven, CT: Yale University Press, 1990).

40. These social-cultural, psycho-social, political-critical, historical-critical, comparative, expressive-critical questions, issues and problematics constitute the research and programmatic agenda for the new research center—the ISS.

41. This is the basis for the divisions of the essays that follow. Essayists were asked to address one particular set of questions. But the final categorization is mine as editor. By virtue of their argumentation, orientation, and the range of issues ultimately addressed, some essays can with justification be located within more than one category. But I have made judgments about what one set or category of issues and questions to which an essay responds most compellingly for the sake of advancing the conversation.

42. Cf. Eliade, *Images and Symbols*; "Sacred Places: Temple, Palace, Centre of the World," in *Patterns in Comparative Religion* (New York: Sheed and Ward, 1958); Michel de Certeau, "The Scriptural Economy," in *The Practice of Everyday Life* (Berkeley: University of California Press, 1984); Pierre Bourdieu, "Structures, Habitus, Power: Basis for a Theory of Symbolic Power," in *Outline of a Theory of Practice*; Maurice Bloch, ed., *Political Language and Oratory in Traditional Society* (New York: Academic Press, 1975); Catherine Bell, *Ritual Theory, Ritual Practice* (New York: Oxford University Press, 1992); *Ritual: Perspectives and Dimensions* (New York: Oxford University Press, 1997); Genevieve Fabre and Robert O'Meally, eds., *History and Memory in African American Culture* (New York: Oxford University Press, 1994).

43. See Toni Morrison, *Playing in the Dark: Whiteness and the Literary Imagination* (New York: Vintage Books, 1992), 91.

PART I

THE PHENOMENON—
AND ITS ORIGINS

1 *Scriptures—Text and Then Some*

CATHERINE BELL

It is a daunting task to address a question about the "phenomenology" of anything. Yet I have had the good fortune to count among my teachers the great phenomenologist, Mircea Eliade, and the undisputed great anti-phenomenologist, Jonathan Z. Smith. If they remain in my psyche as dual influences, although perhaps more Scylla and Charybdis than yin and yang, they also insure there is little that I cannot *attempt* to address one way or another. So I put prevarications aside. I have been drawn to the study of texts and issues of textuality since the beginning of my career, and it is probably fair to say they brought me to the type of study of religion that I do. It is exciting to have an opportunity to contribute something of what I have thought about religious texts and then learn about and engage other ways in which such textual phenomenon might be parsed.

I draw less on phenomenology than ideas about textuality and comparison. Likewise I draw less on the phenomenon of the Christian "scriptures" than my own research in Chinese "scriptures" of various types and many years of teaching about "scriptures" in a comparative framework. I know it is valuable to talk about the scriptural roles of other media: but as I am a text person, I am content to contribute to the broader conversation something of what things look like from there.

In the last thirty years, much attention has been given to the study of *l'ecriture*, textuality vis à vis orality, classicism versus historicity, the ideological tyrannies and liberties of the written word, as well as the "sensual dimension" noted by William Graham (although much less attention has gone to the "affective role of texts in everyday life," especially as a written object among the illiterate or partially literate).[1] Scholarship has also explored the researcher's own presence in these studies, most often cast as a liability that mythologizes objectivity, but also given a complexity on a par with any of the great conundrums of physics, such as the Uncertainty Principle, Gödel's theorem, or Schrödinger's doomed cat. If you look or ask, you have changed things; moreover there are some assumptions you cannot un-assume and still practice the practices that energize us and employ us. In textual studies no question has been too big, no complication too small, no conditional reality too hypothetical to be pursued fully.

This is the context within which I view "scriptures." For me, biblical and scriptural studies must acknowledge the more basic phenomenon of textuality as their starting point or ultimate canvas of interpretation. "Scriptures" have consistently been an early and key form of textuality in many cultures. Indeed textuality itself appears to be an inspiration for the emergence of scriptures as texts that are held sacred in comparison to other objects or other texts. In many cultures, it might be said that "scriptures" are the "text of texts," the first and ultimate text, the template for all books and the font of all images of literary inspiration. "Scriptures" are the model for the enlistment of written words to bear multiple meanings; more than a mere narrative, the story of "scriptures" is a narrative whose full nature is regarded as diminished and confounded by the limits of human memory and speech. It is the written word elevated into a service that eliminates the lines between medium and message, only to reimpose these lines in less sacred contexts.

So I have understood the study of "scriptures" as a study of textuality—textuality extolled for the power of texts within communities to impose another level of meaning. While "scriptures" are a critical form of textuality for such communities, and perhaps a historically early form as well, understandings of *how* something is a text vary; aside from some common models, the most interesting variations are the traditions in which scriptural texts continue to be revealed. These traditions include the "treasure texts" of Padmasambhva unearthed periodically in Tibetan Buddhism and the open canon of Mormonism, which insures that this community's clear textual history continues to have revelations with an expanding canon. Scriptural forms may generate other forms of texts, less sacred but still revelatory, as the Veda, sacred as *śruti* (what is revealed) are thought to be the basis of a more accessible literature known as *smṛti* (remembered wisdom of teachers). The variety of ways in which scriptural revelation may be textual, and the texts embody sacrality, is truly unending. It is probably quite important that there are few regularities to be found.

Under what circumstances might the phenomena of "scriptures" emerge? For many years, I have taught a "Scripture, Canon, and Community" course in which we examined all sorts of phenomena that acted scripture-like for their communities, looking at how the holiness of the scriptural phenomenon is constituted in different types of social settings and institutional roles for religion. Starting with the oral creation myth of the Dogon, as related by Ogotemmeli, we would look to Goody and Watt's famous essay, "The Consequences of Literacy," for the terms needed to analyze the literate and nonliterate worlds of the first Christians.[2] The role of book technology in making it possible to collect a limited and ultimately canonical number of texts leads to a close consideration of the impact of printing on the sacred text itself and on the new Christian communities that gathered around it. The course is able to explore how the stages of revelation, textualization, canonization, and scriptural interpretation are dissimilar in Judaism and Islam. Still they remain comparable phenomena: a group that is struggling to be a community, large enough to preclude convenient ritual gatherings, produces a revelatory text; eventually the multiple versions of the text must be addressed, and a particular enclave empowered, by fixing one version as canonical. Immediately there ensue all the problems one might expect of a fixed text in fluid and historically evolving communities. The need for an interpretive apparatus was solved in different ways in these three traditions—for reasons I force the students to figure out.

When exploring the Buddhist and Hindu "scriptures," the course could analyze the same three stages of a revelation, a canon, and an interpretive apparatus, but these traditions are particularly interesting for their interplay of orality and literacy. The emergence of revelation in a textual form is, in any situation, a substantial challenge to oral modes of knowing and authority, and the textual power grab is, I believe, a major component in any analysis of textuality. Yet it does not always play out that a text replaces orally transmitted revelation; sometimes they coexist with orality integral to aspects of scriptural interpretation and cultural knowledge. Yet in Hinduism the fundamentally oral nature of the Vedas, and the concomitant authority of a whole set of social relationships, such as the ritualized master-disciple relationship, could endure even when textual metamorphoses were able to widen cultural community. The many written (and oral) versions of the *Rāmāyaṇa* and *Mahabharata* in the dominant languages of India loosely knit together a level of shared culture beyond the divisions of caste and language. The course ended with viewing a small part of the very lengthy televised version of the *Rāmāyaṇa*, a retelling of the holy story that became a ritual and spiritual event in many villages. It also helped elect a political party on a fundamentally religious appeal for a return to lost India, Hindutva. For all the nationalist and divisive aspects of such a vision, it also reflected a fresh, postindependence understanding of pan-Hinduism.

The three-stage process of a revelatory scripture, its canonization, and then the necessity of interpretation is, students find, not a neat one in which literate culture vanquishes an older oral reality. The variety makes generalizations very hazardous, but it does seem that a sacred text is most likely to emerge when, in the context of relatively new access to literacy, religious authority seeks to grow beyond the face-to-face local community where ritual is much more effective, to a larger regional community held together, in part, by allegiance to this new sacred text.

My own research, begun a decade—or two—before this course, took an incomplete understanding of the ways in which the Abrahamic traditions developed in the West and asked, "what is a text in China?" where the nature of the writing system alone suggests different cosmological correspondences and social realities. I was asking, in other words, what constitutes textuality and how did that come together in the longest (if not the earliest) continuous literary tradition on earth. What have been the textual templates in a culture that got wind of anything traveling the trade routes while frequently suppressing change with a conservative ideology that glorified, in part, sacred texts of a rather odd sort? In several articles I was able to explore aspects of the textuality of the various forms of "scriptures" in Chinese history.[3] I concluded that scriptural textuality is certainly not one thing. Text is not the same imaginative or substantive construction everywhere it appears—it is not even the same technology or the same cosmology. "Scriptures" as sacred texts vary widely in terms of the cultural constructions of textuality as well as their cultural understandings of sacrality.

Yet clearly Chinese notions of the text have been different from those of the European tradition; its construction of writing has drawn on a very different cosmos; its textual traditions have been built by other social forces. Still the similarities drew me in. Aware of the delusions laid bare by the critical theory, I was still interested to push the issue first named by Marshall McLuhan, that is, to wonder if the medium of writing and then printing did not exert some of the same forces in any cultural setting.[4] I compared two very different sets of Daoist "scriptures." The first was a fifth-century set of Daoist revelations that appeared on the scene to rival another earlier set, effectively closing down all further revelation, establishing a canon of sorts, and making access to its revelations a matter of the ritual expertise of a new priesthood. These were "scriptures" revealed to the pious, and purist, few; some were even written in a celestial script illegible to the unfit. Curious about how printing and mass distribution would affect this type of textual revelation, I looked to the fifteenth and sixteenth century, when the technology for both cheap paper and ink created the conditions for mass printing. (Printing in China, of course, appears to go back to the ninth century, based on currently extant materials.) In these centuries many other types of texts were proclaiming themselves as revealed "scriptures;" not wholly Confucian, Buddhist, or Daoist, the morality books (shanshu) or precious scrolls (baojuan) were the main contenders in a large field of competitive options. Choosing to focus primarily on paradigmatic shanshu, I found that they had many of the bells and whistles associated with the "scriptures" of the Daoists, Buddhists, and Confucians, but they argued that a person needed only this one book to "be saved"; its revelation, words of the Lord Lao, and its sometimes extensive commentary were said to contain everything important in all the famous and inaccessible "scriptures" of China's mainstream institutions.

In an interesting example of the impact of textual technology on the type of religious message these texts were spreading, the shanshu put great emphasis on distributing the tract, often repeating the good karma to be had by supporting the printing and circulation of the text. One late edition of the Taishang ganying pian (Treatise on the Most High on the Retribution for All Action) argued that the greatest good a person could possibly do (for unlimited good karma, in effect) would be to help disseminate this tract; if it transformed one person (who would distribute it), it could potentially transform ten thousand people; if it spread to one city, it could go on to ten thousand cities.[5] The phenomenon of a printed "scriptures" invigorated—not a Protestant revolution, for many interesting reasons—but clearly a populist prerogative to receive revelations and blend religious teachings. It also presents a moral ethic in which so much good would be done by promotion of the material product itself—an ethic curiously in keeping with the mercantile culture battling for a place in the conservative traditions of China. Yet with a political system usually able to crush any version of religious populism that might threaten its authority, this new form of text appears to have encouraged rather conservative forms of popular religion. There are other texts from this period bearing more radical visions, and their textual practices also challenged the cultural norm. The practices associated with these new revelatory "scriptures" closely corresponded to the type of message they conveyed.

In brief, the preceding argument is the basis for pursuing comparison among scriptural phenomena on the level of textuality and everything we can do to inform that complex notion. There is no one phenomenon or scenario behind the notion of "scriptures," but perhaps the material nature of texts that must be written, gathered up, and circulated introduces a basis for comparison that is not confined to features internal to the "scriptures," as assumed in most exegeses.

Biblical scholars have been involved in all of the theoretical issues raised across the academy by the explorations of critical theory. Going back further, the history of the book suggests that Bible study was at the forefront of the development of logical and historical methods of scholarly interpretation. Yet, from outside this field, the study of "scriptures" can appear rather insular. I do not question the zeal with which any new bit of parchment is used to rethink assumptions and recast the larger context. The most rigorous methods of analyzing the Christian "scriptures" have not been as difficult for the field as something else—quite simply, cross-cultural comparison. In other words, while bringing all the current theoretical apparatus to bear, the focus of biblical studies is still only one scriptural corpus (both canonical and noncanonical, of course), which may be extended outward indefinitely but still avoid formal comparisons. Biblical study explores textuality only in regard to one set of texts, however narrowly or widely defined. It does not, as a discipline, engage in serious, systematic comparison with "scriptures" as a phenomenon in other cultural contexts. Certainly the human limits of mastering the requisite languages would appear to be a major obstacle, but that is not a reason for the lack of a comparative reflex. It is interesting to wonder if the reluctance or inability to engage in comparison may be connected to the failure to see other "significations," even within the wider Christian tradition of biblical practices.

While historical and scientific studies undertaken by biblical studies surely challenged earlier understandings of faith in the holy book, comparison does something else. Comparison challenges uniqueness; it subsumes this book of books within a crowded category as one among many. It leads to the conjecture that there is no one scriptural phenomenon. Biblical studies clearly has its way of dealing with the text on the one hand, and its sacred revelation on the other. Comparison, however, brings to the fore not only the plethora of texts and "scriptures," but also the extensive history of a wide variety of "revelations." This may be the reason, or some part of the reason, that the comparative reflex seems slow to catch the interest of biblical studies. Their quest for the earliest manuscripts also sets aside the problem that the historical development of "signifying" practices resulted in multiple versions of the text and multiple communities. Indeed, Bible scholars left all that to the church historians.

Where does the scriptural phenomenon start and end? This is a boundary question, and I set it aside for now. It is more interesting and effective to stalk the phenomenon by asking how many different types of texts and interpretive communities can be usefully unraveled, if even just a bit, by a comparison-driven understanding of a concept of "scriptures" that embraces all the issues accompanying textuality, and might even be applied to other media and modes of creation.

NOTES

1. William A. Graham, *Beyond the Written Word: Oral Aspects of Scripture in the History of Religion* (Cambridge: Cambridge University Press, 1987), 162–163.

2. Jack Goody and Ian Watt, "The Consequences of Literacy," *Literacy in Traditional Societies*, ed. Jack Goody (Cambridge: Cambridge University Press, 1968), 27–68.

3. See Catherine Bell, "'A Precious Raft to Save the World': The Interaction of Scriptural Traditions and Printing in a Chinese Morality Book," *Late Imperial China* 17 (June 1996): 158–200; Catherine Bell, "Printing and Religion in China: Some Evidence from the *Taishang Ganying Pian*," *Journal of Chinese Religions* 20 (Fall 1992): 173–186; Catherine Bell, "Ritualization of Texts and Textualization of Ritual in the Codification of Taoist Liturgy," *History of Religions* 27 (1988): 366–392.

4. Marshall McLuhan, *Understanding Media: The Extensions of Man* (New York: McGraw Hill, 1964).

5. Bell, "A Precious Raft," 158.

2   *Signifying Revelation in Islam*

TAZIM R. KASSAM

The wider context of this essay is to bring about an epistemic shift in theorizing about "scriptures" by making transparent the signifying process and by calling into question the methods and activities by which (scriptural) meaning is made and legitimated. This involves looking from the margins to the center where dominant discourses and frames of reference have established the hermeneutical norms and epistemic regimes for understanding and relating to "scripture(s)." Such a venture invokes the broader question of how to relate to scriptural language given the sacred status that it enjoys. What questions might one ask of "scriptures" and their signifiers by standing outside the religious claims made on behalf of them? This framework, applied to the study of Islamic "scriptures" and sacred texts, is modestly attempted here. My arguments in what follows will be confined to philosophical and phenomenological aspects of Islamic scripture rather than historical, form-critical, and philological issues. I consider what is meant by the phenomenon called scripture in Islam and try to articulate a phenomenology of Islamic scripture by addressing four interrelated questions. First, what do we mean by "scriptures" in the case of Islam? How have Muslims at large come to signify it? Second, what is the phenomenon of revelation? What was Muhammad's experience of the Qur'an in the active sense of divine disclosure? Third, what role did the prophetic experience of revelation play in signifying "scriptures"? Finally, what are the implications of opening up the idea of "scriptures" to signify not just the sediment but also the process of revelation? How would this recast vernacular and counter-hegemonic "scriptures"?

"Scriptures" as Cultural Artifact

First, what do we mean by "scriptures" generally speaking and specifically in the case of Islam? If we classify "scriptures" under the wider rubric of cultural artifacts that are textual in nature, including originally oral utterances that became inscribed into written form, we may say that "scriptures" are a subcategory of textual artifacts that are highly saturated with power and meaning. They are texts (oral and written) that are imbued with sacred authority such that they function as templates and charters of a society's cultural norms. God, a supernatural power, divine being, or ancestral spirit is usually the presumed author or originator of texts called "scriptures." This claim to ultimacy is both self-referential (staked out within "scriptures") and socially sanctioned (accorded to "scriptures" by religious specialists and believers). The avowals of absolute authority that are found in "scriptures" are thus taken to be self-evident and axiomatic by those within a scripture's charismatic field of influence.

Two points need to be made. First, the claims to ultimacy made by "scriptures" and on their behalf circumscribe what can be said of them. This is the self-referential element of ultimacy that is structurally integrated into "scriptures" as an axiom or self-evident truth. For instance, in many verses of the Qur'an, God identifies himself as speaker: "And to you is bestowed the Qur'an from the presence of the All-Knowing, Wise" (27:06) or "God is Merciful and Compassionate; the Beneficent who revealed the Qur'an, created humans, gave them speech" (55:1–4). At the same time, "scriptures" receive their authority and legitimacy through the repeated affirmation of their affiliated community. Thus it is typical from the vantage point of the faithful to believe that their "scriptures" are compelling to all; however such is not the case. The axiomatic nature of claims to absolute authority and truth has to be stated and made transparent so that interpreters can perceive the moves made within "scriptures" to establish the boundaries, limits, and terms of acceptable discourse about "scriptures."

Second, it follows that any analytical or theoretical move that considers "scriptures" as a subset of texts of cultural significance and as a cultural, historical artifact creates anxiety, for this contextualization is seen as relativizing it and thus undermining its (assumed) intrinsic sacred value, status, and authority. It is not necessarily the case, however, that the appreciation of "scriptures" be wedded to allegiance to it. Cragg rightly asks, for instance, does one need "to 'own' a Scripture credally in order to possess it intelligently? Can one belong with a text in sympathy if not in dogma?"[1] Indeed it may be argued that an approach to "scriptures" as a subset of textual cultural artifacts opens them up to any intelligent reader, irrespective of his or her theological commitment, for thoughtful reflection and critical appreciation. For, notwithstanding its claim to ultimacy, every scriptural text is also "the climax—and also the deposit—of an inter-play of historical, liturgical, communal and editorial factors."[2] And thus, as oral-textual artifacts imbedded in social history, "scriptures"—like art, architecture, technology, and so on—are cultural productions worthy of intellectual and aesthetic attention.

Traditional View of "Scriptures" in Islam and Its Implications

The Qur'an has been an inexhaustible font of inspiration to Muslims over the centuries. It has stimulated continuing reflection and action in the realms of Islamic ritual, aesthetics, philosophy, law, and spiritual and moral life. In addition, while this is not commonly recognized, wide-ranging and contending views and interpretations exist about the meaning and status of Islamic "scriptures" both within and outside the Muslim world. Attempting to categorize these diverse approaches to the Qur'an using an accessible and multivocal metaphor of Lover and Beloved to capture the complex relation between the Qur'an and its interpreters, the progressive Muslim scholar Farid Esack offers a sixfold typology: ordinary Muslims, confessional Muslim scholars, critical Muslim scholars, participant observers, revisionists, and polemicists.[3] The typical traditional Muslim view about the Qur'an (which in his schema would include ordinary Muslims and confessional Muslim scholars) is summed up by Esack as follows: "For Muslims the Qur'an is *the literal word of God*. It is *God speaking*, not merely to the Prophet in seventh-century Arabia, but from all eternity to all humankind [emphasis mine]."[4] He cites a passage from Mukarram Ibn Manzur (d. 1312) that reflects the views of the vast majority of Muslims. In his famous lexicon *Lisan al-Arab*, Ibn Manzur defines the Qur'an as "the unique revelation, the Speech of God revealed to the Prophet Muhammad through the Angel Gabriel (always existing) literally and orally in the exact wording of the purest Arabic."[5] Esack carefully demonstrates that "the predominant Muslim thinking is emphatic about the otherness of the Qur'an."[6]

Signifying the Qur'an as a divine text, word for word, has had serious consequences for Muslims with respect to its understanding, exegesis, and uses. The theological claim makes a clear-cut and incommensurable distinction between God's Word and prophetic word. Even though the prophet's life and historical situation is thoroughly implicated in the "descent" and "reception" of the Qur'an, a fact recognized by traditional Muslim exegetes themselves, such theological positions were encrusted early in Islamic history and closed off further investigations about the enigmatic but ever-fertile relation between Word and word. The impulse to safeguard the divine origin of the Qur'an led to exegetical practices that insisted on an unequivocal and sharply contrasted distinction between the divine and the human in the event of revelation. Thus, deep and rigorous intellectual reflections about the relation between prophetic experience and divine word were undercut and made out of bounds through the establishment of dogmatic positions about the essential nature of the Qur'an (such as its inimitability, eternality, and miraculous nature) and of Muhammad (such as his alleged illiteracy). As Esack argues, the "hermeneutical implications of the idea that the Qur'an as scripture exists outside history" was to make "a neat and seemingly unbridgeable distinction between the production of scripture on the one hand and its interpretation and reception on the other hand."[7] In addition to repressing and eliminating divergent opinions and debates, these dogmatic positions, established and enforced through political means as "orthodox," have structured and set strict limits on thinking about the Qur'an, and on exploring questions concerning the phenomenology of revelation, the epistemology of scripture, and Muhammad's role as receiver and messenger of divine guidance.

In particular, it is important to examine the implication of a static and literal identification of the Qur'an as divine speech for the prophet of Islam. What does such an uncompromising position mean for Muhammad's individual gifts and character? As stated earlier, the traditional understanding of revelation is that the Qur'an was dictated to Muhammad in Arabic by God through the angel Gabriel. Muslim scholars such as Muhammad ibn Abd al-Zarkashi (d. 1392) and Jalal al-Suyuti (d. 1440) describe the "descent" of the Qur'an in three stages based on various hadith or traditions ascribed to Muhammad. The first stage is from God to the divine tablet, an eternal, spiritual repository of all revealed books also called the mother of the book (umm al-kitab). The second stage is the descent of the entire Qur'an from this divine blueprint on the night of majesty (layl tul qadr) to the lowest heaven described as the abode of honor (bayt al-'izzah). And finally, from this abode of honor the Qur'an is revealed to Muhammad piecemeal over twenty-three years through the angel Gabriel.[8] Muhammad's role parallels Gabriel's role as messenger in as much as it is regarded literally in terms of transmitting verbatim the divine speech of God. Cragg explains that "this understanding of a syllabic deliverance has long served to reassure Muslims of the infallible nature of the text, as immune from any mental or literary participation in the process on Muhammad's part, he being a totally passive, allegedly illiterate, recipient."[9] Muhammad's position is essentially reduced to that of a conduit, a passive, inert mouthpiece of God.

The myriad historical reasons why Muslim theologians felt the need to safeguard the Qur'an as God's speech uninfluenced by Muhammad cannot be fully examined here. Suffice it to say that Muhammad's authority was challenged by his Arab contemporaries, both the Meccans and the Jewish tribes in Medina, who demanded he produce a holy book (kitab) and perform miracles that proved that God was speaking to him.[10] Clearly, the Arabs who first heard Muhammad reciting the Qur'an did not immediately recognize or accept it as divine revelation. In response to the jeers and taunts of his contemporaries, Muhammad received revelations that asserted that every prophet was given a miracle, and Muhammad's miracle was the Qur'an itself. His contemporaries were challenged to produce verses like it, and the Qur'an declared that no human being could compose verses equal to it in eloquence and power. Other verses in the Qur'an emphasized that the revelations were from God and not invented by Muhammad.

The key point is that in the interest of safeguarding the Qur'an as divine speech or the literal word of God, official doctrines such as the Qur'an's miraculous nature and inimitability ('ijaz) had to be hung on other presumptions, notably that Muhammad was illiterate (ummi) and that his reception of the Qur'an was unconscious. But while these positions appear to deliver the Qur'an from any influence by Muhammad, they do so by impairing Muhammad on many levels. He may not have been the most literate of his Arab contemporaries, but it seems very likely that he could read and write given his early career as a tradesman responsible for managing business contracts for his wife Khadija, as well as his statesman's role in drawing up the constitution of Medina when he moved there. Many scholars doubt that Muhammad was illiterate and consider this claim to be a later invention to lend support to the doctrine of the Qur'an's unique and inviolably divine character and inimitability ('ijaz).[11] Early Qur'anic scholarship by Muslims even suggests that there were contending opinions on these matters.

The conflation of divine revelation with divine speech—where divine speech (kalam allah) is taken literally to be the same as the linguistic symbols and speech acts that humans know, namely, strings of words ordered by grammar and syntax, and in the case of the Qur'an, specifically in circa-sixth-century Arabic—has resulted in theological positions that create many difficulties. In as much as this view reduces Muhammad to a passive and involuntary state in the transmission of revelation, it simplifies the nature of religious experience and the human experience of the divine, and it undermines any systematic investigation of what one may call a phenomenology of revelation. To be sure, Muhammad was human, but did his humanity preclude him by definition from apprehending the divine? A mechanical view of the prophet's role in his reception of revelation compromises Muhammad's individual gifts and his worthiness for being the "chosen one" (*mustafa*), and thus it deserves to be reconsidered even within an Islamic framework. As Cragg notes, it is also arguably disloyal to the Qur'an itself, which says, "We have sent it down upon your heart" (2:97), a recognition that revelation occurs at the center and core of Muhammad's being.[12]

Thus, one might raise the question of the meaning of revelation from an epistemological viewpoint. In terms of knowledge, what kind of episteme does revelation (identified as "scriptures") represent? Or more broadly speaking, if revelation, which is at the basis of Qur'anic scripture, is an experience not commonly accessible to ordinary human beings, what is being revealed (or recovered) in that experience? What is the status of that knowledge, what kind of knowledge is it, what type of contact with reality does it signify, and at which level of reality? These questions raise crucial issues concerning the nature of human language, perception, and cognition, such as how is this type of (divine or hidden) knowledge received or gained; that is, what is the way of perceiving revelation? What instruments of human perception are involved: is it spirit, imagination, reason, intuition, the physical senses, and so on? The point of raising these issues is to draw attention to the problem of radical simplification involved in identifying the Qur'an (or any "scriptures") as the literal word of God; the nature and limits of human perception, discursive practices, epistemological and ontological claims, and historical conditions are all implicated in any religious experience, including the phenomenon of revelation.

A Phenomenology of Revelation in Islam

First, what is the phenomenon that we call scripture in Islam? The typical answer to this question is, of course, the holy book, the Qur'an. Muslims describes themselves, along with Christians and Jews, as People of the Book or *ahl al-kitab*. But is the phenomenon about which we speak, is revelation, literally speaking, a book? At the time when Muhammad taught his message was the Qur'an a book? Was it even a *mushaf* or collection of folios or leaves of writing bound between two covers? Did Muhammad himself think of the Qur'an as a book? Did he make any effort to compile all the revelations he received into the Qur'an? When did the Qur'an come into existence as the book of scripture we know it to be today? What was the Qur'an before it came to be the Qur'an? Put differently, what was revelation before it came to be a book of scripture? Is there not a valid distinction to be made between revelation as experience and revelation as book? What are we theorizing about when we refer to "scriptures" in Islam? Is it possible to theorize about Islamic scripture not only as a book, but in terms of its antecedent and basis, what Cragg aptly calls the event of revelation, namely Muhammad's experience of "receiving" the Qur'an? The point I am urging here is not the obvious one, namely, that the Qur'an as a book of scripture had a historical period of formation. Rather it is a more philosophical question regarding the phenomenology of the Qur'an as epiphany and divine disclosure. It is pushing to the foreground for deliberate attention the notion of revelation as a verb, not a noun, as a living encounter, not an indelible inscription.

The Qur'an in its incipient form refers to Muhammad's episodic experiences of revelation during his twenty-three years as prophet; namely, those eruptive and intimate moments of disclosure of God's will to Muhammad in spite of himself. During his prophetic career, Muhammad's Qur'anic recitations were speech acts consequent on profoundly moving and physically exhausting religious experiences. The prophet described revelation as agonizing; he reportedly said, "never once did I receive revelation without thinking that my soul had been torn away from me."[13] In this first instance then, the phenomenon of "scriptures" is neither book nor text, but a texture of (mainly auditory) heart-rending and ecstatic (as in the Greek *ekstasis*: standing outside, climbing above, or beyond) experiences recalled and recreated through recitation or recital of oracular speech. This sequence clearly involved an act of memory and remembrance, an important point to bear in mind when considering the actual words of the Qur'an, because the articulation of revelation in language involved an intellectual process of world formation. Obviously, because revelation is among the most elemental of religious claims, and lies at the heart of the Qur'an, it must be thoughtfully and sensitively tackled. As Cragg succinctly puts it, the key issue to be grappled with is "What can be understood by the divine and the human in partnership—if such we can believe it to be—of 'revelation' and 'inspiration'?"[14] This issue can be further divided into two parts: the question of divine-human encounter and the question of the expression of this encounter in symbolic form, including language.

The exegetical tradition in Islam acknowledges the contextuality of every verse in the Qur'an, namely, that revelation was a divine response to a human situation. Nonetheless, as previously noted, the will to safeguard the Qur'an as God's speech has sustained the dominant theological Muslim view of Muhammad as a passive recipient of revelation. The desire to make the Qur'an infallible and to secure its untouchable status by claiming it to be utterly divine and otherworldly led to the logic that Muhammad, the individual man and prophet, be made to disappear. Traditional accounts often render Muhammad unconscious in his reception of revelation. This theological position, however, is weak for many reasons. First, it must contend with a philosophical problem: is it not a flawed presumption to assert that God's Word as divine, eternal, infallible, and perfect can exist in a conditioned, changing, and imperfect world? More challenging than this logical fallacy is the tenuous and troubling principle that the divine status of revelation must stand in inverse relation to the prophet's human involvement. What sense does it make that Muhammad was rendered unconscious while receiving revelation but was fully conscious while delivering it? How were his cognitive faculties absent during revelation but present to deliver it? Was it not necessary that he be as fully "awake" and "present" in receiving revelation as he was in conveying its power and meaning through words? One may argue, in fact, that his own gift and authority was located precisely in this fact, namely, that he was able to receive revelation (something ordinary mortals cannot readily do). Not only must the prophet's conscious engagement be diminished by this manner of sanctifying revelation, but so too the divine is compromised when the Qur'an as book/scripture is forced to function in place of God as divine word. Scripture becomes a displacement of divine being. It is not, however, difficult to understand the development of such theological positions given self-referential verses in the Qur'an that declare it to be "a book in which there is nothing dubious" (2:2), although much depends on how "book" is to be understood. As Cragg notes, what all this has meant for many Muslims is "the assumption of a total abeyance of the human factor of Muhammad in the recipience of revelation. Hence, the belief in his illiteracy and in the Arabic syllables of a celestial dictation in which human thought, will, emotion, have played, and could play no part."[15]

This view needs to be challenged for historical and humanistic reasons. That the Qur'an as it stands is saturated with particularities of context and history is well acknowledged by Muslim and non-Muslim scholars alike, even though the latter two may disagree on how they interpret the specificity of language and references in the Qur'an. As Cragg says, "The whole Qur'an, once it begins, is situational. It has what Muslims themselves call 'the occasions of revelation' (*asbab al-nuzul*). With his context Muhammad is vitally, even heroically engaged."[16] That Muhammad was fully involved and implicated in the revelation of the Qur'an is a historical fact. Muslims bear testimony to this mutuality in the *shahadah*: "There is no god but God and Muhammad is his messenger." Muhammad as the "chosen" (*mustafa*) messenger suggests that the reception of revelation is not a purely passive matter in as much as Muhammad's personal character, conscience, and yearnings were engaged (else any other sixth-century Arab may have served the role). The Qur'an need be no less riveting as "scriptures" if Muhammad's condition of receptivity is acknowledged, as also the implications for religious perception that his humility and humanity had for those whom he taught and those who were to follow his example. Poets are better at capturing this point. Rumi says in a couplet in his Mathnavi: "The sufi's book is not of ink and letters; it is nothing but a heart as white as snow" (2:159).[17] Prior to the writing of the Qur'an with ink on parchment or paper, prior to the memorization of verses by his companions, and prior even to the shaping of the words of the Qur'an into a human language, in this case Arabic, was an experience that moved Muhammad's soul. That was the primary phenomenon: revelation as a happening and a mode of being.

It is interesting to note that there is no record of Muhammad attempting to gather all the revelations he experienced during his lifetime into the book that would be later called the Qur'an.[18] One can speculate about this but clearly the primary impulse of Qur'anic revelation for Muhammad was to bring his fellow human beings into the presence of God. This is to be understood on many levels ranging from the social, ethical, and worldly to the artistic, intellectual, and spiritual. At minimum, the cultivation of humility and receptivity of heart that made Muhammad a finely tuned receiver for such an experience were essential criteria for any relationship between the divine and human. His very fallibility is paradoxically the precondition of his humility. Muhammad epitomizes the notion that no human being can be fully so without the divine, and he holds out the promise of rending the thousand veils (of ignorance and blindness), separating the two so that the human ultimately attains his or her highest potential, which is a form of unique insight and self-recognition disclosed through divine guidance. Thus the role that Muhammad plays in receiving revelation suggests a theology of perception and enlightenment along the lines developed in esoteric Islamic traditions. No message can be received if the reception is not clear and if the instrument that receives the message can make no sense of it, has not the capacity to absorb it. In this sense, the receptor is very much involved in that message.

The alternative view suggested by Cragg, that the more revelation is divine, the more it recruits and activates the human,[19] is compelling precisely because it dignifies the prophet and also offers scope for a historically sensitive appreciation of the human quest for the divine. In other words, the attainment of human perfection (as an ideal, because perfection as such is only divine) is a constant struggle and movement toward ever-greater attainment of the attributes of the divine in human development. Revelation thus finds its (relative) perfection in the most attuned human response to it. The argument here is that Muhammad was of a nature, inherited and cultivated, that he could "bear" that experience. As such, he embodies the first living symbol of Islam as a historical faith, a manifestation of the spirit of revelation in pursuit of its core principles, including compassion, justice, generosity, and so forth. Muhammad receives the gift of divine disclosure from that which is wholly other because of his capacity to do so. This then is the first step in that divine-human encounter: to be worthy of the divine generosity manifest in revelation. Then comes the second step, namely, the vocation and compulsion to convey to others that gift of divine speaking with its generous, capacious, and awe-inspiring spirit. The impact of the Qur'an on his contemporaries, and on centuries of Muslims ever since, signals that Muhammad succeeded.

The point I have endeavored to make is that in addressing the central question, what is the phenomenon of which we speak, it is possible to distinguish between revelation as an experience Muhammad received and revelation as "scriptures" Muslims received and compiled. Both are called Qur'an. This distinction has been carefully demonstrated by Daniel Madigan in his unique study titled *The Quran's Self-Image: Writing and Authority in Islam's Scripture*. Madigan systematically investigates what the Qur'an says about itself. In particular, he analyzes the semantic field of the word *kitab* (book) in the Qur'an to ascertain its significance given the prominence of the orality of the Qur'an both at its inception during Muhammad's recitals and in its daily liturgical rehearsal by Muslims ever since.[20] A careful analysis shows that the categories of revelation, writing, guidance, and book are conflated in understandings of the Qur'an after Muhammad. Madigan notes that Muhammad himself does not appear to have given much thought to leaving behind such a book or "scriptures" and did not lead an effort to compile one during his life. Hence, when he died, there was no Qur'an as it exists today. Quite likely the idea of the Qur'an as a holy book of scripture belonging to a community comes later; "book" during the period of revelation stands as a symbol for divine knowledge and guidance. In other words, the "writing" that is referred to in the Qur'an is a guidance; "writing" signifies knowledge that guides. Just as "lightning," mentioned in the Qur'an as a divine sign (*ayah*), lights up and charts a clear path in the darkness of night, so too "book" signifies a divine revelation or telling that makes things clear in the midst of confusion and ignorance. Both lightning and book are symbols pregnant with meaning, and neither is necessarily literal.

Madigan demonstrates that the Qur'an understands itself not so much as a complete and fixed book but as an ongoing process of divine writing and rewriting, as God's compelling and compassionate response to actual people, circumstances, and events. Revelation is a continuous, intimate, and contextual "speaking," a witness to the verse declaring that "God is closer to you than your jugular vein" (50:16). He concludes that "taken all together, what the Qur'an says of the kitab points not to a circumscribed corpus of liturgy, dogma, and law that can be duplicated and parceled out for each group, but to an open-ended process of divine engagement with humanity in its concrete history."[21] It is thus perhaps more accurate to call the phenomenon of revelation in Islam a speaking and reciting, to emphasize its verbal, dynamic, and inspiring aspect, than to call it a scripture or book that constitutes a static and frozen entity. Indeed, while the Qur'an came to be a book, over the centuries, Muslims' encounters with it have been quintessentially oral in the form of recitations. First and foremost, the Qur'an is a recital of inspiration, and Muslims have rehearsed it liturgically by reenacting its original episodic and profoundly moving and piercing spiritual presence.

Vernacular Literatures As Recovering/ Rehearsing the Spirit of Revelation

Finally, I want to conclude this essay by briefly examining the implications of such a reconsideration of the phenomenon of revelation. If the term "signifying" in "signifying scriptures" refers to the activity of signifying or giving meaning to and setting apart certain texts, it is clear that in the first instance, the process of revelation is itself the precondition to signifying what comes later to be known as "scriptures." Revelation as verb precedes "scriptures" as noun. When we shift the focus to the signifiers, the agents and actors who are responsible for signifying "scriptures," in the case of Islamic scripture, Muhammad is the first signifier. It is he who plays the pivotal role of signifying verses of the Qur'an as revelation. This reframing is critical in its implications. For one thing, it relocates the field of analysis from "scriptures" as fixed text to the charismatic office of the prophet. Weber's distinction between prophets and priests, and his discussion of the routinization of the charisma of the prophet, is relevant here. The prophet is the primary figure in the line of signifying "scriptures," followed by scholars, jurists, exegetes, and mystics, who are secondary signifiers.

Examining the phenomenology of revelation highlights the paradox of revelation as both in, of, and outside history. Undoubtedly, the language of the Qur'an shows its intimate relation to the socioeconomic, cultural, and political world of Muhammad. Its vocabulary, discourse, and ethos disclose its historicity, and accordingly its pertinence to Muhammad's time. While the Qur'an is shot through with historical referents that reveal an indebtedness to a specific time, place, and culture, it is also implicated in charting out new horizons and transforming and recreating the world from which it draws its discourse or systems of signification. The prophet's revelation is thus also a revolution; it is tied to a mission of world making and world unfolding. In this sense, it is a departure from the known. It is a departure from history and challenges the precepts of historicism. If we thus maintain focus on the revelatory aspect of the divine word in Islam, it becomes possible to consider a wider spectrum of manifestations of inspiration riffing off the Qur'an itself. That is to say, there is always a fresh, subversive, and potentially unsettling element to revelation, and scripturalization, or the routinization of revelation that results in "scriptures," is often intended to tame and contain this liberating power.

The prophet's charisma and experience of revelation becomes routinized (and institutionalized through exegetical practices) into "scriptures;" so Muhammad's charisma or experience of revelation is distilled in the Qur'an, but the contextuality of his speech-acts is lost the moment it becomes scripture. The Shia attempted to resolve this problem through their Imams, whom they recognized as the primary signifiers of the Qur'an after the prophet. Thus they refer to their Imams as the speaking Qur'an (*quran-i natiq*) and the Qur'an itself as the silent Qur'an (*quran-i samit*). Many traditional exegetes of the Qur'an, insisting that the text speaks for itself, would deny the fact that they are engaged in the signifying process. The concept of *Imamah* in Shia Islam underscores the inevitability of interpretation and the self-conscious necessity of signifying "scriptures," conceding that revelation remains a limitless, ongoing, dynamic expression of God's will and mercy to humankind. Hence the signifying practices that have developed in the Shia and Sunni traditions have gone in different directions, with the Shia placing much greater emphasis on symbolic and analogical interpretation of scripture.

Scripturalization is the human activity of making certain texts prohibitive to interrogation, of screening them off and creating taboos against applying various sets of discursive practices to them. The efficacy of "scriptures" rests on a paradox, namely, to selectively forget or disavow its cultural-historical-political dimensions and confess its sacred-mythical dimensions. Accordingly, secondary and tertiary signifiers of "scriptures," the scholars and priests of "scriptures," must resist applying particular forms of criticism to it because this would undo or unmake "scriptures." The structure of scriptural texts also tends to dictate its own terms. It is thus necessary to interrogate discourses that dictate their own terms of engagement and discursive practices that ensure that there is only a given way to interact with "scriptures." Obviously what is at stake here are self-interests (power, legitimacy, authority) gained by establishing the rules of engagement. What benefits accrue to those who signify "scriptures" and who reserve for themselves the power to do so?

Framing the phenomenon of "scriptures" as the process of revelation as well as its oral/textual materialization, and keeping in mind the charismatic office of the prophet, offers a keener appreciation of the place of vernacular traditions that emerge from the margins. These vernacular "scriptures"-and sacred works may be simultaneously complementary and counter-scriptural. As riffs of Qur'anic revelation, they build on it, extend it, and complement it; but often they act as a counterpoint, challenging the epistemic regimes of "scriptures" and its invested signifiers. Inevitably "scriptures" have also been used as a means of domination and oppression. Engaging them as "scriptures" with their force of divine authority often means becoming implicated in their oppressive uses. Vernacular "scriptures" generally arise from voices of poets and preachers at the periphery who deconstruct or de-center normative structures while at the same time weave new social textures and identities. In this respect, they mirror Muhammad, who acted from a space that was outside the status quo. He experienced his first revelation in a cave, a place far away from the hegemonic discourses of his day. His was a counter-discourse in its time, and it arose from a point of exile or at least from the margins, away from the center, and as a challenge to that center. Apart from this, his revelations began from a personal quest, not a political quest, from a searching for something deep and profound, for his life's ultimate meaning. So, too, the inspired works of vernacular poets and preachers are part of a personal quest for truth that may necessitate a reaction to and assertion against what Vincent Wimbush aptly describes as the "tightly controlled almost obsessive focus on (scripturalized) texts" that results in "rendering invisible or inauthentic the complex worlds of vernacular orientations and traditions, both oral and (unconventionally) scripted."[22]

This "tightly controlled almost obsessive focus" can be seen in some areas of Islamic studies and scholarship (Muslim and non-Muslim) that are exclusively Arabo-centric in their emphasis as well as in the dismissal of literary productions of Muslims in other languages. Traditional Muslim scholars have themselves successfully anchored Islamic scripture, law, and theology in Arabic, signifying it as God's language. The question of signifying thus goes to the very script itself, and there is a contest between the "authentic" and thus authoritative language of Islam, because God's divine speech (*kalam allah*), the Qur'an, is in Arabic, and inauthentic languages and literatures, namely, all the rest. The hegemony of Arabic language and literature in "reading" Islamic history and cultural productions is virtually complete, entrenched, and unquestioned. When the focus (and locus of meaning production) is allowed to shift to the signifiers of texts, in this case the subaltern who hear "scriptures" and sing "a different song, or an old song in a new key," then the power and mystery of the text qua revelation can be felt and expressed through virtually any language and symbol system, including religious drama and performances. Hence the challenge to what Wimbush describes as "the epistemic system in which meanings are located in a conventional semantic order"[23] invariably comes from subaltern and outsider experiences of "scriptures." Often these experiences are not merely appropriations or translations but moments of mini-revelations, of seers, poets, and mystics living at the margins and being keenly touched by a social and spiritual conscience. These new signifiers bear witness to what Madigan describes as the "open-ended process of divine engagement with humanity in its concrete history," namely, the living phenomenon of revelation.

NOTES

1. Kenneth Cragg, *Troubled by the Truth: Biographies in the Presence of Mystery* (Cleveland: Pilgrim Press, 1992), 10.

2. Ibid., 25.

3. Farid Esack, *The Qur'an: A Short Introduction* (Oxford: OneWorld, 2002), 1–10.

4. Ibid., 31.

5. Ibid., 31.

6. Ibid., 100.

7. Ibid., 110.

8. Ibid., 30–33.

9. Cragg, *Troubled by the Truth*, 152.

10. See especially chapter 2, "The Qur'an's Rejection of Some Common Conceptions of Kitab," in Dan Madigan, *The Qur'an's Self-Image: Writing and Authority in Islam's Scripture* (Princeton, NJ: Princeton University Press, 2001), 53–78.

11. Esack, *The Qur'an*, 102

12. Cragg, *Troubled by the Truth*, 152.

13. Esack, *The Qur'an*, 43: Asqalani, cited in E. M. Sartain, *Jalal al-Din al-Suyuti: Biography and Background* (Cambridge: Cambridge UniversityPress, 1973), 1:46.

14. Cragg, *Troubled by the Truth*, 158.

15. Ibid., 159.

16. Ibid., 161.

17. *Rumi Daylight: A Daybook of Spiritual Guidance*, trans. Camille and Kabir Helminski (Boston: Shambala, 1994), 97.

18. Madigan, *The Qur'an's Self-Image*, 23.

19. Cragg, *Troubled by the Truth*, 159.

20. This is lucidly demonstrated by William Graham's classic work *Beyond the Written Word: Oral Aspects of Scripture in the History of Religion* (Cambridge, UK: Cambridge University Press, 1987).

21. Madigan, *The Qur'an's Self-Image*, 178.

22. See Vincent L. Wimbush, introduction to this volume, 13.

23. Ibid.

3

Scriptures and the Nature of Authority

THE CASE OF THE GURU GRANTH IN SIKH TRADITION

GURINDER SINGH MANN

A quick look inside a *gurdwara* (house of the Guru/preceptor, Sikh place of worship) reveals the high degree of reverence with which the Sikhs hold their "scriptures." The *gurdwara* is literally the house of the Guru Granth (the Guru manifested as the book), which is covered in expensive robes (*rumalas*) and displayed at the head of a well-lit congregational hall replicating a royal court (*darbar/divan*). The text is placed on a throne-like structure with a canopy (*palaki*), and an attendant ceremonially waves a yak's tail flywhisk over it (*chaur*). The canopy and the flywhisk, two core symbols of royalty in the Indian culture, validate the Guru Granth's status as the supreme authority within the Sikh community. The text is opened in the morning (*prakash*) and put to rest in the evening (*sukhasan*), and it is transported from one place to another at an elevation above the human height and with appropriate retinue accompanying it.

Historic gurdwaras have pools attached to them where pilgrims take a holy dip (*ishnan*) prior to entering the congregational hall. In other places, all entrants undergo a ritual cleansing that includes washing of feet, hands up to the elbows, and the mouth, the five parts of the body considered most exposed (*panj ishnana*). They walk up to the Guru Granth with hands folded, leave their offerings there, register obeisance by touching their foreheads to the ground (*matha tekanha*), and then move aside and sit on the floor respectfully facing toward the text. The same setting is recreated in Sikh households, where a separate room is allocated to the Guru Granth and families gather there for daily prayers and other ceremonial events. If the house is not large enough for this arrangement, a smaller text (*gutka/sanchi*) containing selected compositions from the Guru Granth is used for prayers, and this text is assigned fitting respect by keeping it wrapped in silk cloth and placed on the top shelf of a cupboard when not in use.

The Guru Granth constitutes the center of Sikh devotional worship, which includes the following five elements: the recitation of its verses (*path*), their singing with accompaniment by musical instruments (*kirtan*), their exegesis (*katha*), a supplication (*ardas*) addressed through the text to Vahiguru (Great Guru, the most commonly used designation for God among the Sikhs), and the receiving of the divine reply (*hukam*) at the conclusion of worship. The text is opened at random, and the first composition on the left-hand top corner of the page is considered the hukam to the congregation's supplication. The Sikhs do not have a priestly class, and anyone regardless of gender or age distinction can attend to the text, recite, sing, lead the prayers, receive the hukam, or carry the text to its place of rest. Particularly, within the family setting, the lady of the house is responsible for the opening and closing of the text and related activities.

The Guru Granth also plays the central role in Sikh ritual and ceremonial life. It includes ceremonies such as the naming of the newborn (*namkaran*) with the first letter of the hukam to the family's supplication after the birth of the baby; the taking of the nectar of the double-edged sword (*khande di pahul*), symbolizing one's commitment to serve the community with complete dedication in the presence of the Guru Granth; the listening to a special prayer from the text and circumambulating it four times to mark a wedding (*lavan*); and the recitation of the complete text followed by a prayer for the peace of the departed soul (*bhog*). Because the primary thrust of the message of the Guru Granth is ethical, the text defines the norms of a meaningful and productive Sikh life.

Given this centrality of the Guru Granth in Sikh life, a variety of its printed editions, ranging from a large-size text used in congregational worship to multivolume texts for family prayers or study, are available. The text contains around 3,000 poetic compositions and is now printed with a standard pagination of 1,430 pages. It opens with a liturgical section (pp. 1–13); its main body includes thirty-one chapters constructed around the musical modes on which these poetic compositions are to be sung (pp. 14–1352); and the final section closes with miscellaneous compositions that are not set to music (pp. 1353–1430). Sikh belief in the importance of understanding the ideas enshrined in the text has historically resulted in an array of annotated editions, translated versions, and detailed commentaries. The nature of scholarship on the Guru Granth has, however, remained exegetical, though studies are available on the history of its compilation and structure.[1]

This essay is divided into three sections. It begins with a brief examination of the sociocultural context that gave rise to Sikh scripture. The main section reconstructs (1) the history of the text from its beginnings to canonization, (2) the rise of its scriptural authority, (3) and some observations about Sikh devotional and social life as reflected in early scriptural manuscripts. In a brief conclusion, I sum up Sikh understanding of their scripture and attempt to situate this understanding within the larger field of scriptural studies.[2] In addition to introducing the Guru Granth to scholars of comparative "scriptures," I hope this paper will also provide insights for those involved in theorizing about "scriptures" and advance the agenda of the Institute for Signifying Scriptures.

The Context

The story of Guru Granth began in 1530 in central Punjab, the region that serves as a bridge between South Asia, the Middle East, and Central Asia. Islam came to the region much earlier than the rest of the subcontinent. Muhammad bin Qasim captured Multan, the southern tip of the Punjab, and built the first mosque there in the 730s. Later, at the turn of the second millennium, Mahmud of Ghazni (d. 1030), the Turkish chief, annexed the Punjab to his large empire, which stretched from Samarkand in Central Asia to Ispahan in Iran. From this point on, the Punjab remained under the control of Muslim rulers, who eventually moved their capital to the city of Lahore, the cultural center of the Punjab.[3]

These developments left a deep impact on the socioreligious scene of the Punjab. The rise of mosques and Sufi centers (*khanqah*) changed the look of the regional landscape. Shaikh Fariduddin (d. 1173), a Sufi poet from southern Punjab, wrote in such beautiful Punjabi that local people turned his poetic expressions into proverbs. The arrival of Muslim ruling classes was accompanied by Afghan, Arab, Iranian, and Turkish immigrants into the Punjab. This created a difficult situation for upper-caste Hindus—Brahmans and Kshatriyas, the priestly and warrior castes, respectively. A large number of them left the Punjab plains for the hills in the north or the desert in the south. The Khatris, an indigenous Punjabi mercantile caste, filled this vacuum, thriving in their traditional profession as well as expanding their venues of employment by learning Farsi and seeking work in the administration.

A significant socioeconomic factor came into play with the introduction of the Persian Wheel, a gear and pulley system, which could lift water from a depth of around twenty feet. This resulted in an important development with the erstwhile nomads beginning settled agriculture. For the first time in their history, these people tackled the opportunity of becoming part of a settled society. In the northwest, in present-day Pakistan, these nomads joined Islam in large numbers; in the central Punjab, they took up the Sikh path.[4]

The Punjabi society around 1500 was composed of various segments—the Muslims who constituted the majority, the Hindus, the Jains, and the nomads-turned-farmers. They all had their distinct understanding of "scriptures" and its role in life. The ruling classes regarded themselves as the *ahl-al kitab* (the possessors of the holy book), and their administrative law was rooted in the Qu'ran. The Muslim community also included converts originating from both Hindu and nomadic backgrounds, for whom the idea of the text of the Qu'ran as the scripture was relatively new. Among the Hindus, there were Brahmans who literally carried the Vedic chants in their memory and firmly believed in the "oral transmission" of this sacred corpus. Women and lower castes were banned access to these sounds; only the upper-caste males could listen to them. The Jains in the Punjab, like their counterparts in other parts of the subcontinent, had a vast religious literature, and sectarian groups from among them had different notions of a religious text: the Shvetambaras accepted the role of "scriptures" but the Digambaras did not. Finally, the nomads, who had only recently been exposed to these ideas of oral and written "scriptures" may have brought their own historical proclivities while absorbing them into their lives.

Sikhs and Their Scripture

These diverse ideas about the physical form and the role of "scriptures" had thus coexisted for over half a millennium before Guru Nanak (1469–1539), the founder of the Sikh tradition, appeared on the scene. The striking thing about the Sikhs is that they began to commit to writing their sacred literature very early in their history, taking care to protect and preserve these manuscripts for posterity. As a result, a sizable number of them, including the pre-canonical documents, have survived despite the difficult weather conditions and ravages of history associated with the Punjab. This unique empirical data helps us reconstruct the history of Sikh scripture with a degree of accuracy not possible in older religious tradition. Scholars have been largely interested in the formation of the Sikh canon and the related textual issues; the details, such as the structure of the early manuscripts, marginal notes, information about those who inscribed and preserved these documents, and religio-social implications of this information, are yet to be examined.

History of the Text

Guru Nanak's beliefs, presented in more than five hundred of his poetic composi-tions, as well as details of his life available in other sources, help us understand his thinking, which resulted in the creation of the Sikh sacred text.[5] First, Guru Nanak was convinced that he had direct access to divine knowledge, and his com-positions resulted from his conversation with Vahiguru (*jaisi mai avaai khasam ki banhi tesrha kari gianu ve Lalo*, M1, GG, 722, and *ta ma kahia kahanhu ja tujhai kahaia*, M1, GG, 566).[6] Second, his writings register the importance of the institution of "scriptures." He accepted that Hindu and Semitic scriptural texts were of divine origin and that following them helps to save their adherents from evil (*chauthi upae chare Beda*, M1, GG, 839; *oankari Bed nirmae*, M1, GG, 930; *Bed path mati papa khae*, M1, GG, 791). Finally, Guru Nanak believed that the inscription of the sacred word was an act of profound devotion requiring the heart and soul of the scribe, and he urged people to devote themselves to inscribing the divine word (*jali mohu ghasi masu kari mati kagadu kari saru*, M1, GG, 16; *sunhi pande kia likhahu janajala, likhu ramnam gurmukhi gopala*, M1, GG, 930).

Having said that, Guru Nanak had no doubt that his own compositions con-tained all the significant knowledge that was needed to live life meaningfully (*sabhi nad Bed gurbanhi*, M1, GG, 879). It appears that he had written down his composi-tions as he had created them and compiled them in the form of a text later, during the 1530s. After all, he expected his followers to understand the contents of his compositions and to put them into practice in their day-to-day activities (*gurbanhi nirbanhu shabad pachhania*, M1, GG, 752; *guri kahia sa kar kamavahu*, M1, GG, 933; *satigur ki banhi sati sati kari manahu*, M1, GG, 1028). The text containing his com-positions was ceremonially passed on to his successor, Angad (Guru, 1539–1571), at the time of his elevation to the office of the Guru.[7]

Here is an instance of consciously created scriptural text during the lifetime of the founder, and the role assigned to it in the succession ceremony of the Guru marked the public declaration of its authority within the community. The new revelation sprang up in the vernacular, associated with the rustic people, and was dressed in a new script specifically created for this purpose and assigned the name of Gurmukhi (of the Gurmukhs/Sikhs).[8] As repository of divine knowledge, the text's contents were to guide the Sikh community. Its physical existence had the potential of allowing the Sikhs to obtain the recognition of ahl-al kitab and the resulting clemency from the tax paid by the non-Muslims (*jizya*), which the law of the time authorized.

Guru Nanak's text subsequently expanded to include the compositions of six Gurus, those of bards at the Sikh court, and a carefully selected set of writings of fifteen non-Sikh saints. Three of these saints came from Muslim backgrounds and twelve from Hindu backgrounds. Eleven among them, however, have symbolic presence in Sikh scripture; in all, nineteen short compositions are attributed to them. One poet has four compositions, another one three, three have two compositions each, and six have only one composition each to their credit.[9] By deciding not to enter his compositions into the text, Guru Gobind Singh (1675–1708), the tenth and the last personal Guru, declared the canon closed in the 1680s.

Building on Guru Nanak's belief regarding the nature of his compositions, Sikhs firmly consider their scripture as revealed. The compositions of six later Gurus are seen as an extension of Guru Nanak's ideas—after all, they had received their knowledge from him or a successor of his. They have their own claims for direct revelation, too (*mahali bulaia prabhu amrit bhuncha*, M5, GG, 562). The presence of the compositions of the bards at the Sikh court, and of Hindu and Sufi saints, is attributed to the decision of Guru Arjan (1581–1606), the fifth in line of the Gurus, and, according to some scholars, of Guru Nanak himself. The early manuscripts, however, support the view that these writings entered Sikh scriptural text during the period of the third Guru, Amardas (1551–1574).

Whatever the time of their entry, the text of the Guru Granth itself helps us appreciate the presence of these compositions in it. The organization of the text manifests a hierarchical understanding of the nature of revelation. Guru Nanak's compositions are situated at the top, as he had direct contact with Vahiguru; following these are the compositions of his successors who learned their lessons from him; then next come the compositions of Sikh bards who worked with his successors; the carefully selected compositions of the non-Sikh saints appear at the end. Only those that fully conformed to Sikh belief in divine unity and a vision of productive social life were kept.

As mentioned above, eleven of these saints have a nominal presence. The only striking feature of these compositions is the diversity of the social backgrounds of their creators. The caste background of all is not known, but some definitely came from low-caste and untouchable backgrounds (Dhanna, Sadhana, Sainh). The inclusion of their writings in the Sikh scriptural text makes an emphatic assertion of the social comprehensiveness of the rising Sikh community. After all, Sikh beliefs fully support social equality: if Vahiguru is the creator of all, how can there be high and low, pure and impure (*sabhana jia ika chhau*, M1, GG, 83; *manda kisno akhiai jan sabhana sahibu ek*, M2, 1238)?

The presence of bards at Sikh court sits well with another dimension of Sikh understanding of revelation. Guru Nanak is the only spiritual leader of his time who created three compositions commenting on the most significant historical event of his time, the 1526 invasion of India by Babur, the founder of the Mughal dynasty in India. Being part of the divine design, the historical events deserve to be recorded. In the verses of the Gurus, we find details of the rise of the Sikh community, including references to the tension with the Mughal rulers. Within this context, the bards' songs about the Sikh court, an important development in religious history, thus belonged to Sikh scripture.

In early manuscripts, the list of dates of the deaths of the Gurus is also available. It seems that these dates were originally recorded at the end of the texts, but, beginning with the manuscripts prepared in 1604, they were brought to the opening folios. Here were the details of a sacred history unfolding right in front of the Sikhs of the time. Guru Arjan sings of his followers scattered all over the region (*kirati hamari ghari ghari hoi, bhagati hamari sabhani loi*, M5, GG, 1141). Beginning with 1604, the manuscripts also carry a note about a large Sikh congregation in south India. They are reported to be running an extensive community kitchen (*langar*); whether it was a marker of the large size of the community or of their philanthropy in serving food to the locals is not clear, but reference to a thriving congregation made it into Sikh scriptural text.

The emphasis on the ethical import of Sikh revelation surfaces in the form of brief entries regarding what the Sikhs should or should not do. A manuscript inscribed around 1600 records an interesting fragment under the title of "five do's and five do not's" (*panj kare panj na kare*). The five "do's" are:

1. Participation in congregational worship
2. Generosity to the needy, suffering, and poor
3. Arranging for the marriage of an unmarried Sikh
4. Assisting a non-Sikh in joining the Sikh fold
5. Praying for the welfare of all with no ill will for anyone

The five "do not's" are: no stealing, no adultery, no slander, no gambling, no consumption of liquor and meat.

As Sikh scripture became canonized in the 1680s, the text was considered closed. At this point, however, Sikh understanding of revelation was interpreted strictly in terms of the poetic compositions included in the earlier text, and consequently all other details, such as the dates of the deaths of the Gurus, references to the congregation in south India, or brief statements of moral imperatives, were deleted. With the passage of time, the historical dimension of Sikh revelation that these details alluded to became increasingly de-emphasized, while the eternal aspect of Sikh scripture was supposedly brought to the forefront.

In addition to belief in revelation ensconced in the scriptural text, it also developed as a marker of the community's identity. Within this context, the Sikh text became their counterpart of the Hindu and Muslim scriptures. For Guru Nanak, there was no doubt that the text containing his compositions had all that his followers needed to know in order to live their lives meaningfully. In the 1570s, the Sikh scriptural text took the shape of four volumes, and references indicate that the number four may have stood in comparison to the four Vedas, on the one hand, and to the four Kateb (literally, books, a term used in Punjabi, to describe the four holy books of the Semites—Toret (Torah), Jambur (Psalms), Injil (Gospels), and Qu'ran), on the other. The Sikhs had absolutely no doubt that the revelation that they had received went beyond the previous ones (*dila ka malaku kare haqu, Quran kateb te paku*, M5, GG, 897). In 1604, however, the Sikhs expanded the contents of the four volumes by adding the compositions of Guru Ramdas (1574–1581), the fourth Guru, and Guru Arjan and simultaneously collapsing them into a single text. With an addition of over one hundred short compositions of Guru Tegh Bahadur (1664–1675), the ninth Sikh Guru, Sikh scripture reached its canonical form in the 1680s.

Rise of Scriptural Authority

In early Sikh history, the Guru enjoyed central authority within the community, which grew stronger with the emergence of the belief that he was the representative of Vahiguru on earth. By the turn of the seventeenth century, Bhai Gurdas (d. 1638) claimed categorically that Sikhs only recognized the authority of the Guru, and that the Mughal emperor was no match for him.[10] By the late 1690s, however, Guru Gobind Singh made the radical decision of formally dissolving the role of personal authority within the Sikh community by declaring the community to be the Khalsa (the pure) and answerable only to Vahiguru.

It may be argued that dissension within the community over the extent of the Guru's authority, and the vulnerability of the office exposed after Guru Arjan's (1606) and Guru Tegh Bahadur's (1675) execution-martyrdom at the hands of the Mughal rulers, may have influenced his thinking. Quite likely, Guru Gobind Singh concluded that the office of the Guru had served its purpose and needed to be replaced by a more enduring source of authority than that of a charismatic, but vulnerable, individual. Sikh scripture became the center of authority, hence the title, the Guru Granth, and the community was assigned the authority to interpret it.

This emergence of scriptural authority had antecedents that can be traced back to the very founding of the Sikh community. In a way, the symbolic authority of the Sikh scriptural text had coexisted with that of the personal authority of the Guru since the beginning of the tradition. The text was understood to be the container of revelation and a communal treasure beginning with Guru Nanak's time. Guru Amardas declared that the compositions of the Gurus represented Vahiguru (*vahu vahu banhi nirankar hdi tisu jevadu avaru na koi*, M3, GG, 515), and they were the light of the world (*gurbanhi isu jag mahi chananu karami vasai mani ae*, M3, GG, 67).

Guru Ramdas emphasized the liberating nature of the compositions of the Guru (*banhi guru guru hai banhi vichi banhi amritu sare. gurubanhi kahai sevaku janu manai partakhi guru nistare*, M4, GG, 982). Guru Arjan believed that the revealed text has the purpose of removing suffering from the world (*dhur ki banhi ai tini sagali chint mitai*, M5, GG, 628), and he declared the text to be the abode of Vahiguru, an object of significance in its own right (*pothi parmesar ka thanu*, M5, GG, 1226).

In early Sikh history, the role of the Guru was twofold: he served as the medium for the revealed message and the guide of the community. By the end of the seventeenth century, this divine message to the Sikhs was felt to have achieved completion with the canonization of the Granth, and the community as the Khalsa was ready to assume the burden of representing itself. At the time of Guru Gobind Singh's death, then, we see the two strands of religious authority within the community coming together in a unique form. The symbolic role of the Granth expanded to encompass the authority of the personal Guru, as manifested in its new title, the Guru Granth, and the community as a whole (Guru Panth) took up the authority to interpret it and follow their destiny in light of its teachings.

Beginning with the turn of the eighteenth century, the centrality of the text resulted in the proliferation of the Guru Granth manuscripts. The physical form of these manuscripts points to the community's welfare at the time of their creation. During the difficult times of the early eighteenth century, the manuscripts were small in size and could be tied on the back and taken to the battlefield if the need arose. The time of Sikh political ascension resulted in beautifully illuminated and neatly calligraphed megatexts with paintings on the binding pages. Scribal notes tell us about the quantity of gold powder that went into the illumination of the text. As the printing press became available, numerous editions of the Guru Granth in various sizes and forms were created.

As the Sikh numbers increased, they left their mark on the landscape of the Punjab by building gurdwaras, which by this time had become the houses of the Guru Granth. The Sikhs used the best expertise and the most expensive materials available to build these places to house the Guru Granth. As referred to earlier, the Sikh belief system does not permit a priestly class, but the gurdwara buildings needed custodians to oversee them. This basic need resulted in the emergence of the office of the *granthi*, literally, the caretaker of the Guru Granth, but in reality the granthi's responsibilities included the overseeing of the building of the gurdwara, leading the daily prayers and ceremonial activities, teaching Sikh children to read and understand the Guru Granth, and officiating on ceremonies such as the naming of children, the weddings, and the post-death rituals. Historic places such as Darbar Sahib, Amritsar, Damdama Sahib, and Talwandi Sabo emerged as large centers of learning where the granthis and other itinerant scholars of Sikh scripture and history could receive training.

Beginning with the eighteenth century, Sikh savants reiterated the beliefs enshrined in the Guru Granth itself: its contents were not only to be recited and revered but also understood and put into practice (*guri kahia sa kar kamavahu*, M1, GG, 933; *dithai mukati na hovai jicharu sabadi na kare vichar*, M3, GG, 594;

sachu kamavai sachi rahai sache savi samai, M3, GG, 560). Guru Nanak's successors attempted to elaborate on his themes and the exegesis of Sikh sacred compositions began soon after the death of the founder of the tradition. At the turn of the seventeenth century, Bhai Gurdas emerged as the first major exegete of Sikh sacred writings. The structure of his ballads (*vars*), where he takes up important themes and explains them on the basis of the Gurus' writings, reveals his commitment to providing a clear interpretation of Sikh tenets. With the passage of time, these efforts expanded to form different schools of exegesis.[11]

In the 1860s, the Sikhs enthusiastically took up the opportunity of large-scale multiplication of the text of the Guru Granth, which occurred with the arrival of the printing press to the Punjab. In the early part of the twentieth century, it was realized that there were some Sikh groups in Sindh and the Northwest province, both in present-day Pakistan, who understood Punjabi but could not read Gurmukhi. To help them, transliterated editions in Devanagari and Indo-Persian scripts were created. More recently, as large numbers of Sikhs moved to the Western world and with some Euro-Americans taking up the Sikh path in North America, an edition that has Roman transliteration and English translation has been created. The emphasis on understanding the text has in a way overshadowed other beliefs such as the sacredness of the Gurmukhi script and Punjabi language.

The period following the elevation of the text to the Guru Granth also resulted in the formation of elaborate details about: how to treat the text—no bookmark was to be put in it; how to show proper respect to it—one was to wash up before going in its presence and then always sit silently there; and how to transport it from one place to another—it was carried in a palanquin or on one's head and a proper retinue was to accompany it. The Gurmukhi, its script, was sacred and any sheet of paper on which this script was inscribed was not to be used for mundane purposes. As the text aged, it was to be disposed of by placing it in flowing water. The belief may have been that water will wash away the revealed writing and the paper will decompose. This ceremony has over time changed and now the Sikhs cremate old texts.[12] The details of the reverence offered to the Guru Granth can be traced back to the references in the early-eighteenth-century literature.

Being the supreme authority within the community, the Guru Granth was treated as the sovereign of the Sikhs, and it stayed with them no matter where they were. Supplications were offered and the hukam was taken before the Sikhs engaged their enemy in battles. In the 1750s, the Afghan army's capturing of the Guru Granth in a battle was interpreted as a crippling blow and duly recorded in Sikh memory.[13] The presence of the Guru Granth and of the gurdwara remained an integral part of the Sikh army ethos, and these traditions continued during both world wars when the Sikhs fought for the British in Europe and other parts of the world.[14]

Sikh belief in the authority of Sikh scripture resulted in two other developments. In early Sikh history, this line of thinking contributed to a vigorous sense of the authority of scriptural manuscripts. Beginning with the mid-decades of the sixteenth century, all the dissident families possessed an important manuscript, which served as the primary ground for their claim for authority. In the process, these families preserved rare pre-canonical manuscripts of unique historical value.[15] In addition, the text came to be presented in human terms; any attempt to tinker with the text's contents was interpreted as severing its body.[16] During the period of political power, land grants were assigned to the text of the Guru Granth, and later the Supreme Court of India assigned the Guru Granth, the status of a "juristic person."

Additional Issues

The seventeenth-century scriptural manuscripts present data that shed interesting light on the religio-social life of the early Sikh community. Guru Nanak believed that the paper, the pen, the ink, the inkpot, and the scribe who wrote the divine word were all blessed (*dhanu so kagadu kalam dhanu dhanu bhanda dahn masu, danau lekhari Nanaka jinni namu likhia sachu*, M1, GG, 1291). This belief permeated the consciousness of early Sikhs, and in the process they left us interesting information regarding the inscription of sacred verses as devotional experience, its implications for literacy, and the social background and status of Sikh scribes within the community.

Bhai Gurdas reports that the paper was made from hemp (*Crotolaria junica*), a plant that grows in the Punjab. The skin of the plant was turned into a paste and then dried to form a light brown paper that was non-acidic and has withstood the test of time. By the late seventeenth-century, the Sikhs had also learned the system of marking straight lines on the paper itself, which made writing easy and also aesthetically pleasant. The large sheet of paper was folded to create a gathering of eight folios that were duly numbered. The opening folio, and in some cases the middle one, too, was illuminated and a multi-lined border was drawn on all four sides of the regular pages before the writing began. The Sikh scribes carefully recorded the details of the recipe for making ink. Items such as alum, copper sulfate, collyrium, gold, indigo, musk, saffron, and sealing wax were ground together for thirty days in a copper utensil with a wooden stick coming from the tree of margosa/nim (*Azadirachta indica*). In addition to creating ink with proper shine, the copper sulfate and the nim stick added bitterness that made the ink unpalatable for mites. Once the writing was completed, the gatherings were collected, sewn together, and neatly bound in cow-hide exteriors with a free edge flap.

The preserving of the details of paper- and ink-making indicates the degree of seriousness and affection that went into the inscribing of these manuscripts. Almost a century and half after the equipment had fallen into disuse, the paper-making troughs at the Damdama Sahib, Talwandi Sabo, were still preserved. They were disposed of rather reluctantly to clear the area for new construction in the early 1990s.[17] The manuscripts record scribal notes of gratitude for divine help in the completion of the work and profuse apologies for any flaws that may have crept in their creation. The normative writings condemn any provision for selling these manuscripts: accursed are those who inscribe the sacred word for the purpose of selling it (*dhrigu tina ka jivia ji likhi likhi vechahi nau*, M1, GG, 1245).

These manuscripts also indicate the debt that the Sikhs owed to techniques of Islamic book making. In the actual style of the drawings on the opening folios, beautifully drawn borders, the technique of collecting folios in gatherings, and finally the leather binding exhibit a close affinity with Islamic manuscripts. Hindu manuscripts of the period followed their own method of putting folios between two pieces of hardboard and then tying them with a thick thread.

The extant manuscripts normally do not include the names of the scribes who prepared them. The absence of the name was a mark of humility on the part of the scribe; they made the point that not their expertise but the divine help resulted in the completion of these impressive tasks. After the text was elevated to the status of the Guru, the possibility of recording the date or the name of the scribe, or any other detail, was seen to challenge the basic integrity of the text.

Limited but intriguing data regarding the identity of the scribes in the early Sikh community are available. The Sikh tradition has preserved the names of some early scribes. The first among them is Lehna, whose name was later changed to Angad when he was elevated to the office Guru Nanak held. He is believed to have helped Guru Nanak compile and inscribe the original text, and some traditions even attribute the formation of Gurmukhi letters to him. We are told that Lehna read Guru Nanak's compositions from stray folios, and the Guru decided how the stanzas fit together, finalized the organization of the text, and Lehna then inscribed it. The first scribe known to the tradition eventually ended up as the successor of the founder.

The tradition has preserved the memory of Sahansar Ram, the grandson of Guru Amardas, as the scribe of a four-volume manuscript created in the 1570s. Next, Bhai Gurdas is associated with the manuscript created in 1604. He enjoys substantial prestige as the interpreter of Sikh beliefs and practice; his compositions are considered the key to the Guru Granth and enjoy the rare privilege of being made part of Sikh devotional singing. As a Sikh leader, he holds a status that is second only to that of the Gurus. High respect for the scribes continued as the tradition evolved. Bhai Gurdas refers to two sixteenth-century Sikh scribes, Pandha and Bulla, who were prominent figures within the community. Leading eighteenth-century figures such as Bhai Mani Singh (d. 1738) and Baba Dip Singh (d.1757) were closely involved in scribal activity.

Although the data is restricted, it does offer an interesting look at the social background of the scribes prior to their joining the Sikh fold. In addition to the above-mentioned names, the seventeenth-century scribes whose pre-Sikh background we know include Jagna (Brahman), Ramrai (goldsmith), and Burha Sandhu, Gurdita Jateta, Pakharmal Dhillon (all Jats, whose names appear in manuscripts recorded in 1605, 1653, and 1678, respectively). We thus have knowledge of the background of ten early scribes: one of them came from the priestly caste among the Hindus (Jagana), four from the Khatri caste (Lehna, Bhai Gurdas, Sahansaram, and Ramrai), and the remaining five came from nomadic backgrounds (Burha Sandhu, Gurdita Jateta, Pakharmal Dhillon, Bhai Mani Singh, Baba Dip Singh). This provides us with an indication of the distribution of the social backgrounds of those who joined the Sikh community, as well as the rise of literacy among erstwhile nomads who joined the Sikh community. We do not have their counterparts, scribes and scholars, among those who joined the Muslim and Hindu traditions.[18]

We may also address the role of Sikh patronage in the creation of scriptural manuscripts. When the Sikhs became politically powerful, their prosperity attracted the services of Muslim and Hindu scribes. In the process of working for the Sikhs, however, these scribes left the marks of their professional training on the products they created. For instance, a Muslim scribe elaborately illuminated the text using the Qur'anic style and created a beautiful painting of a cityscape on the binding pages with the mosque at its center. The Hindu scribes, on the other hand, could not resist painting some of their deities on the opening folios as part of their invocation before beginning the massive task.[19] It seems that Sikhs took these foreign embellishments in stride and did not regard them as presenting any contradiction to the message of the text.

Conclusion

Enjoying the central authority within the community, the text of Guru Granth has made a deep impact on all dimensions of Sikh life; it constitutes the highest authority, the normative source of Sikh beliefs and practice, and a marker of Sikh identity. If you see a Sikh male or female carrying a suitcase on his or her head at the airport, rest assured that the suitcase's contents comprise the text of the Guru Granth. Since the early period, Sikh devotional experience has been centered on its reading, recitation, singing, and reflection as means of communicating with Vahiguru. While the early scribes spared no pains in creating illuminated and calligraphically elegant manuscripts of the Guru Granth, eighteenth-century Sikh blacksmiths inscribed its verses on swords and shields. The printing press helped proliferate the text in various sizes and forms. If ever there was a religion of the book, this is it.

In their understanding of revelation, its manifestation as a bounded written text, and the role of this text within the community, the Sikhs have close affinity with Islam and other Semitic traditions. It should come as no surprise. The Guru Granth was, after all, created in a socioreligious context in which Islam has been around for over half a millennium and the majority of people were Muslims. Yet, following the erroneous assumptions that Sikhs have emerged from the Hindu fold, scholars continue to resist registering the Sikh closeness with Semitic traditions, manifested in the functioning of the Sikh institution of "scriptures" and the nature of its message.[20]

Finally, the Sikh case brings to light an interesting sociological dimension in understanding the nature of authority attributed to "scriptures." Contrary to the received wisdom, the overwhelming majority of those who joined the Sikh community came not from the caste-based Hindu society but from among the nomads, who have been historically known for their traditions of hostility to personal authority.[21] Writing in the mid-nineteenth century, Shah Mohammad, a Punjabi Muslim poet, claims that no matter who sits in the position of authority, the Sikhs have to pull him down (*jihrha bahe gaddi ohnu mar lainde*).[22] Having followed a sedentary lifestyle for over six centuries, this attitude toward authority does not seem to be fading away. One wonders if this is true of all nomadic people around the world, and if so, then a symbolic center of authority such as the sacred text suits their temperament better. After all, it cannot be a simple coincidence that all three traditions, Judaism, Islam, and Sikhism, originated from people of nomadic stock. I leave it for those associated with the Institute of Signifying Scriptures to ponder over this issue.

NOTES

I am grateful to Professor Vincent Wimbush for his interest in incorporating Sikh experience in broad scriptural debates and his patience with my requests for extensions to complete this essay.

1. For detailed studies of the Guru Granth, see Surinder Singh Kohli, *A Critical Study of the Adi Granth* (Delhi: Motilal Banarasidass, 1961); Pashaura Singh, *The Guru Granth Sahib* (New Delhi: Oxford University Press, 2000); and my *Making of Sikh Scripture* (New York: Oxford University Press, 2001).

2. Discussion of Sikh scripture is not available in Miriam Levering, ed., *Rethinking Scripture* (Albany, NY: SUNY Press, 1989); or Frederic M. Denny and Rodney L. Taylor, eds., *The Holy Book in Comparative Perspective* (Columbia: University of South Carolina Press, 1993). Harold Coward, however, recognized the importance of the subject and included it both in his *Sacred Word and Sacred Text* (New York: Orbis Books, 1988); and his edited volume *Experiencing Scriptures in World Religions* (New York: Orbis Books, 2000).

3. For details see Andre Wink, *The Making of the Indo-Islamic World* (New York: Oxford University Press, 1997).

4. Irfan Habib, "Jatts of Punjab and Sind," in *Panjab Past and Present: Essays in Honour of Dr. Ganda Singh*, ed. Ganda Singh, Harbans Singh, and N. Gerald Barrier (Patiala: Punjabi University Press, 1976), 92–103.

5. For two very different reconstructions of Sikh history, see Hew McLeod, *Sikhism* (New York: Penguin, 1997); and my *Sikhism* (Upper Saddle River, NJ: Prentice Hall, 2004).

6. In these references M1 stands for Mahala 1, Guru Nanak; M2 for Guru Angad and so on; and GG for the Guru Granth. The pagination of the text being uniform, these page numbers would apply to any standard edition of the Guru Granth.

7. Puratan Janam Sakhi, ed., *Shamsher Singh Ashok* (Amritsar: SGPC, 1969), 195.

8. J. S. Grewal and Irfan Habib, eds., *Dabistan-I Mazahib* (Delhi: Indian History Congress, 2001), 63.

9. Among the Bhagats whose hymns appear in the Guru Granth, Kabir (224 hymns, 237 couplets, and three long compositions), Farid (four hymns and 112 couplets), Namdev (sixty-one hymns), and Ravidas (forty hymns) are the prominent figures. The remaining eleven Bhagats—Benhi (three hymns), Bhikhanh (two hymns), Dhanna (two hymns), Jaidev (two hymns), Parmanand (one hymns), Pipa (one hymn), Ramanand (one hymn), Sadhna (one hymn), Sainh (one hymn), Surdas (one verse), and Trilochanh (four hymns)—enjoy more of a symbolic presence in Sikh scripture. While Bhikhanh, Farid, and Kabir came from a Muslim background, all others were from the large Hindu fold. For detailed discussion of this aspect of Sikh scripture, see Pashaura Singh, *The Bhagats of the Guru Granth Sahib* (New Delhi: Oxford University Press, 2003); and my *Making of Sikh Scripture*, 102–120.

10. Bhai Gurdas, ed., *Varan*, Gursharan Kaur Jaggi (Patiala: Punjabi University Press, 1987), 160.

11. Gurdas, *Varan*; and Singh, *The Guru Granth Sahib*, 239–261.

12. During the 1990s, Goindval has emerged as the central place where the old texts of the Guru Granth are brought for ceremonial cremation. People even come to watch the ceremony that is held once a month.

13. The tradition appears in Giani Gian Singh. See Harbhajan Singh, *Gurbanhi Sampadan Nirnai* (Chandigarh: Satinam Prakashan, 1989), 106–107.

14. For photographs, see Amandeep Singh Madra and Paramjit Singh, *Warrior Saints* (London: IB Tauris, 1999), 124–125, 127.

15. For the details of these families see my *Making of Sikh Scriptures*, 32–68.

16. Kesar Singh Chhibbar, *Bansavalinama Dasan Patshihan ka*, ed. Ratan Singh Jaggi (Chandigarh: Panjab University Press, 1972), 136. He interpreted the execution of Bhai Mani Singh by the Mughals as a result of his effort to restructure the text of the Guru Granth.

17. In the winter of 1992, I happened to be there when the paper-making equipment had to be removed to clear the area for new construction. I examined these objects but did not have the presence of mind to take their photographs.

18. With the exception of two Jat poets, Dhanna and Jalanh, who have left some poems, I do not know anyone else involved in literary or scholarly activity.

19. Jeewan Singh Deol, "Illustration and Illumination in Sikh Scriptural Manuscripts," in *New Insights into Sikh Art*, ed. Kavita Singh (Mumbai: Marg, 2003), 50–67.

20. Harjot Oberoi's "Sikhism," in *Experiencing Scriptures in World Religions*, ed. Harold Coward (New York: Orbis Books, 2000),133–135, is a characteristic exercise in scholarly fixation on situating the Sikh community within the Hindu fold. He concludes his essay by pointing out three differences and two similarities between the Sikh and Hindu understandings of scripture. He does not see the relevance of placing the Guru Granth along with Semitic scriptures to understand the Sikh concept of scripture or its role within the community.

21. People from the nomadic background have historically constituted the overwhelming majority of the Sikh community. The primary group, the Jats, presently composes 66 percent of the total Sikh population and their ancillary rural groups include another 20 percent or so.

22. Shah Muhammad, *Var Shah Muhammad*, ed. Ratan Singh Jaggi (Chandigarh: Panjab University Press, 1981), 16.

4   *The Dynamics of Scripturalization*

THE ANCIENT NEAR EAST

HUGH R. PAGE JR.

The launching of the new Institute for Signifying Scriptures (ISS) and the programmatic vision articulated for it by Vincent Wimbush in the introductory essay of this volume create an opportunity for reflection on an enormous number of issues related to the creation of "scriptures" and the social, political, and other dynamics that obtain when individuals and other social aggregates inscribe themselves on, read their life experiences through, or employ as basic building blocks for their identity construction and community formation, texts of various genres. In particular, scripturalization itself appears to convey, both covertly and subtly, some interesting issues, themes, motifs, and tropes. In my several endeavors as scholar, priest, academic administrator, and public intellectual, it has been my experience that the chief vehicle for the communication of the aforementioned has been the authoritative texts (i.e., the "scriptures") generated by the process itself.

The database on which I will base my observations consists of the multifaceted anthology of texts that has come to be known as the Hebrew Bible, *Tanak*, Old Testament, or First Testament, as well as the corpus of extant texts hailing from ancient Egypt, Syria-Palestine, Anatolia, and Mesopotamia. I have taken seriously the arguments made by Wimbush in his introductory essay about the starting point for the new institute's endeavors, the life experience of the marginal and subaltern; and so I have used such arguments as an opportunity to establish a tone for my remarks that accentuates exploration and play. The linking of these two processes is rarely given positive sanction by the institutions in which academic research takes place. Nonetheless both have long been the lifeblood of those specialists charged with the stewardship of intellectual and folkloric traditions throughout the world. Whether we are speaking of the *ummia* ("school-father") of the Sumerian *edubba* ("tablet house," "school"),[1] the African *griot*, or the faculty of today's colleges and universities, scholarship requires mastery of established disciplinary concepts, investigation of hitherto unexplored vistas, and the free-associative interaction with and response to a host of data drawn from the length and breadth of the human experience. It is both an art and a way of life. By reengaging the body of primary texts with which I routinely work, my goal is to do some preliminary reconnaissance on the literary territory under consideration—from a perspective that is oblique—and offer an initial report of my findings. I also hope to take an important step toward embracing the kind of intellectual activity that Cornel West described more than a decade ago: "The central task of postmodern Black intellectuals is to stimulate, hasten, and enable alternative perceptions and practices by dislodging prevailing discourses and powers. This can be done only by intense intellectual work and engaged insurgent praxis."[2]

Such work, for West, is best undertaken within settings that privilege collective effort and promote the building of infrastructures that stimulate, promote, and affirm intellectual activity on the part of black scholars. These endeavors, and the institutions that support them, enable the unique experiences of African Americans to be of central rather than peripheral concern in the larger arena of humanistic and social scientific research and open the way for new forms of scholarship that are global in scope:

> Black intellectual work and Black collective insurgency must be rooted in the specificity of Afro-American life and history; but they are also inextricably linked to the American, European, and African elements which shape and mold them. Such work and insurgency are explicitly particularist though not exclusivist—hence they are international in outlook and practice.[3]

The launch of the ISS presents me with an opportunity to look at my discipline and its texts without having to set aside or negate the sociocultural particularities that have shaped my identity. It also allows me to use these ideas and experiences as points of departure for an examination of those aspects of my perception of black diasporan life that resonate with other subaltern peoples and to be mindful of them as I reconsider a discrete set of ancient texts.

Issues, Themes, and Tropes: General Observations

In the work I have conducted thus far on literary *corpora* in the ancient Near East, I have noted a number of distinct activities concomitant with the formation of authoritative text collections—that is, bodies of lore to which individuals and groups ascribe controlling influence in the shaping of life ways and in the establishment of basic parameters for a safe and meaningful relationship with their immediate and extended environments. These manifest themselves through a number of recurrent issues, themes, and tropes as follows: (1) a cartographic impulse; (2) the generation of a distinct set of ontological, anthropological, cosmological, and soteriological conceptions; (3) the privileging of one or more dominant ideologies and the expression of such through various modes of artifice; (4) a tendency to mute ideas and themes that threaten to unravel or deconstruct dominant ideologies through literary strategies of disempowerment; (5) the encoding of bodily techniques;[4] (6) the artistic use of raw cultural data; (7) ascription of special power to scripturalized texts—in the case of literary *exempla*, great emphasis is placed on the efficacious nature of words and writing; (8) circumscription of the power of poets, storytellers, and other creative voices through the creation of a canonical standard; (9) the promulgation of text-specific hermeneutical principles; (10) assignation of special significance to particular subtexts, passages, books, and so forth as keys for unlocking the meaning(s) of the whole; (11) an impetus toward viewing community and authoritative texts as symbolic representations—that is, icons—of one another; (12) an unresolved tension between subaltern and dominant scripturalized voices that accentuates both the unity and diversity of the whole; (13) eschatologizing potentialities; (14) an innate generative capacity-force—that is, "scriptures" tend to produce other "scriptures"; (15) predisposition toward commodification; and (16) an emphasis on the need for one to be a devotee of a dominant scripturalized ideology to become a fully actualized self. In keeping with the transgressive nature of the ISS, I will offer a few brief illustrative examples of, and some "playful" reflections on, these areas.

Illustrative Examples from the Bible and the Ancient Near East

One can see in the Hebrew Bible a decided interest in charting the cosmos. For example, this cartographic impulse is prevalent in the Pentateuch. One can turn to the primeval history in Genesis 1–11, the epic of Abraham and Sarah in Genesis 11:27–25, and the Mosaic saga narrated in Exodus for numerous examples. Places and locations, both actual and fictive, provide important anchors for what might be termed a scripturalized reality.[5] These *loci* become frames of reference for understanding the warp and weft of the cosmos, sites of pilgrimage—both concrete and mythic, and part of the taxonomy needed to classify social *realia*. This same tendency can be seen in the Ugaritic literary corpus—for example, the *Baal*, *Kirta*, and *Aqhat* cycles—as well as in texts such as the *Sumerian King List* and *Gilgamesh Epic* (particularly the Standard Babylonian Version), all of which likely enjoyed some degree of authoritative status within their respective cultural settings.[6]

One could argue that several of the various collections brought together to form both the Pentateuch and Deuteronomistic history in the Hebrew Bible had at one time their own integrity as scripturalized texts and, as a result, their own unique ontological, anthropological, cosmological, and soteriological presuppositions.[7] We can see vestiges of these in hypothetically reconstructed Pentateuchal substrata.[8] We can also see the ways in which these competing conceptions have been brought into conversation with a dominant Deuteronomic ideology, a necessity when the Torah and Former Prophets were joined. If one posits that the latter is, at least to some extent, a theologizing midrash on the former, then we have a good example of how "scriptures" are generative of "scriptures." One can see this operating in the Old Babylonian *Atrahasis Epic* as well. There, a dominant narratological strand stresses the fact that human beings are created as divine servants while a subaltern voice asserts that they are nonetheless capable of mounting resistance to oppression because they are made of the flesh and blood of the slain god who led the first resistance movement against divine autocracy.[9]

In tablet XI of the *Gilgamesh Epic*, Utnapishtim, a hero somewhat akin to the biblical Noah, is himself a text that riffs discordantly on the dominant narrative theme of divine immortality and human finitude. His embodied self, removed from the land of the living and placed in a liminal space because of his ability to escape a divinely decreed death sentence, is a potentially dangerous human text.

His experiences make him a newly generated and reinscribed (re-scripturalized) being who possesses esoteric knowledge. The speech of the god Enlil in tablet XI, column iv, summarizes well the transformation that the gods deem necessary to limit Utnapishtim's power:[10] "Until now Ut-napishtim was mortal / But henceforth Ut-napishtim and his woman shall be as we gods are / Ut-napishtim shall dwell far off at the mouth of the rivers."

Returning to the Hebrew Bible, the story of the medium of Endor's kindness to Saul (1 Samuel 28:7–25) is an excellent example of how "scriptures" can have embedded within them subtexts that signify against their dominant theologies or ideologies. The kindness the medium extends to Saul just before his demise (1 Samuel 28:20–25) highlights her nobility, dignity, and insight in a way that deconstructs the Deuteronomic injunctions marginalizing and othering indigenous religious praxis (e.g., Deuteronomy 18:10–22). This favorable impression remains in spite of the Deuteronomistic editors' efforts to diminish the value of this female shaman by associating her with the tragic fall of David's predecessor.

The Bible and other ancient Near Eastern "scriptures" often contain clues about how one ought to view the human body and understand certain of its functions. A very fine example of this can be seen in tablet I, column iv, of the Babylonian *Atrahasis Epic*, where one is told that the heartbeat is the living testimony of the god Geshtu-e, whose sacrifice made possible the creation of humankind. Anthropologist Mary Douglas's work[11] on the ways that responses to social stressors are inscribed in rituals related to bodily purity within the Hebrew Bible is well known. One is also reminded of the fact that the encoding of clues about the proper care of the human body is frequently part of the process of scripturalization. Legislation in the Holiness Code in Leviticus 17–26 can be seen in this light. Furthermore the description of the body, both divine and human, can often convey truths about social reality. I have suggested elsewhere that this is the case in the Ugaritic *Baal Cycle* where the enumeration of divine body parts may correlate positively with the degree to which the agents of scripturalization indicate either strong or weak affinity with a particular deity.[12]

Cultural information in biblical and cognate sources is frequently used as an element of literary artifice to heighten dramatic effect and reinforce key themes. To date, the extent to which scholars have been attentive to this strategy has been limited. Closer examination of the artistic use of ethnological information in written texts will make it possible for scholars to understand better an important element of these texts' capacity for evocation.[13]

The recent work of Theophus Smith[14] and Yvonne Chireau[15] on the tradition of conjure have called attention to the transformational powers ascribed by many black diasporan readers to the Bible as scripture. This belief is consistent with that found in the ancient Near East where words, both spoken and written, are considered to possess efficacy in the seen and unseen world. This is particularly true of names (see, e.g., Genesis 4:26, Exodus 3:15, and Deuteronomy 12:5). Canon formation accentuates the power of the written word, and readers, looking for ways to employ authoritative texts for the purposes of self-transformation and empowerment, tend to find ways to mine such sources for their assorted riches.[16]

Once a text or body of texts has gained scriptural status, the generative and interpretive powers of literati begin to be circumscribed and text-specific hermeneutical norms begin to be generated. Evidence of this can be seen in apparently mundane media such as Mesopotamian royal inscriptions that frequently conclude with formulaic curses upon those that dare to change in any way the original content of a monument.[17] It is also in evidence within biblical sources, an example of which can be seen at the conclusion of the book of Revelation (22:18). In time, standards are established for the delimitation of a scripturalized corpus and the appropriation thereof by readers. There is evidence of both processes in Jude (1:9) and the Pastoral Letters (2 Timothy 3:16). Scripturalization can also result in the formation of sub-canons or the setting off of certain texts that are considered to have special significance. Poems embedded in narratives within the Hebrew Bible (e.g., Genesis 49; Exodus 15; and Judges 5) and the New Testament (e.g., Luke 1:46–55) are examples of such. One wonders to what extent such texts also contain the axiomatic core of the books in which they are found, as well as subtle indications of the theological impulses that elicit the formation of "scriptures." This is something to which Gerhard von Rad pointed many years ago in his now classic *The Problem of the Hexateuch and Other Essays*.[18]

An examination of the plurality of theological perspectives represented in the canon of both the Hebrew Bible and the New Testament suggests that, to some extent, a conscious effort has been made in each instance to juxtapose community and text in a manner that facilitates viewing the two entities as semiotic equivalents. In such light, community and text are construed as archetypal reflections of one another. The dynamic that allows both to cohere—that is, a creative tension between subaltern and dominant scripturalized voices—permits the unity and diversity of both to be seen as virtues.[19] This sets the stage for a multilayered engagement of "scriptures" that is open to an assortment of reading strategies, including those that have an eschatological orientation. Joseph Blenkinsopp has noted that the book of Isaiah, for example, has been redacted so that eschatological and historical themes are deftly interwoven into its final canonical form.[20]

A few comments are in order about three final matters: these are the generative capacities of "scriptures," their predisposition toward commodification, and the tendency for self-actualization to be measured in terms of an individual's embrace of a single dominant scripturalized ideology. Umberto Eco has suggested that novels provide their own hermeneutical impetus.[21] The same could be said of "scriptures." Texts, particularly those considered to have binding authority on human behavior, invite conversation and are generative of signifying texts and scatting communities. Such dialogue, particularly that which takes place in faith communities and within nonacademic settings, is facilitated by specialized critical editions of the Bible. Unfortunately this is one of the least studied parts of the hermeneutical enterprise. Such texts are in many respects the result of scriptural commodification. Using the Christian Bible as an example, there are now scores of what might be termed "theme Bibles" consisting of standard biblical translations and "study helps" whose foci include background information on biblical books, exegesis, and the application of truths purportedly derived from the Bible to life challenges encountered by men, women, teens, and other target groups. Their prevalence indicates that they are quite profitable to the publishing houses that produce and market them. This phenomenon invites further speculation on the mediators, motives, and outcomes of scripturalization. At stake is our ability to understand the extent to which this complex process has been, and continues to be, influenced by factors social, political, religious, and economic. Moreover it begs all scholars to question the extent to which such commodified texts reinforce ideologies driven by a capitalist global economy. Covert and overt signals from religious communities, publishers, and commodified texts, which indicate that fully actualized persons need to become both owners of a specific version of the text and devotees of its attendant midrash, must be subjected to critical scrutiny.

NOTES

1. On Sumerian education, see Kramer's now dated, though still excellent treatment: Samuel N. Kramer, *The Sumerians* (1963; repr., Chicago: University of Chicago Press, 1971), 229–248.

2. bell hooks and Cornel West, *Breaking Bread: Insurgent Black Intellectual Life* (Toronto: Between the Lines, 1991), 144.

3. Ibid., 145.

4. Marcel Mauss, "Les Techniques Du Corps," *Sociologie et Anthropologie* (1950; repr., Paris: Presses Universitaires de France, 1968).

5. Recent work suggests that greater methodological breadth be employed in the reading and interpretation of ancient myth. See, for example, the recent exhortation of Walls (Neal Walls, *Desire, Discord, and Death: Approaches to Ancient Near Eastern Myth* [Boston: American Schools of Oriental Research, 2001], 6) for pluriformity in our hermeneutical engagements of myth. The new Institute for Signifying Scriptures could serve as an institutional home for scholars interested not just in the application of existing methods to such texts, but also for those who would like to develop the critical tools necessary to generate new approaches that draw upon the life experiences and values of marginalized communities throughout the world.

6. These major myths/epics may well have achieved the status of spiritual classics in their respective contexts—that is, works that focused attention on ideas, themes, and values deemed to be of perennial concern to those who were part of the larger Ugaritic social matrix. While the vast majority of scholars engaged in the study of these texts remain interested in matters philological, historical, and religious, an examination of what might be termed their lived implications and theological meaning potential would be of great value. At some point, it might enable the reconstruction of those spiritualities created by the original priestly and lay audiences who produced, heard, and (in some instances) read them. For accessible contemporary translations of the aforementioned texts, see N. Wyatt, ed., *Religious Texts from Ugarit: The Words of Ilimilku and His Colleagues* (Sheffield: Sheffield Academic Press, 1998); Stephanie Dalley, *Myths from Mesopotamia: Creation, the Flood, Gilgamesh, and Others* (New York: Oxford, 1991).

7. See, for example, the list of Deuteronomic theological tenets proposed by Moshe Weinfeld in *Deuteronomy and the Deuteronomic School* (Oxford: Clarendon Press, 1972). Taken together, these tenets present a relatively clear picture of what those responsible for the production of the Deuteronomistic history felt about the nature of reality, humanity, the cosmos, and salvation. See as well Boling's synopsis of the process by which the stories of individual local heroes were incorporated into the biblical book of Judges: Robert G. Boling, "*Judges*," in *The Anchor Bible*, ed. W. F. Albright and D. N. Freedman (Garden City, NY: Doubleday, 1975), 6A:30–38.

8. Clearly, the work of the Yahwist, Elohist, and Priestly traditions—if such can be supposed to have had a tangible existence—must have exercised considerable influence over those who produced and were formed, intellectually and spiritually, by them.

9. See tablet I, column iv, in which the fate of Geshtu-e is described. His flesh and blood are mixed with clay by Nintu and are the raw materials from which the first humans are fashioned.

10. Here, for the sake of convenience, I follow the translation of Dalley, *Myths*, 116.

11. Mary Douglas, *Purity and Danger* (London: ARK Paperbacks, 1966); *Natural Symbols* (London: Barrie and Rockliff, 1970).

12. Hugh R. Page Jr., "Divine Anatomy and Social Reality in the Ugaritic Baal Myth: An Exploration into the Use of the Body as Interpretive Lens," *Ugarit-Forschungen* 30 (1998): 603–613; "The Three Zone Theory and Ugaritic Conceptions of the Divine," *Ugarit-Forschungen* 30 (1998): 615–631.

13. This is part of the agenda of ethnological criticism; see Hugh R. Page Jr., "Ethnological Criticism: An Apologia and Application," in *Exploring New Paradigms in Biblical and Cognate Studies*, ed. Hugh R. Page Jr. (Lewiston: Mellen Biblical Press, 1996), 84–107.

14. Theophus Smith, *Conjuring Culture: Biblical Formations of Black America* (New York: Oxford University Press, 1994).

15. Yvonne P. Chireau, *Black Magic: Religion and the African American Conjuring Tradition* (Berkeley: University of California Press, 2003).

16. See for example the devotional works of Nathan Stone, *Names of God* (Chicago: Moody Press, 1944); Herbert Lockyer, *All the Prayers of the Bible* (Grand Rapids, MI: Zondervan, 1959); and Henri Gamache, *The Master Book of Candle Burning* (1942; repr., Plainview, NY: Original Publications, 1998). The latter is an example of a body of esoteric hermeneutical tradition that treats the Bible as a book whose words have an implicit power to alter reality. Chireau has noted that some of these works have enjoyed considerable popularity among African American hoodoo practitioners (Chireau, *Black Magic*, 25–26).

17. See for example the Sumerian vase inscription of Ur-Nammu which invokes a curse from Gilgamesh on anyone who alters its dedicatory prose. John H. Hayes, *A Manual of Sumerian Grammar and Texts*, ed. G. Buccellati, 2nd rev. and exp. ed. (Malibu, CA: Undena Publications, 2000), 155–156.

18. Gerhard von Rad, *The Problem of the Hexateuch and Other Essays*, trans. E. W. Trueman Dicken (New York: McGraw, 1966).

19. Note should be taken of the way in which Yahwistic, Elohistic, Deuteronomic, and Priestly perspectives are combined in the Pentateuch as well as the manner in which several different prophetic ideologies (e.g., those in Amos, Hosea, Micah, etc.) are fused in the Book of the Twelve.

20. Joseph Blenkinsopp, *A History of Prophecy in Israel*, rev. ed. (Louisville, KY: Westminster John Knox, 1996), 97–110, 181–193, 212–222.

21. Umberto Eco, *Postscript to the Name of the Rose*, trans. W. Weaver (San Diego: Harcourt Brace Jovanovich, 1984).

Known Knowns and Unknown Unknowns

SCRIPTURES AND SCRIPTURAL INTERPRETATIONS

R. S. SUGIRTHARAJAH

Reports that say something hasn't happened are always interesting to me, because, as we know, there are known knowns, there are things we know we know. We also know there are known unknowns; that is to say, we know there are some things we do not know. But there are also unknown unknowns—the ones we don't know we don't know.[1]

These were the words of the U.S. Defense Secretary Donald Rumsfeld at a press conference. This is indeed a highly complicated use of the English language, at least equivalent to and perhaps surpassing the Bhabha-ist and Spivakian verbiage. The defense secretary may not have had the world of scriptural interpretation in mind when he uttered these profound thoughts, but what he said has some relevance to the discipline.

There are known knowns, there are things we know we know.

There are certain things about sacred texts, their interpretation and their interpreters, that are fairly well known.

Colonialism played an important part in giving a new status to sacred texts. At a time when the King James Version was losing its appeal at home, as the reports of the British and Foreign Bible Society bemoaned, it was the colonies that provided it with a new lease on life. The colonial "discovery" of other peoples' lands and the discovery of their sacred texts, which Monier Monier-Williams patronizingly referred to as the "Bibles of non-Christian systems,"[2] happened simultaneously. This colonial curiosity led to the unearthing of the sacred texts of Hindus, Buddhists, Muslims, Sikhs, Parsees, and Chinese. It also succeeded in persuading these communities that their texts defined their culture and went on to set ground rules for their interpretation. The *Gita*, the *Granth*, the *Tripitika*, and the Confucian texts, which had been remote and even unknown outside their vernacular contexts, were now made easily accessible in standardized and printed format. The Vedas, which had previously been largely conserved and perpetuated through oral memorization and recitation, were now turned into a portable and readable book. The colonial instrumentality was further reinforced when the expenses of Max Müller's translation of the *Sacred Books of the East* were underwritten by the corporate entrepreneurs of the time—the directors of the East India Company.

The art of interpretation was intertwined with Western colonialism. The fact that Friedrich Schleiermacher was the "father" of modern hermeneutics is well acknowledged, but what often goes unnoticed is that it was the typical engagement with the colonial "other" that led to the principles of exegesis being first teased out. Schleiermacher's interest in interpretation was prompted when he was asked to translate David Collins' *An Account of the English Colony in New South Wales* of 1804. Since then, biblical scholarship, under the guise of apparent neutrality and detachment, has been engaging in the business of studying, codifying, and controlling the sacred texts of other people. This has resulted in a tradition like Hinduism, which had a fairly relaxed attitude toward texts, becoming obsessively textual, assertive, and, even worse, willing to compromise the very qualities for which it was famous—tolerance and acknowledgement that there are many ways to God.

One of the enduring myths of biblical scholarship has been that Protestantism encouraged the free examination of scriptures. After September 11, the call has been that the other scriptural traditions should go through a similar reformation process. This call, besides betraying Christian arrogance, is also a spurious one. The aim of the Reformers was not to grant the masses uncontrolled access to the scriptures but to impose their own theological positions on them and reject any ecclesiastical intervention. Although Martin Luther initially invited everyone to read the Bible, he changed his mind after the Peasants' War, which produced the *plural readings* that naturally worried him. Hence, he said: "The catechism is the laymen's Bible; it contains the whole of what every Christian must know of Christian doctrine."[3]

Western biblical scholarship was successful in projecting the idea that historical critical methods were part of the discipline since time immemorial. This is one of the academic cons perpetuated by mainstream pundits. Historical criticism as we know today is less than two hundred years old. It reached its peak between 1880 and 1910. What followed afterward was clarification and amplification of the method. Evidence? Take a look at the amount of repetition that goes on in line-by-line commentaries held up as exemplary forms of modern criticism. They more or less say the same things.

Sacred texts woo the common reader, spur his or her imagination. They are good at alluring the reader into assuming that the ordeals of Job and Sita are theirs, too, and events such as the Exodus and the battle of Kurukshetra are ongoing happenings in their lives and histories. They are particularly good at convincing the marginalized that the texts are on the side of the victims. But all such readings have only a selective and limited value. Canaanites, Palestinians, and indigenes around the world, whose lands have been stolen, have exposed the dubious value of the Exodus narrative. Similarly, women's retellings of the *Rāmāyaṇa* often maintain an eerie silence over the morality of Rama killing the monkey Vali. No sacred text contains entirely liberative material.

The guardians and interpreters of sacred books are constantly torn between treating sacred texts as history or as myth. Christianity, which claimed itself as a historical religion, is now buckling under the weight of postmodernity's skepticism about the "facts" of history, and it is trying to re-mythicize its basic tenets. Hinduism, on the other hand, which was seen as a mythical religion, is now, under new national pressures, trying to historicize its core teachings, and historical authenticity is claimed for Ram, Ayodhya, and the battle of Panipat.

Sacred texts are simultaneously self-contained entities and open systems. They are filled with quotations from and allusions to other texts. Monier Williams, one of the pioneer comparative theologians of the colonial era, was forced to admit after studying the Hindu scriptures that they contained not only the basic tenets of biblical faith but also "every other rudimentary idea of our religion."[4] A similar conclusion was reached by A. J. Edmunds, A. Lillie, and H. de Lubac when they examined Buddhist texts.

At the same time, sacred texts are not totally open. They are part of a contextual package that sets certain limits and prevents them from being totally mixed and matched. The guardians of these texts prescribe certain ways in which they have to be read. Nevertheless one of the colonial discoveries was that the Bible cannot be studied in isolation. It had to be studied in conjunction with other texts. What Monier-Williams said grudgingly at the height of the colonial enterprise is even more true now: "It may indeed shock Christians in this Christian country of ours to think of our missionaries placing the Bible on the same platform with the Koran and the Veda; there is no alternative."[5]

It was Karl Marx who said that every person is an intellectual because everyone thinks. This is applicable to interpretation as well. Every person is an interpreter because everyone reads, though only some belong to the profession and are paid to be interpreters.

We Also Know There Are Known Unknowns; That Is to Say, We Know There Are Some Things We Do Not Know

Sacred texts are like refugees eternally seeking a "home." Their modern physical appearance is an illusion. The printed version gives a false impression that they are the final revelation, the last word. As peoples' perception of God's word, however, they are incomplete and tentative. What is increasingly clear is that texts are liable to spawn and signify new meanings in new contexts. Even within their natural habitat it is not easy to muzzle and control them. Any move to canonize or finalize a sacred text will pave the way for many other parallel and supplementary texts. The closed "New Testament" canon has been accompanied by a spate of deuterocanonical gospels and writings. Buddhagosa's parables were clarifications of Buddha's teachings eight centuries after the Gautama's death, and Shah Wali Allah of Delhi's *Ta'wil al-ahadith* in the nineteenth century was in keeping with the edifying literature known as Prophetic Tales generated by the Qur'an. The ability of sacred texts to transfer from their natural context to an alien context shatters any attempt by a community to stake an exclusive claim on the tenets of their sacred texts.

Hebrew Scriptures are reconfigured in the Christian testament. Islam has incorporated Jesus. Dasaratha Jataka tells the story of the Buddha taking the form of Rama. What the guardians of the texts cannot control is the movement of the texts and what form they will take. What is known to be unknown is what the new canon will look like in the postcolonial context, when identities and texts coalesce.

But There Are Also Unknown Unknowns– the Ones We Don't Know We Don't Know

Biblical studies and empires are conjoined. When empires flourish, biblical studies also flourish. When Europe was in its imperial pomp, biblical studies thrived in Germany and England. It is no coincidence that the current boom in biblical studies is taking place in America when America has become the empire. The old empire spoke in terms of eradicating ignorance and enlightening the benighted natives with Christian values. The new empire is also on a mission but sees its task as righting the wrongs of rulers who undermine American authority, violate human rights, and threaten American corporate interests. The new missionaries who effect these changes are the American soldiers, who are seen not as military personnel but as emancipators. Their weapons are not guns but belief in American values. Their new missionary command is to preach the gospel of democracy, human rights, free speech, and a market economy, distinctly as defined by its American projectors. Like the disciples of old, they, too, cast out demons in such forms as that of Saddam Hussein. Those who question this project are seen as anti-Christ, those who are not with us. The words George Smith uttered during the height of the British empire continue to find their echoes, however distorted: "The younger, of Great Britain and America, have been prepared to serve the elder, of India, in the highest ministry of sacrifice."[6] Now Great Britain has become less great; the mantle has fallen on America. Substitute India with Iraq, Chechnya, Bosnia, and Kosovo, and you will get the picture.

What is the "unknown unknown" to many caught up in the new imperium? Who, in the battle of interpretation, is going to have the last word—those who wish to impose a single reading or those who advocate multiple readings? The current hermeneutical battle is deceptively simple. Is there one single and closed reading that fixes for good universal values such as democracy, human rights, and the market economy as defined by American power? Or is there going to be, beyond the comprehension of its projectors, a variety of readings? These values are too precious to be left to one culture and one nation to define.

This kind of censorial impulse manifests itself in cultural and religious arenas as well. Interpretative control imposed by the current keepers of Hinduism, Buddhism, and Islam sets limits on how an interpreter may exegete, a novelist may tell a story, a painter may imagine, or a filmmaker may recreate reality. The difficult and often acrimonious interpretative battle that is going on in India is expressed by two characters in the novel *The Sixth Veda*. One wants to bring a "kind of closure" to Hinduism and Hindu identity in face of growing secular and liberal values, whereas the other wants to "search without the possibility of closure," thus preserving the accommodative power of Hinduism.[7]

In the new imperium, the task of the hermeneut is to remind those who work out their hermeneutics within rigidly set boundaries, and who undervalue other experiences, that there are no predetermined meanings but only actual meanings determined by larger cultural and political contexts. Such current narratives as human rights, democracy, and market do not define themselves in advance, can mean different things to different people, and are capable of different interpretations or no interpretation at all. Similarly, religious traditions thrive when they accommodate and critically interweave new influences from outside. The least the interpreters can do is to assert that narratives are "meanings in motion." This is what those in the business of interpretation can do. It is, as Rumsfeld would have put it, "doable," which, as you can imagine, will deeply annoy him.

NOTES

1. "Rum Remark Wins Rumsfeld an Award," *BBC News*, December 2, 2003, world edition, http://news.bbc.co.uk/2/hi/americas/3254852.stm.

2. M. Monier-Williams, *The Holy Bible and the Sacred Books of the East: Four Addresses to Which Added a Fifth Address on Zenana Mission* (London: Seeley and Co., 1887), 30.

3. Jean-François Gilmont, "Protestant Reformations and Reading," in *A History of Reading in the West*, ed. G. Cavallo and R. Chartier (Oxford: Polity Press, 1999), 220, 213–237.

4. M. Monier-Williams, *Modern India and Indians* (London: Trübner and Co., 1889), 234.

5. Ibid., 233.

6. George Smith, *The Conversion of India: From Pataenus to the Present Time A.D. 193–1893* (London: John Murray, 1893), 5.

7. Prashant Parikh, *The Sixth Veda* (London: Hamilton and Co., 1999).

Talking Back

These essays provoke our thinking about what "scriptures" are, why they are invented, the work we make them do for us. Whatever else scriptures may be made to be for us, whatever else they may be made to do for us, we seem to make them a centering force.[1] We allow them to locate us, help define us, orient us—always, of course, in obvious relationships to some circle or framework. This means that no matter the passionate rhetorical claims and arguments, no matter the long-standing and widely held assumptions, no matter the entrenched practices and rituals in relationship to them, there are no free-floating "scriptures." The latter always come out of and reflect the operations of some small-scale local circle or network or some large-scale extensive world or some formation between the two. In other words, "scriptures" are not the same as texts, though they may sometimes appear as such. But they represent a more complex social-psychological phenomenon than a text or text-ed-ness. That we sometimes think of "scriptures" as free-floating, as having independent existence, as something to out there or here to be grasped, to be touched, to be manipulated, to be strictly adhered to or rejected is a measure of the occluding, obfuscating power of the phenomenon of center-ing that takes the form of scripturalizing.

That center-ing forces can be called "scriptures" with little qualification or explanation is also worth continued consideration. Although not always the case in human history, the text-ed-ness of the center-ing operation has obtained powerfully for some time. The power of the written, of textuality, in the social-political arrangements we know and experience is obvious. Why would we not come to a point of making scriptures one of the most important center-ing forces?

The phenomenon of making texts into scriptures as center-forces carries implications and ramifications aplenty for our ongoing cultural-critical analysis and structuring of relationships. Here we have to do less with the origins of scriptures in terms of a pointed time and place for an appearance from which everything else develops. No, what we are inspired to think about here are the situations and dynamics within societies and cultures that account for the invention of "scriptures"—in non-textual and textual forms.

So the baseline question with which we begin this probing—what is it about us, our constitution, our social arrangements and the webs we have spun, that make "scriptures" compelling?

—ed.

NOTES

1. Rudolph Arnheim, *The Power of the Center: A Study of Composition in the Visual Arts* (Berkeley: University of California Press, 1988).

PART II

SETTINGS, SITUATIONS, PRACTICES

6   Signifying Scriptures in Confucianism

YAN SHOUCHENG

"Signifying scriptures" as a social-cultural phenomenon is of critical importance for revealed religions such as Christianity and Islam. As pointed out by the historian Jonathan Riley-Smith in his recent article "Religious Authority,"

> Christians and Muslims believe in an interventionary God who has revealed something of his nature, his intentions for mankind and the future of the created cosmos through prophets and inspired scriptures and, in the case of Christianity, through a personal intervention in human history. Given such a belief it is, of course, vitally important to decide what God's messages are, particularly as they are expressed through a medium, the written word, which is notoriously difficult to interpret. This is, as true of the Gospels as it is of the Old Testaments and of the Koran. There are ambivalences which have to be clarified and contradictions which must be resolved. . . . But who decides how the ambivalences should be clarified and the contradictions resolved and what the principles are which can then be universally applied? This was an issue in Christianity from the start.[1]

The same is true in Islam, another revealed religion.

It is clear from this perspective that the church government that controls the practices of signifying "scriptures" has the authority and power over clerics. But what about the case of other civilizations such as Sinic, which, unlike Western and Islamic, have neither revealed religion nor the concept of interventionary God? Only one century ago there was even no equivalent of the word "religion" in Chinese language. *Jing*, the Chinese equivalent of "scripture," actually means a classic. For example, *wujing* means a classic of military affairs or arts of war, and *yijing* means a classic of medicine; jing as a word is never limited to religious "scriptures." If we research how Confucian classics or "scriptures" were invented and made to work and how they evolved throughout Chinese history, however, we will find that "signifying scriptures" is a social-cultural phenomenon of significant relevance in Chinese civilization. The Chinese case, with its rich history and ample literary records, provides a good example for analyzing "scriptures" in terms of signifying practices.

Vincent Wimbush's program for the study of "scriptures" places focus on "textures" instead of content-meaning.[2] Strikingly the original meaning of jing, the Chinese equivalent of "scriptures," is none other than "textures" of cloth, especially of silk. When jing is used as a verb it means to "thread," especially to thread the bamboo slips which were used for writing before the invention of paper. From "threading" bamboo slips it extends to the meaning of managing or governing the world, or as a noun it means statecraft or the way of governance, and thus implies "standard" or "principle." It also denotes the works which represent the "way" or "principle," wherein it derives the meaning of "classics" or, in a certain sense, "scriptures."[3] After the rise of Confucianism the name of jing was usually ascribed to Confucian "scriptures." Yet we must keep in mind that Confucian "scriptures," unlike the Bible or the Qur'an, are not tantamount to "holy books" given by the gods. After all Confucius was not a god or demigod. Due to this fact "signifying scriptures" was probably more important in Confucianism than in revealed religions.

As suggested by the archaeologist K. C. Chang, shamanism played the central role in ancient Chinese politics. He cited a myth that describes that in the past there was communication between heaven and earth, but later it was severed by the order of a king. Thereafter only the shamans had access to heaven, where the wisdom of human affairs lies. This myth implies that after the "severance of heaven-earth communication" the access to heaven was limited to the shamans; only they could get the wisdom for running human affairs, which can be found nowhere except in heaven. That implies that in ancient China political authority was derived and inseparable from shamanistic power.[4] As pointed out by the Chinese scholar Chen Mengjia (Ch'en Meng-chia), there are quite a number of oracle bone inscriptions that describe "the king dancing to pray for rain and the king prognosticating about a dream"; obviously the king himself was the head shaman.[5]

The rites wherein the shamans danced to pray for rain and so on were accompanied by music, especially played with bronze bells and drums. The Chinese character for rites (li) originally denotes the vessel to offer sacrifices to the gods or the jade and drums used in the rites. As is well known, Confucianism puts great emphasis on the rites. But the name "Confucianism" is in fact an invention by the Jesuits; in Chinese language there is no such word as "Confucianism." The Chinese equivalent of "Confucian" is ru, who was the expert of "rites and music." From this perspective, the Peking University historian Yan Buke proffered plenty of evidence to prove that the early "Confucian" was actually the musician or shaman. The character ru, Yan argues, is closely related to rainmaking. The early ru was no other than the musician who prayed for rain through dancing; moreover, the character for "dance" and that for "shaman" are interchangeable in ancient Chinese written language. So the musician was the same as the shaman. Therefore Yan concludes that the "Confucian" (ru) originated in the ancient musician-shaman, who was also responsible for the teaching of rites, music, and so forth to young nobles. It is from that tradition that Confucianism developed.[6]

Confucianism as a religion differs from Christianity and Islam regarding "scriptures" in the sense of holy books given by the gods, as can be seen from the following saying of Mencius: "If one believed everything in the Book of History, it would have been better for the Book not to have existed at all."[7] (The *Book of History* is one of the Confucian Five Classics.) Yet on the other hand the Confucians are notoriously known for their bookishness; over the course of two thousand years, they developed a huge corpus of classics or "scriptures." Great emphasis was put on "scriptures," not because they were holy books given by the gods, but because in ancient China writing was regarded as playing an extremely important role in the heaven-earth communication. According to Chinese mythology, when the legendary Cang Jie (T'sang Chieh) invented writing, "millet grains rained from heaven and ghosts wailed at night." Through writing that the mystery of nature and humanity began to be revealed to humans.[8] Therefore the historiographer (*shi*), who is depicted in the *Rites of the Zhou* as one who "is in charge of government documents and thereby assists in ruling," was invested "with the authority to point the way, so to speak, for the benefit of their rulers."[9]

Yan Buke therefore maintains that the tradition of the historiographer and that of the musician composed two main elements of ancient Chinese culture and that, in early times of the Western Han dynasty (206–208 BCE), the two were integrated, whereupon the gentleman-scholar class was born. In his view, the bureaucracy of imperial China was conceived in the historiographer tradition, while some roles played by the Confucian scholar, such as the educator of the populace, the spokesman for society, and the critic of the state, may be traced back to the musician tradition.[10] Before the "severance of heaven-earth communication," however, the historiographer was also responsible for the sacrificial rites.[11] In other words, the role of the musician or shaman and that of the historiographer were inseparable at the beginning, as is seen in the case of the great historian Sima Qian (145–190 BCE), whose ancestors were both historiographer (*shi*) and shaman (*wu*). The two traditions were intertwined in Confucius and his school as well. His two most influential successors, Mencius and Xunzi, may be thought to represent respectively the musician and the historiographer traditions. But the two finally merged in the early Han dynasty (206 BCE—220 CE). Thereafter Confucian scholars stressed the words of the "scriptures," and simultaneously felt free to interpret or "signify" on them.

Confucius said, "I transmit; I invent nothing."[12] This statement sheds light on the way Confucius himself theorized or signified "scriptures." What he "transmitted" was the so-called Six Classics, namely, the *Books of Poems, History, Rites, Music, Changes*, and the *Spring and Autumn* (the *Book of Music* is now lost), which were later regarded as jing (scriptures) in the Confucian tradition. All of them were actually the documents of recorded history, shamanistic rites and music, and so on, which used to be textbooks for young nobles in classical China before Confucius. After establishing the first private school in Chinese history Confucius "transmitted" the canons to his disciples. In this sense he was the transmitter, instead of the inventor. But Confucius did not stress the texts themselves, but the "secret meanings and great principles" he thought implied in the texts. As recorded by Sima Qian, Confucius said, "It will be better to express my thought through concrete things than to convey it in empty words."[13] The "scriptures," for Confucius, were merely convenient means for communication; more important were the "signifying practices." In this sense he did make a "philosophical breakthrough" in the axial age. So in the Confucian tradition the "scriptures" or texts (jing) were not as important as the "records" (ji) or commentaries (zhuan and shuo) made by Confucius and his disciples.[14] For instance, the "scriptures" of the Book of Changes are in fact nothing but the oracle's messages, and the Confucian scholars do not really think highly of them. As regards the rites, it is not the "scriptures" but the Records of the Rites, the collection of commentaries on the rites by Confucius and his disciples, that is considered more important. In sum, for Confucian scholars the commentaries have utmost importance in that they theorize or signify the "scriptures."

Although Confucianism and other Chinese religions, unlike Protestantism, do not regard "scriptures" as the only authentic authority, with the establishment of the "scriptures" learning and the worship of the written word,[15] toward the end of the Western Han period (206 BCE–9 CE) focus was gradually transferred from the "secret meanings and great principles" to the "scriptures" themselves. Those Han Confucians thought that the Six Classics were not just historical documents or conventional texts but sacred words transmitted from the ancient sage kings. Therefore they must be interpreted strictly literally. Those learned scholars thereby kept a firm grip on the power of "signifying scriptures." As a result, Confucianism became more doctrinally rigid for several hundred years. In the Confucian tradition, however, the sages were not gods. The learned scholars could not monopolize the practices of signifying "scriptures" for long. With the rise of Neo-Confucianism, a new approach to "scriptures" emerged.

The Neo-Confucian master Cheng Hao (1032–1085) stated, "Although I have learned some of my doctrines from others, the concept of the Principle of Heaven, however, has been realized by myself."[16] In his view, the authority of the "scriptures" is rooted in the notion that they embody what is common for everybody, that is, the principle. Once again, the "scriptures" are only the media to attain to the principle. The Taoist Zhuangzi said, "It is through words that we get meaning; once the meaning is obtained, the words are forgotten."[17] Similarly, for Cheng Hao once the principle has been obtained the "scriptures" may be forgotten. When Neo-Confucianism became popular among the literati, the new approach to the "scriptures" was adopted by more and more Confucian scholars. Eventually the "scriptures" themselves were modified and finally even the corpus of the "scriptures" was changed. The most prominent Neo-Confucian thinker, Zhu Xi (Chu Hsi) (1130–1200), finally replaced the Five Classics with the Four Books, namely, the Analects, Mencius, the Great Learning, and the Doctrine of the Mean (the latter two are originally two books in the Records of Rites), which later became the core curriculum not only in China, but also in all of East Asia. We can say that it is through the practices of "signifying scriptures" that the transition from classical Confucianism to Neo-Confucianism was achieved.

For the Neo-Confucians, the ultimate authority is the principle instead of the written word, as is explicitly declared by the Ming (1368–1644) Neo-Confucian scholar Lü Kun (1536–1618):

> *Dao* is the universal principle all over the world and of all the times; everybody takes part in it. Dao is not exclusive, and the sages do not monopolize the Dao; yet Confucians always make it exclusive and call it the Dao of the sages. . . . However, Dao has no boundary and cannot be limited by the sages' words; things depend on conditions and cannot be exhausted by the sages' criteria. If in later times there emerges somebody who says that which the sages have never said but which tallies with what they want to say, and who does that which the sages have never done but which is in line with what they will certainly do, the sages would be deeply happy about it, but it startles the narrow-minded Confucians.[18]

Obviously, for Lü it is the universal principle or Dao, rather than the sages' words or "scriptures," that has the final say. Zhu Xi's contemporary Lu Xiangshan (Hsian-shan) (1139–1193) even said, "If in our study we know the fundamentals, then all the Six Classics are my footnotes."[19] According to Zhu and his School of Principle, the "fundamentals" are the principles underlying all things, which theoretically can be grasped by anybody through "investigation of things." The ancient sages first discovered what is common for every mind, so we must trust them in the matter of understanding the principle. The true meaning of the sages, however, these Neo-Confucian thinkers held, were long lost in the voluminous commentaries and notes of early Confucian scholars. In order to grasp the true meaning, they insisted it was necessary to turn to the classics. The problem is that if different people hold different views about the principle, who will decide which one is right. Zhu maintained that we must "follow the path of inquiry and study" and get it by ourselves. With the establishment of Zhu's Neo-Confucianism as orthodoxy, however, the recorded sayings of Neo-Confucian masters, especially those of Cheng brothers and Zhu himself, became new "scriptures," even overshadowing the Five Classics. As for commoners, because they were unable to "inquire and study," they of course had no say and must follow the teachings of Neo-Confucian masters to obtain self-realization.

In contrast, according to Lu Xiangshan, the "fundamentals" are not the principles outside one's mind, but the mind itself, which is same for everybody. Based on Mencius's statement that even the ancient sage kings Yao and Shun were the same as anybody else,[20] Lu argued. "Even if I am totally illiterate, I still can be dignified as human being."[21] This statement implies the assertion that a commoner who has no access to classical learning can also become a sage through his own efforts. The most influential Ming Neo-Confucian thinker, Wang Yangming (1472–1529), developed this trend; he claimed, "Man [*sic*] is the mind of heaven, earth, and all things, and mind is the master of heaven, earth, and all things. So mind is simply heaven; when mind is spoken of, heaven, earth, and all things are at the same time referred to." In his view, the Principle of Heaven is no more than the mind, the essence of which he calls "innate knowledge of good."[22] His disciple Wang Gen (Ken) (1483–1541) went further; by emphasizing "on making the Way answer to the everyday needs of the people," the sage is essentially not unlike the "ignorant men and women" and "must be concerned with what nourishes people's bodies and hearts."[23]

With economic and social changes in the sixteenth and seventeenth centuries, these radical teachings, beginning with Lu Xiangshan, developed by Wang Yangming, and culminating in Wang Gen and his Taizhou (Tai-chou) school, helped bring about a mass movement among the common people. Hence, as pointed out by de Bary, "in the Tai-chou school Confucianism for the first time became heavily involved in the sphere traditionally occupied by the popular religions."[24] This popularization of Confucianism was due, to a great extent, to the practices of "signifying scriptures," to put it concretely, to the reinterpretation of some Confucian classics, especially the *Great Learning*, as in the cases of Wang Yangming and Wang Gen. It may be said that "signifying scriptures" played a critical role in Confucianism's penetration into the lower classes in late imperial China. A good example is Yuan Huang (1533–1606), who was famous for his preaching of "ledgers of merit and demerit" among the ordinary people. The ledgers originated in popular Taoist works such as the *Treatise of the Most Exalted One on Moral Retribution*,[25] which illustrate that reward and retribution are meted out by the gods according to merits and demerits one has done. By theorizing the "scriptures," Yuan invented a point system, according to which,

> The value of human deeds could be calculated with so many credits or merits attached to each good deed and so many debits or demerits for the evil deeds. Using the point system provided him in the Ledgers, each individual could evaluate his deeds one by one, add the merits and demerits, and then strike a balance for himself. The greater the balance of merits, the greater the reward he might expect, and vice versa.[26]

Though this system was somewhat mechanical and put too much emphasis on quantitative calculation regarding ethical acts, "it nevertheless strengthened the confidence of the ordinary man [sic] that he [sic] could cope with the challenges and crises of life."[27] In short, Yuan successfully transformed the popular Taoist morality of heteronomy into the Confucian one of autonomy through practices of "signifying scriptures."

Yuan's ledgers became so popular that they "were widely printed and sold, not only in China, but also in Japan."[28] A contemporary Confucian teacher even lamented that "students of his day viewed Yuan's *Ledgers* as a text as sacred as the standard works of the Neo-Confucian curriculum."[29] This splendid achievement was realized mainly thorough Yuan's efforts in signifying "scriptures," of popular Taoist ones this time. Moreover his ledgers, in turn, became new "scriptures" because of their widespread acceptance by the ordinary men and women. This is a good example of how relatively powerless groups asserted themselves through "signifying scriptures."

For the orthodox Confucians, however, Yuan's ledger system "threatened the stability and authority of the Confucian Classics." Yuan and his *Ledgers* were therefore regarded as heterodox and severely attacked.[30] In the late seventeenth and early eighteenth centuries, as a response against what was thought to be the vulgarization of Confucian ethics, there emerged a trend that stressed the importance of literally reading the Confucian Classics. On the other hand, Yuan's new approach to "scriptures" was characteristic of the new popular religions, which flourished in late imperial China and are still popular today, as in the case of the Unity Way (I Kuan Tao) in Taiwan. Most of them were syncretic; instead of inventing their own "scriptures," they usually signified on the existing ones, whether of Confucianism, Taoism, or Buddhism, to establish their own authority.

Writing and the written word were highly respected or even worshiped by the Chinese. So "scriptures" occupied a very important role in society and culture. The history of Chinese culture and religions, which is characterized by a dynamics of "signifying scriptures," offers a great amount of materials for our analysis of the phenomenology of "scriptures" in terms of signifying practices.

NOTES

1. Jonathan Riley Smith, "Religious Authority," in *The Future of the Past: Big Questions in History*, ed. Peter Martland (London: Pimlico, 2002), 1–2.

2. See Wimbush's introductory essay to this volume.

3. Huang Shouqi, *Introduction to Confucian Classical Learning* (Shanghai: East China Normal University Press, 2000), 1–2.

4. K. C. Chang, "Shamanism and Politics," in *Arts, Myth, and Ritual: The Path to Political Authority in Ancient China*, ed. K. C. Chang (Cambridge, MA: Harvard University Press, 1983), 44–55.

5. "Ch'en Men-chia, Myth and Magic of the Shang Dynasty," cited in Chang, "Shamanism," 45–46.

6. Yan Buke, "The Musician and the Origin of the Confucian," *The Musician and the Historiographer: Collected Papers on Traditional Chinese Political Culture and Political Institutions* (Beijing: Sanlian Shudian, 2001), 1–32.

7. *Mencius*, 7B:3, trans. D. C. Lau (Middlesex: Harmondsworth, 1970), 194.

8. See K. C. Chang, "Writing as the Path to Authority," in *Arts, Myth, and Ritual: The Path to Political Authority in Ancient China*, ed. K. C. Chang (Cambridge, MA: Harvard University Press, 1983), 81, 91.

9. Ibid., 94. See also Liu Yizheng, *Essential Significances of Chinese History* (1948; repr., Taipei: Zhonghua Book Co., 1984), 1–5.

10. Yan Buke, "The Similarities and Differences Between the Musician and the Historiographer Tradition and Their Implications," *The Musician and the Historiographer: Collected Papers on Traditional Chinese Political Culture and Political Institutions* (Beijing: Sanlian Shudian, 2001), 83–114.

11. Liu, *Essential Significances*, 9.

12. *The Analects of Confucius*, 7:1, trans. Simon Leys (New York: W. W. Norton and Company, 1997), 29.

13. *Shiji* (Historical Records) (Shanghai: Chinese Classics Publishing House, 1997), 2485.

14. Lü Simian, *Introduction to Pre-Qin Thought* (Shanghai: Chinese Encyclopedia Publishing House, 1985), 52–60, 67–75.

15. Because Chinese characters were regarded as carriers of the mystery of nature and humanity and being transmitted by the sages, in traditional China any waste paper with written or printed words on it had to be treated respectfully; they must not be scrapped or demolished, but should be collected and burned. This custom continued even to the 1940s or early 1950s. Today we still can see the furnaces, usually in or by temples, with those words inscribed on them: "Pay respect to the paper with characters on it."

16. Cited from Wing-tsit Chan, ed., *A Source Book in Chinese Philosophy* (Princeton, NJ: Princeton University Press, 1963), 520. I replace "Principle of Nature" with "Principle of Heaven."

17. Zhuang Zi, *The Complete Works of Zhuang Zi*, trans. Burton Watson (New York: Columbia University Press, 1968), 302.

18. Lü, *Moaning Words* (Shanghai: Shanghai Chinese Classics Publishing House, 2000), 49.

19. Cited from Chan, *A Source Book*, 580.

20. Mencirs, 4B:32.

21. *The Records of Song-Yuan Scholars* (Shanghai: Shijie Shuju, 1936), 1069.

22. *The Records of Ming Scholars* (Beijing: Zhnghua Shuju, 1985), 196–197.

23. Wm. Theodore de Bary, "Individualism and Humanitarianism in Late Ming Thought," in *Self and Society in Ming Thought*, ed. Wm. Theodore de Barry and the Conference on Ming Thought (New York: Columbia University Press, 1970), 168, 188–225.

24. Ibid., 174.

25. It was rendered into English by D. T. Suzuki and Paul Carus, titled *Treatise on Response and Retribution* (LaSalle, IL: Open Court, 1973).

26. Tadao Sakai, "Confucianism and Popular Educational Works," in *Self and Society in Ming Thought*, ed. Wm. Theodore de Barry and the Conference on Ming Thought (New York: Columbia University Press, 1970), 342–343, 331—366.

27. De Bary, "Individualism," 174.

28. Ibid., 176.

29. Cynthia J. Brokaw, *The Ledgers of Merit and Demerit: Social Change and Moral Order in Imperial China* (Princeton, NJ: Princeton University Press, 1991), 123.

30. Ibid., 121–128.

7   *The Confessions of Nat Turner*

MEMOIR OF A MARTYR OR
TESTAMENT OF A TERRORIST?

WILLIAM L. ANDREWS

During the pre–Civil War era, *The Confessions of Nat Turner* was the most widely read and the most influential African American spiritual autobiography published in the United States. At the outset of the Civil War, one commentator on the *Confessions* estimated that 50,000 copies of that brief document had been printed and circulated throughout the United States.[1] Although we don't know why so many people read Turner's *Confessions*, I doubt that a large proportion of its audience took the narrative seriously as a spiritual autobiography. Nor has more recent scholarly and critical analysis treated Turner's *Confessions* as a major contribution to the African American spiritual autobiography tradition.[2] If we are interested in spiritual autobiography as a signifying practice on "scriptures," however, we need to regard Nat Turner as a pivotal figure.

The writer of Turner's *Confessions*,[3] Thomas R. Gray, a lawyer and former slaveholder who served as Turner's amanuensis, had a clear political agenda when he met the condemned black man in his Jerusalem, Virginia, jail cell on November 1, 1831. Gray wanted to know why Turner conceived and led his "insurrection," as Gray termed the killings of more than fifty-five white men, women, and children that began before dawn on August 22, 1831. What did the former slave hope to accomplish? These questions continue to haunt us today.

Before and after interviewing Turner, Gray contended that Prophet Nat was a desperately self-deceived religious fanatic. In the *Confessions'* prefatory "To the Public," Gray states: "It will thus appear, that whilst every thing upon the surface of society wore a calm and peaceful aspect; whilst not one note of preparation was heard to warn the devoted inhabitants of woe and death, a gloomy fanatic was revolving in the recesses of his own dark, bewildered, and overwrought mind, schemes of indiscriminate massacre to the whites" (41). At the conclusion of Turner's narrative, Gray observes, "He is a complete fanatic, or plays his part most admirably" (54). The Southampton County, Virginia, judge who sentenced Turner to death four days after Gray began interviewing him also blamed religious fanaticism for the uprising.[4] Yet anyone who reads the narrative that Turner dictated, or is supposed to have dictated (for we will never know how much of the that narrative is Turner and how much is Gray[5]) will be struck by Turner's utter conviction, even as he faced the gallows, that what he did was in full accordance with the mission he had been given by what he called "the Spirit."

The initial mention of "the Spirit" in Turner's narrative occurs as the condemned man recalls a religious meeting in which he first heard Jesus's command, "'Seek ye the kingdom of Heaven and all things shall be added unto you'" (45). As he reflected prayerfully on the passage, "the Spirit spoke to me, saying 'Seek ye the kingdom of Heaven and all things shall be added unto you'" (46). Apparently surprised by Turner's evocation of the Bible, Gray stops recording in order to interrogate Turner. "What do you mean by the Spirit?" Gray demands. Turner replies: "The Spirit that spoke to the prophets in former days" (46). This allusion to "the Spirit" seems to have either perplexed or bothered Gray enough to cause him to ask if, in effect, "the Spirit" that spoke to this black conspirator was the same "Spirit" that spoke through the white Bible. That every mention of "the Spirit" is capitalized thereafter in the *Confessions* suggests that Gray felt satisfied that his interlocutor's idea of "the spirit" referred not to an alien African or slave supernaturalism but to the Spirit of God, the source of revealed truth to the Christian South. We can only wonder if Gray realized that by requiring Turner to identify "the Spirit," he had unwittingly given this "fanatic" license to ally himself explicitly with "the prophets in former days," thereby abetting, willy-nilly, the spiritual legitimation of Prophet Nat.

Turner speaks later in his story of having been "baptized by the Spirit," which in turn serves as the prelude for a climactic eschatological vision of life-and-death struggle: "the Spirit instantly appeared to me and said the Serpent was loosened, and Christ had laid down the yoke he had borne for the sins of men, and that I should take it on and fight against the Serpent, for the time was fast approaching when the first should be last and the last should be first" (47–48). Although Turner does not explain who "the Serpent" was that he was called on to fight, the logic of his narrative leaves the strong impression that those who denied the will of "the Spirit" in the earthly realm are one and the same with Satan, "that ancient serpent" that, according to the Book of Revelation, must be conquered before the final judgment of the elect and the damned can proceed (Revelation 19–20). Turner's visions and the words of "the Spirit" gave him even broader, and disturbingly sociopolitical, standards by which to distinguish the elect from the damned, those to be saved from "my enemies" who must be slain "with their own weapons" (48). Perhaps it was this unique blend of religious and political apocalypticism, which racialized into "white spirits and black spirits" the cosmic war envisioned in the Hebrew Armageddon and in the New Testament prophesies of the last days (47), that triggered Gray's second interruption of Turner's narration.

As though he could not bear to accede passively to Turner's unsubtle judgment of the slaveholding Serpent and his blasphemous self-anointment as a type of Christ, Gray demands of Turner, "Do you not find yourself mistaken now?" (48). Apparently Gray wished to trump Turner's bid for mystical authority by reinvoking the brute facts of the prisoner's legal status, namely, his apprehension, impending trial, and certain execution. But Turner's terse retort to Gray—"Was not Christ crucified" (48)—reasserts and indeed enhances the slave's claim to messianic spiritual and moral authority. In a stunning irony, Christ's martyrdom on the cross, which Turner cites as a historical prefiguration of his impending fate on the gallows, becomes just the sort of demonstrable, prima facie evidence of the slave's unjust victimization that Gray's rhetorical question had seemingly ruled out. More powerfully and pointedly than anything the slave could have done, Gray's question gave Turner the chance to deliver himself from condemnation via an appeal to Christ's martyrdom, while implicitly sentencing his captors to the ignominy of the Romans who put Jesus to death. Turner's death, ultimate proof according to Gray that his was a defeated "insurrection," is thus swallowed up if not in victory, at least in vindication of the black messiah's divinely sanctioned mission—to bear witness to Christ's promise that "the first should be last and the last should be first" (48). The last of the rebels to be captured, Turner was the first and only member of his band to claim the moral authority of "the Spirit" for what he had done.

Before his interview with Gray, none of Turner's interrogators had elicited from the prisoner such a radical claim to a specific homology between himself and Christ.[6] Whether Turner had intended to keep this to himself, or whether he had not come firmly to the conclusion of his Christological identity until confronted by his own doubting Thomas, lawyer Gray, is uncertain. What is much clearer is Turner's refusal during his interview-debate with Thomas R. Gray from November 1–3, 1831, to yield any ground to the white lawyer's insinuations that his sense of messianic identity and apocalyptic mission had been nothing but the murderous delusions of a religious madman. As far as Turner was concerned, or at least as much as we can infer from what he purportedly told Gray in the *Confessions*, Prophet Nat's behavior, from beginning to end, was simply and truly radical faith in action. This Turner confirmed to the world on November 5, the date of his trial. When asked in court how he pled in response to the host of capital murder charges against him, Turner replied evenly, "not guilty," adding "that he did not feel so."

If Turner believed that he was a type of Christ whose identity and mission could be confirmed only by his martyrdom, then Turner's personal narrative may be read as a kind of scripture in itself, the final testament of a holy man dedicated utterly to "the Spirit" even unto death. If we are to come to grips with Turner and his singularly influential spiritual autobiography, we must consider Turner's *Confessions* as a revision, a strong misreading, an act of signifying of and on biblical traditions, particularly the prophetic books of the Bible and the Book of Revelation. Turner's narrative constitutes his personal confession of faith, in short, though its larger public design was to recapitulate the terrible events of August 22 and 23, 1831, so as to ensure that they would not be rendered meaningless by faithless whites but would be revealed, to those who had ears to hear and eyes to see, as the fulfillment of providential destiny.

Among the leaders of the three major slave uprisings in U.S. history, only Nat Turner demonstrated a clear willingness to explain what he did and why he did it. Inspired by the liberation of Saint Domingue by the slave general Toussaint Louverture in 1793, Gabriel Prosser, an educated slave blacksmith who lived just outside

Richmond, Virginia, planned an elaborate rebellion in 1800 that aimed to capture the state capital and compel the authorities to grant freedom to the rebels. But on August 30, the night on which the blacks were to mass for the attack, the aptly named Gabriel was betrayed by two slaves and by a major storm, which prevented the insurgents from assembling in force. "The Main Spring and Chief Mover" of the conspiracy, Prosser refused to confess when captured and divulged nothing at his trial or execution on October 10, 1800.[7]

Denmark Vesey, the mastermind of the conspiracy to overthrow white rule in Charleston, South Carolina, in 1821, had grown up a slave before purchasing his freedom in 1799. Strongly influenced by the success of the slave revolt in Saint Domingue, Vesey preached his own liberation theology in Charleston's African Methodist Episcopal church, where, by the summer of 1821, he had assembled a group of lieutenants to lead an army of several thousand urban and rural slaves against the city. Before he could put his plans into effect, however, he too was betrayed by black informers. On his day in court Vesey steadfastly refused to confess. Faithful to the stern oath he had administered to his followers, "We will not tell on one another, we will not tell on any body, We will not tell if taken by the whites, nor will we tell if we are to be put to death,"[8] Vesey was found guilty of treason and hanged on July 2, 1822.

In contrast to Prosser's silence and Vesey's denial, Nat Turner made, evidently voluntarily, "a full confession" to Gray, who, as neither Turner's defense counsel nor an officer of the Southampton County Court, had no power over Turner other than the permission of the county jailer to interview the prisoner.[9] According to regional newspaper accounts of the week between Turner's apprehension and his trial, Turner had been "willing to answer any questions" and "very free in his confessions" not only with Gray but also with at least one other white man, a correspondent for the *Richmond Enquirer*, and probably more.[10] Because Turner was not motivated by a sense of guilt over his actions in the uprising, and since he had no reason to think that by confessing he would receive anything less than a death sentence, his willingness to talk to whites at all, let alone make "a full confession," may seem puzzling. Perhaps, however, Turner realized that Gray's presence in his cell represented an unprecedented autobiographical initiative, hitherto denied any enslaved American living in the South, to personalize himself, even as the prevailing journalistic and political discourse about him and his uprising was busy dehumanizing him. Perhaps by recounting his life as a process of spiritual evolution, Turner meant to create the necessary foreground for the *Confessions* to be received as the final testamentary phase of, not merely a hapless addendum to, his messianic mission.

Having been asked by Gray for "a history of the motives which induced me to undertake the late insurrection, as you call it," Turner initiates his narration with a bland statement of acquiescence. "To do so I must go back to the days of my infancy, and even before I was born" (44). A decisive announcement follows: "I was thirty-one years of age the 2nd of October last, and born the property of Benj. Turner, of this county" (44). Here Turner marshals the language of autobiography so as to parry Gray's legalistic agenda and interpose another of Turner's own choosing. Converted from object to subject, Turner invokes a rhetoric of individual origins so coveted by fugitive slave narrators in the future that the phrasing "I was born" became a conventional authorial gambit in the classics of nineteenth-century African American autobiography by Frederick Douglass and Booker T. Washington. The simple but unprecedented decision to commence his "confession" with a statement of his personal origins testifies to Turner's determination to bequeath a history of *himself*, despite Gray's request simply for a "history of the *motives*" (emphasis added) that had led Turner to undertake the August uprising. Turner's autobiographical act constitutes the first significant chronology of an African American life in the literature of the American South.

Expecting to obtain an incriminating legal confessional, Gray found himself complicit in recording an unrepentant, highly individualized confession of religious faith. That Turner did not try to escape Southampton County after his failed uprising but was captured less than two miles from where it began,[11] along with the fact that he willingly, even eagerly, embraced the autobiographical initiative offered him by Gray, suggest that Turner had come to see that the culmination and fulfillment of his earthly mission lay in the text that would be published after his death. The autobiography he narrated to Gray would become, to the extent that he could determine it, both the record of his martyrdom and the testament of his resurrection, his textual life after death, in effect.

In this connection we should remember that Turner never called the events of August 22 and 23 a rebellion or a revolt, and he directly rejected Gray's labeling his campaign an insurrection. The descriptor Turner resorts to repeatedly in the *Confessions* is simply "the work of death" (41, 48, 50 [the phrase is used three times on this page], 51, 56). Whether he conceived of his campaign in this shockingly matter-of-fact way when he began it in late August, by characterizing it in such language in early November Turner underlined the absoluteness of his remorseless dedication to his mission. The stark contrast between the heightened sense of subjectivity and spiritual agency that Turner claims for himself and the objectivizing, amoral perspective in which he regards his victims may constitute for some ultimate proof of Turner's religious dementia. Others may judge the same disparity as conclusive evidence of Turner's unwavering commitment to "revolutionary terror."[12] But in light of the late-twentieth-century rise of religious terrorism, it is also worthwhile to ask if what we think we know about this brand of terrorism might provide an interpretive framework in which to reconsider Turner's *Confessions*.

In the *Confessions* Gray records Turner announcing, "twas my object to carry terror and devastation wherever we went" (50). Three days before Turner was executed the *Richmond Enquirer* reported that during his interrogation he had disavowed "indiscriminate massacre" as the long-term purpose of his campaign, having adopted the mass killing of whites only "in the first instance to strike terror and alarm."[13] In a rare discussion of the *Confessions* that locates it in relation to a literary genre, namely, the black jeremiad, Eric Sundquist surmises terror as a likely purpose not just of the "work of death" but also of the work of autobiographical narration that resulted in the *Confessions*. "Turner's exercise of power by means of terror depended not just on the overt brutality of the revolt but, more important, on his calculated intervention, by means of his 'Confessions,' into the historical memory of Southampton."[14] Although Sundquist doesn't develop this insight into the role of the *Confessions* in what some have called terrorism's "violent communication strategy,"[15] my contention is that Turner's decision to "confess" by recounting his spiritual autobiography, which leads from visionary call to messianic mission to sacrificial martyrdom, provides the crucial linguistic mediation between the horrendous August 22 and 23 killings and whatever cognitive meaning and emotional significance whites were likely to draw from the violence itself.

In the aftermath of the cataclysmic events of September 11, 2001, an attempt to represent Nat Turner in the lineaments of a terrorist, religious or otherwise, may seem to some a desecration of his memory as a great American revolutionary and freedom fighter. We should remember, however, that the predominantly sympathetic, if not approving, sociopolitical estimate of Turner's actions that prevails in most studies of Turner today, especially since the furor over William Styron's novel, *The Confessions of Nat Turner* (1967), is comparatively recent. Few antebellum observers of and commentators on the so-called Southampton Slave Revolt would have dignified Turner's motives as comprehensible, let alone defensible or respectable. It took three decades before Thomas Wentworth Higginson, on the eve of a war he hoped would bring an end to slavery, dared to try to rehabilitate Turner to the readers of the *Atlantic Monthly* in 1861 by eulogizing him as a man "who knew no book but his Bible, and that by heart,—who devoted himself soul and body to the cause of his race, without a trace of personal hope or fear."[16] To suggest affinities between Turner's violence and that of the terrorists of September 11 may seem unfair to Turner today, but given the similarities between the rhetoric of dehumanization and demonization that constituted official reaction to Turner and his followers in most media in the antebellum United States and to the Al-Qaeda terrorists in much contemporary U.S. media, we have reason to ask what we can learn from a fresh look at Turner, and in particular his *Confessions*, through a post-9/11 perspective.[17]

Like many men and women in our world today who resort to terrorism out of a combination of religious motives and political goals,[18] Turner may well have believed that the corruption of the dominant socioeconomic institution of his own time—that is, American slavery—had become so pervasive and banal that nothing short of a cataclysmic strike against that institution could force American whites, especially slaveholders, to recognize the terror embodied in the institution itself. If this be true, then as a proto-religious terrorist, Turner may well have realized as he prepared for his interview with Gray that the only way to make "the work of death" both terrifying *and* meaningful, the only way to compel slaveholding whites to face the monstrous retribution that their own religion promised them for their crimes against humanity, was to represent the instigator of "the work of death" as a dedicated man of "the Spirit" prepared and willing to be martyred for his actions. In the final pages of the *Confessions* Gray assures his reader that none of the commonly held explanations of Turner's behavior—that he was drunk, that he was a sneak and a coward, that he aimed to rob his victims so as to "obtain money to make his escape" (54)—could adequately account for Turner. The only answer to the mystery of Turner, Gray acknowledges, was the one Turner himself insisted on throughout his narrative: "He is a complete fanatic, or plays his part most admirably" (54). Labeling Turner a "fanatic," Gray in effect granted the black man the basis for his religious zeal, condemning him for his extreme expression of his faith rather than questioning that faith itself. That some readers of the *Confessions*, then and now, have regarded Gray as something of a convert, however grudgingly or inadvertently, to Turner's apocalyptic message reminds us, once again, of the *Confessions'* implicit design, which was not just to record or even to explain Turner's motives but to endow the terror of the seemingly "indiscriminate massacre" with the most audacious spiritual meaning.[19]

Theorists of terrorism argue persuasively that a terrorist event is not merely "what happens" but "is that which can be narrated," that which becomes convincingly explanatory in and through the form of a story.[20] Because the violence of a terrorist event can often seem to defeat reasoned explanation, terrorism needs, in fact, demands textual emplotment. What seems to have confounded Turner's interrogators the most about his plot was the connection, the causal link, between the spiritual and the political. One of those who interviewed Turner before he met with Gray wrote this in the *Richmond Enquirer*: "he gave, apparently with great candor, a history of the operations of his mind for many years past; of the signs he saw; the spirits he conversed with; of his prayers, fastings and watchings. . . . These he considered for a long time only as a call to superior righteousness; and it was not until rather more than a year ago that the idea of emancipating the blacks entered his mind." But "how this idea came or in what manner it was connected with his signs, etc., I could not get him to explain in a manner at all satisfactory— notwithstanding I examined him closely upon this point, he alway [sic] seemed to mystify."[21]

How to "connect" the political idea of liberation to a personal "call to superior righteousness" was what Turner hoped the *Confessions* would demystify. Was there any other way for Turner to break through white indoctrination as to the divine right of slavery other than to represent his narrative of a slave uprising in what theorist Mark Jurgensmeyer calls "the symbolic 'script' of cosmic warfare—a struggle that links current political issues with a timeless battle between the forces of Good and Evil"?[22] Such a narrative yoking of temporal and cosmic struggle, which is characteristic of the worldview of many contemporary religious terrorists according to Jurgensmeyer, points up affinities among the rhetoric of Turner and that of antebellum black and white antislavery propagandists and activists from David Walker to John Brown.

As perhaps America's first religio-political terrorist, Nat Turner understood that his mission demanded more than repaying the state terror of American slavery with a response horrifying enough to induce in white consciousness something like the terror in which slaves lived every day. Perhaps only when he realized that his ostensible revolt would fail did he decide that he had to live long enough to explicate the spiritual logic of his terrorist career, so that his own self-sacrifice, his execution, could fulfill "the work of death" that the Spirit had sent him to do. If the work of death visited on New York and Washington DC on September 11, 2001, provides a way to reckon with the *Confessions of Nat Turner*, perhaps further study of this text as a harbinger of the spiritualizing violence of today's jihads and crusades will enable us better to understand how "scriptures" and fanaticism have come to seem so often indistinguishable in the apocalyptic world we live in now.

NOTES

1. Thomas Wentworth Higginson, "Nat Turner's Insurrection," *Atlantic Monthly* 8 (1861): 173–187. An antislavery activist who would lead black troops into battle during the Civil War, Rev. Higginson concludes his large, sympathetic article about Turner by calling him "a memory of terror and a symbol of retribution triumphant."

2. Over the past thirty years, African American historical and religious studies scholarship from Vincent Harding's *There Is a River* (New York: Random House, 1983) to Theophus H. Smith's *Conjuring Culture: Biblical Formations of Black America* (New York: Oxford University Press, 1994) have regularly treated Nat Turner as a key figure, often linking him to prophetic as well as revolutionary traditions. Little work, however, has been done on Turner's *Confessions* as an important spiritual autobiography such as that of Richard Allen or Jarena Lee, for instance. For a brief analysis of the *Confessions* as a "tropological reading of Scripture," see William L. Andrews, *To Tell a Free Story: The First Century of Afro-American Autobiography, 1760–1865* (Urbana: University of Illinois Press, 1986), 72–77.

3. All references to and quotations from Turner's *Confessions* are taken from *The Confessions of Nat Turner and Related Documents*, ed. Kenneth S. Greenberg (Boston: St. Martin's Press, 1996).

4. Pronouncing the death sentence on Turner, Judge Jeremiah Cobb remarked, "Borne down by this load of guilt, your only justification is, that you were led away by fanaticism. If this be true, from my soul I pity you . . ." Turner, *Confessions*, 57.

5. Because we know little of Turner's thinking apart from the "Nat Turner" who speaks in the *Confessions*, we are well advised to remember that the "Nat Turner" of the *Confessions* is "a joint semiotic construction" of two men whose identities themselves have been increasingly overdetermined by legend and myth. See Eric Sundquist, *To Wake the Nations* (Cambridge, MA: Harvard University Press, 1993), 39. In *To Tell a Free Story*, I picture Turner and Gray in a "diametric collaboration," in which a fundamental competition between two opposing wills yoked together in temporary but mutual need for the other underlies the entire text.

6. According to those who informed local newspapers of their interrogations of Turner, the prisoner referred to himself as a prophet "commanded by the Almighty to do what he did," who conversed with spirits, performed miracles, and interpreted signs in the heavens. But in none of these reports is there mention of Turner alluding to Christ. See the extensive selection of contemporary reports on the Turner rebellion in Henry Irving Tragle, *The Southampton Slave Revolt of 1831* (Amherst: University of Massachusetts Press, 1971), 27–169.

7. Gerald W. Mullin, *Flight and Rebellion: Slave Resistance in Eighteenth-Century Virginia* (New York: Oxford University Press, 1972), 147–151.

8. Robert S. Starobin, ed., *Denmark Vesey* (Englewood Cliffs, NJ: Prentice Hall, 1970), 1–12, 62.

9. Thomas C. Parramore, *Southampton County, Virginia* (Charlottesville: University Press of Virginia, 1978), 107.

10. Eric Foner, ed., *Nat Turner* (Englewood Cliffs, NJ: Prentice Hall, 1971), 31; Tragle, *Southampton Slave Revolt*, 132–140.

11. Tragle, *Southampton Slave Revolt*, xvii.

12. Eugene D. Genovese invokes this term to characterize the commitment to revolutionary violence, even against noncooperative blacks, that was necessary to the freedom struggles led by Denmark Vesey and Nat Turner. See *From Rebellion to Revolution: Afro-American Slave Revolts in the Making of the Modern World* (Baton Rouge: Louisiana State University Press, 1979), 9–10.

13. Tragle, *Southampton Slave Revolt*, 137.

14. Sundquist, *To Wake the Nations*, 72.

15. Alex P. Schmid and Janny de Graf, *Violence as Communication: Insurgent Terrorism and the Western News Media* (London: Sage, 1982), 15.

16. Tragle, *Southampton Slave Revolt*, 347.

17. Richard E. Rubenstein observes that President George W. Bush's evocation of the adjective "evil" to characterize the Al-Qaeda attackers draws on an "Augustinian sense" of the word, which renders evil as notably "uncaused in any historical sense" and thus is particularly grievous and alien. See "The Psycho-Political Sources of Terrorism," in *The New Global Terrorism*, ed. Charles W. Kegley Jr. (Upper Saddle River, NJ: Prentice Hall, 2003), 144, 139–150. Thomas Gray acknowledges from the outset of the *Confessions* that "public curiosity" had been especially keen to learn "the motives" that had led the uprising's "diabolical actors" (characterized elsewhere in the *Confessions* as Turner's "fiendish band . . . actuated by hellish purposes" to perform deeds of "fiend-like barbarity"), because until Turner's capture, "every thing connected with this sad affair was wrapt in mystery" (40–41).

18. See Walter Laqueur, *The New Terrorism: Fanaticism and the Arms of Mass Destruction* (New York: Oxford University Press, 1999).

19. When it reviewed the *Confessions*, the *Richmond Enquirer* sensed a persuasive force and individuality in the narrative that belie the editor's professed efforts to discredit or explain away what the slave says. "The language [of the slave's narrative] is far superior to what Nat Turner could have employed," the *Enquirer* complained. "Portions of it are even eloquently and classically expressed," a decision that was likely "to give the Bandit a character for intelligence which he does not deserve" (Tragle, *Southampton Slave Revolt*, 143). Thomas C. Parramore, the historian who discovered the identity of Gray, suggests that the Southampton lawyer found in Turner "the mirror image of his own ravaged soul." *Southampton County*, 113.

20. Allen Feldman, *Formations of Violence* (Chicago: University of Chicago Press, 1991), 14.

21. Tragle, *Southampton Slave Revolt*, 137.

22. Mark Jurgensmeyer, *Terror in the Mind of God* (Berkeley: University of California Press, 2000), 146.

8   *Signifying Scriptures from an African Perspective*

OYERONKE OLAJUBU

Indigenous religions are often characterized by plurality, but the term "plurality" is an inadequate descriptor of people's lived experience. Rather than plurality, in this essay, I emphasize mutuality, accommodation, and balance. The Yoruba religion is one of such indigenous religions that prioritize balance and mutuality in relationships between God and humans, humans and nature, and in interpersonal relationships. Dividends of this stance can be discerned in power relations, gender relations, and power utilization among adherents of Yoruba religion.

The agenda of the Institute for Signifying Scriptures (ISS) seeks to problematize the use of normative paradigms, including "plurality," in the definition and conceptualization of what "scripture" is. Notions of "scripture" in "major" world religions seem restrictive and in need of expansion to better reflect other people's religious inclinations. This attempt touches directly on some issues in African religion, especially in the realm of rituals, the exposition of which may facilitate, albeit in a minimal way, the agenda of the ISS.

In this essay I identify some important themes, issues, and motifs raised by Vincent Wimbush in the introductory essay of this volume. These themes, issues, and motifs to do not so much represent Wimbush's view; they reflect his naming of problems to be addressed. My aim is to address them in light of Yoruba traditions.

Scriptures As the Ultimate, Discontinuous Medium of the Sacred

It is misleading and pernicious to present "scriptures" (written or oral) as the ultimate or single medium of communication between divinity and humanity.[1] The dynamism of religious life and experiences makes the above submission implausible.[2] In nondominant religions, rituals and performance constitute a free-flowing means of communication on diverse issues from different perspectives. These may include invocations, rites of passages, and spirit possession. In African religion, such rituals exhibit features of spontaneity and fluidity in as much as activities in performance and recitations are neither fixed nor static. Cultic functionaries who officiate or offer direction during each ritual often operate under the influence of a supersensible power with whom they are in constant communication and whose dictates they communicate to worshippers.

There is therefore a continuous web of interpersonal exchange of information and disposition in this process of assessing "scripture." A phenomenon as dynamic as the communication between the sacred and humans may not be constrained to a single medium.

"Scripture" has been taken in history to refer to written prescriptions for humans from the Supreme Being.[3] Embedded within "scriptures" are explanations for nature (cosmology and cosmogony); expectations for interpersonal relationships (ethics); and stipulations for contact between the supersensible world, humans, and the ecosystem (ritual). A salient feature of "scriptures" has been their normative character. Though "scriptures" display different levels of dynamism in interpretations, they nonetheless remain normative. In African religions, "scriptures" would be a fluid phenomenon, marked by multiplicity. This would be especially true of the ritual sphere where a continuous process of communication and interaction occur in African religions. A crucial product of these interactions between the divine and humans involves prescriptions of diverse modes, which would qualify to be labeled as "scriptures."

Worthy of mention is the role played by custodians of "scripture" in these enterprises. The profound influence of these custodians over dogma and ritual in religion turns around notions of restrictive knowledge, which is assumed to bestow authority. In a certain parlance, this authority may not be challenged. These observations point toward a restricted definition of what constitutes "scripture," the boundary of which is immutable. Realities in some societies render such definitions and conceptualizations impractical and inadequate.

A "discontinuous" medium suggests one that is not stable, one that is on and off. The question to ask is this: is this discontinuous-ness the prerogative of the sacred? In which case the sacred may use this medium designated "scripture" sometimes to communicate with humans but may choose to employ other means at other times. At any rate, the term "scripture" conveys notions of complexity and dynamism.

What Is Scripture?

Traditionally, "scripture" as a term in religious discourse is a text linked to a sacred being or sacredness. It is usually written and fixed. Sometimes it is subject to scientific analysis (hermeneutics); sometimes it is not. These predictable and boundary-bound classifications of "scripture" have, however, proven inadequate for certain societies on account of the mark of dynamism in the religious experience of such a people. So what is scripture? As a concept, "scripture" would appear, on the one hand, to exhibit a close affinity with the history, culture, and social order of a given people. It would seem to encompass a people's meaning system and process of legitimization. It would therefore be regarded as a broad concept with a complex agenda. On the other hand, "scripture" is not expected to be culture bound, in which case any "scripture" should be universally accessible insomuch as its prescriptions are agreeable to individuals who subscribe to it, irrespective of the nationality or cultural affiliations of such individuals.

The case of Yoruba religion may be cited as an example. "Scripture" in Yoruba religion is coded, but not static or closed. It encompasses oral narratives (Ifa, stories, legends, incantations, and proverbs); some of these oral sources are now documented. In addition, Yoruba "scripture" includes prescriptions that emanate from the daily enactment of ritual through diverse modes of performance and recitations. Often this involves recitation of praise names (*oriki*) for the gods and spirits (*orisa*), which may result in spirit possession from which messages are transmitted to worshippers. Hence the content of Yoruba "scriptures" is dynamic and multifarious. Nonetheless its prescriptions are agreeable and accessible to people worldwide, irrespective of nationality or cultural affiliation. Consequently, there are adherents of Yoruba religion who are Yoruba by origin and others who are non-Yoruba. Also, Yoruba religion is practiced with minor modifications in places such as Cuba, Brazil, Trinidad and Tobago, Germany, and North America.

Maybe an attempt at considering what "scriptures" are *not* will provide a helpful angle. "Scripture" is *not* a sole reference to a written text, a finished product, that exercises normative influence on people's lives and is untouched by peoples' experiences. "Scripture" is *not* an oral text that exists apart from the experiences of a people or an individual; it seeks to exert normative influence on a group of people. "Scripture" is *not* a written or oral text that is closed or sealed to analysis, appraisal, and some level of "negotiations."

Furthermore, "scripture" must be located in African social settings in light of the permeating feature of religion in African worldviews. This is especially true of the people's use of language, which could be direct or indirect. In the recitations of praise names of individuals, lineages, or communities, for example, the process of recitation and memory recall could produce salient sociocultural paradigms in conjunction/conversation/contrast to "scripture."

Whence Scriptures Developed

The availability of many "scriptures" in the religious experiences of human beings reflects human diversity. How do "scriptures" fare in the face of religious pluralism? Does the presence of many "scriptures," whether written or oral, not suggest the futility of constraining "scriptures" not only in number but also as a concept? For example, all the definitions I checked for "scriptures" assumed they were written documents, ignoring the fact that there are oral scriptures in existence. Therefore the need to reflect a broader perspective in the definition of "scripture" is clear.

The development of the concept of "scripture" could not have occurred in a vacuum. In some instances, records of the encounter between the sacred and humans are kept in oral or written forms to serve as encouragement, reproof, and examples for the living adherents of such "scriptures" (Bible). In some cases, in addition to the records of encounters between the sacred and humans, the sayings and conduct profile of a religious leader are also recorded to serve as a model for those who subscribe to such "scriptures" (Qur'an). Again, at other times, records are kept in written or oral forms of ancient accounts that proffer explanations for events and past occurrences that history could not explain (Bhagavad-Gita). On other occasions, "scriptures" develop as accumulated recordings of philosophies and practices espoused by a key figure with profound influence on the lives of the society (Tao Te Ching).

Germane to the various forms of developmental procedures identified above is human agency. The trail of information from and about the sacred and the encounter between the sacred and humans necessarily passes through human agency. Consequently the influence of the experiences of human beings as a significant factor on the interpretations of received information in the religious sphere cannot be undervalued. The interpretation of any information by an individual carries with it aspects of who the individual is, where he or she has been, and what the individual prioritizes. The development of "scripture" is thus intertwined with the lived experiences of the human agency through which it was communicated.

Some of the adherents to these "scriptures," however, who are also having varied living experiences, may not have the opportunity to influence these "scriptures" in a way that the "scriptures" handed over to them have been able to influence them. One such example is the sharia legal system in the religiously pluralistic society that is Nigeria. Zamfara State, one of the northern states of Nigeria, predominantly Muslim, was the first to begin, in the year 2000, the operation of sharia. Punitive prescriptions of the sharia system, such as the cutting of limbs of a thief, separate transportation for men and women, and the poverty reduction measures for the less-privileged in the society, have apparently had little impact on the people of Zamfara, due to the differences in the daily living experiences of Nigerian Muslims today.

Not long ago, the major Nigerian television news bulletin (*NTA Network News*) reported that the Zamfara government had resolved to enlist the help of retired armed-forces and police personnel to assist with security problems in the state. This move was made more stressful by the case of Safiya Husain, the single mother whom a Nigerian sharia court condemned to death by stoning. The court decision was rescinded because of pressure from the international community and civil rights and women's groups in Nigeria.[4] Here, the intersection of religion and modern legal systems complicates some conceptions of "scripture."

How Do Scriptures Function?

"Scripture" is a normative concept that functions in fundamental ways in people's lives. Its legitimacy in this regard often rests on its claim to divine origin and approval. "Scripture" also functions as a guiding principle for delineating social order. It offers legitimacy for social structures and provides prescriptions for social conduct all at once. "Scriptures" offer explanations for profound questions in life: Who created the world, the world of humans and the world of nature? Why death? Why do bad things happen to good people? Why do bad people escape punishment and flourish? Why are there diseases? Why should a good and faithful wife die of HIV/AIDS contracted from a promiscuous husband? What of an innocent child dying from HIV/AIDS?

Some "scriptures" function as tools of imperialism between and within groups. Examples of this include the alliance between the missionaries and colonial masters in colonized communities. This was true of the British colonial powers and Christian missionaries in Nigeria before 1960, where both parties cooperated to ensure the "compliance" of Nigerians to roles prescribed for them by society.

"Scripture" has also been used as a tool for indoctrination and destruction of unsuspecting and fervent worshippers; the case of the Movement for the Restoration of the Ten Commandments of God in Kanungu, Uganda, is apposite here. In Kanungu on March 17, 2000, about five hundred bodies were found burned to death in a church. These were some members of the Movement for the Restoration of the Ten Commandments of God in Uganda. Further searches revealed mass graves at other sites linked to the church. According to reports, the leader of the movement, Joseph Kibwetere, ordered the mass murder after members who had sold all their properties and donated the proceeds to the church began demanding the return of their money when the world did not end on December 31, 1999, as had been predicted. The sixty-eight-year old leader and his female assistant, Gredonia Miwerinda, however, escaped the church blaze.[5]

"Even the Bible was made to suit our imagination" (Zora Neale Hurston)

Who made the Bible? Is the Bible "scripture"? What constitutes "our imagination"? Who do we mean by "our"?

In Africa, the Bible has been "domesticated" while Christianity has been undergoing a process of African enculturation. Biblical concepts are adorned in African philosophical garbs; hence references to Jesus as a kinsman, ancestor, and king are common. In addition, "African Christianity," a brand of Christianity with distinct features rooted in African ethos and worldview, is now recognized worldwide.[6]

Both African conceptualizations of Jesus and African Christianity are linked to biblical hermeneutics, which could be perceived as a product of human imagination in interaction with divine endowments. The influence of "scripture" in this parlance, however, is often thought of as a one-way flow of influence—from the Bible to the people. Typically no avenue for human lived experiences of the people to influence the "scriptures" is accorded. Recently, however, some African women began to read the Bible through the lens of their daily lived experiences.[7] In other words, whereas the Bible and its interpretations may influence African Biblical conceptions, African daily-lived experiences may not influence the content or structure of the Bible in any formidable manner.

Social Weaving and Textur(e)ing

Indeed, the place of the "social" seems crucial to reconceptualizing "scripture," including the social at the level of reception as well as at the level of constitution. The positioning of the "text" relative to social textures would involve social engineering in a broad sense, especially as every text is a product of particular sociocultural and historical settings. This dynamic nature of religious experiences makes a constant reappraisal of "scriptures" imperative. "Scriptures" as a means of forming and deforming social identities reinforces this pertinent need. Because religion constitutes an important ingredient in identity formation, especially in Africa, the relationship between "scripture" and social identity requires ongoing attention, as in the obvious case of conversion.[8]

The act of forming and deforming social identities as a consequence of religion suggests "fluidity" for the concept of "scriptures." This "fluidity" would suggest open-mindedness and the willingness for continuous assessments. The crucial place of the "social" in conceptualizing "scripture" also brings to the fore issues of politics and power dynamics. Embedded within the traditional concept of "scripture" is the power to "name" or prescribe. This points toward power distribution and utilization. Feminist concerns in religion are to a large extent geared toward redressing the imbalance that has marked power distribution in religion, especially as regards "scripture" and its interpretation. A consequence of the above discourse is that the conceptualization of "scripture" should go beyond an analysis of texts and encompass sociocultural modes, such as symbols, rituals, practices, and oral narratives (folktales, myths, legends, proverbs, parables, and conventions).

That humans shape and reshape themselves on the one hand and are shaped and reshaped by prevailing circumstances on the other hand confirms that "scripture" as a concept should be marked by "fluidity." The canonization of the Bible warranted the elimination of some books from the recognized list of literature in early Christianity. Canonization assumes a closed "scripture," an obvious variant to the situation in Africa, where "scriptures" are open-ended.

Conclusion

"Scriptures" as it presently exists in religious studies is an inadequate term. The motifs and themes from Nigeria reveal the essential place of fluidity in conceptualizing "scriptures," the crucial place of the "social" in the constitution of "scriptures," the importance of human agency and the distribution of power in arriving at "scriptures," and the need to see "scriptures" as a means of communication. Issues on the "universal" or "exclusive" character of "scriptures" need reappraisal, as do the functions of "scriptures" from the perspective of how "scriptures" were received in Africa and what had been done with them.

NOTES

1. All subhead titles are based on ideas and phrases found in Wimbush's introduction to the current volume.

2. James L. Matory, *Sex and the Empire That is No More* (Minneapolis: University of Minnesota Press, 1994).

3. Examples of such scriptures include the Bible, the Qur'an, and the Vedas.

4. Safiya Husain of Sokoto was convicted for adultery, and a *rajm* (stoning to death) sentence was pronounced on her. The sharia court of appeal, however, faulted the sentence of the area court. Safiya was subsequently bestowed in Rome with Italian citizenship.

5. http://www.uiowa.edu.

6. J. A. Omoyajowo, *Cherubim and Seraphim: The History of an African Independent Church* (New York: NOK Publishers International, 1982).

7. Musa Dube, ed., *Other Ways of Reading: African Women and the Bible* (Atlanta: Society of Biblical Literature, 2001).

8. R. Shaw and C. Stewart, "Introduction: Problematizing Syncretism," in *Syncretism/Anti-Syncretism: The Politics of Religious Synthesis*, ed. C. Stewart and R. Shaw (New York: Routledge, 1994), 1–27.

9

Transforming Identities, De-textualizing Interpretation, and Re-modalizing Representation

SCRIPTURES AND SUBALTERN SUBJECTIVITY IN INDIA

SATHIANATHAN CLARKE

The methodology presented in Vincent Wimbush's theorizing of "scriptures" introduction to this volume is both complexly situated and conspicuously vested. The methodology of investigating "scriptures" is decidedly embedded in the multiplex and pluriform world of concrete power exchanges within which the phenomena operate. "Scriptures" become powerful agents of discursive practice in a complex of worlds entrenched in power. "Scriptures" are thus stripped of their exclusive transcendental wrappings, which have been historically utilized to save them from critical interrogation. Rather "scriptures" have been reassembled as subjects/objects of immanental influence in the messy and concrete world of interconnected power generators and power mediators. From another viewpoint, the methodology eschewed by Wimbush also appears deliberately warped. Let me not be misunderstood: I state this as a commendation. The object of his investigation seems to seek to comprehend these multiplex and pluriform dimensions of the power of "scriptures" as experienced from those on the underside of history. Such a method opts to investigate the variegated strategies of subordinated communities both in their reception and reconstruction of the phenomena. This option is a preferential one that takes sides with specific ways of construing the effects of "scriptures" for and by the subaltern. I hope that both features of this methodological proclivity will be a part of the enduring commitment of the Institute for Signifying Scriptures.

How would this methodology work in an effort to signify "scriptures" in the Indian context? Let me attempt to explore this question in somewhat more detail through the rest of this essay. The question of how to proceed with studying significations of "scriptures" is a challenging one in the Indian setting. In a country that prides itself on being the birthplace of Hinduism, Buddhism, Jainism, and Sikhism, do we select a kind of intertextuality of "scriptures," which involves some form of comparative studies of the various sacred books? Or, in a country that comprises multifarious forms of Tribal and Dalit local religious traditions, are we to focus on the manner in which their respective oral "scriptures" both resist and replicate theological themes of written "scriptures" in their intricate and innovative significations? Or in a country that possesses some of the oldest forms of "scriptures," might it be appropriate to inquire into the ways in which the Christian Bible negotiated its entry and sustained its expansion in India? While commending such directions as worthwhile and fitting, I limit this reflection to something less interreligious in nature. I am interested in looking at the reception and reconstruction of the Christian Bible as it made its way into colonial India, especially in relation to one of the main subaltern communities, that is, Dalits.

The complex nature of the historical context into which the Christian Bible arrived in India instructs us that we can no longer simply signify "scriptures" through prefabricated and convenient binaries like colonial versus native, white versus black, literacy versus orality, the West versus the rest, and modern versus traditional. The Christian text no doubt came to India couched, even if somewhat uneasily, within the enthusiastic and carefully designed expansion of Western colonialism. Even though there were Christian communities in India from at least the fourth century of the Common Era, the Bible emerged as a key emblem of Christianity and a major tool of Christianizing India only after 1706 with the arrival of the Protestant missions in Trancobar, South India. The two and a half centuries that followed this important historical marker of Christian mission in India witnessed the introduction, translation, and circulation of the Bible, almost solely funded by the finance, expertise, and machinery of Western mission agencies. And yet the Bible cannot be simply understood as an instrument of colonization of India by the West. The Bible also found itself unwittingly deposited among the objects of an internal system of colonization that had a history going back at least a millennium in India. In the custody of Dalit communities, the Bible served as a useful tool to access the forbidden world of literacy, which was one key means of empowerment denied them by the powerful native elite of Hindu caste communities. Some clarification is necessary to understand the relationship of Dalit communities to the rest of Indian society.

There are competing views about the sources of caste-based stratification in Indian society during the British colonial period (circa 1700 to 1947) that coincided with the major expansion of Protestant Christianity in India. On the one hand, there is the suggestion that the system of caste was rigidified and reified as an organizing framework of Indian society by the colonial rulers. This view purports that in order to enumerate, segregate, and govern the native populace, the colonial agents inventively reconstituted and reinforced caste. On the other hand, there is the argument that the caste system is intrinsically rooted in an old civilizational paradigm of Indian social arrangements that discloses an Indic way of communitarian living. This native way of living thus was reified as a mechanism to reiterate a form of Indianness in a context of colonialism. Whichever way one interprets the strengthening of caste in relationship to colonial rule, the system as such was convenient for Christian mission. It helped the process of "othering" the culture and religion of the native Indians (i.e., Hinduism as being hierarchically grounded in a dehumanizing way of life) in their scheme to convert the same to a different religious faith (i.e., Christianity offering a more egalitarian and humanizing way of life).[1]

Whatever may have been the case, for our purposes it suffices to assert that Indian society during the expansion of Protestant missions, especially in relation to South India, was divided along lines that had much to do with caste, even if not along the customarily established mode. The main contours of the South Indian social system during this period can be seen to have three distinct divisions. Let me sketch the threefold caste segmentation in South India during the eighteenth, nineteenth, and first half of the twentieth centuries. First, there was a configuration of Brahmanic caste communities, which consisted of an alliance between the Brahmins and the purer caste communities from among the Śūdras. These *sat*-Śūdras (pure Śūdras), who were a landowning class, were given ritual privileges, thus appropriating the status of the Kshatriyas and Vaishiyas (the other twice-born castes apart from the Brahmins), who for some reason were absent from the Tamil region. They also donated liberally to the upkeep of the priestly community (Brahmins). In return for these gifts the Brahmins legitimated their social, cultural, political, and economic authority. Second, there was the coalition of the not-so-pure Śūdra caste communities. This consortium comprised laboring classes who were within the caste society but who were ritually subordinate and economically dependent on the Brahmanic caste communities. These *asat*-Śūdras (impure Śūdras) lived within the geographic confines of the caste society and were in social interaction with the Brahmanic caste community. Yet they suffered religious and economic restrictions that hindered their free and full participation in the functioning of Indian society. Third, there was a category of communities that lived outside the borders of the Hindu caste society. Repulsed by and ejected from the Hindu caste society (both the Brahmanic caste communities and the asat-Śūdra caste communities), they lived as outcaste peoples. This third section of peoples were cast out of society in the postulate that they were too polluted to live within the geographical and social space of caste Hindus. They were treated as objects both by the Brahmanic caste communities and the asat-Śūdra communities. And they were economically exploited and socially exiled. Called by various terms (e.g., Exterior-Castes, Depressed Classes, Panchamas, Outcastes, Harijans, and Scheduled Castes), this community has lately taken on the name Dalits, which means "broken ones," who resist this oppression and brokenness. Dalits, thus, in the words of Deliege, "refer to those sections of Indian society that are economically dependent and exploited, victims of many kinds of discriminations, and ritually polluted in a permanent way. It is the combination of these elements that characterize Untouchables [Dalits]."[2] An important addition to Deliege's somewhat passive depiction of defining Dalits is the dimension of their own agency, which both protests such subjection and advances a more empowering and emancipated subjectivity.

Situated among the many economic, sociocultural, and religio-political differences among these three unequal communities was the caste communities' right to literacy, a right calculatingly and comprehensively denied to the Dalit communities. The literacy divide between these two sections of caste communities (Brahmanic and the asat-Śūdras), on the one hand, and the Dalits (outcaste), on the other hand, can be interpreted as a major debilitation for the emancipation of the Dalits. Education, as an important form of social capital, was historically denied to the Dalits by the caste communities. In a concrete way this denial of access to literacy was symbolized in their being kept far away from the Hindu scriptures. Popular mythology disseminated the admonition that while Dalits were not permitted to read the sacred scripture, even those caught listening to the recitation of the scriptures would have molten lead poured down their ears. This unavailability of the scripture to Dalits reinforced several messages. First, literacy is the domain of the religiously, economically, and socially privileged castes. It was confined to the reflective classes and denied to the laboring masses. Second, literacy must be withheld from Dalits in order to keep the scriptures free from misinterpretation. The sacred as mediated by the revealed word must not be entrusted to polluted ones who do not have the capacities to comprehend the divine in its purity. And, third, social capital (education in this instance) must be withheld from Dalits because it may aid them in upsetting the strict conventions on who can and cannot have power in the caste-based society. Knowledge-as-power must be restricted to maintain the status quo in a caste-determined system.

This is the specific historical context into which the Bible made its entry into India. Even while it came with the dominance associated with the colonial power, it arrived into the world of the Dalits who have been objects of an internal form of colonization for several centuries. The Christian Bible quite fortuitously found itself in a position to overturn the literacy restrictions imposed on the Dalits by the dominant caste communities. Here I think that the conspicuously vested character of the methodology evident in Wimbush's essay, which opts to be linked up mainly with the subalterns' signification of "scriptures," is useful in the Indian context. It permits us to resist spending time and energy on being preoccupied with either the intentions and executions of Western colonial-assisted bearers of the Bible in their effort to restore true wisdom for thought and life among Hindu Indians or the cross-cultural experiments of hybridization that were the result of Christian sacred texts being wedded to Hindu religious texts by the elite native Brahmanic scholars in their pursuit of indigenization of the Christian Gospel. Instead it commissions us to explore the tactics of the Dalit communities in their encountering, dismantling, reconstituting, and assimilating of the phenomena of "scriptures" that was thrust into their impoverished, othered, illiterate world.

The Bible in a World That Had Been Deprived of "Scriptures" and Yet Saturated with Other Complementary Symbols: Transforming Subaltern Identities

Like all other religious phenomena, "scriptures," too, are made to work differently from the intended effects for which they were initially circulated. Western missionaries may have gifted the Bible to Indian natives to aid their transformation into a certain kind of West-like "enlightened" people. But from the moment that the phenomenon is handed over to any society it finds itself in a world of alien religious and cultural objects within which it construes its particular subjectivity. From the Indian experience, one can say that the Bible truly suffers signification within an unfamiliar setting.

This entails two consequences for the study of the reception and re-symbolization of the Bible. On the one hand, scripture and its signification cannot be understood apart from the preexisting world of religious symbols that are part of the social memory and practice of the receiving society. In this context the painful memory of the absence of scripture has deep significance. The memory of being denied access to Hindu scriptures surely plays a role in the reception and reconstitution of the Bible among Dalits. It was not as if they merely did not have the sacred text; instead it was more that they were refused it because such a pure form of divine revelation could not be placed near their polluted being. Kancha Ilaiah, a well-known social scientist, draws our attention to the manner in which the arrival of the Christian Bible transformed the identities of SCs (Dalits), STs (Tribals), and OBCs (Other Backward Castes) by incorporating them into the sacred world of literacy and religious reflectivity. "These ships [Doulos and Logos II of Operation Mobilization] have taken books to people who have never seen books earlier. When a book reaches an illiterate person, he or she has to learn to read. The OM volunteers, I am told, encourage reading aloud of books for the benefit of illiterate people. This is where Hinduism has failed. It neither allowed the SCs, STs or OBCs to hear books read out nor to learn reading and writing for centuries."[3] Also the Bible as a sacred object that seeks to mediate divine power enters a world in which there are competing and complementing objects that function to achieve similar goals. Such sacred objects may be coterminous or dissimilar to the scripture, but their future now becomes intertwined with a new religious symbol that professes to be the key to religious thought and life. The signification of the Bible then takes place within an already existing frame of reference that particularizes and interconnects a host of symbols within a universe of religious meaning. Wimbush is thus right to suggest that an inquiry into "scriptures" cannot be severed from the study of religion as a whole.[4] The place and role of the Bible in relation to other analogous and contrasting symbols within the universe of various religious systems can only enhance the peculiar significations that "scriptures" take on in vastly different historical and geographical contexts.

The performative function of "scriptures," on the other hand, can be extended into newer and broader vistas that have no precedence in the tradition of signification that has been previously documented. In the process of signifying "scriptures," subaltern communities are both able to extend the life of their respective systems of representation through the new phenomenon ("scriptures") and able to make the phenomenon learn and play new tricks in order to authentically express their own subjectivity differently. A focus on the mechanics of signification, which are unleashed by the subaltern communities through transforming their own identities in the light of the Bible and transforming the Bible to project their own subjectivity, becomes the locus of raking, making, taking, shaping, waking, forsaking, and, even, faking meaning. Subaltern communities thus form, deform, reform, and transform their subjectivity in novel and unanticipated ways through the politics of instrumentalizing various forms of signifying "scriptures." I want to utilize these two insights to highlight the manner in which Dalits signify the Christian Bible and then suggest one major implication that this would have for the work of the Institute for Signifying Scriptures.

Orality As Terrain, Techne, and Tactic for Subaltern Significations of "Scriptures": De-textualizing the World of Interpretation

It is noteworthy that signification of scripture is often deliberately, one may even say cunningly, relocated by subaltern communities away from an unfamiliar and, often, formal world of text to a more familiar and largely informal world of oral recitation. The universe of literacy, which has a history and philosophy of hermeneutics, is strategically exchanged for the world of orality, which has a different history and philosophy of representation. This could very well be one of the most significant empowering tactics for making sure that the rules and conventions of the unfamiliar world of textuality, which in the case of the Dalits has been denied to them for centuries, do not govern the signification process that is undertaken by the subaltern. Rather the re-symbolization of the Bible is attempted within a more familiar world of orality. The norms of interpretation, the frames of references, and the dynamics of discourse are formulated from within their own native world of representation. This also means that the literary heritage of the Bible is required and requisitioned to perform in unconventional and extraordinary ways within a different world of orality. This transposition of the terrain of signification from literacy to oral story is a tactic that incorporates the *techne* of the native world of the subaltern. There is a subversive overthrowing of the elite domain of text and an election for conducting the activity of interpretation within the province of orality. Saurabh Dube, in a study of native agents of creative interpretation of Christianity, points to just such a phenomenon:

> M. M. Paul had commented [in a 1938–1939 report], "My small tract on Satna-mis . . . is now printed and sells to people. Also illiterate people are found buying my Satnami tract and requesting some literate persons to read it to them." The tract had found its ways to sections of the group that had been targeted as its potential readers and audience. The missionary's comment also suggests that the reading of the tract as a collective rehearsal of telling of and listening to a story had become part of the fluid world of popular religious discourse.[5]

Let me quote another example of the power of oral signification from the Indian context and explicate some features of this subaltern strategy of signification. A Church Missionary Society (CMS) missionary called Mr. Breed requests prayers, in his report of 1903, for a native Dalit woman in Vagaikulam village, Tinnevelly District, in Tamilnadu. He writes, "She was formerly a devil-dancer, but now is converted to Christ, and makes her living by coolie work. She cannot read herself, but always carries a Testament with her, and frequently, when meeting a passer-by, she opens the book at the Sermon on the Mount, and asks the person to read, explaining the passage as she herself has been taught."[6]

Five points are relevant regarding the Dalit woman's move to wrest the scriptures from the powerful and alien interpretive world of the dominant literati and make it available to the interpretive trope of the common folk. First, the illiterate woman creates the oral world of story as the field of interpretation. She offers a commentary on the spoken word. Keep in mind that she was reported to be a "devil-dancer." Thus, performative signification through dance finds partnership in oral rendition through story. Second, she creates an intermediate and mediatory zone between the word written and the word testified to in speech. She bestows the gift of meaning in oral commentary rather than correct reading. The Dalit woman empowers herself by taking possession of the Bible and makes literate persons vulnerable by letting them only read the text: meaning is construed not in its reading but in its interpretation through the imagining of the illiterate woman. Third, she makes a choice on what must be read. In doing so she redefines the crux of the Bible. It is indeed noteworthy that the woman uses the Sermon on the Mount as the canon for sharing the good news at a time in which the missionary world had centered its interpretation of Christianity on the atoning work of Jesus Christ. Fourth, scripture is ushered away from the nondiscursive realm of private and ecclesial habitations and set loose within public and communitarian settings. The Bible was usually confined to the private space of the home. This was the location for personal meditation on scripture and family devotion in which the Bible has an important role. Apart from this the Bible is ritualistically read and expounded within the bounds of the church. The Dalit woman frees the Bible from its confinement and brings it out into the open and into the midst of the hustle and bustle of the public street. In fact, this act of scattering the sacred word away from the church and into the polluted streets must be interpreted against the backdrop of conventional Hinduism. We have already pointed to the manner in which the Hindu sacred scriptures were stored far away from the common people and deposited into the secure vault of the temple, which was well guarded by the Brahmin priests from any mishandling and misinterpretation. Fifth, it is interesting to observe that the elite of the literati continue to struggle to retain control over subaltern interpretation of "scriptures." The editorial insertion of the agency of the missionary over this process of oral interpretation is subtle but intentional. The illiterate Dalit woman, according to Mr. Breed, is "explaining the passage as she herself has been taught." This addendum seems to communicate that although the Dalit woman has chosen and utilized the fluid and flaky world of oral story to reconfigure her interpretation of the Christian Gospel, there is really nothing to fear because her interpretation is in accordance with the instructions given to her by the missionaries.

The destabilization of meaning implicit in the process of interchanging somewhat more fixed textual inscriptions for somewhat more fluid oral narrations clearly increases the agency of the subaltern. And yet we must be careful in the academic enterprise of signifying "scriptures," which generally will be lured into reversing this process. Thus, the world of oral rendition is usually transposed for our sake into the templates of literariness. The Institute for Signifying Scriptures needs to deliberate on both how researchers can study reinterpretation of oral renditions of "scriptures" without reducing them to our world of textuality and how such scholars can also become vulnerable in the universe of the subalterns that is purposively designed to be carried forward through oral narratives.

Subaltern Reflexivity Is Stored, Mediated, and Circulated in Multimodal and Multimedial Forms: Signification of "Scriptures" Involves Re-modalizing Representation

Signifying "scriptures" will need to admit, circulate, and embrace the various modes through which subaltern peoples choose to communicate their reflexivity. This is already an objective of the Institute for Signifying Scriptures. More important, the institute has to creatively and inclusively interpret the significations that emerge from such multimodal and multimedial interplay of imaginings. My own work in India has documented the amazing ways in which the drum has been utilized as a surrogate language system to conserve and disseminate Dalit communities' reflections on God, world, and human beings and their interrelations within a historical context that excluded them from the written and oral performances of the scripture.[7] Eliza Kent, in a study of Tamil Bible women in Colonial South India, also notes the ease with which native Bible women convey meaning and contextualize interpretation of scripture by moving judiciously and comfortably among story, music, and text. She says:

> Bible women grounded their preaching and teaching in indigenous tropes that could convey the greatness and majesty of the Christian God to an Indian audience. Even the medium in which they worked proved remarkably effective at attracting and keeping attentive audiences. Like other indigenous religious specialists, Bible women used music a great deal in their evangelism: they sang in order to attract people's attention and used hymns to answer questions put to them by inquirers and to comment on passages taken from the Bible. The agility necessary for this kind of improvisation is considerable.[8]

Meaning is generated, transposed, preserved, circulated, and negotiated in many forms or modes. The modalities of the mind, the body, and the heart work in concert; but concrete signs and constellations of signs take specific material form. Painting, acting, music, dancing, writing, weaving, and sculpting are authentic modes of representation. But we do not yet know how and what exactly they communicate. And this plethora of sign systems is daunting. How do we mediate sense out of the interconnected dialogue of the senses? Multimodal and multimedial signification cannot but be part of the reflections of the Institute for Signifying Scriptures.

Subaltern communities in the task of reflexivity, which involves both the capacities to be reflective and negotiate meaning, utilize material culture in its multimodal and multimedia forms. By multimodal I am referring to various modes of receiving knowledge. The mode of reason, a function of the mind, is often assumed to be the only instrument of knowledge reception and production. Yet communities receive and generate knowledge using the modalities of heart, body, and soul also. The term multimedial refers to the material forms in which such knowledge is contained, preserved, and circulated. Again, it is easy to buy into the view that written texts are the predominant medium by which human beings record, store, and distribute the knowledge that they receive and produce. But that would not be true of many subaltern communities in India. Local and traditional knowledge for such communities is received, produced, stored, and circulated in an array of multimodal and multimedial forms. Including the knowledge systems of subalterns in India means becoming aware of what is represented by heart, body, mind, and soul through reflection on all the modes of seeing, hearing, touching, smelling, and tasting. It is pertinent to register the point that communities that work with their hands and are intimately related to the products that they create do not have a need to separate their reflective activity from the material activity that they are involved with. Thus production, reflection, and communication are connected and integrated into a human way of living. Praxis is a way of life: action-reflection-action is not an artificial exercise that one must take time to inculcate into one's everyday existence; rather it becomes the natural cycle of individual and corporate living. Thus, on the one hand, drumming, dancing, weaving, painting, and making artifacts become media through which Dalits contain, shape, and express their reflections on the divine, the world, and human beings. On the other hand, drumming, dancing, spinning, weaving, bamboo work, painting, and carving are vehicles that naturally function to capture, corroborate, and communicate the Adivasis reflection on their experience of all aspects of reality as they encounter it. In quite a different context Ananda Coomaraswamy brilliantly sums it up in the following succinct manner: "craftsmanship is a mode of thought."[9] In this sense the Institute for Signifying Scriptures may even be a hope in need of a science (as in systematic reflection on sign systems). Let the science and the art of signification go on and go forth!

NOTES

1. Andre Beteille gives us some idea of the discussion concerning the relationship between colonial governance and caste in the nineteenth and the first half of the twentieth century.

The changes that have been taking place in caste since independence began at least a hundred years before independence, under colonial rule. If the constitution is a landmark in the history of caste, an earlier, though less conspicuous, landmark is the Removal of Caste Disabilities Act of 1850. Until then a Hindu was so deeply embedded in his caste that expulsion from it amounted virtually civil death.

Colonial administrators, like administrators everywhere, were inclined to take more than their due share of credit for bringing about beneficial changes in the country they administered. They exaggerated the rigidity and oppressiveness of the traditional social order and their own role in establishing liberal ideas and institutions in India. Many of their acts did indeed lead to the weakening of caste, but some also lead to its strengthening. On balance, however, the long-term consequence of colonial rule was the weakening rather than a strengthening of caste.

It has now become increasingly common to represent colonial rule as the source and origin of every economic, political, and social malady in contemporary India. Some smart American historians have even floated the idea that caste as we know it today is basically the creation of colonial rule, and that idea has naturally found many subscribers among Indians. There is no need now to white-wash colonial rule; but there is no need either to deny the advances in Indian society that started under it.

See Andre Beteille, "Caste and Colonial Rule," *The Hindu*, March 4, 2002, 10.

2. Robert Deliege, *The Untouchables of India* (Oxford: Berg Publishers, 1999), 2.

3. Kancha Ilaiah, *Buffalo Nationalism: A Critique of Spiritual Fascism* (Kolkata: Samya, 2004), 179.

4. See Wimbush's introductory essay to this volume.

5. Saurabh Dube, *Untouchable Pasts: Religion, Identity, and Power among a Central Indian Community, 1780–1950* (Albany, NY: SUNY Press, 1998), 201.

6. Church Missionary Society, *Proceedings of the Church Missionary Society 1903–1904* (London: CM House, 1904), 290.

7. Sathianathan Clarke, *Dalits and Christianity: Subaltern Religion and Liberation Theology in India* (New Delhi: Oxford University Press, 1998).

8. Eliza F. Kent, "Tamil Bible Women and the Zenana Missions of Colonial South India," *History of Religions* 39 (November 1999): 137.

9. Quoted in Roger Lipsey, ed., *Coomaraswamy: His Life and Work* (Princeton, NJ: Princeton University Press, 1977), 40. I have addressed this issue of multimodal and multimedial forms of reflexivity elsewhere. See Sathianathan Clarke, "Viewing the Bible Through the Eyes and Ears of Subalterns in India," *Biblical Interpretations* 10 (2002): 245–266.

10   *Signification as Scripturalization*

COMMUNAL MEMORIES AMONG THE MIAO AND IN ANCIENT JEWISH ALLEGORIZATION

SZE-KAR WAN

In his landmark study, Wilfred Cantwell Smith suggests that scripture is a widespread phenomenon associated mainly with human community.[1] It is the community that attributes sacrality and authority to a set of texts, an overarching set of symbols, or a collection of canonical images that have extraordinary, transcendent meanings for the community that subscribes to that scripture. If so, one could be excused perhaps for thinking that "scriptures" are an inherently unstable category bound up with the life and changing fortunes of a community. To conclude thus, however, would be wrong. While a community renews itself in the vicissitudes of time and circumstances, its attitudes toward what it considers classical or scriptural are remarkably consistent and stable over time. Even as the life of the community changes, the collective memories incorporating the backgrounds and experiences of the community remain a constant thread that unites members to a distant but nonetheless vivid past, while tying them to communal symbols that look to the future. These communal memories, once crystallized in visible forms, become "scriptures."

This short essay surveys two examples from vastly different cultures and times and concludes that the one principle of unity is found in the inseparable relation between memories and "scriptures." These memories, granted, are themselves malleable and selective; they shift as experiences change over time under varying circumstances. But these memories return time and time again to some canonical story or text that defines for the community its central core of self-understanding. In conversation with this canon, these collective memories negotiate for renewed, transformed meanings that continue to sustain the life of the community.

The first example I adduce is one that illustrates the scriptural principle of memory: that of the Miao, an ethnic minority group in China's southwestern province of Yunnan, whose "recovery" of their own canon is no less than a scripturalization of communal memories of a painful past, now taken shape in the form of written words, words that are at once strange and familiar. They read the missionaries' Christian Bible into a text of their own experience. The second example comes from the Greek-speaking Jewish communities during the Greco-Roman period as typified in the writings of Philo of Alexandria. For a highly educated Jew like Philo, the problem was not so much to create a new canon as to adapt an old scripture to a world thoroughly Hellenized and therefore thoroughly alien to his traditional Jewish values. In his case, communal memories negotiated with the text to form highly specialized commentaries on the Torah. While the Miao overlaid a system of meanings *on top of* a text received from foreigners, Philo's efforts resulted in extending the canonical texts *beyond* their boundaries. If one thinks of the Miao experiment as the creation of a *vertical* structure on top of the biblical narrative, Hellenistic Jews might well be extending the biblical text *horizontally* into the life and time of the commentators.

The Miao Scripture: A Myth of Origins, Hope of Restoration

In January 1905, British Methodist missionary Samuel Pollard had been working among the Miao people. His first task was to develop a writing system for the Miao language. The Miao claimed that they had a written language long ago, but it was lost when they were forced to flee from the north. This part of their history was canonized in a myth of origins. Pollard reported: "The Miao lost their written language many centuries ago. When crossing a river the books fell into the water and were swallowed by a fish. . . . The drama was apparently one of a single act, for as far as we know the fish never restored the books again."[2] The same legend of the lost books was reported some years later, but with important variations:

> Before the Pollard script, books and a library were unknown. The great major-
> ity of these tribesmen had never handled even a sheet of writing paper or a
> pen. They had heard that once upon a time there were books; a tribal legend
> described how long, long ago the Miao lived on the north side of the Yangtze
> River, *but the conquering Chinese came and drove them from their land and homes.*
> Coming to the river and possessing no boats they debated what should be done
> with the books and in the end they strapped them to their shoulders and swam
> across, but the water ran so swiftly and the river was so wide, that the books
> were washed away and fishes swallowed them.[3]

The story played an integral part in the Miao's acceptance of the Bible. In 1907, when the British and Foreign Bible Society distributed a translation of the Gospel of Mark into Miao using Pollard's script, "the legend grew—the once-upon-a-time lost books had been found, found in the white man's country, and they told the incomparable story that Jesus loved the Miao. Only the imagination can conceive what this meant to those hillmen; some of whom travelled for days to view the books."[4]

The Miao myth of origins ostensibly tries to prove that they had books just like the Chinese, that they had a writing system just like the Chinese, and that they had come from north of the Yangzi River, an area traditionally claimed by the Chinese as the birthplace of their civilization. The Miao had to abandon their homeland and cross the Yangzi and flee to Yunnan, only because the conquering Chinese drove them out of their ancestral and cultural home. There is no evidence that the Miao ever claimed that they were the progenitors of the Chinese civilization, but they did claim to have been on the same par with their Chinese conquerors. They too had writing. For the Chinese, of course, writing, or *wen*, was a metonym for culture.

Far more than just simple "metooism," the Miao legend is at heart a lament, a lament for the disappearance of their writing and their culture at the hands of the advancing Chinese civilization. The experience was formalized in the legend as marauding soldiers' overtaking their ancestral land and displacing their texts and their culture. The legend is therefore at heart a protest against cultural hegemony and cultural annihilation that threatened to eradicate all vestiges of Miao writing, language, and ultimately thought itself. The conquerors waged an ethnic cleansing, the legend tells us, by means of a linguo-hermeneutical displacement.

What could not be erased, however, was the memory of the *existence* of the once-was and will-be scripture, a memory that persisted in the collective embers of communal consciousness, stoked continually through centuries of telling and retelling the lost-book legend. The memory was preserved also in the spoken language itself. Freed from the boundaries of the written text, the spoken words were given the capacity to store for themselves potentials that can be realized, that is to say, *textualized*, once the patterns scattered about in legends and traditions could be reorganized and reborn into an authoritative text. The legend canonized within itself clues to this rebirth already. The books were swept away at the river crossing but they were not destroyed or wiped clean. They were *swallowed up* by fish. They were not eaten, digested, discarded, which is to say they were *not* absorbed and assimilated into disappearance, but they were swallowed whole and stored in the belly of the fish in a twist that would do Jonah proud until their final restoration and revelation.

When the missionary observed that the legend had only a "single act" of books being swallowed by fish and a second act of restoration was missing, he unwittingly teased out the inner logic of the legend: the apocalyptic conclusion of the legend, insistent by its absence, lies with the restoration of the golden age of Miao writing. The fish swallowed the books, but that was not how the Miao culture was lost; it was how the culture was saved and kept alive. Nature and its agents conspired to become a storehouse holding the Miao texts in abeyance until such time as when Miao self-understanding and, by extension, self-determination was once again given expression, when the texts are palimpsestically rewritten and reinvented.

Scripture As Palimpsest: Scripture Going Native

When the Miao finally received and embraced the translated Gospels, they embraced not so much the missionaries' Bible as their own history of the lost book. The end product was a sacred text that embodied not so much the missionaries' teachings as the Miao's own past subordination and future aspirations. In this regard, the missionary played no more than midwife to the reestablishment and re-textualization of the Miao experience. Nowhere is this clearer than how the Miao were able to provide immediate contextualization for the missionary's teachings. In a telling story, Pollard the foreigner, again unwittingly, gave us clues as to how the Miao finally appropriated the text for themselves: "[I tried] to tell them how K'eh-mi came down and died for us. How he was put to death by wicked men. 'Yes,' they said at once: 'the wicked Chinese killed Jesus.' Everything bad they think must come from the Chinese."[5]

The episode happened early on in Pollard's work among the Miao and most certainly came before the publication of the Miao Bible. Yet the Miao were already able to interpret "Jesus came down to die for us . . . he was killed by wicked men" as "the wicked Chinese killed Jesus." Even before the restoration of their writing system, in other words, the Miao started to write their own text, a hidden text that made itself known in a timely parousia. The Miao scripture at one level made use of linguistic and grammatical signs left behind by the missionaries. These signs, when analyzed linearly and syntactically, superficially spell out a conventional Christian message. But when these syntactical signs were overlaid with the depth of the history of annihilation and survival, books lost and "scriptures" found, when they formed a story told with a communal wink of an eye to each other, when the story was echoed with the deep satisfaction of a knowing nod that can only come from owning the story from the beginning, even before the beginning, when the straight biblical stories were transformed by the verticality of communal experience, that is to say when the Christian Bible was signified on, the Miao created and recreated their scripture.

Signification: Vertical Extension of Sign into Significance

In Henry Louis Gates Jr.'s language, the Miao Bible was a signifier that extended the syntagmatic structure paradigmatically. The Miao did this by layering their experience on top of the Christian story so that while the syntagmatic structure of the narrative was now used as a paradigm on which the Miao's own story was modeled.[6] The biblical narratives, now inhabiting a new language and strung together in new Miao, followed what Gates would call a horizontal structure as dictated by the syntactical rules inherent in the new language. The Miao Bible, on the surface at least, told the same Christian story at its denotative level. Above this horizontal narrative, however, that is to say vertically, the Miao overlaid their own system of signification that told a drastically different story. It told of the disappearance and silence of a national culture at the hands of invaders and the recovery of their own voice and their own story. That recovery process continued unabated ever since the demise of their written culture, but it culminated at the completion of the Miao translation in the new script, when the Miao finally had before them a physical book. Scripturalization, the process of signification that had started long ago, in this case, meant not the elevation of long-recognized texts and stories to canonical status, as countless canons in major cultures were formed; rather it meant the creation or production of meaning out of an alien text by modeling one's experience, paradigmatically, after the syntagmatic narrative.

Thus, by a substitution, the Miao created a new text. The syntagmatic structure of grammar was now paradigmatically extended, with the result that the text became a new signifier, and the historical experience and present oppression were the newly signified. Hence the double-voiced nature of the Miao script: the text spoke, but the Miao also spoke.

In signifying the text, the Miao also signified on the missionaries with the Christian story of Jesus refigured to tell a different story, one that resembled both the Christian story and the Miao story. In an act of defiance, the Miao scripturalized themselves into existence. On the erased, but still visible, tablet of their memory, the Miao reinvigorated their notion of the sacred. "The wicked Chinese killed Jesus" was not so much an interpretation of the Christian story as a new line modeled after the primary signifier mimicking the Christian narrative. Thus the Bible became to the Miao a palimpsest, over which the Maio, now new tellers of the Christian story, scripted their own sacred text. Meaning production was coterminous with the formation or, better yet, reformation of a sacred text.

The end product of this process was the Bible going native. Before it was rewritten and layered on with the experience of the native readers, it remained a foreign object. Even the translation of the text into their native language using a new script was not enough to insinuate it into the hearts and souls of the Miao. It took a new reading of the central story of the Bible *and* a miraculous story of restoration to convince the hearers that this was *their* book, not the missionaries'. Scripture cannot be "scripture," therefore, until it becomes native. Scripture cannot be "scripture" until the natives embrace it. In this light, legends, myths, divine intervention, such as miraculous literacy in the African American tradition, all these miraculous stories serve to disrupt the transmission of a text. The lost-book legend of the Miao connected the text to the long-lost literacy of yesteryears, but it also disconnected it from the transmitters, so that continuity with the natives' past necessitated a discontinuity from the transmitters. Then and only then could the Miao claim the text as *their* scripture.

Signification: Horizontal Extension into Allegorization

Lest we think what I call vertical signification typified by the Miao interlocutors and Gates's Signifying Monkey represents only an isolated incident, one can make a case that the ancient art of allegorical interpretation, made venerable by its centuries of occupying the center of hermeneutical orthodoxy, is itself a form of signification. When Philo of Alexandria, for example, allegorized the Genesis story as the ascent of the human soul striving for self-transcendence, he was following a system of signification well established among his Greek-speaking predecessors and contemporaries. Because the Genesis narratives were unacceptable to Greek sensibility because of their mythical qualities, Philo surmised that they could not refer to literal truths. If one were to insist on the literal value of the narratives, that would only devalue the nature of scripture. To preserve the text, therefore, one must resort to a system of signification that identifies the narratives with a reality external to the text. For Philo that external reality was the *allegory of the soul*.[7]

Scholars have persuasively demonstrated that what distinguishes Philo from his predecessors is his consistent effort of reading external events—the creation story, the fall, and the patriarchs in Genesis—as internal struggles of our soul on its tortuous journey to perfection.[8] This is clear from his treatment of Genesis 2:8–9, which reads in the LXX (Septuagint): "God planted Paradise in Eden facing the sunrising and placed there the man whom he had fashioned. And out of the ground God made every tree that is pleasant in sight and good for food and the tree of life and the tree of knowing good and evil." In the *Creation of the World*, Philo first dismisses the notion that Paradise could mean a physical garden, for no one has yet witnessed such things as the Tree of Life and the Tree of Knowing Good and Evil. The idea of a literal garden full of mythical trees is so absurd and empirically false to the rational mind, according to Philo, that it must be an invitation to read the biblical passage "allegorically." This Philo does by identifying Paradise as "mind" and the trees as "virtues" planted as "standards in the soul." The result is a full-blown interpretation of the Garden of Eden as the mind:

> While the man was still leading a life of solitude, the woman not having been yet formed, a park or pleasaunce, we are told, was planted by God, quite unlike the pleasaunces with which we are familiar (Gen 2:8–9): for in them the wood is soulless; they are full of trees of all sorts, some ever-blooming to give uninterrupted joy to the eye, some bursting forth with young life every spring: some again bearing cultivated fruit for man, not only for use by way of necessary nourishment, but also for his superfluities, for the enjoyment of a life of luxury; while others yield a different kind of fruit, supplied to the wild beasts to satisfy their actual needs.
>
> But in the divine park or pleasaunce all plants are endowed with soul or reason, bearing the virtues for fruit, and beside these insight and discernment that never fail, by which things fair and ugly are recognized, and life free from disease, and incorruption, and all that is of a like nature. This description is, I think, intended *symbolically* rather than literally; for never yet have trees of life or of understanding appeared on earth, nor is it likely that they will appear hereafter. No, Moses evidently signifies by the pleasaunce the ruling power of the soul which is full of countless opinions, as it might be of plants; and by the tree of life he signifies reverence toward God, the greatest of the virtues, by means of which the soul attains to immortality; while by the tree that is cognisant of good and evil things he signifies moral prudence, the virtue that occupies the middle position and enables us to distinguish things by nature contrary the one to the other.
>
> Having set up these *standards in the soul*, He watched, as a judge might, to see to which it would tend. And when He saw it inclining to wickedness, and making light of holiness and godly fear, out of which comes the winning of immortal life, He cast it forth, as we might expect, and drove it from the pleasaunce, giving the soul which committed offences that defy the healer's skill, no hope of a subsequent return. (LIV–LV; emphasis added)

These identifications prepare Philo for the interpretation of the planting of the Paradise as the placement of virtues in the human mind, which in turn allows him to read the story of the fall allegorically, or psychologically to be exact. In this schema, "Adam" represents the mind, "Eve" is sense perception, and finally the "serpent" is pleasure that constantly tempts sense perception into giving up the pursuit of virtue. Beginning with some simple identifications, Philo was able to map all the events in the fall narrative external to the mind into internal struggles of the soul.

Another example of this same allegorical procedure can be found in Philo's interpretation of Genesis 12:6: "[Leaving Haran] Abram passed through the land to the place at Shechem, to the oak of Moreh." In *The Migration of Abraham*, Philo first identifies Abraham as the mind that is capable of, and in fact must be freed from, the confines of our body. Here, even though the biblical narrative includes no absurdities of the sort we see in the creation story, Philo nevertheless extends it into a new philosophical interpretation whose internal logic is governed by the allegory of the soul. Though Abraham's travel to Canaan might, to the untrained mind, speak of the patriarch's journey, it in reality points to the inner soul's striving for learning.

> The mind, when it has gone forth from the places about Haran, is said to have travelled through the country as far as the place of Shechem, to the lofty oak-tree (Gen 12:6). Let us consider what is meant by "travel through."
>
> Love of learning is by nature curious and inquisitive, not hesitating to bend its steps in all directions, prying into everything, reluctant to leave anything that exists unexplored, whether material or immaterial. It has an extraordinary appetite for all that there is to be seen and heard, and, not content with what it finds in its own country, it is bent on seeking what is in foreign parts and separated by great distances. We are reminded that merchants and traders for the sake of trifling profits cross the seas, and compass the wide world, letting stand in their way no summer heat nor winter cold, no tempestuous or contrary winds, neither youth nor age, no sickness of body, neither the daily intercourse with friends nor the pleasure too great for words which we take in wife and children and in all else that is our own, nor the enjoyment of our fatherland and of all the gracious amenities of civic life, nor the safe use of money and property and abundance of other good things, nor in a word anything else either great or small. If so, it is monstrous, such speakers urge, when we stand to gain a thing most fair, worth all men's striving for, the special prerogative of the human race, namely wisdom, to refrain from crossing every sea, from exploring earth's every recess, in the joy of finding out whether there is in any place aught that is fair to see or hear, and from following the quest of it with utmost zest and keenness, until we can come to the enjoyment of the things that we are seeking and longing for.
>
> Travel through man also, if you wilt, O my soul, bringing to examination each component part of him. For instance, to take the first examples that occur,

find out what the body is and what it must do or undergo to cooperate with the understanding; what sense-perception is and in what way it is of service to its ruler, mind; what pleasure is, and what desire is; what pain and fear are, and what the healing art is that can counteract them, by means of which a man shall either, if he falls into their hand, without difficulty make his escape, or avoid capture altogether; what it is to play the fool, what to be licentious, what to be unjust, what the multitude of other sicknesses to which it is the nature of pestilential wickedness to give birth, and what the preventive of these; and on the other hand, what righteousness is, or good sense, or self-mastery, courage, discretion, in a word virtue generally and moral welfare, and in what way each of them is wont to be won.

Travel again through the greatest and most perfect man, the universe, and scan narrowly its parts, how far asunder they are in the positions which they occupy, how wholly made one by the powers which govern them, and what constitutes for them all this invisible bond of harmony and unity. If, however, in your investigation, you do not easily attain the objects of your quest, keep on without giving in, for these "need both hands to catch them," and only by manifold and painful toil can they be discovered. (XXXIX)

This interpretation follows a well-planned rhetorical form. First, the text is mentioned (Genesis 12:6). Second, a *lemma* is singled out for interpretation ("Let us consider what is meant by 'travel through'"). Third, the phrase "passing through" is related to "love of learning." "Love of learning" is an appropriate analogy, because it is "by nature curious and inquisitive, not hesitating to . . . pry into everything." Once this identification is established, Philo is able to discuss the *soul's* "learning" and its pursuit of wisdom. A supplement is added to show the importance of the search of wisdom: if merchants, seekers of earthly goods, risk danger "traveling through" different lands to reach their destination, the pursuer of wisdom surely ought to be that much more diligent "exploring earth's every recess, until we can come to the enjoyment of the things that we are seeking and longing for." Fourth, Philo exhorts the soul to "travel through" a human body, so as to examine its every part. Fifth, Philo exhorts the soul further to search through the mystery of the cosmos, for the cosmos is the "greatest and most perfect man." The same five-step procedure is then repeated, this time focusing on a different *lemma*, "Shechem." Examples of this sort can be multiplied throughout the Philonic corpus.

If the Miao treatment of the missionary Bible is one of modeling their own experiences in the fashion of the narratives in the text, which at the end replaces the narratives by placing on them their own text, then Philonic allegory can be seen as a horizontal extension of the biblical narratives, not by replacing them, but by affirming simultaneously their fundamental soundness *and* their contemporary applicability to the readers. Philo and virtually all Western interpreters, whether they practice allegorical methods and whether they are aware of it, start by affirming the inherently sacred nature of the biblical text. Because they hold the text to be valid and relevant at all times to all readers, they understand their responsibilities as interpreters to be drawing out the meanings of the text for their readers in their situations. In spite of what might strike us the uninformed as fanciful interpretations, Philo would go so far as to insist on the literal meaning of the text, however "literal" might be understood, to which he would add his allegorical and psychological identifications of the text. If this is true with allegorical interpretation, it is even more true with historical criticism, the supposedly "scientific" method that insists on discovering "what actually happened" to the biblical characters and "what the author really said." The historical critic certainly does not replace the biblical text but applies to it standards of historical criticism applicable to modern scholarship. The result is a constructed narrative that purports to satisfy contemporary historical requirements and sensibilities, but it is a narrative constructed as an extension of the text retelling the narratives in a historically acceptable manner.[9] In both allegorical and historical-critical methods, the present is seen as an extension of the past, and the readers are seen as inheritors of a biblical tradition that extends from the main actors of the biblical narratives onward.

It is, accordingly, not surprising that the proper response to such a linear view of "scriptures" is commentary writing. Philo himself composed three massive series of commentaries on the Torah. Successors to rabbis and Jewish sages codified ancient sayings on legal and interpretive matters into tractates that extend the sacred law into contemporary periods. During the Reformation, the reformers debated with each other on exegetical matters, precisely because they thought the text must be extended into their times. The result of their debates was encapsulated in commentaries. One need not mention the modern proliferation of commentaries. In all this, commentaries exist side-by-side with the main text and even compete with it for authority. While the Miao create their own text, Western exegesis produces commentaries.

Conclusion

The key term shared by both Miao and Western exegesis is memory: memory that unifies the present to the past, contemporary readers to ancient authors, communal experiences to biblical characters. Whether this memory is kept alive by creating one's own text, as in the case of Miao, or by writing commentaries, which is but a different form of scripturalization, memory is what keeps a tradition alive and a community connected to its historical formations.

Lest one romanticizes this view of "scripture," it is at heart an essentialist understanding of tradition and, as such, is open to the influence of power and control. Frequently in the history of Western exegesis, whoever controls communal memories occupies an authoritative, sometimes unquestioned authoritarian, position in tradition and power. It is no accident that the Bible has always been the battleground in the West, because whoever holds the key to the collective memory of a community or nation, made "real" in biblical exegesis, can unlock the door of power.

In addition to the dimension of memory, the course of this brief survey has also uncovered some enduring themes in "scriptures," here summarized without demonstration. First, scripture is always a double-voiced text. Western linguistic tools made it possible for the Miao to have a writing system, but voiced through the collective consciousness of the people, the text became a new signifier.[10] And this principle can be generalized. In the same vein, second, scripture is itself interpretation, because the process of scripturalization is always freighted with the meaning of the text for the community and the question of legitimacy for the receiving community. Put in the terms established in the conference, scripture and signification are not two discrete poles but are one and the same thing.

Third, our usual binarisms—orality versus textuality, the oppressed versus the oppressors, text versus interpretation, and scripture versus signification—cannot be maintained too rigidly. Sometimes the distinction is blurred, as we see in the distinction between scripture and signification. Sometimes the distinction needs to be made more complex, as in the adoption of a foreign text, itself introduced in an intrusive context, in a struggle against local tyrants. The Miao's use of the missionaries' Bible to fight against Chinese overlords is a case in point, but it is not unique in the annals of missionary history. The local versus foreign, therefore, cannot be insisted on too stringently.

NOTES

1. W. C. Smith, *What Is Scripture?: A Comparative Approach* (Minneapolis: Fortress Press, 1993).

2. Joakim Enwall, "The Bible Translations into Miao: Chinese Influence Versus Linguistic Autonomy," in *Bible in Modern China: The Literary and Intellectual Impact*, ed. I. Eber et al. (Sankt Augustin: Institut Monumenta Serica, 1999), 211–212, 199–234.

3. Enwall, "Bible Translations," 213, quoting William H. Hudspeth, *Stone-Gateway and the Flower Miao* (London: The Cargate Press, 1937), 38–39.

4. Ibid.

5. Ibid., 211.

6. Henry Louis Gates Jr., *The Signifying Monkey: A Theory of African-American Literary Criticism* (New York: Oxford University Press, 1988), 49–50.

7. See Sze-kar Wan, "Allegorical Interpretation East and West: A Methodological Enquiry into Comparative Hermeneutics," in *Text and Experience: Towards a Cultural Exegesis of the Bible*, ed. Daniel Smith-Christopher (Sheffield: Sheffield Academic Press, 1995), 154–179, for further details.

8. P. Boyancé, "Études philoniennes," *Revue des Études Grecques* 76 (1963): 64–110; J. Daniélou, *Philon d'Alexandrie* (Paris: Artème Fayard, 1958); Thomas H. Tobin, *The Creation of Man: Philo and the History of Interpretation* (Washington DC: Catholic Biblical Association of America, 1983), 145–154. For definition of the allegory of the soul, see Tobin, *The Creation of Man*, 34–35.

9. See a comparison of Philonic allegorical interpretation with historical criticism in Wan, "Allegorical," 154–179.

10. The historical experiences of conquest and the continual subjugation of an oppressed people became the new signified. Their stories are then made concrete, through a paradigmatic figuration, thus restoring the stories to the people and giving voice to the hitherto voiceless. (See Gates, *Signifying Monkey*, 80, extending Claudia Mitchell-Kernan's observation.) If scripture is thus double- and multivoiced, and if a canonical text achieves what David Tracy calls "excess of meaning" by means of signification, the meaning of scripture must by definition be indeterminate; if it is scripture at all, it becomes scripture by being a signifier.

Talking Back

The baseline center-ing function and operations of "scriptures" notwithstanding, it is important to acknowledge, as have the essayists in this section, that "scriptures" are used for different purposes in different situations and settings in ongoing and in special terms. The different uses in the different settings and situations may sometimes represent resistance to and undermining of the center-ing force; they may also simply reflect in different ways the reality and power of the center. These differences are the stuff of ongoing social-cultural dynamics—differentiation, conflict, negotiation, formation, deformation, reformation.[1]

In relationship to the issues raised in the essays in part 1, we must also think more seriously about how centering in the form of "scriptures" in the form of texts both facilitates and frustrates differentiation of uses and the corresponding power dynamics. Textuality and reading and writing can overdetermine ideas and notions;[2] they can also provide the opportunity for continuous play and experimentation and resistance. Who or what in any situation determines which situation obtains?

—ed.

NOTES

1. Cf. Vincent L. Wimbush, "Reading Darkness, Reading Scriptures," in *African Americans and the Bible: Sacred Texts and Social Textures* (2000; repr., New York: Continuum, 2001).

2. Roy A. Rappaport, *Ritual and Religion in the Making of Humanity* (New York: Cambridge University Press, 1999).

PART III

MATERIAL AND EXPRESSIVE REPRESENTATIONS

11 Conjuring Scriptures and Engendering Healing Traditions

YVONNE P. CHIREAU

There are numerous meanings that may be given to textuality using comparative approaches, and the religions of the Afro-Atlantic world provide an especially rich terrain for conceptualizing the phenomena of "scriptures" as it appears in the experiences of historically dominated peoples. So in the following discussion I want to put forward some examples from black American religions that demonstrate how practitioners make use of "scriptures," sometimes in unique ways.

The traditions on which I will focus form a locus of beliefs and practices that have been identified as "black folk religions." The religion scholar Theophus Smith has characterized these traditions thematically and phenomenologically as a complex of cultural values, thoughts, rituals, and orientations that share efficacious and therapeutic intent. Folk religions, he suggests, constitute "formations" of the "conjuring culture" of African American people. The phrase "conjuring culture" refers to the processes of biblical appropriation and hermeneutical transformation that African Americans have engaged in their religious experiences. I would add that aspects of conjuring cultures could be identified wherever black people have performed or presented their own insurgent spiritualities. The notion of conjuring culture is especially relevant to alternative understandings of the "phenomenon" in question today, "scriptures," their contexts, their uses, and their attendant practitioners. For, as Smith has argued, the uses of "scriptures" in conjurational performances correlate with traditional biblical discourses of figuralism but are aptly applied to the traditions of healing, harming, and supernatural invocation that occur in African American religions.[1]

In many respects, because these traditions are themselves distinctive, they require distinctive methodologies for their illumination. With respect to "scriptures," black folk practices such as conjuring demand a supplementary approach to that of the scriptures-as-written-literature interpretive framework. This alternative perspective views "scriptures" as a cultural phenomena that fulfills religious functions such as personal and community edification, spiritual empowerment, and the transmission of sacred wisdom. Considering these functions, how do practitioners utilize the texts in the context of religious practice and belief? In many cases, the scriptures are seen as embodying spiritual ideas and communicating these ideas through expressive practices and instrumental modes apart from conventional forms of knowledge. Often these texts are heard, not read; they display symbols and figurations, without narrative, that communicate their power and purpose. Sometimes the text is embedded within artifacts that convey insights that are revealed through alternative epistemological processes such as divination. Indeed the emphasis for many practitioners in African American folk traditions appears to lie beyond the content-meaning of texts, or at least it is presumed that the interaction between exegesis and object is foregrounded in the actual religious activity—the practice.

Now in order to identify the focus of spirituality and practice in African American conjuring traditions, and the persons who institute such traditions, one must recall their origins. This is only part of an extensive cultural history that reaches far back into the African past and only later converges with the European presence on American soil. The roots of the conjuring tradition can be sought in the reinterpretations of indigenous African religions by African American people, beginning in slavery. These indigenous traditions and religions, diverse as they were, elaborated complex cosmologies that articulated a dense but unified framework. Africans expressed their understandings of the world in terms of invisible, animate forces and visible, living beings. Creative power flowed in a reciprocating process, traversing the boundaries of nature and the spirit, interacting in eternally persistent cycles of rebirth and renewal. In the wake of the devastation of the slave trade in which human lives and institutions were lost and scattered in the diaspora, the focus of these perspectives was transformed, and specific religious ideas were diluted over time, replaced with other concepts and images. What remained—remnants, fragmented theologies and rituals, and the strong, intuitive kinship between the living and the dead, the seen and the unseen, the realms of the body and of the spirit—took root in the values, aesthetics, and cultural forms that defined aspects of the black experience in America and facilitated the development of black folk religions.[2]

In considering possibilities for looking at "scriptures" and folk religion, we are led ever closer to perceiving the depth and complexity of African American spiritual experiences in the United States. Like other cultural offspring elsewhere in the Afro-Atlantic milieu, black folk practices have merged and blended with other, disparate forms, sometimes taking on the conventions and colorations of their analogues in the New World. Along the way, these folk traditions have been glossed by detractors as "magical" and "superstitious" practices and thereby separated from a normative religious framework. As a corrective, I wish to interrogate within the following discussion these "folk" interpretations and interpreters of black religion and their use of what Grey Gundaker has called "vernacular literacies" in order to relate to sacred texts.[3] I suggest that these engagements with "scriptures" reflect particular orientations to power. Power in all of its permutations becomes a fundamental source of meaning and agency in African American religions, emerging as they have within the larger historical context of the domination of black people in the African diaspora. Smith and others have identified within the black folk traditions of conjure coded forms of communication that combine with efficacious intent on the part of practitioners to create unique modes of knowledge and experience. These traditions constitute an enduring and innovative style of mediating the sacred. While Smith speaks of "magical" practices that "map and manage the world in the form of signs," they are viewed by others as "expressive rituals" or "transformative actions" that achieve individual rather than collective goals. In referring to these practices and beliefs I will use the native terminology and call them, after Smith, conjure or conjuring practices.

In the following discussion I want to also demonstrate how conjuring culture can be a productive model for engendering African American religious history. Women are at the heart of black folk religions and often dominate the conjuring culture in which such religions are embedded. In fact, within the conjuring culture complex, one can identify one of the most significant areas around which women's spiritual activities have been historically organized—their healing traditions. Why are women central to this tradition? Beginning in slavery, healing and doctoring roles were thrust on African American women, because women were often responsible for nursing the sick within plantation households, prescribing folk medicines, and administering other forms of domestic care for the families of slaveholding whites. Healing work was considered the private and personal duty of enslaved black women. Practices involving care of the body occurred predominantly within a woman's world, with women assuming the tasks of nursing and attending the sick, gathering herbs for medicines, and preparing the dead for burial. Moreover, in many slave communities, gender-specific doctoring practices such as female reproductive health fell to women, who utilized skills that had been passed down to them by other women. Women's healing practices benefited everyone, from the most vulnerable members of the enslaved population, such as the elderly and infants, to those who were constantly at risk due to their daily involvement with physically hazardous and unhealthy tasks. Therefore, although slave women were constrained by the institutions that appropriated their labor, they were able to develop unique traditions in support of their roles as agents of folk healing and religious practice.[4]

Let us return now to the phenomenon of "scriptures" in conjuring cultures. We see that in black conjuring traditions, texts may be simultaneously rendered as oral, graphic, and artifactual resources by which human beings gain unfettered access to powerful forces. In black religious life, one most often sees practices involving the sacred text par excellence, the Bible. Historically, the stories, lore, and images of the Bible have provided a fertile field for African Americans who engaged in magical practices such as spiritual healing, divination, and protective ritualism. The Bible was held in great esteem as the supreme text of mysteries and occult formulae by which one could perform effective works. Accordingly, following her extensive research on African American religion and culture in the southeastern United States during the early twentieth century, Zora Neale Hurston wrote that the Bible was considered by many blacks to be the "greatest Conjure book in the world."[5]

The history of black folk traditions in the United States provides numerous variations on the link between conjuring and the Bible. In some cases individuals who were thought to possess supernatural gifts and aptitudes utilized the Bible. William Adams, for example, believed himself to be chosen to "show de powah" of God, as written in the New Testament book of Mark. Adams, a former slave from Texas who was interviewed during the early twentieth century at the ripe old age of ninety-one, had cultivated a distinguished reputation for his esoteric interpretations of biblical lore. For years Adams had been sought after by members of his community for his skills as a healer. He attributed his expertise to "understanding from the Lord" and based his authority on scriptural sources. In his own words, Adams commented that

> there am lots of folks, and educated ones too, that says we-uns believes in superstition. Well, 'tis cause they don't understand. 'Member the Lord, in some of His ways, can be mysterious. The Bible says so. There am some things the Lord wants all folks to know, some things just the chosen few to know, and some things no one should know. Now, just 'cause you don't know 'bout some of the Lord's laws, 'tain't superstition if some other person understands and believes in such . . . How I larnt such? Well, I [don't] learn it. It come to me. When the Lord gives such power to a person, it just comes to 'em.[6]

Adams interprets his particular understanding of "scriptures" as the product of a personal relationship to the divine, by which he has been empowered with the knowledge of esoteric or hidden "mysteries." His inference is clear: to those persons who are endowed with the requisite talents and spiritual insight, the Bible can yield mystical wisdom. He acknowledges that what he knows has been learned by only a select few, and while unconventional and intuitive, his epistemological stance is supported by an internal logic, for to him, it is not "superstition." But William Adams was by no means unique among the African Americans who utilized the Bible in order to conjure, decode, remap or re-signify their sacred cultures. The twentieth-century black political writer George Schuyler spoke of his grandmother, a woman who defended her belief that persons could be "fixed" or hexed by evil conjurers and witches, ideas she deduced from evidence that she had sought and found while reading the Bible. Schuyler admitted that his family had denounced his grandmother's beliefs as "ignorant" and "superstitious," but to no avail. Bemused but impressed by her tenacity, he recalled:

> My grandmother held stubbornly to her beliefs and cited an impressive list of apt anecdotes in support of them . . . she charged mother with being little better than an infidel because of her iconoclastic views, while my mother chided her for believing in Christianity and occultism at one and the same time. An able Bible student, Grandma could cite the Good Book for belief in witches, and she could produce an apt quotation for almost everything else, pro or con.[7]

With the above examples, I have focused on the textual uses of "scriptures" as a vehicle of otherworldly, supernatural knowledge that may be put in the service of the adept interpreter. What are some of the other ways that "scriptures" are used in black American conjuring traditions? For some, the text-as-scripture is an important object of mediation across the boundaries of learned, human wisdom and revealed, divine knowledge. While one might suppose that mediation most often occurs via the text as a form of sacred writ, it also occurs by one's engagement with the text as a sacred article. According to this practice, the text/scripture is represented as an artifact with exceptional properties—for instance, as a kind of talisman. The text, whether the Bible or some other religious writing, constitutes the actual, physical condensation of unseen powers. In these cases, materiality and spirituality converge within an object that is vested with religious meaning.

In what follows I want to offer some preliminary illustrations of "scriptures" as an artifact of spiritual power, a theme that occurs in a number of contexts and cases in black American conjuring traditions. Again, the Bible is the most popular textual resource by which a practitioner may attain spiritual power, but this occurs in different ways. The biblical scriptures are widely associated in black American folk practices with supernatural healing. Perhaps because the Bible is believed to *contain* revealed wisdom and divine knowledge, however, it is equally useful as a material manifestation of magical efficacy. In other words, the content of the Bible is significant for many conjure practitioners and believers, for it communicates and reveals its knowledge in various forms of engagement; but in its material function as a charm, an icon and a talisman, it is a potent object as well.

The following example demonstrates this use of the Bible as a kind of ritual tool. The narrator, Jacob Stroyer, was born a slave on a plantation near Columbia, South Carolina, in the mid-1800s. In 1898 he wrote a memoir in which he described the everyday experiences, habits, and sufferings of himself and his fellow bondsmen. Stroyer, although representing himself as a skeptic, seems to have been very familiar with the practices of the conjurers, root doctors, and hoodooists that he describes in great detail in his narrative. In the following account he depicts a ceremonial process that was sometimes employed by members of the community for purposes of theft detection:

> Four men were selected, one of which had a Bible with a string attached to it, and each man had his own part to perform . . . These four would commence at the first cabin with every man of the family, and the one who held the string attached to the Bible would say John or Tom, whatever the person's name was, you are accused of stealing a chicken or a dress from Sam at such a time, then [one] of the other two would say, "John stole the chicken," and another would say, "John did not steal the chicken." They would continue their assertions . . . then the men would put a stick in the loop of the string that was attached to the Bible, and hold it as still as they could, one would say, "Bible, in the name of the father, and the Son and of the Holy Ghost, if John stole that chicken, turn," that is, if the man had stolen what he was accused of, the Bible was to turn around on the string, and that would be a proof that he did steal it.[8]

In Stroyer's testimony we see an example of a collective prayer ritual in which a sacred text is used as an artifact for divination. The Bible thus becomes a source of supernatural knowledge, but not in the conventional sense; the scripture is not "read" to attain the revelation, but the movement of the book is "read" in order to ascertain a hidden, immediate, situational meaning. A similar example of Bible divination was recalled by Byrl Anderson, an African American once enslaved in Tennessee, who told how the white slave master on his farm would "tell many a fortune . . . by hanging the Bible on a key and saying certain words." Anderson added, "When the Bible would come to me, it would just spin. That meant that I was [a] lucky and righteous man." Byrl Anderson's recollections are interesting because they expand the social boundary of practitioners to include those who stand outside of the immediate community in which such practices ordinarily occurred. In this case the practitioner, a dominant social elite, is a white slave owner who occupies the central position of power in relation to the other participants in this ritual event. Setting aside, for the moment, the meaning and significance of his role as an authority of supernatural knowledge, we must consider the fact that these traditions sometimes transcended their communities of origin, or at least possessed analogues within the wider cultures in which they were located. Indeed, as I have noted elsewhere, whites were often as inclined as black Americans to adopt folk traditions that incorporated magical elements and beliefs, especially in times of insecurity and need.[9]

Beginning in the eighteenth century, African American people turned to conjuring specialists, including "root" doctors and Hoodoo practitioners, not only because they lacked viable alternatives for treatment, but because they shared these individuals' perspectives on illness and health. A complex of traditions emerged that were devoted to healing and doctoring, the use of sacred objects, the invocation of otherworldly forces, and the effective powers of spirit-inspired individuals. It is also clear that many healers integrated biblical scriptures into their practices. Furthermore we know that folk traditions were pervasive among African American women, especially those whose formal roles were associated with "doctoring" or healing. Because they were chiefly responsible for the care of the sick in black slave communities, women became the local repositories of therapeutic knowledge. African American women often interpreted this healing work using a spiritual idiom, describing the visions, dreams, and other mystical experiences from which they derived their inspiration and sense of mission. Furthermore, through their use of charmed objects as well as prayers, herbal treatments, Bible-based cures, such as the laying on of hands and "rootworking," and the skillful employment of natural and organic substances for physical deliverance, women were able to attain a special authority as healing practitioners. Whether root doctors or conjurers who viewed themselves as vessels through which supernatural power was channeled, black women adopted a variety of measures in their efforts to treat physical affliction and to ward off sicknesses untreatable by conventional means. Given the authority that has historically been bestowed on female folk healers, it might be argued that healing is a gendered sacred activity.[10]

African American women healers were sought out for their knowledge and assistance. Some women were described as "native African" or "native-born" practitioners. Jack Waldburg, a former slave in South Carolina, for example, described his African grandmother, who was skilled at preparing herbs for medicinal cures, and whose knowledge was passed on from one generation to the next. The grandmother, a midwife, taught Waldburg how to "take medicine from root" and create remedies out of plants. Another ex-slave, Ned Chaney, spoke of his African-born great grandmother, whose knowledge of healing was well known and respected by other members of her community. The white missionary Laura Towne, writing about slave life on the Sea Islands in 1863, recalled Maum Katie, "an old African woman" who was a great "spiritual mother," a fortuneteller, or prophetess, and "a woman of tremendous influence over her spiritual children." African American women's folk healing traditions were also related to the development of female-specific health practices such as midwifery, fertility, contraception, and abortion in black communities. The "Granny" or "granny-midwife," was usually an elderly female figure who was not only responsible for many aspects of healthcare in her own community, but was often called to administer to the needs of whites as well. The "Granny" figure was the community nurse, doctor, and caretaker. The office of the "Granny" is made more significant by the fact that pregnant female slaves were dependent on other women for their health maintenance. Slave women were usually attended by slave women rather than professional gynecologists and obstetricians, whose medical practices were in their infancy in nineteenth-century America. In the slave quarters, women and expectant mothers worked, interacted, and exchanged cultural values and traditions. Recognizing the presence of a distinct woman's culture is key to understanding the survival of spiritual healing practices and conjuring traditions in African American life. It is also clear that many practitioners integrated biblical scriptures into their practice.[11]

I have highlighted cases in which the Bible is utilized as an artifact of divination in contrast to accounts in which the Bible is adopted for conjuring with primary concern for its *content* rather than its form and materiality. Even as the Bible and other texts were sometimes viewed as written charms through which power was exercised, prayer was often adopted as a spoken charm or incantation. In the Christian tradition of prayer, black folk appealed to God for protection and moral strength. But a larger province of powers was also available through prayer for specific supernatural entreaties. The use of biblical sayings and prayers as ingredients in magical spells and charms is an element of the occult tradition, which dates as far back as the origins of Christianity itself. In the previous examples, the Bible operates as more than "scripture"; it functions as an object of supernatural mediation, a magical tool for attaining hidden knowledge. In this it demonstrates resonances with other physical channels of sacred power and knowledge in traditions of the African diaspora, such as the divining implements of Yoruba *babalawos*, which are used for consulting the text of the powerful Ifa oracle in traditions of sacred disclosure, or another case, in which the use of magazine pages published by the black American bishop Daddy Grace, shredded and infused in teas and poultices, functioned as conduits of physical healing for his followers. In these examples, performers and practitioners favor form and materiality in addition to content, in order to activate spiritual force. Not only does the scripture/text provide access to power through its subject material, it is also an *object* of power.

In conclusion, I offer some brief thoughts on the theoretical implications of this investigation of "scriptures" within the context of conjuring cultures. If we focus on the Bible as a paramount resource for conjure practitioners and their subjects, we must also consider the significance of these innovative uses of the texts. How should we study "scriptures" from the perspectives of these actors in a way that gives meaning to their actions? Is it here perhaps that the idea of signifying practices—as expressive styles and as subversive, often critical representations by which persons engage the Bible—comes into play. Again, the Bible is one of the most prominent textual resources by which African American folk religious practitioners have attained power. We have seen that empowerment comes through knowledge, but it is also conveyed via practices involving the body and also ritual techniques that directly involve the Bible as a material resource. Engagement with "scriptures" occurs in different ways. As I have pointed out, the Bible fulfills religious and spiritual purposes, but in conjuring cultures, the "scriptures" are primarily associated with the functional practices of healing and harming. The Bible sanctions, authorizes, and instructs practitioners in their creation and understanding of the means by which they can transform reality. Perhaps because the Bible is also believed to be comprised of revealed wisdom and divine knowledge, however, it is equally useful as a material manifestation of spiritual efficacy. In other words, the content of the Bible is significant for practitioners and believers in that it communicates and reveals itself to individuals; but in its material function and form— its uses as a charm, an icon, a sacred object, or a talisman—it is an effectual artifact as well. We must consider the kinds of interpretive approaches that one might utilize in order to investigate the phenomena of "scriptures" from these alternative functions and points of view.

Other questions remain. Does the Bible retain a unique status in African American religious life, or are there other texts that practitioners of folk religions engage with equal devotion, as they do this particular text? We know, for example, of the widespread use of occult books and magical manuals by conjurers, an esoteric tradition of literacy and spirituality that was at the center of black folk religiosity in the nineteenth and twentieth centuries. Do such texts ever attain the status of "scriptures"? Other uses of texts and textuality in African American religious culture that might be explored in other contexts include the popular techniques of spiritual "reading" as an arcane, nonliterate practice among black urban-storefront spiritual advisors. How are the religious functions of "scriptures" reconceived when placed in the service of these folk practitioners? What is the relation of this kind of signifying to the world-defining and world-making practices of the dominated, the stuff of life and survival, of which health, healing, and well-being compose such an important part? These are political and historical questions, as well as questions of religious inquiry. They should lead us back to consider the meanings of "scriptures" in black life and to ask whether the designation adequately describes the phenomenon that engages the signifiers and their signifying practices as they contest and create alternative modes of power. Does the idea fully embrace the range of meanings of the phenomena that are evidenced within conjuring cultures—the reality that is given to "scriptures" as divine word, supernatural will, and spiritual work?[12]

NOTES

1. Theophus Smith, *Conjuring Culture: Biblical Formations of Black America* (New York: Oxford, 1994), 10.

2. Yvonne Chireau, *Black Magic: African American Religion and the Conjuring Tradition* (Berkeley: University of California Press, 2003).

3. Grey Gundaker, *Signs of Diaspora/Diaspora of Signs* (New York: Oxford, 1998).

4. Sharla Fett, *Working Cures: Healing, Health and Power on Southern Slave Plantations* (Chapel Hill: University of North Carolina Press, 2002), 190. See also Jacqueline Jones, *Labor of Love, Labor of Sorrow: Black Women, Work, and the Family from Slavery to the Present* (New York: Basic Books, 1985).

5. Zora Neale Hurston, "Hoodoo in America," *Journal of American Folklore* 44 (1931): 317.

6. *The American Slave: A Composite Autobiography*, ed. George P. Rawick, vol. 2, *Texas Narratives*, ed. Jan Hillegas and Ken Lawrence (Westport, CT: Greenwood Press, 1979), 16–17.

7. George Schuyler, *Black and Conservative: The Autobiography of George S. Schuyler* (New Rochelle, NY: Arlington House, 1966), 21–22.

8. Jacob Stroyer, *My Life in the South* (Salem, MA: Salem Observer Book and Job Print, 1885), 57–58.

9. Charles L. Purdue et al., *Weevils in the Wheat* (Charlottesville: University Press of Virginia, 1976), 11.

10. See Sharla Fett, "It's a Spirit in Me: Spiritual Power and the Healing Work of African American Women in Slavery," in *A Mighty Baptism: Race, Gender, and the Creation of American Protestantism*, ed. Susan Juster (Ithaca, NY: Cornell University Press, 1996), 189–209, and in the same volume, Yvonne Chireau, "The Uses of the Supernatural: Towards a History of Black Women's Magical Practices."

11. Rupert Sargent Holland, ed. *Letters and Diary of Laura M. Towne* (Cambridge, MA: Riverside Press, 1912), 20.

12. Patrick A. Polk, "Other Books, Other Powers: the Sixth and Seventh Books of Moses in Afro-Atlantic Folk Belief," *Southern Folklore* 56 (1999): 115–133. On African American spiritualists and urban psychics, see Yvonne Chireau, "Varieties of Spiritual Experience: Magic, Occultism, and Alternative Supernatural Traditions among African Americans in the Cities, 1915–1939," in *The Black Urban Community: From Dusk Till Dawn*, ed. Gayle Tate (New York: Palgrave Macmillan, 2006), 193–203.

12 *Visualizing Scriptures*

COLLEEN MCDANNELL

Let me begin by reciting my proof text. A reading from Vincent Wimbush's introductory essay: "Such folk generally do not stay within the lines; often they go undetected, uncounted, and unaccounted for. They almost always scramble the generalities by which dominance defines itself and the world."[1] It is thus to "such folks" that I turn. To discuss "such folks"—as we all know—is no simple task. Such folks are everywhere but they are not easily found. They populate our memories but not our textbooks. While it is easy to say that we would like to know the signifying predilections of "such folks," we're not sure how to approach the subject. Of course, we could ask them . . . but what if they were . . . dead? The grave certainly slows down their signifying potential. Our core problem is this: we have few representations of "such folks," especially those who have been silenced by history.

One way to resurrect such people so that they can signify again is to look at their pictures. Between 1935 and 1943 around 164,000 photographs were taken of such folk—such folk like the child of migrant workers from Crystal City, Texas, or a traveling preacher from Belle Glade, Florida. The Historical Division of the Farm Security Administration (FSA) took these photographs in order to generate support for New Deal reforms. Historical Division director Roy E. Stryker also wanted to produce a composite picture of American society. So, in the "scripts" he sent out to his photographers, he asked them to include pictures of America's religious life. These "sociologists with cameras" entered the homes and churches of the poor as well as the middle class. They photographed people in prayer, domestic shrines, dinner graces, parishioners going into their churches, revival meetings, and even the gospel trucks of itinerant preachers. FSA photographers—among them Russell Lee, Dorothea Lange, Walker Evans, Marion Post Wolcott, Gordon Parks—are now well known in art and history circles.

Rather than focus on these photographers, I urge us to use these photographs as evidence of the ways that "such folks" scramble together various ways of representing the "scriptures." While we scholars often recognize the importance of literacy for such folk, we tend to ignore how they move quickly and effortlessly between textual, visual, and oral representations of key biblical events. In a close-up photograph taken by Russell Lee of a black woman reading, we can see an apt summary of the importance of literacy.

Figure 12.1 Chicago (south side), Illinois; April 1941, Sunday. Reading the Bible in a "store-front" Baptist church on Easter Sunday. Photograph by Russell Lee. All photographs in this chapter courtesy the Library of Congress.

This picture is a beautiful—but conventional—illustration of the intensity of faith as mediated through a book, through the Bible. This is a picture of—dare I say it—"dominant generality." We are witness to an individual soul appropriating the divine via the text. Alone, she communicates with her God. Here is the classic image of "searching the scriptures." Every study of "the" black church tells us that such people find solace in the Bible. They remember its words. They caress it like a lover. They embrace books because for so long they were kept from possessing literacy. Sola Scriptura. Viva the Reformation.

In another photograph taken moments later we can see a different perspective on the importance of the Bible.

The photographer has pulled back and has taken a picture of the context in which the woman is "searching the scriptures." You can still see her in the middle of this photo. Her Bible now rests on her lap. We now see that she is not alone. The picture shows the final moments of a Sunday school service conducted by a Church of God in Christ congregation. Russell Lee took the photograph on Easter Sunday in 1941, on the south side of Chicago. The congregation was featured in Richard Wright's book *12 Million Black Voices* but was not identified in the text. Indeed, photographer Russell Lee, as well as later historians, has mistakenly referred to it as a Baptist church.

In the picture we see how the literary text of the Bible has been transformed into images. The Passion narrative is not only read, recited, and memorized as a series of words; it is looked at. The Resurrection is not only sung about; it is

Figure 12.2   "Storefront" Baptist church on Easter Sunday. Photograph by Russell Lee.

constructed out of white crepe paper. Look closely at the photograph; the Word
has been made flesh. On the far left you see a print of the young Christ. It is a face
from a larger painting by the Victorian artist Heinrich Hoffmann. Moving to the
front of the church, you see a repetition of crosses—there is one behind the hat
among the hangers, a larger white one strung with dark paper symbolizing the cast
off burial shroud, a crucifixion scene, and two more crosses on the right side of
the standing woman. Immediately to the left of those crosses is a reproduction of
Leonardo da Vinci's *The Last Supper*. That these images are of a white Jesus reflect
both the limited visual repertoire offered to African Americans in the 1930s and
1940s and also their disinterest—cultivated by centuries of white Christianity—in
imagining a black savior. In another photograph the Church of God in Christ congregation has placed a print of the sacred heart above the rack of hangers in their
sanctuary. The figure of Jesus points to his inflamed heart. Care has been taken to
transform all of these mass-produced prints into something special by having them
framed and placed in prominent places.

      These pictures remind us that such people who build their lives around the
Bible and the gifts of the Holy Spirit may also create a visible worship environment. While the biblical text is certainly central in this congregation, such people
also use images to draw themselves out of the everyday and focus their minds
and feelings on the life, passion, and resurrection of Christ. They transform the

Figure 12.3 "Storefront" Baptist church during services on Easter Sunday. Photograph by Russell Lee.

scriptures into a wide variety of expressions in order to create a dense, eclectic, and vibrant worship environment. Visual images are layered and repeated. These are not anti-iconic Protestants.

Other photographs illustrate how the pastor of the community, Elder W. A. Hicks, layers his own body and environment with traditional and modern symbols. He wears both a cross and carries two pens in his pocket. Elder Hicks speaks to his congregation using a modern amplification system. Recall that in addition to Bibles and hymnals being in use, we saw a clock and a proliferation of coat hangers. "Such folks" integrate rather than separate. Crosses are not isolated from fountain pens and hangers. Words are not isolated from prints of the sacred heart or the Last Supper. Neat divisions between text and image, high and low culture, traditional and modern, black and white, Protestant and Catholic are ours—not theirs.

This mingling, this spreading of "scriptures" into the visual, is not unique to Chicago. Other FSA photographers traveling to different regions of the country saw similar things among African American Christian communities. In Woodville, Georgia, in the same year, 1941, photographer Jack Delano took a picture of what he called a "Negro church."

On the wall of the church was tacked a pennant that read "Baptist World Alliance." In this apparently Baptist church, a large crucifix hangs down over the chair

Figure 12.4 Pastor of a "storefront" Baptist church. Photograph by Russell Lee.

where the minister sits. Such visualizing did not merely appear in photography. Also in 1941, Spencer Williams wrote, directed, acted in, and financed a film he called "The Blood of Jesus." The movie was a "race film" and, like other Spencer Williams movies, had an all-black cast. It also contained many bleeding Christ images. Women wore crucifixes when they went to the river for baptism, and the main protagonist prayed in front of a print of the sacred heart in her bedroom. In the dramatic climax to the movie, blood drips from the wounds of a crucified Christ onto the forehead of a virtuous woman. Many such people do this visualizing of scriptures, allowing the words of the Bible to be made visible in different ways at different times. It is our responsibility as scholars to recognize the ways that "folks generally do not stay within the lines"—not the lines on paper or the lines anywhere else.

NOTES

1. See Wimbush's introduction to this volume, 14.

Figure 12.5 Woodville, Greene County, Georgia, October 1941. Church service in the "Negro church." Photograph by Jack Delano.

Signifying in Nineteenth-Century African American Religious Music

JACQUELINE COGDELL DJEDJE

This essay concerns the role of religious music in nineteenth-century African American culture. Just as religion in African and African-derived cultures is a topic that has received much study, so too has the discussion of the role of music in religion. I find these topics fascinating because both phenomena—music and religion—are central to African peoples. Music scholar J. H. Kwabena Nketia writes, "The most compelling reason for music making in Africa derives from religious experience, for it is generally believed that the spiritual world is responsive to music and deeply affected by it. . . . Hence worship always finds its most intense expression in music making."[1] When practiced in African-derived "folk" and "traditional" (or "roots") culture, religion and music are not placed on a shelf to be observed, gazed on, or used only on special occasions, but integrated fully into the everyday lives of global Africans. And for many Africans, life would be meaningless without these phenomena. Music and religion are also interesting because of their link to relationships that are as complex, diverse, and difficult to define as either term in itself. Ethnomusicologist Ter Ellingson explains:

> Religious believers have heard music as the voices of gods and the cacophony of devils, praised it as the purest form of spirituality, and condemned it as the ultimate in sensual depravity; with equal enthusiasm they have promoted its use in worship and sought to eradicate it from both religious and secular life. Seldom a neutral phenomenon, music has a high positive or negative value that reflects its near-universal importance in the religious sphere.[2]

Definitions, Sources, and Methodology

Although signifying, a concept most often used to explain black language, verbal behavior, folklore, and literary tradition, has been discussed by a number of folklorists, sociolinguists, and literary scholars,[3] Claudia Mitchell-Kernan is among the first to frame the discussion broadly so that it encompasses more than the analysis of verbal expressions. In defining the term, Mitchell-Kernan states, "Signifying . . . refers to a way of encoding messages or meaning which involves, in most cases, an element of indirection . . . This kind of *signifying* might be best viewed as an alternative message form, selected for its artistic merit, and may occur embedded in a variety of discourse."[4] This definition is significant because it alludes both to the technique of signifying and the parameters of signifying. On the first point, Mitchell-Kernan suggests that signifying is synonymous with figuration,[5] which refers to the "act or process of creating."[6] Musically, figuration can be defined as "the ornamentation of a musical passage by using decorative figures."[7] When applied to African derived music, Mitchell-Kernan's definition highlights innovation and creation, which are central to performance in African and African-derived cultures. On the second point, Mitchell-Kernan's use of the phrase "variety of discourse" implies that signifying can be found in other expressive forms in African American culture. In other words, just as researchers are able to observe, analyze, and find meaning in the encoded messages of African American language, the same can be done for art, dance, and musical sound.

Most scholars who note the use of signifying in black performance tend to focus on song lyrics rather than sound (the singing or the playing of music instruments) or other aspects of expressive culture (movement and visual elements). Also, black secular musical styles (jazz, blues, and popular music) are discussed more prominently than sacred music. For example, in *The Signifying Monkey: A Theory of African-American Literary Criticism*, Henry Louis Gates makes several comments about jazz and blues musicians who have included signification in the lyrics and titles of songs. One of the few instances when Gates discusses religious music is when he includes comments by Wash Wilson, an ex-slave who states that the term "sig'fication" was a special term and practice for slaves: "When de niggers go round singing' 'Steal Away to Jesus,' dat mean dere gwine be a 'ligious meetin' dat night. Dat de *sig'fication* of a meetin.' De masters 'fore and after freedom didn't like dem 'ligious meetin's, so us natcherly slips off at night, down in de bottoms or somewheres. Sometimes us sing and pray all night."[8]

Samuel A. Floyd is one of the few music scholars to employ signifying as a conceptual framework for interpreting African American music generally, with extensive discussion of the intricate layers of meaning in all types of black performance. Inspired by Gates's use of the "Signifying Monkey" as a trope to interpret black narratives, Floyd employs the rubric "Call and Response" to analyze black music. In *The Power of Black Music: Interpreting Its History from Africa to the United States*, Floyd argues that just as the black vernacular tradition can be used for the development of critical strategies for black literary inquiry, "African-American music can be examined through the same vernacular tradition, with the rhetorical tropes of verbal provenance replaced with those of its own genesis. In this way, the calls, cries, hollers, riffs, licks, overlapping antiphony, and various rhythmic, melodic, and other musical practices can serve as Signifying figures."[9] For Floyd, musical signifying is "the transformation of preexisting musical material by trifling with it, teasing it, or censuring it. Musical Signifyin(g) is the rhetorical use of preexisting material as a means of demonstrating respect for or poking fun at a musical style, process, or practice through parody, pastiche, implication, indirection, humor, tone play or word play, the illusion of speech or narration, or other troping mechanisms."[10] Most important in African American performance, according to Floyd, is the practice of black musical styles signifying on each other:

In African-American music, musical figures Signify by commenting on other musical figures, on themselves, on performances of other music, on other performances of the same piece, and on completely new works of music. Moreover, genres Signify on other genres—ragtime on European and early European and American dance music; blues on the ballad; the spiritual on the hymn; jazz on blues and ragtime; gospel on the hymn, the spiritual, and blues; soul on rhythm and blues, rock 'n' roll, and rock music; bebop on swing, ragtime rhythms, and blues; funk on soul; rap on funk; and so on.[11]

In *Race Music: Black Cultures from Bebop to Hip-Hop*, music scholar Guthrie Ramsey acknowledges the importance of Floyd's work for providing a theoretical framework, or language, for discussing black music. Yet he believes that if we situate the theory "more firmly in specific historical and social texts, we can add nuance to the provocative Call-and-Response idea. By attending to the specific historical moment and social setting in which a music gesture appears, we avoid the appearance of reifying, or 'essentializing' cultural expressions."[12] To demonstrate signifying in black music, Ramsey focuses on contemporary idioms in African American music. In one part of the book, he discusses hip-hop not only to explore "what a musical performance means but also how it achieves a particular signifying inflection."[13] Later in the study, Ramsey analyzes *Handel's Messiah: A Soulful Celebration* (1992), an African-American music project marketed as gospel, but the performance is actually a fusion of George Frideric Handel's composition with jazz, rhythm and blues, and gospel.[14]

As noted from this concise literature review, few scholars have used signifying to interpret nineteenth-century black religious music. Therefore, I believe this study is necessary, if only to eliminate the skewed view that signifying occurs only in twentieth-century black secular culture.

My focus is on nineteenth-century hymnody and musical idioms and performance practices that developed from hymns (e.g., denominational hymnals, camp meeting and spiritual songs, and style of worship). I have deliberately chosen examples prominent during slavery, when the large majority of blacks were under the control of whites, because signifying took on a deeper meaning then. When blacks attempted to do things their own way during the slave era, this could result not only in criticism but also in physical and emotional harm. In some cases, signifying was life threatening. Before discussing signifying, indirections, and figurations as they relate specifically to religious music, a concise historical overview of black music and religion music would be helpful. As Ramsey explains, "we need to situate these figures and gestures into as fully contextualized a setting as possible . . . to arrive at a penetrating and convincing interpretation."[15]

Religion and Music

During the seventeenth and eighteenth centuries, it was primarily Africans in the North who were introduced to Christianity. Slave owners in the South were reluctant to provide religious instruction to Africans because many believed that slaves who converted to Christianity would automatically achieve freedom. When laws were passed by various colonies to refute the belief that baptism would exempt Africans from bondage, Europeans used other reasons to deny religious instruction. Some slave owners thought that Christianity made Africans proud and not good servants. Others felt the religion would place the enslaved on the same ethical, moral, and spiritual level as the slave owner. Many feared that allowing Africans to congregate together would lead to revolts and uprisings.[16] In addition to the slave owners' reluctance, enslaved Africans were not interested in converting to Christianity because most wanted to continue practicing their indigenous religions and Islam.[17]

As a result, few Africans became Christians during the seventeenth and eighteenth centuries. Large numbers of conversions did not begin until the nineteenth century. What was most interesting about the conversion was how Africans responded. In the literature, whites often remarked that Africans preferred the *musical* activities of the religious experience above all else.[18] This is noteworthy because it demonstrates the continued importance of music to worship among blacks. In spite of the fact that Africans were in a new land (the Americas) and embracing a new faith (Christianity), they wanted to be involved in religion in the same manner they had experienced it in their homelands.

When Africans were first introduced to Christian songs between the seventeenth and nineteenth centuries, most researchers believe they performed the same musical forms (e.g., psalms and hymns) used by whites. Thus, most writings indicate that it was not until later years that blacks began to create musical styles and genres (moans, shouts, jubilees, spirituals, and gospel songs) that could be identified uniquely as African American. If we accept this version of history, it suggests that what blacks performed during those early years were merely *imitations* of white music and that innovations did not occur until much later. I argue differently. While Africans may have performed musical forms introduced to them by whites, I do not believe they always performed *exactly* what whites taught them. To make the performance meaningful, blacks signified or performed the music indirectly. R. R. Earl Jr. states, "Lyricized conversion language gave slaves a radical sense of being free to dialogue together in the face of their slave masters' oppressive monological structure of communication. It afforded them, indirectly, a creative way to critique the oppressive nature of their master's monologues."[19] Through songs, according to church historian Ray Allen Billington, African Americans

> were able to develop a vocabulary and means of expression that was entirely their own. This was done by sprinkling their melodies with symbols, images, and concepts borrowed from their African past and completely unknown to the whites. By developing this symbolism as a universal language among themselves, they were able to harbor and express thoughts that were not understandable to others. Their masters never realized this; instead they poked fun at the Negroes for using a jargon which apparently made little sense. The Negroes gladly endured this ridicule, knowing that by doing so they helped preserve a

degree of intellectual freedom. Little did the whites realize, as they ridiculed the slaves for their "ignorance," that those slaves were enjoying the satisfaction which goes with a sense of superiority.[20]

With that being the case, signifying began very early in the history of black religious expression in the Americas. Through the manipulation of language and sound, blacks developed their own way of communicating and conversing musically.

Hymns became an important genre in the Americas with the Great Awakening, a revival movement that swept the colonies in the early eighteenth century. Based on lively tunes and religious poems written by individuals, hymns became popular among both blacks and whites, so much so that people began to neglect the singing of psalms that had been used during the seventeenth century. During the first three decades of the eighteenth century, several European composers (e.g., Isaac Watts, John and Charles Wesley, and George Whitefield) published hymnals. Of all the hymn writers, however, hymns composed by English minister Isaac Watts (often called "Dr. Watts") were especially popular among blacks "because of the freshness and vitality of the words."[21] Camp-meeting hymns (or spiritual songs) became popular during the camp meeting, an interracial institution that began during the revival movement (called the Second Awakening) and dominated the religious life of the American frontier from 1780 to 1830. Just as the Great Awakening stimulated a revolt against the staid psalmody of the religious establishment and ushered in the livelier hymnody, the Second Awakening brought about a similar reaction against the antiquated hymns. In the noisy, folksy environment of the camp meeting, different songs were demanded. Because no hymnbooks were used in the early years, worshippers had either to sing from memory or learn songs in the meetings.[22]

Musical Signifying

Hymnody

Signifying on hymns by African Americans led to several developments. Not only did it affect the creation of new musical forms, but it also had a major impact on performance practices. One development was the compilation of a hymnbook, *A Collection of Spiritual Songs and Hymns Selected from Various Authors by Richard Allen, African Minister* (1801), by Richard Allen, a black minister who organized, in the early nineteenth century in Philadelphia, the first congregation of the African Methodist Episcopal (AME) church. Because Allen understood the importance of music to blacks, he knew he had to provide his congregation with a repertoire of songs that blacks preferred and appreciated, particularly if his church was going to be successful. Allen's hymnal included fifty-four hymn texts, without tunes, drawn primarily from the collections of Dr. Watts, the Wesleys, and other hymn writers popular among Methodists and Baptists during that period.[23] The importance of the first hymnal designed expressly for an all-black congregation cannot be overemphasized. Instead of using the official Methodist hymnal, as a good Methodist should have done, Allen collected hymns that had special appeal to his congregation, hymns that were favorites of black Americans. Not only does the hymnal provide an index to the hymns popular among black religious groups (the AME in particular) in the United States, the hymns represent the black worshippers' own choices, not the choices of white missionaries and ministers.[24] After 1801, the AME church consistently published its own hymnals rather than use those of the white mother churches, as did most other black congregations. Throughout its history, the AME hymnal has contained hymns written by black authors and composers (e.g., songs that Allen, elders, and members of the AME church had composed). Also included were black favorites by white hymn writers.[25]

Several examples of indirection can be found both in Allen's hymnal and the manner in which his congregation performed the hymns. Of particular importance was the type of material Allen added to hymns. Southern explains:

> Allen's hymnal was the first to employ the so-called wandering refrains—that is, refrain verses or short choruses attached at random to orthodox hymn stanzas. The idea of adding a refrain to a hymn was highly novel at the beginning of the nineteenth century; the only other extant examples are in a hymnbook published by the Native American minister Samson Occum in 1774. But Allen's practice of adding *any* refrain to *any* hymn—hence the "wandering refrain"— was unique. This was a kind of improvisation, and it must have introduced a great deal of informality into the worship service.[26]

Another distinction (or indirection) was the type of melodies Allen's congregation used to perform hymns. Since Allen's hymnal did not contain any melodies, the hymn texts could have easily been sung to the appropriate short meter, long meter, or common meter tunes that had been used by Protestants for centuries past or the texts could have been linked with the tunes found in other hymnals.[27] Scholars believe that, instead of following in the tradition of whites, Allen's congregation drew on popular songs of the period as a source for tunes or they composed their own tunes.[28] Theologian Jeremiah A. Wright Jr. explains the significance of this innovation: "In taking the words of popular hymn writers like Isaac Watts and Charles Wesley and singing them with their own melodic and rhythmic style, often to their own African tunes, black usage of meter music was clearly distinguishable from non-black usage."[29] The innovations that Allen's congregants initiated led to even more improvisations by other black Protestants. Music researcher Wendell Whalum compares the singing of hymns by black Methodists and Baptists: "The Black Methodists and Baptists endorsed Watts' hymns, but the Baptists 'blackened' them. They virtually threw out the meter signature and rhythm and before 1875 had begun a new system which, though based on the style of singing coming from England to America in the eighteenth century, was drastically different from it. It was congregational singing much like the Spiritual had been in which the text was retained."[30]

Although the use of folksongs for hymn tunes was common practice among Protestants (i.e., Martin Luther's best chorale melodies had been borrowed from

German folksongs or popular songs), white Methodists in the United States criticized blacks for using melodies from the secular world in hymns. In the opinions of whites, blacks were debasing the music of the church. Whites who visited black churches in the early nineteenth century often made satirical remarks about the singing they heard. In some cases, they criticized *what* (or the kinds of songs) blacks performed. John Fanning Watson, one of the leading white Methodist church fathers of Philadelphia, complained in 1819: "We have too, a growing evil, in the practice of singing in our places of public and society worship, *merry* airs, adapted from old *songs*, to hymns of our composing: often miserable as poetry, and senseless as matter. . . . Most frequently [these hymns are] composed and first sung by the illiterate *blacks* of the society."[31]

Other times, whites complained about *how* the music was performed. William Faux, a white who visited Allen's church in 1820, wrote:

> After the sermon they began singing merrily, and continued, without stopping, one hour, till they became exhausted and breathless. "Oh! come to Zion, come!" "Hallelujah, &c." And then, "O won't you have my lovely bleeding *Jasus*," a thousand times repeated in full thundering chorus to the tune of "Fol de rol." While all the time they were clapping hands, shouting and jumping, and exclaiming, "Ah Lord! Good Lord! Give me *Jasus*! Amen."[32]

The practice of adding refrains to hymns became so widespread that the AME church, in 1841, "felt it necessary to pass a resolution at its Annual Conference directing preachers to 'strenuously oppose' the singing of the specially composed hymns in 'public meetings.'"[33]

Spirituals (Camp-Meeting Songs)

The creation of the camp meeting or spiritual song is another development that emerged from blacks signifying on hymns. No one knows when the term spiritual was first used in print to refer to religious music of African Americans, but many studies have been written on the origin, character, role, function, and meaning of spirituals in black culture.[34] While some spirituals were strictly religious, many had dual meanings that related to protest and returning to Africa. As religion scholar Randall C. Bailey explains, "the spirituals became a way of political communication among the initiated, which would be safe in the presence of the oppressor."[35]

Church historian Miles Mark Fisher suggests that hymn writers influenced spirituals both in "their arrangements, with verses first and then chorus, and in their theology, vocabulary, meter, rhythm, and tunes."[36] When composing spirituals, however, blacks either improvised on songs already in existence, combined material from several old songs to make new ones, or created songs entirely from new material.[37] Regardless of the method of composition, spirituals were a refashioning of verses and motives from parent hymns and not merely different versions of hymns. In other words, spirituals constituted a totally different song type with their own text, music, and distinct stylistic features. The melodies of spirituals represented original composition rather than a borrowing of old tunes.

Characteristic of African American folksongs, spirituals were reshaped by the process of "communal recreation," no matter the original sources of text and melodic materials.[38] Commenting on the originality of music created by slaves, song collector Thomas W. Higginson, in 1870, wrote: "As they learned all their songs by ear, they often strayed into wholly new versions, which sometimes became popular, and entirely banished the others."[39]

Southern indicates that several spirituals (e.g., "My Lord, What a Morning," "Steal Away to Jesus," "In That Great Gettin'-Up Morning," and others) were inspired by the Watts's hymn "Behold the Awful Trumpet Sounds," which appeared in the first edition of Allen's hymnbook.[40] "My Lord, What a Morning" is an example of enslaved Africans using a preexisting text to create a new one.[41] Using the imagery from Watts's hymn, slaves developed their own way of expressing that morning ("great day"), which, for some, may have meant Judgment Day, while for others, the day of emancipation (escape to the North). The significance of the phrase "trumpet sound" (emancipation) can be seen in its use in both "My Lord, What a Morning" and "Steal Away." Interestingly, the adjective "awful" is not employed in either spiritual because slaves regarded the "trumpet blast" (emancipation) as something positive, not negative. References to the dead ("wake the nations underground" in "My Lord, What a Morning" and "tomb stones are bursting" in "Steal Away") may have been ways of slaves communicating with the enslaved (dead in spirit) who were waiting to escape. Thus the reason for the song leader's repetition of the phrase "nations underground" in each verse of "My Lord, What a Morning" was to inform blacks, particularly individuals who had been waiting a long time and possibly had lost all hope, that freedom (a plan to escape or the conductor of the Underground Railroad) was in sight. All they needed to do was listen for the signal that would come from either the "trumpet sound," the "sinner cry," or the "Christian shout." References to the dead in songs may have also been a way of slaves communicating with their ancestors in an hour of need. As historian Sterling Stuckey explains, "Being on good terms with the ancestral spirits was an overarching conceptual concern for Africans everywhere in slavery."[42]

Although "Steal Away to Jesus"[43] may have been inspired by the Watts's hymn, several scholars believe this spiritual was composed during the planning of the uprising by nineteenth-century black freedom fighter Nat Turner.[44] Expanding on this interpretation and the statements of ex-slaves (see foregoing by ex-slave Wash Wilson), John W. Work II indicates that "Steal Away" signified "a secret meeting [for slaves] which the master had prohibited; and to the overseer and the rest of the world, a longing for the quiet communion with God."[45] Not only did blacks sing the song while working during the day, they sang it at night as they "would steal from their cabins and quietly creep through the cotton, corn, and tall grasses" to their meeting place.[46] Like other spirituals, "Steal Away" was not produced in one night but developed over time. Also, the chorus ending "I ain't got long to stay here" was not originally sacred, but a sharp reminder to slaves that they must not stay too long on that side of the river, or they must pay the penalty of disobeying their master.[47]

Style of Worship

The worship style identified with black "folk" religion is a third development that came about as a result of blacks signifying on hymns. The comments that whites made about activities that took place during camp meetings are especially noteworthy because, although some remarks are pejorative, they help us to understand what was distinctive about the behavior of blacks in these settings. Fredrika Bremer, a Swedish novelist who attended a camp meeting in Georgia during the 1850s, was impressed that blacks led in the singing and were often the loudest and most superb performers. Other white writers, however, were extremely critical of black practices because they thought: (1) the behavior of blacks was unusual, especially singing short repetitive phrases late into the night and early morning hours after the regular worship had ended; (2) blacks were breaking the rules by holding songfests in their segregated quarters away from the supervision of whites; (3) blacks were having too much influence on whites, especially when some whites began joining blacks in after-worship singing; (4) blacks were using songs of their own composing based on melodies that were dangerously similar to popular dance tunes; and (5) blacks were moving their bodies in ways that was believed to be indecent and immoral.[48]

On this latter point, the comments by Daniel Alexander Payne, a black AME minister from Georgia, who witnessed the performance of a ring shout during a camp-meeting service in the early nineteenth century, are enlightening:

> After the sermon, they formed a ring, and with coats off sung, clapped their hands and stamped their feet in a most ridiculous and heathenish way. I requested the pastor to go and stop their dancing. At his request they stopped their dancing and clapping of hands, but remained singing and rocking their bodies to and fro. . . . After the sermon in the afternoon, having another opportunity of speaking alone to this young leader of the singing and clapping ring, he said: "Sinners won't get converted unless there is a ring. . . . The Spirit of God works upon people in different ways. At camp meeting there must be a ring here, a ring there, a ring over yonder, or sinners will not get converted."[49]

Payne was not successful in getting blacks to abandon their worship practices because the "[ring] shout was a primary means of contact with and respect for the ancestral spirits and the source of artistic expression."[50] As Stuckey explains, Payne "was asking them [slaves] to give up the products of ancestral genius as well as the means by which spiritual autonomy was preserved, and with it a certain unity of being. And because the shout . . . was the single most important cause of the formation of common consciousness and ethos, Payne drew almost uniformly hostile reactions in attempting to extirpate it from black Christianity."[51]

Conclusion

Why did blacks use religious music to signify? What did they gain from these indirections? I believe several reasons account for the figurative musical behavior of blacks during religious worship in the nineteenth century. Signifying was a way to create an identity that separated blacks from whites. It also allowed blacks to mask, communicate, and send messages to each other without the larger society understanding. In some instances, signifying masked the true meaning of what was being communicated among blacks on a personal level. Whites did not understand the indirections, nor did they know how indirections enabled blacks to create an identity separate from the majority audience. When blacks performed songs and actively participated in worship like they did in Africa, it created a spiritual communion with God that was African and, hence, familiar to them. Most important, signifying was a form of resistance. While it appeared that blacks were assimilating through the appropriation of Christianity, most in fact were creating a distinct identity that could be called African American. Signifying was not only one of the primary vehicles for the maintenance of Africanisms in black religious music in the nineteenth century, it was also used to empower black people.

NOTES

1. J. H. Kwabena Nketia, "Music and Religion in Sub-Saharan Africa," in *The Encyclopedia of Religion*, ed. Mircea Eliade (New York: Macmillan, 1987), 172.

2. Ter Ellingson, "Music and Religion," in *The Encyclopedia of Religion*, ed. Mircea Eliade (New York: Macmillan, 1987), 163, 163–171.

3. Roger D. Abrahams, *Deep Down in the Jungle: Negro Narrative Folklore from the Streets of Philadelphia* (Hatboro, PA: Folklore Associates, 1964); Claudia Mitchell-Kernan, "Signifying," in *Mother Wit from the Laughing Barrel: Readings in the Interpretation of Afro-American Folklore*, ed. Alan Dundes (Englewood Cliffs, NJ: Prentice Hall, 1973), 310–328; Henry Louis Gates Jr., *The Signifying Monkey: A Theory of African-American Literary Criticism* (New York: Oxford University Press, 1988).

4. Mitchell-Kernan, "Signifying," 311.

5. Gates, *The Signifying Monkey*, 80.

6. *Webster's New Collegiate Dictionary*, 1974 ed., s.v. "figuration."

7. Ibid.

8. Quoted in Gates, *The Signifying Monkey*, 68.

9. Samuel A. Floyd Jr., *The Power of Black Music: Interpreting Its History from Africa to the United States.* (New York: Oxford University Press, 1995), 7.

10. Ibid., 8.

11. Ibid., 95.

12. Guthrie P. Ramsey Jr., *Race Music: Black Cultures from Bebop to Hip-Hop* (Berkeley: University of California Press, 2003), 21.

13. Ibid., 164.

14. Ibid., 193.

15. Ibid., 21–22.

16. Eileen Southern, *The Music of Black Americans: A History*, 3rd ed. (New York: W. W. Norton and Co., 1997), 72.

17. LeRoi Jones (Amiri Baraka), *Blues People: Negro Music in White America* (New York: William Morrow and Co., 1963).

18. Southern, *The Music of Black Americans*, 39.

19. Quoted in Randall C. Bailey, "The Danger of Ignoring One's Own Cultural Bias in Interpreting the Text," in *The Postcolonial Bible*, ed. R. S. Sugirtharajah (Sheffield: Sheffield Academic Press, 1998), 69, 66–90.

20. Ray Allen Billington, foreword to *Negro Slave Songs in the United States*, by Miles Mark Fisher (1953; repr., New York: The Citadel Press, 1969), ix.

21. Southern, *The Music of Black Americans*, 34.

22. Ibid., 85.

23. Ibid., 76.

24. Ibid., 75–76.

25. Ibid., 82.

26. Ibid., 79.

27. Ibid., 77–78.

28. Ibid., 76–78.

29. Jeremiah A. Wright, "Music as Cultural Expression in Black Church Theology and Worship," *The Journal of Black Sacred Music* 3 (Spring 1989): 2.

30. Whalum 1973; quoted in Wright, "Music as Cultural Expression," 2.

31. Watson; quoted in Southern, *The Music of Black Americans*, 78.

32. Faux; quoted in Southern, *The Music of Black Americans*, 78.

33. Southern, *The Music of Black Americans*, 180.

34. James H. Cone, *The Spirituals and the Blues: An Interpretation* (New York: The Seabury Press, 1972), 8–19.

35. Bailey, "Danger," 72.

36. Miles Mark Fisher, *Negro Slave Songs in the United States* (1953; repr., New York: The Citadel Press, 1969), 179.

37. Southern, *The Music of Black Americans*, 185.

38. Ibid., 188–189.

39. As quoted in Southern, *The Music of Black Americans*, 189.

40. Because of difficulty in obtaining permissions, the texts of the hymns and spirituals discussed in this article are not included. The lyrics for Isaac Watts's hymn "Behold the Awful Trumpet Sounds" can be found in Southern, *The Music of Black Americans*, 185–186. For further discussion about the origin of spirituals, see Southern, *The Music of Black Americans*, 184–189.

41. For the lyrics to the spiritual, "My Lord, What a Morning," see Southern, *The Music of Black Americans*, 186, or John W. Work III, *American Negro Songs and Spirituals: A Comprehensive Collection of 230 Folk Songs, Religious and Secular* (New York: Bonanza Books, 1940), 92.

42. Sterling Stuckey, *Slave Culture: National Theory and the Foundation of Black America* (New York: Oxford University Press, 1987), 43. Also see Jacqueline Cogdell DjeDje, "Remembering Kojo: History, Music, and Gender in the January Sixth Celebration of the Jamaican Accompong Maroons," *Black Music Research Journal* 18 (Spring-Fall 1998): 81–82, 105–107.

43. For the lyrics to the spiritual, "Steal Away to Jesus," see Work III; *Negro Songs*, 123.

44. John W. Work II, *Folk Song of the American Negro* (New York: Negro Universities Press, 1915), 77–78; Fisher, *Negro Slave Songs*, 66–67; Jacqueline Cogdell DjeDje, *Black Religious Music from Southeast Georgia* (Birmingham: Alabama Center for Higher Education, 1979), 7–9.

45. Work II, *Folk Song*, 123.

46. Ibid., 78.

47. Ibid.

48. Southern, *The Music of Black Americans*, 85.

49. Quoted in Southern, *The Music of Black Americans*, 130.

50. Stuckey, *Slave Culture*, 93.

51. Ibid.

14   *Signifying Proverbs*

MENACE II SOCIETY

ERIN RUNIONS

I begin with several questions. The first is my own question about how the Bible is used in film to propagate white privilege. In the past I have looked at how citation of scripture in film can enable misrecognition of the experiences of oppressed and marginalized peoples. The premises of the Institute for Signifying Scriptures (ISS) have challenged this way of thinking, however, by asking how "scriptures" can also be used to talk back to oppressive stereotypes and politics. This question has given me cause to think more specifically about how black filmmakers in the United States might use scripture to signify on white audiences' assessment and categorization of black experience. Then, the question, "What is the thing in the middle of it all?" posed by Vincent Wimbush in the inaugural call for the ISS,[1] pushes the analysis further, by demanding an examination of the material base around which biblical citations signify.

Finally, there is the question of theorizing that which has been undertheorized, in keeping with the goals of the institute. In an attempt to explore all these questions together, I will interrogate an expression of the material base around which biblical citations can signify on race in film: that is, the drug trade. Focusing on the Hughes brothers' *Menace II Society*,[2] I will suggest that the juxtaposition of scripture with the drug trade can disturb stereotypes about race relations, opening up new ways to think about the problems and solutions for the troubles in the hood.[3] To be clear, this work is part of an ongoing personal scrutiny as well as a cultural scrutiny, by which I hope my own continuing forms of misrecognition can be dissected and corrected.

Productions of the Thing in the Middle

For cultural critics, the question "What is the thing in the middle of it all?" is suggestive of a certain materialist and psychoanalytic tradition that seeks to identify and analyze the repressed elements that drive culture and produce ideology. According to this materialist/psychoanalytic tradition, that which has been repressed (i.e., repressed relations of production, primal scenes, or bodily drives) forever generates new products and productions, such as commodity fetishes and objects of desire. Slavoj Žižek—a recent interlocutor in this tradition—describes "the thing" as the Lacanian Real: it is that element "in the very heart of the subject which cannot be symbolized, which is produced as a residue, a remnant, a leftover of every signifying operation."[4] The "thing" can only be known through what it produces.

Žižek provides a Lacanian elaboration of a Marxist/Althusserian understanding of ideology, which is helpful for materialist analysis of culture. Repressed relations of production (and attendant conflicts) are projected onto elevated objects and images of desire, which together make up ideology. Access to repressed elements can only be gained through desire, or in its social form, ideology.[5] In short, for Žižek, ideology is desire for the repressed writ large.

According to this account of ideology, individuals affirm and secure their positions in the social hierarchies of production and consumption (including gender, race, and class) by identifying with images and objects of desire that reflect and assure the continued success of the economic system. The process of ideological identification is neither conspiratorial, nor necessarily conscious; it is simply what keeps the system functioning. Individuals identify with images that seem natural and completely coherent but are actually produced by a repressed material order, so as to maintain that order. Indeed ideological points of identification are welcomed, on an unconscious level, because they fill in and make sense of incoherencies on the material level, or gaps in one's knowledge of material contingencies. (So for instance, as I will discuss below, the racist stereotype of the drug-dealing black youth glosses over the material reality of white people's drug use in order to explain poverty and hold the myth of white superiority in place.) Ideological identification is, therefore, always a misrecognition.[6]

Though there are problems with this theory,[7] it nonetheless provides a useful model for thinking about film. Film is one of the most obvious cultural expressions of ideology, holding out as it does stereotypic images and objects of desire with which the viewer might identify. For instance, the stereotypes of people of color and of interracial relations that abound in film can be understood as elevated objects of desire—by-products of repressed hierarchies of production and consumption—with which viewers identify. Film can allow white viewers to misrecognize their own privileged positioning within economic and race relations. In order to overcome oppressions that are perpetuated along gender, race, and class lines, then, scrutiny of the misrecognition inherent in ideological processes is crucial. Signifying may help in this scrutiny.

Signifying Sites of Liminal Identification

Though no one escapes the misrecognition factor of ideological identification, interrogation and repositioning may be possible, if not easy, through alternate forms of identification. Those who are excluded by the dominant order tend not to identify fully (if at all) with the images and discourses held out to them by mainstream culture. Yet as Homi Bhabha suggests, it is through such alternative identifications that images and stereotypes of the status quo can be exposed as such. Likewise, attention to the differences in the way that the stereotypic norms of culture are repeated or performed can show up their instability and

provide new liminal sites of identification. This kind of performative signification through alternate repetitions of oppressive categories and norms is what, in
Bhabha's words, opens up "a liminal signifying space that is internally marked by
the discourses of minorities, the heterogeneous histories of contending peoples,
antagonistic authorities and tense locations of cultural difference."[8] Thus, scrutiny of ideological positions and identity constructs becomes possible through
the imperfect repetition of the images and objects of desire that make up social
norms.

It seems to me that signifying is one such way that normative points of identification are interrogated and shown up as ideological constructs rather than as
natural positions. In Henry Louis Gates Jr.'s account of signifying, mimicry plays
a key role in the parody of signifying.[9] Mimicry is repetition with a difference.
The mimicries that take place in signifying "luxuriate in the chaos of ambiguity
that repetition and difference (be that apparent difference centered in the signifier
or in the signified, in the 'sound-image' or in the concept) yield in either an aural
or a visual pun."[10] Just as black colloquial use of the term "signification" repeats
literary theory differently, in Gates's words, black signifying is "a shadowy revision
of . . . white term[s] . . . to demonstrate, first, that a simultaneous but negated,
parallel discursive (ontological, political) universe exists within the larger white
discursive universe."[11] By playing on certain expectations, but repeating them differently, signifying illuminates and interrogates such expectations.[12] Performance
through mimicry breaks open homogenous signs of race and culture, producing
hybrid spaces for different kinds of identification.

Thus, signifying disrupts a straightforward identification with the images and
objects of desire produced by the repressed thing in the middle, and it opens up
new, liminal sites of identification. As indicated, I am interested in how signifying
can operate in film to counteract the ideological images and stereotypes that hold
white privilege in place. The mimicry of a stereotype through film could have
several effects, all of which might, in Bhabha's words, have the subversive effect
of unsettling the "mimetic or narcissistic demands" of ideologically governed
signification, by turning the gaze of the viewer "back upon the eye of power."[13]
By creating a disturbance in the smooth repetition of a norm or ideal, mimicry
brings into view the repetitive operation that might otherwise go unnoticed, by
which a stereotype comes into being in the first place. The very possibility that a
norm might be repeated differently destabilizes the authenticity of the norm itself.
In this way, signifying "unsettle[s] the myth of origins," the myth of an authentic
and pure cultural signifier.

Mimicry can also have the effect of revealing the constraints and exclusions by
which norms are established. Bhabha, following Žižek, suggests that the subject's
accession to a stereotype always leaves an excess or a remainder behind;[14] this
remainder is what is excluded from the signifying operation, that which cannot be
contained by it. Bhabha argues that this remainder returns not as the repressed, but
as the hybrid or liminal. The liminal site of identification juxtaposes the "norm"
with what has been excluded from it, rendering the excluded visible.

Further, a stereotype displayed differently in film should, in theory, be able to displace the viewer's own notions about self-identity. If the viewer is formed as subject through identification with an ideological signifier, what happens to her identification with it, when it is transformed and hybridized through the operation of a film? Perhaps once its constructed and exclusionary nature is revealed, the viewer would be able to recognize her identification with it, as well as the oppressions inherent to such an ideological positioning.

There is plenty of room for signifying on stereotypes in film. When it comes to representations of African Americans in film, both scripture and drugs have been points of stereotyping and misrecognition. The super-spiritual, scripture-quoting African American is an image readily drawn on (sometimes conflated with what Christopher John Farley[15] calls the stereotype of the Magical African American Friend, who gives advice and solves crises).[16] Likewise, the drug trade is a topic around which there is much misrecognition: the average American middle-class citizen is likely quite misinformed about the war on drugs, the prison industry, and the resulting devastation of lower-income communities of color. Such ignorance comes, in part, from films that count on misrecognition for box-office sales. But these stereotypes can also be repeated differently, signifying, and opening up spaces for identifying otherwise.[17] Indeed the very combination of scripture and drugs in depictions of black communities may challenge their stereotypic valences, illuminating them as expressions of the repressed material base.

Mimicry and *Menace*

Scripture and drugs intersect in perhaps the most controversial of the New Jack films: *Menace II Society*, which still generates academic discourse ten years after its release.[18] The film has even been said to depict the death of signifying,[19] though it is my purpose to contest that view here. It is my contention that the film's use of scripture, in tandem with the thematic of the drug trade, speaks back to the recognition it elicits from white viewers, establishing it as misrecognition and misdiagnosis, while at the same time proposing other solutions.

In an interview, the Hughes brothers stated that the main purpose of the film was to explain the black underclass to white viewers, to explain how black youth become criminals in desperate situations.[20] Filmic mimicry is key here in obtaining recognition: the directors deliberately make use of the gangster genre, citing the heavy influence of directors like Brian De Palma, Francis Coppola, and Martin Scorsese. Here the mimicry is not only of the gangster narrative, but also of the racial stereotyping of Italian gangsters, criminals, and mafia.[21]

Scripture is also at work in obtaining white viewers' recognition of the harsh realities of life in lower-income black communities. Most obviously, the drug-dealing antihero's name is Caine (played by Tyrin Turner), a choice which seems to read straight off both racist identifications of the biblical Cain as black[22] and the scriptural promise that Cain would be forever marked, always tragically flawed. More subtly, the film puts a scriptural subtext—designed to speak to a white audience—into the mouth of Caine's devout grandfather, who has raised him after his drug-enmeshed parents have died, and who is always, according to Caine, "coming at him with that religion." The grandfather's lecturing consists of biblical commands, such as "thou shalt not kill," and motivational queries, like "do you care whether you live or die Caine?" This patriarchal teaching, as Caine puts it, goes in one ear and out the other.[23] From his perspective, and it seems also from the directors' perspective, Caine's *It's a Wonderful Life*–watching grandfather and his religion are white identified, making their teaching irrelevant for Caine's life (Caine tells his friend O'Dog that his grandfather is always praying to that white Jesus).[24] Caine's inability to listen to his grandfather, however, does have ramifications. Toward the end of the film, after Caine beats someone up in the front yard, his grandfather kicks him out of the house, citing Proverbs 22:10: "cast out the scorner and the contention shall go out, yea, strife and reproach shall cease."

The teaching of Caine's grandfather, I would argue, speaks straight to the heart of a white American Protestant religious sensibility, cultivated since the arrival of the first settlers. Using language very similar to early Puritan sermons, Caine's grandfather offers Caine the choice of life or death as a result of keeping the commandments.[25] By citing Proverbs, he reinforces the wisdom that promises blessing for keeping the law and curses for breaking it. This formula for reward and punishment is the same biblical logic that reinforces a sense of white Protestant superiority (and has also grounded various forms of U.S. imperialism); it creates a very tight circle of logic that says, "if I'm doing it, and I'm successful at it, I must be blessed, even chosen, by God" (no matter if—or perhaps especially if—the task happens to be conquering the world). The corollary to this view is, of course, that those who are less fortunate are somehow responsible and deserving of their circumstances.

Along similar lines, use of Proverbs invokes the Protestant work ethic. As Max Weber observed, no book was read more frequently by the Puritans.[26] The recognition that *Menace II Society* elicits from white viewers, then, is one that agrees with the sentiments of Proverbs, in which discipline, hard work, and wise choices are rewarded, while folly and sluggishness is chastised. Indeed, in this view, some of the other maxims in Proverbs 22 could also be applied to the film: "Train up a child in the way he should go: and when he is old, he will not depart from it" (v. 6); "he that soweth iniquity shall reap vanity" (v. 8); "foolishness is bound in the heart of a child; but the rod of correction shall drive it far from him" (v. 15); "hear the words of the wise" (v. 17); and "make no friendship with an angry man" (v. 24).[27] The conservative white viewer might call the relevance of these maxims to the hood a matter of the "other's nature"; the liberal white viewer might feel it his or her duty to get into the "ghetto" to help those poor children's upbringing. Either way, an application of these maxims to lower-income black neighborhoods bestows a sense of moral superiority on the observer.[28]

Scripture as a Menace to Society

But, the film's mimicry of stereotypical uses of scripture and drugs speaks back to this kind of easy recognition and reconciliation of the problems in lower-income black communities. First, the name Caine signifies. The name tells us that the young black antihero is not part of this neat tautological WASP economy, in which one works hard, is an upright citizen, and is rewarded for it. Caine is marked as outside that system. But being outside the dominant order is not necessarily something to bemoan. The biblical Cain is also the father of cities, music, and technology. Indeed Cain's main etiological role in the Bible is to discount this competition for the chosen people: his curse explains why those other cultural innovators (his progeny) are not chosen people. The naming of the hero in film thus asserts that the excluded "outside" is fundamentally indispensable to cultural innovation and organization. Perhaps it is precisely for this reason that the film does not let Caine capitulate to the symbolic order of Proverbs; instead it allows him to die.[29]

Second, if the language of Proverbs is the language of the dominant order's work ethic, the economy of drugs undercuts an economy built on traditional labor time, an economy where time is money. Selling drugs is not a nine-to-five job, by any means, nor is it a job paid at minimum wage. As Caine tells the audience, in a voice-over to a series of shots that show the satisfaction he gains in mixing drugs, "Working for minimum wage was never my style. I like big dollars." Clearly this work ethic contests the one advocated by Proverbs, with its disdain for the easy life (e.g., 12:14, 13:4, 14:23, 18:9, 22:13).

Moreover, a drug-based economy undercuts not only the proverbial wisdom so closely allied with capitalism (with its platitude of financial reward in return for law-abiding, hard work), it also contests traditional remedies for the problems produced by capitalism. For instance, an alternative economy based on drugs challenges standard leftist understanding of labor power within capitalism, as well as the potential of harnessing that labor power for positive change in a community. According to a Marxist understanding, withdrawing or suspending labor time can put a wrench in the process of exchange and profit, in a bid to bring about social change. Such an analysis, however, does not accurately describe labor time in economic relations based on drug trade, where risk, rather than time, is money. Other analyses are therefore needed; analyses that refuse to valorize *labor* and are perhaps more appropriate to late-stage capitalism, with its high rate of unemployment. There is much to be done in theorizing the place of "underclass" economies in subverting the structures of capitalism and racism. To my mind, this theorizing would need to analyze the place in such economies of desire, risk, and dependence, especially of privileged class dependence on the less privileged groups.

The work of Albert Memmi on dependence may be helpful in beginning this task of theorization—and a beginning is all that is possible here. Memmi looks at the intersection of need and desire in relations of dependency. He provides an analytic—one very applicable to the drug trade—that moves beyond thinking about labor power in challenging domination. Indeed Memmi's examination of dependency complicates a straightforward description of power in relations of domination. For Memmi, dependency is not the same as subjection, though there may be overlap.[30] As he describes dependent relationships, dependents look to providers for fulfillment of their needs and desires; therefore providers hold some power over their dependents. Nonetheless providers are also reliant on their dependents in some way. One commentator, Liz Constable, succinctly puts it thus: "Memmi's theorization of dependency provides an agile analytic tool able to make visible the full—and often conflictual and ambivalent—affective range produced through the dynamics of relationality; for example, those who dominate are often also vulnerable in their own dependency on something which their very 'dependents' provide them."[31]

Memmi's overall argument, however, is that humans are not independent beings, but interdependent; so in the final analysis, the question is not how to end dependency, but how to manage it positively, in order to move toward the more positive outcomes of healthy social relationships, reciprocity, and political solidarity.[32] Of course, management requires identification and analysis of the processes at work in dependent relationships, in all their complexity. One such complexity that Memmi describes—pertinent here—is that the dependent has an idealized image of the provider, which is more important in maintaining dependency than is the provider's actual character. Once the idealization fades, the provider loses their powerful hold on the dependent.[33] One way of managing dependent relationships and equalizing power imbalances is to identify idealizations in order to try to loosen their attraction.

Such an investigation of dependency may help to sort out certain issues in alternative economies; it may also illuminate what is at stake in ideological images and stereotypes. To come back to my earlier discussion, dependents' idealizations can be understood to be something like the (idealized) objects of desire and stereotypes produced by the repressed "things in the middle" (on psychical or societal levels). Stereotypes may, therefore, hold dependencies and power imbalances in place. Identifying the relations of dependence and desire within, and as a result of, stereotypes may also be important in attempts to reformulate social relations in a healthy way.[34]

The relationship of dependency brought to the fore by the stereotypic representations of the drug economy in film is complex. If stereotypes indicate some form of dependency, what might it be, in this case? Many films, even those that try to contend with the social ramifications of the drug trade, rely on the stereotype that there is a high involvement of people of color in the drug economy. As Allen Hughes puts it, "the media is looking for 'niggaz' and they want them raw, hardcore, smelling of asphalt."[35] Yet one cannot understand the drug economy in the United States without the relevant statistics that white folk use and sell illegal drugs as much or in greater abundance than people of color, while people of color are prosecuted at a proportionally much-higher rate.[36] But factuality notwithstanding, in the popular imagination, there is a dependence of drug users not only on particular drugs, but also on African American and Latino providers who risk being penalized for their activities. For such a stereotype to continue in the face of fact, there must be a dependence on this perception by white drug users and sellers, and perhaps counter-dependence on this perception by filmmakers who wish to sell films. So dissection of the stereotype of the dope-selling, young, black gangster suggests that there are dependencies of the privileged on the underprivileged at work in maintaining the problems that plague lower-income black neighborhoods. Indeed it indicates that such dependencies are at work within the very fiction that success is as simple as self-motivation and (autonomous) hard work, as Proverbs would have it.

If the place of drugs in the film undermines the conventional proverbial framework of hard work for monetary reward and shows up dependencies at work in the tidy, racialized economy of the Protestant work ethic, the biblical citation of Proverbs 22:10 also signifies on those who benefit from the dependencies of that symbolic order. For instance, the cited proverb "Cast out the scorner" might harbor other meanings. One clue appears in a short scene that clearly shows the origins of many of the detrimental demands on the hood.[37] Set just prior to the arrest of Caine and O'Dog for car theft, a sleazy-looking stolen-car dealer (white) comes into the neighborhood to ask one of Caine's friends, Chauncy, for a car. When the dealer exhibits fear at coming back at night to get the car, Chauncy sends him packing: "You ain't too scared to have a black man steal for your fuckin' ass is you, motherfucker? Man, get the fuck outta here; don't bring your narrow ass over here no more." "Cast out the scorner" seems to fit. A solution is signified through the very scripture being contested in the film.

The phrase could also aptly be applied to others who are dependent on the so-called black underclass to take risks and punishment for them (including, at the present moment, military risk). It could also be applied to the better intentioned: white liberals or other white allies might do well to consider this biblical intervention when wondering where to focus activist energies. The impulse to rush in and help might be checked by the demand to take stock of what might be done in our own lives and communities to counteract such scornfulness, as well as our own dependence on it.

In sum, the film brilliantly juxtaposes scripture with the drug economy, repeating stereotypes differently. Aimed at the white viewer, the film indicates through biblical citation that the dominant order is a white-identified realm, from which the hero has been excluded, for better and for worse. Moreover, Caine's involvement in the drug trade directly contests the desire invested in the dominant order's image of the law-abiding, hard-working success story; the film's ending suggests that solutions do not lie in requiring the excluded to accede to this order. Instead, an economy of drugs highlights dependency and points toward alternate forms of social organization that take dependent relationships into account and manage them in productive, rather than harmful, ways. Thus the juxtaposition of biblical text with the drug trade troubles an easy ideological identification with the capitalist order of white privilege and opens up space for new liminal identifications. Some might also find there a prescription for action.

NOTES

I am grateful to Rosamond Rodman, Mutaamba Maasha, Michael Casey, Elizabeth Castelli, and Susan Abraham for critical reading of earlier drafts, and to Greg Baker for research assistance.

1. Question raised in Wimbush's conference presentation.

2. *Menace II Society*, VHS, directed by Alan and Albert Hughes (New York: New Line Cinema, 1993).

3. For a discussion of *Menace II Society* in relation to the genre of "hood films" (also called New Jack cinema after Van Peebles's *New Jack City*), see Grant Farred, "No Way Out of Menaced Society: Loyalty Within the Boundedness of Race," *Camera Obscura* 35 (1995): 6–23; Paula J. Massood, "*Menace II Society* (film reviews)," *Cineaste* 20 (1996): 44–45.

4. Slavoj Žižek, *The Sublime Object of Ideology* (New York: Verso, 1989), 180.

5. Ibid., 45–49; Slavoj Žižek, "The Spectre of Ideology," in *Mapping Ideology*, ed. Slavoj Žižek (New York: Verso, 1994), 19–22, 1–33.

6. Louis Althusser, "Ideological State Apparatuses (Notes Toward an Investigation)," in *Essays in Ideology* (New York: Verso, 1984), 1–60.

7. Erin Runions, *Changing Subjects: Gender, Nation and Future in Micah* (London: Sheffield Academic Press, 2001), 69–73, 105–111.

8. Homi K. Bhabha, *The Location of Culture* (New York: Routledge, 1994), 148.

9. Gates's discussion of signifying prefigures (and perhaps influences) Bhabha's theorization of mimicry and performative practices. Though Bhabha's allusive style makes it hard to pinpoint all his sources, the influence of Gates seems clear.

10. Henry Louis Gates Jr., *The Signifying Monkey: A Theory of African American Literary Criticism* (New York: Oxford University Press, 1988), 45.

11. Ibid., 49.

12. Ibid., 123.

13. Bhabha, *Location*, 112.

14. Ibid., 184.

15. Christopher John Farley, "That Old Black Magic," *Time* 156 (November 27, 2000): 14.

16. Judith Weisenfeld makes the important point that "black characters often appear as most fully drawn when pictured as participating in Christianity," thus providing an opening, through the stereotype, for the portrayal of African Americans as complex characters. See "For Rent, 'Cabin in the Sky': Race, Religion, and Representational Quagmires in American Film," *Semeia* 74 (1996): 149.

17. One of the problems with a theory of liminal identification is that it may have a tendency to gloss over the fact that the person who does not identify with the dominant social order is often vilified, labeled a hysteric, imprisoned, rehabilitated, "saved," or killed. As alternative identifications become visible, they also become exoticized and consumed, as if human life and misery were not involved. To be very clear, what is being advocated here is *not* appropriation and consumption of orientalized identity formations of the underprivileged by the overprivileged, but rather the difficult work of interrogating one's own oppressive ideological positions through liminal identification, with acknowledgement of dependence on the re-signification of social norms by the marginal.

18. E. G. Celeste A. Fisher, "'America's Worst Nightmare': Reading the Ghetto in a Culturally Diverse Context," in *Saying it Loud: African-American Audiences, Media, and Identity*, ed. Robin R. Means Coleman (New York: Routledge, 2002), 229–248; Robin R. Means Coleman, "The *Menace II Society* Copycat Murder Case and Thug Life: A Reception Study with a Convicted Criminal," in *Saying it Loud: African-American Audiences, Media, and Identity*, ed. Robin R. Means Coleman (New York: Routledge, 2002), 249–284.

19. James McKelly, "Raising Cain in down Eden: *Menace II Society* and the Death of Signifying," *Screen* 39 (1998): 36–52.

20. Albert Hughes and Alan Hughes, "Interview by Elvis Mitchell," *American Pimp*, DVD, directed by Albert and Alan Hughes (Charlotte, NC: Underworld Entertainment, 1999).

21. As Elizabeth Castelli pointed out to me after reading a draft of this paper, these directors capitalize on, and also help to create, racial stereotypes of Italians as gangsters and mafia. The

mimicry of gangster culture may sabotage the aims of the Hughes brothers, in reinforcing already problematic stereotypes of black youth to make a point about life on the streets (Massood, "Menace II Society," 45).

22. So also Farred, "No Way Out," 12. As a number of scholars have pointed out, Cain has long been read as black; see Anne Chevillard-Maubuisson and Alain Marchadour, "Caïn et Abel: Lecture et relectures," in Le Temps de la lecture: Exégèse biblique et sémiotique: Recueil d'hommages pour Jean Delorme, ed. Louis Panier (Paris: Les Éditions du cerf, 1993), 275–276; Ruth Mellinkoff, The Mark of Cain. (Berkeley: University of California Press, 1981), 75–80, figs. 16, 20, 22; Charles B. Copher, "The Black Presence in the Old Testament," in Stony the Road We Trod: African American Biblical Interpretation, ed. Cain Hope Felder. (Minneapolis: Fortress Press, 1991), 148–150, 146–164; Ricado J. Quinones, The Changes of Cain: Violence and the Lost Brother in Cain and Abel Literature (Princeton, NJ: Princeton University Press, 1991), 48, 52–53, 258 n. 11.

23. Critics have pointed out that Menace II Society critiques John Singleton's contention in Boyz N the Hood that male role models can make all the difference (Massood, "Menace II Society," 44–45; Farred, "No Way Out," 6–23).

24. Here, on the surface at least, the directors clearly situate themselves on the youthful side of a generational divide over the status of Christianity (as either co-optive or resistant) in African American struggles against oppression.

25. See, for instance, John Winthrop's "A Model of Christian Charity" in Readings in the History of Christian Theology, Volume 2: From the Reformation to the Present, ed. William C. Placher (Philadelphia: Westminster John Knox, 1988), 108; for an extended discussion of Winthrop, see Robert N. Bellah, The Broken Covenant: American Civil Religion in Time of Trial (Chicago: University of Chicago Press, 1975), 13–15.

26. Max Weber, The Protestant Ethic and the Spirit of Capitalism (1904; repr., New York: Routledge, 1930), 123.

27. Cited in the King James Version.

28. As Mutaamba Maasha commented after reading a draft, "black folk are considered morally flawed characters where one can 'observe' these parables."

29. The other character the directors allow to die with Caine is Sharif (Vonte Sweet), also one who also stands outside the symbolic order of Proverbs. Sharif is the straight-edge one of the bunch, having joined the Nation of Islam. He neither conforms to Protestantism, nor to the stereotypic demands of the gangster image for poor black youth. He makes a number of radical, politically aware statements throughout the film, along with suggestions for change, though his friends constantly shut him up.

30. Albert Memmi, Dependence: A Sketch for a Portrait of the Dependent, trans. Philip A. Fancey (1979; repr., Boston: Beacon Press, 1984), 4–6.

31. Liz Constable, "Economies of Lethal Emotion: La Condition humaine," Modern Language Notes 115 (2000): 581.

32. Memmi, Dependence, 149–156.

33. Ibid., 35; Constable, "Economies of Lethal Emotion," 583.

34. Bhabha, Location, 66–84.

35. Henry Louis Gates Jr., "Niggaz with Latitude," New Yorker 70 (March 21, 1994): 44.

36. Here is one such statistic: "While African-Americans constitute 13% of the nation's monthly drug users, they represent 35% of those persons arrested for drug possession, 55% of drug possession convictions, and 74% of those sentenced to prison for drug possession" (Drug Policy Alliance 2002); for statistics on drug sales, see Drug Policy Alliance 2004.

37. See Farred, "No Way Out," for a discussion of the relationship between Caine's community and the international drug trade.

15 *Scriptures Beyond Script*

SOME AFRICAN DIASPORIC OCCASIONS

GREY GUNDAKER

Early birdcalls rode the mist as a small procession of three women and two men, slowly and silently wove through tall grasses and reeds to the edge of a tidal creek. The leader, a tall, bearded man, now slightly stooped with age, halted and gazed east toward the nearby sea. As the first pink of dawn tipped the grasses, he raised his arms and spread his fingers wide, praying in a language only one member of the group, an elderly woman, remembered from her youth. A tear coursed slowly down her cheek and the young man and woman came up beside her, placing supportive hands gently beneath her elbows to bear her up. She, too, gazed east, toward her home across the silvery water. The young couple's eyes followed hers and their ears filled with the rhythms of prayer.

Falling silent, the leader turned to the woman behind him, who held a shallow sea-grass basket lined with white cloth she had carefully washed and bleached in the sun. The contents of the basket were heavy, but she held it easily with arms toughened by years of labor in the rice fields. The leader took from the basket, one at a time, several objects shaped like duck eggs covered in script and signs and placed them gently into the water. As he did so, the group prayed aloud the words repeated on each egg, Allah, Allah, and asking that the Most merciful one who sees all to take the soul of their newly departed husband, father, and friend, away from this alien land and back to his home across the waters.

——

The discourses that have long tied "scriptures"—a canonical corpus of sacred knowledge—to scripts—conventionally defined by linguists as graphic encoding of spoken language—obviously encompass much more than coding and decoding, or even interpretation and exegesis. As numerous critics of—and within—the "Western tradition" have pointed out, alphabetic script is one of the cornerstones of that tradition and premises about the nature of writing are, in effect, also premises about societies and individuals, their modernity (or lack thereof), cognitive development (ditto), and capacity to contribute usefully to the intellectual and spiritual life of the planet.[1] To cover such ground—and to provide grounds for colonizing so much more—"scriptures," especially the Christian Bible, but also the Qur'an and the notion of "religions of the book"—have provided a physical, portable packaging of Holy Writ, while alphabetic script has provided a portable, supposedly context-independent stepping-stone to "civilization."[2]

Yet, for "scriptures" to have meaning, indeed for "scriptures" to have enduring significance for humanity at all, moments of *scripturalizing*, in Vincent Wimbush's activating terminology, must inherently be intensely personal on some level, mobilizing spirit and social action alike. This is what makes "scriptures" compelling; it is also what makes scripturalizing political, even oppositionally political, especially when participants marginalized by dominant institutions invest "scriptures" with their own hopes.

The story that opened this essay is a case in point. An ethnographic reconstruction, it is the most plausible account I can give thus far of practices involving a group of artifacts currently under investigation at the Institute for Historical Biology of the College of William & Mary: egg-shaped objects inscribed with Arabic letters incised in a white coating.

Each egg is slightly different, and each is subdivided in ways consistent with the sacred numerology and talismanic traditions of West African Islam. Dr. John Bellome found the eggs in 2003 while clearing debris at the marshy edge of his property in coastal South Carolina. Located in a golf-course development on the grounds of former a rice plantation, Africans, most likely Muslims from the Senegambian region, were enslaved there during the eighteenth and nineteenth centuries. The eggs join the very small corpus of surviving Arabic documents from this population, of which the Bilali or Ben Ali document in the Georgia State Library is one of the best known.

The maker(s) of these eggs[3] and the African Americans whose work is discussed in this essay build a texture of cues into objects and events that involve

Figure 15.1 Arabic-inscribed eggs. Photograph by Grey Gundaker.

scriptural components, including *spatial* cues, such as the divisions that frame Arabic script on these eggs. Such scripturalizing challenges the dissociation of script from embodied action and of "religion" from "superstition," as well as the idea that peoples who are thus supposedly uneducated or premodern in their "beliefs" lack the same degree of rationality, sequential reasoning ability, or capacity for abstract thought found in literate population.[4]

From the perspective of such assumptions these eggs would not fare well, being as vulnerable to erasure from the categories of "theorizing" and "scriptures" as their home community was to being bulldozed from the American landscape. For example, the scribe's hand might be labeled clumsy rather than calligraphic, the wording characterized as repetitive and not indicative of any literary innovation, and the four faces on one egg, along with the use of eggs as offerings or memorials, might be dismissed as dilutions of purist Islam: perhaps even as heresies, if one supposes, as I do, that the fourfold drawing of faces represents God's omnidirectional sight and power. Yet these subdivisions cue culturally informed readers that each egg is *not only a text but also a ritual space*, a result of and invitation to sacred performance.[5]

In linguistic terms, when such cues are built into the fabric of a writing system, as in ancient Egyptian, Maya, and Chinese for example, they are known as radicals or morphosemantic signs; that is, signs that index and classify the phonological signs they complement within a glyph or character.[6] When they are not built into the script but nevertheless inform readers about what and how to read (like the margins of this page), they are usually known simply as "context." But either way, they tell culturally informed readers not *what* they are reading but how the act of reading fits into a larger situation. And, either way, these are precisely the affective and contextual dimensions of scriptural practice that alphabetic bias ignores and notions like religion of the book leave out—even when the religion in question has at its heart a book and a script said to have come directly from Allah to his prophet.

The conventional distinction between oral and literate people and cultures also reinforces this diminution, privileging text over context even when the two are obviously complementary within the both/and configuration of a larger religious statement. Those who label Others preliterate, oral, superstitious, and so forth, however, are not without their own beliefs. Thus there is a worrisome parallelism between the academic claim that alphabetic script is context independent and the religious assertion that certain scripts are independent of everyday realities because they are revelations direct from God. Although seemingly emerging from radically different worldviews, both disembody scriptural encounters, privileging that which floats above and apart from human particularities.

The academic stance, what anthropologist Brian Street has termed the *autonomous* theory of writing, marginalizes, literally, both the margins of the page and the contexts of reading and writing that differ from schooled models.[7] The religious dogma aims to reduce variations and sometimes to rename those aberrations, even as heresies. Both belief systems are thus deeply implicated in maintaining the boundaries of dominant institutions. Both promote purisms that help to define the institutions and maintain their authority—for of course the academy itself, no less than the religions of the book taught in university religion departments, is a creature of texts.

Yet, ironically, these qualities of set-apart-ness, purity, the divinity-touched essence associated with touchstone symbols, in alternative contexts also foster oppositional ideas and actions. Thus, regarding the Arabic-inscribed eggs: not only can we infer the existence of counter-hegemonic religious and political orientations from their very existence as the productions or imported possessions of supposedly illiterate and inferior forced laborers, but they also draw on and contribute to a venerable West African Muslim tradition of spatially orienting to activate spiritual power.[8]

For such reasons the scriptural is dangerous, a powerful mobilizer of will and action. But the scriptural is also experienced diversely and personally, operating on a different level than the mystification of institutions. Further, from a social-cultural perspective, no thing, action, or event can ever be unmediated or independent of context; rather, some forms are simply more stable (recognizable, and repeatable) than others because people make them so. And the more stable they are, the more familiarity occasions, if not contempt, at least invisibility.[9] Thus, to make a space for the experiential sacred, even scriptural traditions within sanctioned institutions must be continually regenerated and brought home by participants.

African diaspora scripturalizing practices often foreground and celebrate precisely these regenerative processes by that channeling and by amplifying the participatory nature of scriptural encounters. All for example involve *doing something* (tying, wrapping, untying, opening, traversing, seeing, hearing, orienting in space) and *knowing something* (how to process the said, the unsaid, and the unsayable, the implicit and the explicit with equal grace).

In this respect, the eggs, which rattle as if metal is hidden inside (causing airport-security X-ray technicians briefly to handle them like hand grenades), also cue the nature of the invocations inscribed on their surfaces as active, a message reinforced by their spatial divisions. For example, similar spacing appears in documents confiscated from the Mâles, Yoruba Muslims who organized a slave revolt in Bahia, Brazil, in the 1830s.[10] Although such talismans—like those made by Gullah (Angola) Jack for the Vesey Revolt in Charleston, South Carolina, in 1821—were said to armor the body of the wearer against enemy weapons, also consider the enormous psychic buffer such scripturalizing provided against the oppressors' claims that God willed the enslaved to obey their enslavers. Not surprisingly, then, when both revolts were foiled and the participants awaited trial and certain execution, whites' taunts frequently centered on the talismans' supposed failure.[11]

Indeed, throughout the history of people of African descent in the Americas, innovators have signified and "riffed," not only on the content of "scripture," but also on the very letters from which it is composed, a fact obvious to anyone with even a passing acquaintance with hip-hop, where added diacritics, punctuation, double-voiced spellings, and pumped-up visual language "phattens" text and exposes the malleable—transformable—potentials of the body and the material world.

But novel as individual instances may seem today, they have also clearly figured in the scripturalizing of earlier generations, as in the double voices of figure 15.2, a sketch of a neon Baptist church sign from Chattanooga, Tennessee, dating from the late 1950s or early 1960s: Jes—Us. By means of homonyms, punctuation, punning, and spacing, these letters layer the Christian cross inside and over an older form of talismanic form, so that the implied "Jesus" squares with the vernacular spelling of "just us"—not only the saved, but the black, vernacular-speaking neighborhood church-membership saved of this congregation. Furthermore, this was at a time when the civil rights movement still had a long way to go in Chattanooga and "urban renewal" was destroying numerous nearby homes to construct a new freeway.[12]

While hip-hop artists and Christian churchgoers have focused their talents on the Roman alphabet, others have moved to take charge of the code itself, extending the trajectory of non-Roman scripts like Arabic and Cherokee syllabary among North America's peoples of color to include the ancient writing systems of Kemet (Egypt) and Nubia.

Along with many Egyptological fellow travelers dating from at least the early republic,[13] the Yemassee (formerly Nuwabian) Nation of Moors repossessed the hieroglyphic signs and deities of ancient Egypt. Artists combined them with emblems of space travel and interstellar communication on monumental buildings and sculptures throughout the compound.

Figure 15.2 Sketch of church sign, Chattanooga, Tennessee, 1987. Drawing by Grey Gundaker.

Figure 15.3 Stele with hiero-glyphics, Edenton, Georgia, 1993. Photograph by Grey Gundaker.

For a brief period in the 1990s, their adopted community of Edenton, Georgia (also home to the Uncle Remus Museum), became a multi-script learning center, where members could be seen at the local Chinese restaurant pouring over passages in hieroglyphics, cuneiform, and Hebrew.

As Egyptian hieroglyphics signify the endurance of African intellectual contributions from the past, so new scripts bear witness to the creation of new forms for the future. For example, Paul Alfred Barton, born in St. Lucia, now a Californian, invented Afrikuandika, a script whose graphemes sketch phonological places of articulation in the mouth of the sounds represented.

This permits the script to be learned through sensory practice by speakers of many different languages, an aim of Barton's that fits into the larger dynamics of scripturalizing by attempting to heal breaches and prevent miscommunications among the diaspora's diverse constituencies.[14]

James Hampton, whose *Throne* Professor King-Hammond discusses in her essay in this volume, filled at least ten notebooks with his own revealed script. Possibly a form of visual chant, the books may also be a silent witness to the persistence into the early twentieth century of remnants and echoes of Arabic script, which parts of his writings resemble, in Elloree, South Carolina, where Hampton lived as a child. In a region with a documented history of Muslim presence,

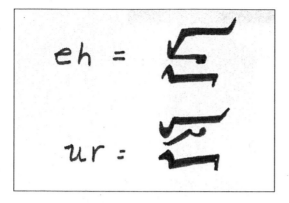

Figure 15.4 Afrikuandika signs after Paul Alfred Barton. Drawing by Grey Gundaker.

J. B. Murray of Sparta, Georgia, centered his healing practice on writing, which God dictated to him as he prayed. Only the pure in heart could read the script. He read God's curing directives through water drawn from a sacred well on his property.[15]

The preceding examples all involve either scripts that represent specific sounds or represent a divine voice that the writer alone can hear. Other diaspora graphic systems, many with African antecedents, offer resources for scripturalizing based on emblems and spatial-material arrangements. Some are logographic, translatable into words, like the red octagon of a stop sign.

Others "say" what speech and writing cannot, forming visual analogs and metaphors for the complex relations that underpin concepts like justice, honesty, forgiveness, faith, forbearance against those who have done oneself harm, and the omniscient, omnidirectional sight of God represented by the all-seeing eagle and the compass-turning whirligig.

Signs that indicate God's all-seeing vision are widespread. Harkening back to the four faces on the egg, Dilmus Hall, a renowned artist from Athens, Georgia, mounted the diamond/star on the four corners of on his house and painted a four-sided cosmogram around the light bulb in the ceiling of his living room.[16]

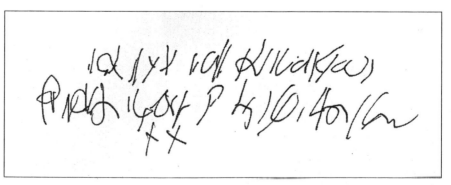

Figure 15.5 Passage of writing in the spirit, after J. B. Murray. Drawing by Grey Gundaker.

Figure 15.6 Stop sign beside back entrance to the home of Gyp Packnett, Centreville, Mississippi, 1989. Photograph by Grey Gundaker.

Material objects also "write" the scripture. Mrs. Florence Gibson staged the Bible story of Noah's Ark in the object theater of her yard in Savannah, Georgia. In Alabama, Reverend George Kornegay was a master of this art. Figure 15.7 instanti-ates "Joshua Fought the Battle of Jericho" by tying up a space in blue surveyor's tape, aligning the circling movement that caused the walls of the city to tumble with the tying and wrapping gestures that seal spiritual power into objects like hands, mojos, and Islamic talismans.

Such objects also enclose the unseen nexus of power. Under certain condi-tions such as direct communication with God the "words" do not—and I would argue, must not—read clearly to outsiders and unprepared eyes. (After all, in the Book of Revelation it is recorded that God said to John: "You got to EAT that book"—here paraphrased in the words of a radio sermonizer I heard on WNOO, Chattanooga, Tennessee, on New Years Day, 1987.) Reverend Kornegay showed this in an assemblage scripturally named "On This Rock I Will Build My Church," an altar with a telephone conduit for God's voice resting on top of an empty (phone) book stand.

Reminiscent of J. B. Murray's writing, a metal tray on the front of the rock, painted with red, black, and white squiggles, depicts the voice unfolding as mere "marks" to those who do not already hear it in their hearts. The marks of word

Figure 15.7 "Joshua Fought the Battle of Jericho," Rev. George Kornegay, 1993. Photograph by Grey Gundaker.

Figure 15.8 "On This Rock I Will Build My Church," Rev. George Kornegay, 1993. Photograph by Grey Gundaker.

energy sparking up, down, and around—voice rendered as line—are not too distant from the Qur'anic notion of God's voice rendered into ink.

While limited space permits only brief discussion of each of these illustrations here, as a group their emergence, perfectly fitting script and "scriptures" to specific situations, times, and places in African diasporic experience, should make clear that scripturalizing practices themselves are rich repositories of indigenous theorizing. One obvious component of the participants' theoretical stance is the demand that viewers/learners grapple with an open-ended package of textual and contextual information, some of it complementary and some contradictory. In other words the demand that academics confront not only the Acts of the Apostles but also the Axe of the Apostles!

Figure 15.9 "The Axe of the Apostles," Rev. George Kornegay, 1993. Photograph by Grey Gundaker.

NOTES

1. For example Michel de Certeau, *The Practice of Everyday Life*, trans. Steven Rendell (Berkeley: University of California Press, 1984), 134; Walter D. Mignolo, "Signs and Their Transmission: The Question of the Book in the New World," in *Writing Without Words: Alternative Literacies in Mesoamerica and the Andes*, ed. Elizabeth Hill Boone and Walter D. Mignolo, (Durham, N.C.: Duke University Press, 1996), 220–270.

2. Proponents of this "hard-core" view of the alphabet include Eric A. Havelock, *Origins of Western Literacy* (Toronto: Ontario Institute for Studies in Education, 1976); Walter J. Ong, *Orality and Literacy* (London: Methuen, 1982); and, carried on into the realms of quasi-theology, Robert K. Logan, *The Alphabet Effect: The Impact of the Phonetic Alphabet on the Development of Western Civilization* (New York: St. Martins Press, 1986).

3. For stylistic reasons it seems possible that two makers or scribes wrote on the artifacts. Seven are extant. It is impossible to know how many the original group comprised. Materials analysis has not yet been completed. Possibly they were constructed of tabby—a durable lime plaster much used in coastal South Carolina. X-rays have shown that the artifacts have metal cores.

4. Although such evolutionist suppositions are ostensibly out of favor in the academy, they continually creep back in very thinly veiled forms. For example, the distinguished historian Henri-Jean Martin wrote (*The History and Power of Writing* [Chicago: University of Chicago Press, 1994], 507):

> It serves little purpose to introduce writing techniques into closed societies; at best they will just use them to immobilize and set down sacred words as secrets that give an oligarchy its power. . . . [N]othing indicates that the incomplete experience of the Amerindians would have gone much further if it had not been interrupted by the Spanish conquest. certain parts of the globe, however,—China, Mesopotamia, Egypt—gave rise to dynamic writing systems destined for a great future. . . . Their rise corresponded to the start of brilliant civilizations.

5. Of course such practices accompany many writing and graphic systems. For diverse instances, see Judge Eliyahu Moziani, *Torah of the Alphabet, Or, How the Art of Writing Was*

Taught Under the Judges of Israel (1441–1025) (Herborn: Baalschem Press, 1984); Ayele Bekerle, *Ethiopic: An African Writing System*, (Lawrenceville, NJ: Red Sea Press, 1997), 82–103; Roy Harris, *Signs of Writing* (New York: Routledge, 1995).

6. For a lucid explanation of this type of system, see Floyd G. Lounsbury, "The Ancient Writing of Middle America" in *The Origins of Writing*, ed. Wayne M. Senner (Lincoln: University of Nebraska Press, 1989), 203–237.

7. Brian V. Street, *Literacy in Theory and Practice* (Cambridge: Cambridge University Press, 1983).

8. Labelle Prussin, *Hatumere: Islamic Design in West Africa* (Berkeley: University of California Press, 1986); René A. Bravmann, *African Islam* (Washington DC: Smithsonian Institution Press, 1983).

9. Conversely, the more novel the context as experienced by participants, the less its cues can be taken for granted. This, of course, is where interventions like "art" and "revelation" bring us full circle. As disruptions to the seemingly inevitable, both threaten institutions, until the work of art or the account of revelation itself is either suppressed or incorporated into the canon.

10. Joaõ José Reis, *Slave Rebellion in Brazil* (Baltimore: Johns Hopkins University Press, 1993); see cover illustration, 100–101. Also see, for an argument regarding these documents diametrically opposed to the one presented in this paper, Jack Goody, "Writing, Religion, and Revolt in Bahia," *Visible Language* 20 (1986): 318–343.

11. Robert Starobin, ed., *Denmark Vesey: The Slave Conspiracy of 1822* (Englewood Cliffs, NJ: Prentice Hall, 1971).

12. For a wider context for this and other script uses discussed in this paper, see Grey Gundaker, *Signs of Diaspora/Diaspora of Signs: Creolization, Literacies, and Vernacular Practice in African America* (New York: Oxford University Press, 1998).

13. Wilson Jeremiah Moses, *Afrotopia: The Roots of African American Popular History* (Cambridge: Cambridge University Press, 1998).

14. Paul Alfred Barton, *Afrikuandika: The African Hieroglyphic Writing System* (New York: Vantage Press, 1991).

15. Judith McWillie, "Writing in an Unknown Tongue," in *Cultural Perspectives on the American South*, ed. Charles Reagan Wilson (New York: Gordon and Breach, 1991), 103–117.

16. Judith McWillie, *Another Face of the Diamond: Pathways Through the Black Atlantic South* (New York: INTAR Latin American Gallery, 1988).

16 Texture, Text, and Testament

READING SACRED SYMBOLS / SIGNIFYING IMAGERY IN AMERICAN VISUAL CULTURE

LESLIE KING-HAMMOND

Deeply embedded in the mythography of American civil religion . . . special revered or "hallowed" sites have long been fundamental elements of a powerfully sustaining worldview in American self-understanding.
　　　　　　　　　—Rowland A. Sherrill, "American Sacred
　　　　　　　　　Space and the Contest of History"[1]

It is quite commonly thought that the intellect is responsible for everything that is made and done. It is commonly thought that everything that is can be put into words. But there is a wide range of emotional response that we make that cannot be put into words. We are so used to making these emotional responses that we are not consciously aware of them until they are represented in artwork.
　　—Agnes Martin, "Beauty Is the Mystery of Life"[2]

And when waste and age
and shock and strife
shall have sapped
these walls of life
Then take this dust
that's earthy worn
and mold it
into heavenly form.

　　　　　　　　　　　—Rosa Lytle, *Prayer*[3]

Reading sacred symbols and signifying imagery in American visual culture is still one of the most under-explored aspects of visual expression in modern and postmodern art of the twentieth and twenty-first centuries. Global history has provided the artist with a wealth of examples in the expression and creation of objects, artifacts, and monuments inspired by personal motivation and religious belief systems. Modernity has posed challenges to the artist's need to connect with a spiritual core fundamental to living a meaningful life in a world of global conflicts and civil wars. Encoded meanings have mandated that the elements represented in contemporary artwork sometimes, as painter Agnes Martin has observed, "cannot be put into words." Yet works of art express or signify ideas and attitudes regarding the nature of the sacred or spiritual world of the invisible and the unspoken. This essay is a journey into that aspect of American visual culture. Using the metaphors of textures, texts, and testaments, this proposed rereading of sacred, signifying symbols and imagery attempts to expand the possibilities of artistic application, interpretation, and meaning. A select group of artists and artworks will expose us to visual strategies regarding belief, signifying objects, and sacred space.

The observations and selected artworks used to illustrate the questions and issues presented in this essay were drawn from ongoing research projects in the investigation of the role of sacred texts and the impact of spirituality in the aesthetic life of contemporary art and visual culture of America. The works of Willie Birch, Allyson Smith, Elizabeth Talford Scott, Aminah Lynn Robinson, Joan Gaither, and Douglas Smith reflect a varied range of aesthetic orientation, spiritual worldviews, and political sensibilities. These artists provide the scholarly community and the public audience with artistic creations that challenge the visualizing potential of signifying upon the world's dominant religions.

In this essay, the artistic metaphors of texture, text, and testament stem from the impact that sacred texts (i.e., the Talmud, the Qur'an, the I Ching, and most especially the Bible) have had on the inspiration and historical production of artworks. The impact of the Bible in the West, and more specifically within the visual culture of America, has forced a too-narrow perspective on the intent and subtexts of the artist-artmaker. New directions and revision are crucial to new meanings or readings. How has the artist used the Bible or other sacred texts as a catalyst to interpret and express their individual creativity, spirituality, and personhood? Biblical scholar Vincent Wimbush challenges prevailing assumptions regarding the impact of such texts: "Insofar as the Bible is recognized as rather important in helping to accord legitimacy to the public religion in the United States, and insofar as the Bible continues to this day to be engaged by elites and nonelites alike, through the prism of American myth, the very meaning and agenda of and approaches to biblical interpretation for our times must change dramatically."[4] It is within this spectrum of change that the mechanisms of artistic textures, symbolic sacred texts, and signifying testaments are important strategies to facilitate the understanding and meaning of this very humanistic and aesthetic phenomenon of scripturally signifying artworks.

The twentieth century and the first phase of the twenty-first century have witnessed modernist artmaking processes and production in rapid states of evolution and change. Intellectual, conceptual, and technical processes have morphed into postmodern ways of seeing, thinking, feeling, and interpreting issues that are more centered on questions of identity, power, and place. Over the last three decades, artistic production has reflected a hyperconsciousness about race, class, gender, sexuality, politics, religion, and economics. Accelerated by the impact of interactive electronic cyberspace technologies and digital media, contemporary artmakers have created works that are more acutely responsive to humankind's emotional, psychological, and spiritual well-being in a global culture driven by the constant stimuli of history, evolution, and technology.

In the midst of this catharsis of evolution, the artist-artmaker has had to become an even more studied observer, scholar, and technician. The elements within the visual culture of their environment have created an expressionism that transcends traditional readings of art established by canonical standards of Euro-Western modalities. To comprehend an artwork or creation of "heavenly form," the community of viewers or audience must *re*read this imagery from a more spiritually attuned center of awareness, experience, and belief.

Historically, the artist-artmaker was commissioned to visualize the sacred text to the masses, because most people could not read. The modernist impulse has given way to the artist-artmaker who now initiates the commentaries, narratives, and responses using image and text to signify on America's perception of its own religious experience and belief.

America represents, from its earliest New World origins, artistic traditions that are as intricately complex as they are deeply conflicted. Dismissing the aesthetic heritage of the indigenous communities, early America mirrored the sensibilities of its European ancestors. The production of architectural structures and utilitarian objects was predicated on issues of need crucial to the development of a New World civilization within the wilderness terrain of the United States. Labor was acquired through the forced importation of chattel slaves from Africa. The Africans were highly skilled artisans in technologies essential to the construction of a New World. These new African citizens, however, were also phenomenally equipped with intellectual, philosophical, physical, and spiritual attributes that enabled them to create systems of survival to maintain a sense of identity and connectiveness to their motherland, Africa—in spite of the horrors of slavery. Even more troubling are the relationships of the African to the *other* populations of New World Americans. The role that women, Asians, and natives played in this vast and complicated matrix of human creative and spiritual energies also compounds the complexities of interpretation. This spectrum of creative production has suffered from a benign neglect. Insufficient research has been accorded to the artwork and imagery that was created by individuals rendered invisible and that still obtains. How do these artists visualize and express their experience of the sacred? What strategies of signification were used to interpret or symbolize those realities, beliefs, and visions of the "heavenly form"?

Reading the Body Texture

Viewing Willie Birch's composition, *Bride of Jesus* (2003), the viewer is confronted by a large-scale drawing of an elderly African American woman who is of a humble, working-class status. It is a commanding, powerful representation and commentary on the evocation of spiritual beliefs and behavior; it is heavily loaded with encoded meanings. Birch's *Bride* is a textual tour de force in the subject's strength of character, conviction, and manner of dress. Birch's *Bride* does not wear white, like the New Orleans painter Sister Gertrude Morgan (who really believed herself to be the bride of Jesus Christ). She wears layered clothing in bold contrasting patterns and designs. By dominant expectations of fashion styles, Birch's *Bride* does not fit the Eurocentric model of upscale fashion norms.

Birch deliberately draws the subject in black and white and in a representational rather than an abstract style to maintain an innate connectivity with the subject's humanness. Given the inhuman treatment accorded to Africans and women, the artist felt it was important to "show that we basically are the same people we were

Figure 16.1 Willie Birch's *Bride of Jesus* (2003). Artist's collection.

when we came to this continent, it's just that things manifest themselves differently based upon the environment . . . differently in terms of materials; the clothes you wear, the look."[5] The *Bride* represents a standard of beauty rarely accorded respect or reverence by Western contemporary norms. This portrayal of the *Bride of Jesus* is a magnificent icon of a New World Madonna, dressed in the royal robes of a spiritual aristocrat. Art historians and anthropologists Judith Perani and Norma H. Wolf have studied the traditional role of cloth and dress in Africa. Their observations confirm Birch's personification of the *Bride* in her manner of "putting on cloth involves intent; the individual enters the sacred arena dressed to achieve certain perceived goals. In the quest to express one's personal worth, an individual can draw upon a rich vocabulary of cloth and clothing to express prestige, proclaim group membership, or challenge tradition."[6] Birch is committed to preserving the power of these images because he believes that "the audience for my work was the same as the people in my work—everyday people . . . It is very important that black people or people of color, see themselves as represented . . . so they can begin to recognize the beauty of themselves."[7]

The bride also occurs as a religious trope in the painting *Banned from Marrying (They Took Up Arms)* (2004) by Allyson Smith. Smith contends that her work, "explores the ambiguities inherent in the picture of the modern, perfect middle class family."[8] Yet reading Smith's painting is as difficult a task for the casual viewer as for the sophisticated critic or art historian because her images contain

Figure 16.2 *Banned from Marrying (They Took Up Arms)* (2004) by Allyson Smith, in the collection of Mary Wieler.

subtextual meanings not easily revealed. The picture plane is constructed from multiple narratives fabricated to form a comic-book or film format—a deliberate act by the artist to combine several images on one picture plane, in which she is "[j]uxtaposing disjointed images next to each other . . . to knit together different meanings, different parts of narrative disparate feelings and parts of life to invoke the multidimensional of life itself where we often experience conflicting emotions and contradictory events at the same time."⁹ The multidimensional and conflicted experience that Smith addresses in her *Banned from Marrying* refers to matrimony, a union of commitment to a life together "for better or for worse, in sickness and in health, until death do us part."

But this is no ordinary wedding. The brides in *Banned* are carrying weapons, which has been misinterpreted, much to the artist's distress, as referring to a "shotgun wedding." In fact, this is the communication of a sacred act of matrimony between same-sex partners. The seriousness of their spiritual commitment to wed according to the laws of the sacred texts was denied by the intervention of legal statutes reinforced in the spring of 2004 by President George W. Bush. Allyson Smith is a lesbian with a long-term partner. They are deeply committed to having their union spiritually and legally sanctified and binding. The painting is a manifesto of resistance to the conflicted attitudes of American society's crisis of *otherness* of same-sex unions. Smith's painting signifies and asserts lesbians' and gays' moral, spiritual, and political rights of normality, humanity, and inclusion.

Sacred Text/Signifying Cloth

Before the invention of the book, early preliterate societies created sacred "texts" in the form of pictographs and iconic imagery on the walls of caves, on pottery and basketry, and on clothing constructed from animal skins and, later, cloth made from fibers cultivated from plants. The surfaces of these sites and objects were marked with images that created the earliest visual texts read by humanity to express the experience of human life-worlds. With the evolution of calligraphy and cursive systems of writing, modern societies accorded a higher priority of meaning and importance to the written text. Once the text was located in book form, modern elites increasingly found the pictorial languages in the textile form to be "more primitive," hence less "intellectual," in its orientation and in its articulation of culture. Reading the text within the textile construction and design of the ancestral legacies of many cultures has become an enigma and a paradox when contrasted with the jet-stream societies immersed in the vortex of digital scripts and cyberspace technologies.

When the diverse groups of peoples of African descent arrived in the "New World" of the Americas during the transatlantic Middle Passage, their cloth signified memories and ancient traditions. In the scrambling of these cultures, ethnicities, languages, and belief systems, a new aesthetic order of constructing and reading cloth emerged. New World Africans—in particular the women, as a result of dire conditions within the slave culture of America—created a formidable mechanism of caring and communicating through the innovation of quilt making.

Quilts provided warmth and protection for families and individuals. They were also used for barter or exchange for goods or services. But they were, most importantly, powerful instruments of communication, cultural retention, and resistance to domination from their oppressors in a political structure that forbade the African to read or write. Rereading these woven texts as carrier of language provides reassessment that considers the extended and alternative possibilities of encoded sacred texts and signifying imagery under the guise of what had been considered only utilitarian, functional objects designed for ordinary domestic usage.

The works of Elizabeth Talford Scott, Aminah Robinson, and Joan Gaither provide crucial examples and artistic strategies that demonstrate the alternative modalities of reading a signifying, woven, stitched text. In Rozsika Parker's seminal study, *The Subversive Stitch: Embroidery and the Making of the Feminine*, she calls for attention to reading quilts as texts of resistance and self expression: "Limited to practicing art with needle and thread, women have nevertheless sewn a subversive stitch—managed to make meanings of their own in the very medium intended to inculcate self-effacement."[10] While Parker's study is particularly focused on the traditions of European women from the eighteenth through the twentieth centuries, her observation has validity for women of African descent as well.

Figure 16.3 *Plantation Quilt* (1980) by Elizabeth Talford Scott, owned by the Delaware Museum of Art.

For example, in the *Plantation Quilt* (1980), Elizabeth Talford Scott stitched a pattern of stars in the South Carolina skies of her youth. Taught to quilt by her mother and sisters (she had twelve siblings), Scott would sit on the porch on hot summer nights after a long day sharecropping the cotton fields that she and her family worked. The design of the quilt is brilliant, with colorful stars against a white background that heightens the power and spiritual energy of the composition. The cosmology of African belief systems is deeply embedded in Scott's visual reference to the phenomenology of these celestial bodies. She recorded the various constellations identifying "the mother of the stars in the center. That's the dipper of the sky."[11]

Scott's quilt, however, is not just simply observing nature and signifying on the wonders of the universe that she witnessed and read in the Bible. The *Plantation Quilt* evokes resistance and defiance. Within the white ground of the composition and cleverly camouflaged between the star patterns, Scott has embroidered linear running stitches (a technique employed to hold the multiple layers of cloth and batting together) that are sewn in track patterns to reflect the contours of a field of crops. Scott's daughter Joyce recalls her mother and other relatives telling her that quilts had been used in the past as maps for slaves to escape the plantation.[12] While the slaves were "resting" they were also plotting their escape. As they read or retold the stories of biblical scriptures to one another, they reclaimed the spiritual function of the ancestral African textile and stitched their way to freedom. These were performative, ceremonial acts of collective and communal resistance. Joseph Murphy, in studying the ceremonies of the African diaspora, has observed, "In the African diaspora the texts of the tradition—the songs, prayers, rhythms, gestures, foods, emblems, and clothing have been transmuted orally and ceremonially."[13] While Elizabeth Talford Scott was not able to complete her education, she was able to innovate and preserve the art of a stitched text that could be read and acted on by the members of her community.

Cloth within the African tradition is a potent metaphor and symbol that reinforces the moral, philosophical, and spiritual universe of African religious and life-world belief systems. In the diasporan world of Columbus, Ohio, mixed-media artist Aminah Robinson creates work that defies the traditional nomenclature and theories of contemporary art world jargon. She refers to her creations as "Symphonic Poems," "Memory Maps," "hogmawg," and "RagGonNons."[14] Her works are a "New World" language for a "New World" visually expressed text that transcends ordinary assumptions regarding the experience, intent, and meaning of an artwork. Robinson has taken the ordinary, almost invisible, mundane elements of her community, using the fundamental structure of a quilt, and expanded the process to record through the application of thousands of material cultural objects (buttons, beads, fibers, music boxes, fabrics, paint, pins, shells, etc.), the history of her community and family. It is a continuous process that is constantly changing as people respond to the work. One of the most complex forms of Robinson's artistry is the conceptualization and execution of a RagGonNon. This concept does not fit easily within Western mainstream genres. A rag is a scrap of old cloth used often for cleaning after the garment is no longer viable. In African American slang or vernacular, "rag" has come to mean anything from a sanitary napkin, a newspaper, to complain, or to dress in the finest clothes. "Rag" then becomes "ragmop" or "raggedy" (unkempt), "rag-head" (man with headscarf), "ragtime" (music), and "ragmen" (pre-jazz musicians who played quick-tempo, "hot" music with fast breaks and complex figures).[15]

Robinson, drawing on this cultural history, defines the RagGonNon as to "rag on and on." When one views *Poindexter Village Quilt, 1966–1984*, it is difficult to recognize it as a quilt because of its mixed-media assemblage of sewn felt embellished with buttons, thread, leather, shells, wool, and rags. In fact, RagGonNons are not quilts but ongoing memory tracks, which tell epic stories to read panoramic vistas of her urban community, Poindexter Village in Columbus. The stories she creates are not revealed to her until the pieces are completed. Robinson works on the RagGonNon rolled up and adds to it as she goes. The work evolves as she observes how life is lived and experienced: it is not a linear, monochromatic phenomenon but a constant flow of change, growth, remembrance, and celebration of rites of passage. These works will never really be finished, because she continually adds memories, new events, and found materials to the compositions.

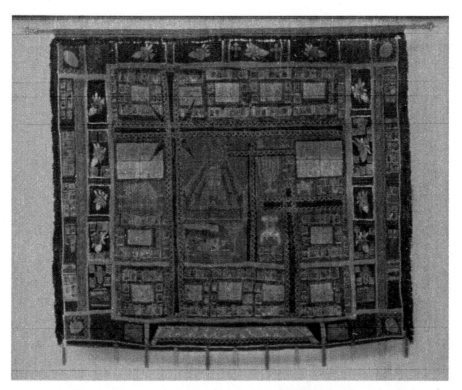

Figure 16.4 *Poindexter Family Quilt, 1966–1984* by Aminah Brenda Lynn Robinson. American, b. 1940. RagGonNon with buttons, beads, cowrie shells, thread, wool, rags, and cloth. 96 × 104 inches. Collection of Esther and Alan Saks. © Aminah Brenda Lynn Robinson.

The artistic modalities of Joan Gaither's quilting processes reflect her kinship to the artistry of Elizabeth Scott and Aminah Robinson. But Gaither has, in the innovative vocabulary of this very fluid medium, used the inspirations of her religious and spiritual upbringing in the black church to embrace the digital technologies to embellish the textual voice of her quilt. In *My Spiritual Family Quilt* (2003) she has undertaken the Herculean task of recording all the images of her family members, with whom she was raised and nurtured in the family church, by reproducing their images in Xerox photo transfers and then sewing the fabric images into the quilt. Family units are stitched into grid blocks. Gaither explains that she "felt compelled and driven to complete the 12′ × 10′ *My Spiritual Family Quilt*, matching objects of divinity to symbolic color and images of over 600 faces of the members of the Saint Mark Methodist Church family in Hanover, Maryland."[16] Gaither bridges the gap between the ancestral legacy of the African textile, the Christian biblical black church experience, and digital electronic technologies to articulate a signifying textural language, consistent with and unique to the postmodernist futuristic trends of twenty-first-century art.

Signifying Revelations/Spatial Testaments

The designation of a spot in the landscape or culturescape as "sacred" results from human decision-making, a result flowing from perceptions of the special, spiritual meanings associated with the site. If the designation is collectively compelling, it subsequently entails the imaginative operations of coordinating those religious meanings with others in the community of belief and commitment and of interpreting and maintaining the place, role, and significance of the "site" in the continuing traditions of the community.[17]

Where women have used domestic textiles to register their resistance and self-expression, artist Samuel Smith used the house itself as his canvas (and instrument). Smith began to alter the environment of his home by designating it as a sacred site. The reconfiguration and appearance of his Freeport, Long Island, New York, residence went from being a family "home" to a spiritual "work" place that evolved into a "church." By 1971 Smith had anointed by his own artistic and religious authority the Freeport home as the Church of the Living God.

Smith's innovative response to a divine calling from God manifested itself as would an artist creating a work of art. The exterior walls of the house are painted bright colors against a white background. The front lawn is organized in grid units with colored pebbles with inset tablets of biblical scriptures and genealogical testaments of family and friends. The side window has been transformed into a "stained glass" window achieved by the effect of written scriptures painted into the windowpanes of the house.

The most spectacular moment is realized on entering the front door of the house and moving into the "living" room, which has been transformed into a vortex of red walls and ceilings covered with scripts of the New Testament. The texts were handwritten and painted by Smith onto a variety of materials, including

Figure 16.5 By 1971 Samuel Smith had anointed by his own artistic and religious authority the Freeport home as the Church of the Living God. Photograph by Leslie King-Hammond.

mirror tiles, picture frames, and window shades. Dining tables became altars, pews replaced sofas, chairs became thrones, all covered in red—the color symbolic of the blood of Jesus Christ. The potent and resonating effect of this spatial testament and signifying revelation of Smith's newly ordered worldview is crystallized by the application of clear plastic, which covers the walls, sofas, pews, chairs, and tables.

The reflective properties of this environment are magnified by the use of mirrored tiles. There are almost a dozen lights that hang from the ceiling and create the effect of the "heavenly form" of Smith's divine universe. Smith's Church of the Living God has great similarity in sculptural execution to Jane Hampton's *Throne of the Third Heaven of the Nations Millennium General Assembly* (ca. 1950–1964) mode of found objects covered with tin gold and silver foil, located at the Smithsonian Institution in Washington DC. Both spaces reverberate with Kongo-American sensibilities of decoration in their dependency on shining surfaces of gold, silver, mirrors, clear plastic, and light bulbs. Robert Farris Thompson refers to this phenomenon as "painting metaphoric motion"[18] or act of artistic and creative black imagination. Reading the aesthetics of sacred spaces as texture, text, and testament gives alternative and unending meaning to reading signifying scriptures and sacred symbols as applied to American visual culture.

NOTES

1. Rowland A. Sherrill, "American Sacred Space and the Contest of History," in *American Sacred Space*, ed. David Chidester and Edward T. Leventhal (Bloomington: Indiana University Press, 1995), 313, 313–340.

2. Agnes Martin, "Beauty Is the Mystery of Life," in *Uncontrollable Beauty*, ed. Bill Beckley with David Shapiro (New York: Allworth Press, 1998), 399–402.

3. Katie Geneva Cannon, *Katie's Canon: Womanism and the Soul of the Black Community* (New York: Continuum, 1996), 37.

4. Vincent Wimbush, "Introduction: And the Students Shall Teach Them . . ." in *The Bible and the American Myth: A Symposium on the Bible and the Construction of Meaning*, ed. Vincent Wimbush (Macon, GA : Mercer University Press, 1999), 5.

5. Jeanette Ingberman, "A Conversation with Willie Birch," in *Willie Birch: A Personal View of Urban America* (New York: Exit Art, 1992), 24.

6. Judith Perani and Norma H. Wolff, *Cloth, Dress, and Art Patronage in Africa* (New York: Oxford University Press, 1999), 29.

7. Ingberman, "A Conversation with Willie Birch," 24.

8. Allyson S. Smith, (master of fine arts thesis, Maryland Institute College of Art, 2004).

9. Ibid.

10. Rozsika Parker, *The Subversive Stitch: Embroidery and the Making of the Feminine* (New York: Routledge, 1989), 215.

11. Maryland Institute College of Art, ed., *Eyewinkers, Tumbleturds and Candlebugs: The Art of Elizabeth Talford Scott* (Baltimore: Maryland Institute College of Art, 1998), 29. This attention to celestial detail can also be found in the *Bible Quilt* (1895) by Harriet Powers, available in Regenia Perry, *Harriet Powers Bible Quilts* (New York: Rizzoli International, 1994).

12. Leslie King-Hammond, "Eyewinkers, Tumbleturds and Candlebugs: Symbols of Power and Protection in the Art of Elizabeth Talford Scott," in *Eyewinkers, Tumbleturds and Candlebugs: The Art of Elizabeth Talford Scott*, ed. Maryland Institute College of Art (Baltimore: Maryland Institute College of Art, 1998), 17.

13. Joseph M. Murphy, *Working the Spirit: Ceremonies of the African Diaspora* (Boston: Beacon Press, 1994), 183.

14. See Carole Miller Genshaft, Leslie King-Hammond, Ramona Austin, and Annegreth Nil, "Aesthetic Realities/Artistic Visions: Aminah Brenda Lynn Robinson," in *Symphonic Poem: The Art of Aminah Brenda Lynn Robinson* (New York: Harry N. Abrams, 2002), 45–52.

15. Clarence Majar, *Juba to Jina: A Dictionary of African American Slang* (New York: Random House, 1983), 374–375.

16. Joan E. Gaither, artist statement, in *Choice, Identity, and Layers of Meaning* (Baltimore: Maryland Institute College of Art, 2004).

17. Sherrill, "American Sacred Space," 313.

18. Robert Farris Thompson, *Flash of the Spirit: African and Afro-American Art and Philosophy* (New York: Random House, 1984), 157.

Talking Back

The essays in this section remind us that the centering force or operation has not always been and is not always associated with or represented by texts. Furthermore, "scriptures" do not even always appear in the form of texts. But even when "scriptures" are represented as texts, engagements have not always been strictly in terms of textuality, namely exegesis. In spite of the force of center-ing operations, there have always been vernacular traditions. Such traditions tend to expand greatly the range of understandings about and uses of the textual and of literacy (cf. Henry Louis Gates Jr., *The Signifying Monkey*; Grey Gundaker, *Signs of Diaspora*).[1] Scriptures are not only to be exegeted, namely textually glossed; they can be and are in the vernaculars performed. But insofar as the academic study of religion and theological studies remain for the most part focused on and oriented to textual exegesis, it is fair to ask who's *mis*reading whom? Who is *mis*educated?

The point of the signifying (on) scriptures orientation is to shift focus away from seeking the content-meaning of texts to seeking meaning of the peoples' meaning-seeking operations and practices, their "readings," their signifying acts, and their consequences.

—ed.

NOTES

1. Cf. Henry Louis Gates Jr., *The Signifying Monkey: A Theory of African-American Literary Criticism* (New York: Oxford University Press, 1988); Grey Gundaker, *Signs of Disaspora/ Diaspora of Signs: Literacies, Creolization, and Vernacular Practice in African America* (New York: Oxford University Press, 1986).

PART IV

PSYCHO-SOCIAL-CULTURAL/
POWER NEEDS AND DYNAMICS

17 Differences at Play in the Fields of the Lord

SUSAN F. HARDING

All men are caught in an inescapable network of mutuality.

—Martin Luther King Jr.

The televangelical preachers of the 1980s each emerged out of, embodied, and performed particular lineages within the American evangelical Protestant tradition. Their particular lineages were visible in their attire, audible in their voices and sermons, and legible in their actions and writings.

The Arminian pulse of reversible, repeatable salvation punctuated the testimonies and lives of Pentecostal preachers Jimmy Swaggart and Jim and Tammy Faye Bakker with episodes of moral backsliding, devil wrestling, and deep spiritual crisis. The content of Swaggart's preaching was marbled with fundamentalism in regard to morality and the end times, but his histrionic preaching style was hardcore Pentecostal crusade evangelism. The Bakkers were more pastoral on stage, low-key and chatty, and they took the non-fundamentalist fork in the Pentecostal road, preaching an aggressively "positive gospel."

The charismatic white Southern Baptist Pat Robertson cast his life and life stories in a Calvinist, once-saved-always-saved mold of irreversible salvation infused with the gifts of the Holy Spirit. His faith was tested many times, but he never backslid. He seamlessly performed his special blend of faith in miracles, moral fundamentalism, and apocalypticism as if it were as routine as the nightly news. The fundamental white Southern Baptist Jerry Falwell, the man, his life, and his story, was likewise framed by a Calvinist presumption of irreversible salvation, but one untainted by any Pentecostal-derived spiritual gifts. Falwell's stiff-bodied demeanor and stolid voice conveyed the unambiguous message that God lives in the Word, not the human body.[1] Falwell did leaven his militant Baptist fundamentalist posture, not with Pentecostalism, but by drawing from conservative evangelicalism its more active engagement with "the world."

This kind of account of the distinctive practices of televangelical preachers attempts to understand them as outcomes of their particular theological traditions and church histories. The part is explained, or interpreted, in terms of its whole. Customs, history, and beliefs are the source of characteristic religious behavior and language. A "religion" is thus much like what anthropologist Fredrick Barth refers to as the classic definition of an "ethnic group": "a unit for the reproduction of a shared culture."² Religion and ethnicity in these kinds of accounts are "ideal type" models of recurring empirical content and form that foreground continuity, identity, and internal dynamics. "History," according to this view, "has produced a world of separate peoples, each with their culture and each organized in a society which can be legitimately isolated for description as an island to itself."³

Barth has devoted much of his writing to a critique of the ideal-type model of ethnic groups.⁴ For him, ethnic groups are not based on shared cultures but rather on the play of cultural difference. "To think of ethnicity in relation to one group and its culture is like trying to clap with one hand. The contrast between 'us' and 'others' is what is embedded in the organization of ethnicity: an otherness of the others that is explicitly linked to the assertion of cultural differences."⁵ What is shared among members of an ethnic group is their difference from those around them and the icons and idioms that come to stand for that difference. In this view, what matters is "the ethnic *boundary* that defines the group, not the cultural stuff it encloses."⁶

Arguably, it makes more sense to think of religions as shared cultures than it does ethnic groups. Religions are, after all, composed of organized, institutionalized, and ritualized practices whose outcome, if not express purpose, is to produce and reproduce shared assumptions, knowledge, experience, sentiments, desire—in a word, culture. But Barth's point about the importance of difference and boundary making is still germane. Religions—preachers, faiths, rites, scriptures—do not arise, exist, act, speak, and change as islands unto themselves but only and always in relation to the field of others around them.

The televangelical preachers of the 1980s arose out of and enacted their traditions, but the meaning of their words and actions was also an outcome of the differences, the boundaries, they signaled and signified. When the televangelists spoke their faith in a living savior Jesus Christ, they collectively announced who they were, and also who they were not—not modern, not secular, not theologically liberal. They also performed who they were not in relation to one another, and in relation to often invisible, social, cultural, and religious others. Thinking in terms of scriptural difference as well as scriptural identity makes new sense of practices and details that might otherwise seem unimportant or tangential and reveals additional formative "significant others," some of them recognized, others not.

Jimmy Swaggart's distinctive Pentecostal fundamentalism took some of its shape and substance from the ways he signaled himself as not a fundamentalist in the Baptist mold. The Bakkers' Pentecostalism was not just non-fundamentalist, it was *not-fundamentalist*, hammered out of their continuous, at times flamboyant, not-fundamentalist moves and messages. While Robertson looked and preached in the style of a white Baptist, what he preached was a decidedly not-Baptist, charismatic Pentecostalism. Finally, Falwell's distinctive Baptist fundamentalism emerged out of the myriad ways he pronounced himself decidedly *not charismatic/ pentecostal*.⁷

In the Thomas Road Baptist fundamentalist church, Jerry Falwell stood behind an oversized solid oak pulpit planted front and center on the chancel, read from a sturdy leather-bound Bible that sat upon the pulpit, and preached his sermon in a full-volume, monotonic baritone voice, feet planted firmly in place and using a limited repertoire of small, somewhat choppy, hand gestures.

Contrast this with Pentecostal crusade evangelist Jimmy Swaggart, who left his Plexiglas pulpit in the wings and roamed about the chancel, his flexible Bible open in his hand, often raised and restless as if it were arising out of him or he out of it. His voice and body dramatized his roller-coaster message, one moment loudly denouncing sin, another sobbing in commiseration for all our sins. The two pulpits, their location and substance, the Bibles, their heft and texture, the preachers' voices, their tones and modulations, the preacherly bodies' fluidity, their gestures and movements—these details and cues all have meaning and force in a field of contrasts. Their meanings arise out of what they are not. A fundamental Baptist pastor emerges out of the ways in which he is *not* (among other things) a Pentecostal crusade evangelist—and vice versa.

All religious folk explicitly contrast themselves with certain others, sometimes quite vociferously, but such polemicized differences do not exhaust the range of significant contrasts that shape religious communities. The full range comes into view only by focusing on scriptural difference rather than identity. The fundamental Baptists whom I lived among in Lynchburg, Virginia, in the 1980s, spoke and performed their difference from charismatic and Pentecostal Christians in many ways. Other, less audible and visible, but no less palpable, differences were marked as well, for example the ways in which fundamental Baptists were not-Methodists and not-Catholics.

Figure 17.1 Jerry Falwell. (AP Photo/Stephanie Klein-Davis, File)

Figure 17.2 Jimmy Swaggart.
(AP Photo/Mark Avery)

The Reverend Melvin Campbell, who brought me "under conviction" early on in my stay in Lynchburg, shaped the language he used to witness to me in opposition to a Methodist understanding of salvation and baptism, which he had grown up with and which he, mistakenly, presumed I held.[8] Among these fundamental Baptists, the emphasis on evangelism, soul winning, and the invitation—an explicit request by a pastor or witness to "get saved today"—continuously fashions their opposition to Methodism, whether they speak it aloud or not.

While I heard little explicit anti-Catholicism, I heard and saw much implicit not-Catholicism—from their empty crosses (that display the risen Christ, as opposed to Catholic crucifixes that display Christ's suffering), to their unornamented churches, unliturgical services, and unsacramental sacraments, and to their story of Jesus Christ in which his mother, Mary, hardly figures. I realized how profoundly this contrast shaped the experience as well as the practice of being a fundamental Baptist when Charlotte, my host in Lynchburg, visited me in New York City. As we walked along Fifth Avenue one afternoon, we decided, on a whim, to go into St. Patrick's Cathedral. Charlotte became visibly agitated and disturbed as we walked around the nave looking at the statues of saints and Mary and Christ in the alcoves. She did not, perhaps could not, articulate her distress in the form of a spoken critique, but her body and her emotions registered horror, as if she were witnessing sacrilege, so rooted was her faith in the suppression of the worship of Mary and the saints.

The precise terms of contrast with a scriptural other and the forms of their enactment may shift more quickly and easily than one might expect. As Barth noted in regard to ethnic groups, "the cultural features that signal the boundary may change, and the cultural characteristic of the members may likewise be transformed, indeed even the organizational form of the group may change—yet the fact of continuing dichotomization between members and outsiders allows us to specify the nature of continuity and investigate the change in cultural form and content."[9]

Of course, the primary named significant other of fundamental Baptists, like that of all fundamentalists, was, until the 1980s, "the modern world," including modern theological, as well as a host of social and cultural, practices. Fundamentalist preachers militantly pronounced their differences from both theological liberalism and modern life and separated themselves from those who did not. Church people enacted their not-modernness in their old-fashioned Bible belief, their active evangelism and "spiritual jargon," and their adherence to strict codes of righteous behavior that prohibited such things as gambling, dancing, drinking, smoking, swearing, bowling, listening to rock and roll, reading modern novels, going to the movies, and unsupervised dating.[10] These and other terms of opposition, fashioned during the first half of the twentieth century, held up during the 1950s but began to sway and buckle during the 1960s and 1970s as endless images and stories detailing dramatic changes in their significant other flowed into fundamentalist communities. Some held on tight to the old terms but many, eventually most, fundamentalists started to reimagine their modern other and invent new terms and modalities of contrast.

By the mid-1980s, fundamentalist Baptists under the influence of Jerry Falwell had renamed and substantially reconfigured their most explicit significant other. It was now "secular humanism," which included feminism, the sexual revolution, homosexuality, youth culture, Hollywood, liberalism, universities, public education, the media, and, by and large, the federal government. They remade the boundary between themselves and "the world" in countless micro-practices in which they broke old taboos constraining their interactions with outsiders, claimed new cultural territory, and refashioned themselves in church services, Bible studies, classrooms, families, everyday life, and the public arena. Who they were and what it meant to be a fundamental Baptist changed in the process. Indeed, by the mid-1990s, both Falwell's church and college had undergone an identity-morphing process that replaced much of what had marked them as distinctly fundamentalist and Baptist with more generic "Christian" markers. This deft re-delineation set up a monopolistic spiritual economy in which all those not in their fold were simply "not Christian."

As the boundary changed between these fundamental Baptists and the world, so did their modes of speaking and performing their difference. Through the course of the 1980s, the strict code of behavioral conduct that prohibited fundamentalists from all kinds of "worldly pleasures" gradually disintegrated. The aggressively militant fundamentalist preacher mellowed, and the customary strictures on their associations and affiliations fell away. In place of these distinctive separatist features, new rhetorics and practices arose that fashioned an appropriating and infiltrating posture toward "the world." Difference was no longer performed through distance, but rather through engagement, contest, and conquest.

Whereas Falwell's 1970s Lynchburg Bible College had focused on training students to work in churches and missions, the university it became in the 1980s (Liberty University) trained and prepared them to become middle- and upper-middle-class professionals—public-school teachers, journalists, producers, professors, nurses, doctors, lawyers, and politicians. Christians came to look and in many ways live like their worldly neighbors, but they had a distinctive mission: "to be the salt of the earth, to take a stand in the field that you're in the way only you can." If you are a nurse, "blow the whistle on the abortionist who does the late-term abortion." If you are a filmmaker, make commercially successful Hollywood films with an "underlying Christian philosophy running through them."[11]

At home, Falwell's community enacted their difference by appropriating and "Christianizing" worldly rhetorics and practices. Liberty University occupied a hitherto not-fundamentalist space of the university with unadulterated Bible-based teaching in all academic areas. The Museum of Earth and Life History on campus performed a relentless, at moments parodic, critique of evolutionary theories, and it subordinated the fossil record to the Bible in the form of creation science.

Figure 17.3 *The Fundamentalist Journal.*

The *Fundamentalist Journal*, which Falwell's Old-Time Gospel Hour Ministries published from 1982 to 1989, was *Time* magazine and the *Saturday Evening Post* after a faith-change operation. The "Liberty Godparent Home" took up the social form of the home for unwed mothers and converted it into a staging ground for the battle against feminist story lines about women in need of abortions. Every Halloween in Lynchburg, "Scaremare" transmogrified the secular haunted house into an evangelistic outreach.

In effect, during the 1980s, fundamental Baptists committed themselves to transgressing the very social and cultural taboos that had defined them for decades, yet they saw themselves as essentially the same because the dichotomy between them and their worldly other was as, or perhaps even more, crystal clear than ever. The dichotomy no longer depended on separation and distance but, on the contrary, on acts of rhetorical and ritual domination that brought fundamental Baptists into intimate contact with what they reviled and gave them occasion to continuously enact their difference and moral superiority.

The field of significant contrasts out of which a religious community emerges is of course not limited to contrasts with other religions. Cultural and political others come into the play of difference, as do social others defined in terms of race, ethnicity, and class.

Religious communities in America are famously segregated. Among the factors often cited to account for this are the distinctive styles of worship and preaching associated with racially different churches, stylistic differences that are sometimes cited as barriers to more integrated congregations. But what this view obscures is the extent to which distinctive scriptural practices produce racialized identities. The fundamental Baptists I sat among on many Sundays in Lynchburg were performing whiteness as much as they were their faith, not by what they said about blacks, but by how their practices signified not-black.

During the 1950s and 1960s, Jerry Falwell and his fellow fundamental Baptist preachers defended segregation and its "biblical basis." In the early 1970s, he quietly dropped these positions as he reached more aggressively beyond his region to fashion a national constituency for his college, media ministry, and nascent moral movement. A few blacks joined his church over the years, and by the 1990s many young blacks were being recruited to come to his university on sports scholarships. In this literal, if limited, sense then, Falwell integrated his community. According to historian Paul Harvey, Falwell, along with many other white-supremacist preachers, "capitulated" on the matter of racial inequality, "choosing to focus their efforts instead on more contemporary (and successful) conservative themes such as family values, the defense of 'life,' and millennialist visions. Patriarchy replaced race as the defining principle of God-ordained inequality."[12]

Officially, in terms of admission policies and public declarations, fundamental Baptists in Falwell's fold integrated, but, the question of how race continued, and continues, to fashion their identity reopens when we attend to the implicit play of difference. In terms of many of their practices, they continue as ever to mark themselves as white by performing themselves as not-black.

In his polemic of biblical inerrancy, Jerry Falwell espouses versions of God and biblical truth not in evidence in African American Christianity. He and his people vigorously oppose the kind of social critique and social gospel embedded in so much black preaching, regardless of whether it manifests itself in political activism.[13] In terms of preaching style, the same stiff, didactic, and emotionally flat qualities that distinguish fundamental Baptists from Pentecostals also mark them off from blacks—not coincidently, because Pentecostalism was fashioned out of a merger of African American and holiness styles. And the sparse, stilted, disembodied music and worship styles of fundamental Baptists are aggressively white insofar as they signify, if only unconsciously, not-black.

These contrasts are especially striking when comparing black Baptists to white fundamental Baptists. Both communities derive historically from the same Baptist organization and their doctrinal statements are almost identical, yet they have evolved radically contrasting scriptural practices. One may think of these differences as the effects of their distinct histories, cultures, and socioeconomic and political conditions. But no faith is an island. Distinctive features are always also dialogic; they emerge and have meaning in a field of differences. Fundamental Baptist scriptural practices make them "white," culturally speaking, because they contrast dramatically with black Baptist and African American scriptural practices, which in turn make them "black" by dent of signifying not-white.[14] Thus, while race did lose salience as a manifest identity marker among fundamental Baptists, it still operates with much the same force through these latent, implicit signifying practices.

Shifts in the field of significant others that define a religious community necessarily cause shifts in that community. It is easy to think of these adjustments as "reactions" to changes taking place outside the community, but significant others—and the significance of others—are already inside and constitutive of the community. Fundamental Baptists arise out of practices that signify not-others in such a way that others, or rather how they are signified, become part of who they are. Fundamental Baptists underwent radical transformations in the final decades of the twentieth century in spite of their avowed aversion to change because the cultural others—most notably blacks and "moderns"—on whom they depended to define themselves, and whom they had in many ways internalized, radically transformed themselves.

Scriptural communities are in this way like M. M. Bakhtin's speech genres: less things in themselves than they are in-between, always interstitial, overlapping, intersecting, things. On the one hand, every sphere of human activity develops its own type of utterance, or speech genre, distinct in content, style, and compositional structure. On the other, speech genres interpenetrate and "absorb and digest" elements from other genres to varying degrees, which leads to "a more or less fundamental and continuous restructuring and renewal of speech genres."[15] Our speech and our writings, including our creative works, are "filled with others' words, varying degrees of otherness" as much as "our-own-ness." "These words of others carry with them their own expression, their own evaluative tone, which we assimilate, rework, and re-accentuate."[16]

I have stressed the not-other signifying practices so far, the ones that say, "we are not them," but scriptural communities are generated out of more positive appropriations and assimilations of others as well.

As a nationally renowned public speaker, Jerry Falwell dexterously mixed and matched voices to remake, expand, and diversify his reputation and audience. In crafting his public postures on political and moral issues, he borrowed language from the conservative side of debates within evangelicalism and blended it with certain fundamentalist distinguishing features while discarding others. Falwell moved so much in this direction that evangelicalism switched from being a negative to a positive cultural other; indeed by the turn of the century he and his community considered themselves evangelicals more than fundamentalists. Falwell's moral rhetorics on issues such as abortion, homosexuality, and gay marriage also enabled him to enter into public alliances with socially conservative Catholics, Mormons, and African American Protestants, affiliations unthinkable only a few years before and still difficult to process given the myriad ways difference from, even aversion to, those communities continues to be signified by fundamentalist Baptist practices.

Great preachers and orators are all masters of multiple voices. The language with which Martin Luther King Jr. led the civil rights movement was in some ways

Figure 17.4 Martin Luther King Jr. (AP Photo/Jack Thornell)

secular but also always sermonic. "The substance of his sermons he translated into civil religious addresses and fiery mass-meeting speeches, but it was always preaching that he was doing."[17] King's preaching joined two traditions: an Afro-Baptist evangelical tradition and a predominantly white liberal Protestant social-gospel tradition. King did not invent this conjuncture of traditions—he inherited it from his mentors—but it was King who enlarged, electrified, and transfigured the mixed genre and used it "to propel and interpret a vast social upheaval" during the course of his public life.[18]

King drew from black and liberal pulpits selectively. One thing he discarded from the liberal tradition was "its deep and unresolved ambivalence about homiletic borrowing," which interrupted the unselfconscious free flow of oral and written materials among its preachers.[19] King's Afro-Baptist tradition harbored no such ambivalence and gave him license not only to circulate its own materials but also to cobble them together with those of other traditions, regardless of their conventions of exchange. King also rejected the critical approaches to the Bible in favor of the Baptist evangelical understanding of the Bible as a book of truths. And he rejected white liberal Protestantism's preference for topical sermons in favor of the black pulpit's preference for sermons that sounded more like "musical dramas," like "cultic performances of a biblical text," like "emotionally curved" religious vocal events.[20] At the same time King played down some of the formal and expressive strategies of the black pulpit—such as associationally structured sermons—and accepted and customized others from the liberal pulpit—such as formal schemes or templates for organizing sermons.[21]

King did not "translate black demands into a white universe."[22] Rather he created a universe in which blacks and whites heard differently his messages of justice and deliverance. Nor did he "merge" two sermonic voices or traditions. He re-voiced both and entwined them; both traditions were audible. They retained their own orientations and were placed in dynamic tension with each other. In effect, King integrated black and white in his preaching without assimilating one to the other. The civil rights movement took place in his speech as well as in movement meetings, church pews, streets, courthouses, jail cells, schools, lunch counters, and voting booths. Again, black and white pulpits were integrated not in the sense of fused, but in the sense of juxtaposed, interacting, relating, and exchanging.

Nor did King submit to a white code in order to achieve a black end, a formulation that suggests he reproduced white hegemony even as he contested it, as if his central project was to convince his white audience that black demands were just. If anything, he submitted the white code to black ends in order to help "inspire his black audience to disobey unjust laws."[23] The dynamics between the two voices, black and white, in his preaching also divided his white audience, viscerally as well as politically. As much as his preaching enabled some white liberals to hear and join the cause of civil rights, it excluded many theologically conservative whites who were as, if not more, antipathetic to his style of preaching as to the cause of racial justice.

As effectively as preacherly voices and styles create insiders, they create outsiders. The same goes for the whole range of practices that define scriptural communities. They are all radically enmeshed and implicated in their significant others, those they disdain as much as those they esteem. Even the most separatist communities are more like networks than islands, openwork fabrics of signified relations to others, heterogeneous mixes of self-ascribed differences in constant flux. The scriptural world is, as anthropologist Talal Asad describes the world in general, "divided into overlapping, fragmented cultures, hybrid selves, continuously dissolving and emerging social states."[24] Sameness is a transitory and illusory by-product of difference making, and cultural boundaries between self and other are always evidence of others inside ourselves.

NOTES

1. Outsiders often called Falwell and his church people "fundamentalists" or "fundamentalist Baptists," but Falwell, at least when he was offstage, and his church people used the term "fundamental Baptists." For further discussion of the term "fundamentalist" and its relatives, see "A Guide to Terms" in Susan F. Harding, *The Book of Jerry Falwell: Fundamentalist Language and Politics* (Princeton, NJ: Princeton University Press, 2000).

2. Fredrik Barth, "Ethnicity and the Concept of Culture," (seminar, Weatherhead Center for International Affairs, Program on Nonviolent Sanctions and Cultural Survival Seminar, Cambridge, MA, February 23, 1995), http://www.wcfia.harvard.edu/ponsacs/seminars/Synopses/s95barth.htm.

3. Fredrik Barth, *Ethnic Groups and Boundaries: the Social Organization of Cultural Difference* (Prospect Heights, IL: Waveland Press, 1969), 11.

4. I am relying on the work of Fredrik Barth here, but Pierre Bordieu and Michelle Lamont develop similar critiques and alternative models with respect to class. Matt Wray applies their ideas to rethink "race" in "Symbolic Boundaries, Social Conflict, and Cultural Power: Some Possible Lessons for Cultural Studies" (unpublished manuscript, 2004).

5. Barth, "Ethnicity and the Concept of Culture."

6. Barth, *Ethnic Groups*, 15.

7. When Falwell "took over" the Bakkers' PTL Club and Heritage USA theme park, these efforts reached new peaks. He wanted to assure Pentecostal park visitors that he did not scorn their forms of recreation, so he slid down the three-story Typhoon waterslide, but, assuring his fundamental Baptist folk at home that he was just as *not-Pentecostal* as ever, he took the plunge with his arms crossed at his chest and dressed in a buttoned-up business suit (Harding, *The Book of Jerry Falwell*, 263–264).

8. See Harding, *The Book of Jerry Falwell*, 41.

9. Barth, *Ethnic Groups*, 14.

10. Patricia Klein et al. *Growing Up Born-Again: A Whimsical Look at the Blessings and Tribulations of Growing Up Born-Again* (Old Tappan, NJ: Fleming H. Revell Company Publishers, 1987) is the best source on the cultural and religious particularities of the fundamental Christian, white, middle-American church experience. Written by five evangelicals who were raised fundamentalist, it is also funny and fun to read. For another fondly critical insider look at fundamentalism, see my discussion of Frankie Schaeffer's 1982 sermon at Liberty Chapel in *The Book of Jerry Falwell*—I take the term "spiritual jargon" from his sermon.

11. The phrases come from Frankie Schaeffer's 1982 sermon at Liberty Chapel, discussed in *The Book of Jerry Falwell*.

12. Paul Harvey, "Racism, Biracialism, and Interracialism in the Southern Religious Experience," in *Freedom's Coming: Religion, Race, and Culture in the South, 1860–2000* (Berkeley: University of California Press, forthcoming).

13. See, for example, Gayraud S. Wilmore's *Black Religion and Black Radicalism* (Maryknoll, NY: Orbis Books, 1998), which makes a strong case for the powerful and persistent, if often suppressed, radicalism of black Christianity throughout its history in America.

14. Black Baptists have always been aware of the racial dimension in their scriptural practices. See, for example, James Melvin Washington, *Frustrated Fellowship: The Black Baptist for Social Power* (Macon, GA: Mercer, 1986).

15. M. M. Bakhtin, *Speech Genres and Other Late Essays* (Austin: University of Texas Press, 1986), 60, 62, 68.

16. Ibid., 89.

17. Richard Lischer, *The Preacher King: Martin Luther King, Jr. and the Word That Moved America* (Oxford: Oxford University Press, 1995).

18. Lischer, *The Preacher King*, 68; Keith Miller, *The Voice of Deliverance: The Language of Martin Luther King, Jr. and Its Sources* (New York: The Free Press, 1992), 12. B. E. Mays, president of Morehouse College, was King's first great mentor in this regard. Mays had the "hypnotic voice" of a powerful preacher, but he preached stewardship, engagement, liberation through knowledge, and the black church's mission as an instrument of social protest (Stephen Oates, *Let the Trumpet Sound: The Life of Martin Luther King, Jr.* [New York: HarperCollins, 1982], 19–20).

19. Miller, *The Voice of Deliverance*, 125.

20. Lischer, *The Preacher King*, 65, 66, 8, 6.

21. Ibid., 65.

22. Miller, *The Voice of Deliverance*, 83. Keith Miller describes King's accomplishment as "voice merging," a fusion of two traditions, which enabled him to "translate black demands into a white universe." In effect, Miller describes King as belonging to the black pulpit and *borrowing* from the white pulpit. Both Michael Eric Dyson and Richard Lischer rework Miller's formulation, arguing that King did not "borrow" from liberal Protestantism. He possessed it as much as his black tradition. He appropriated, retuned, swerved, and remixed materials from both traditions.

23. Michael Eric Dyson, *I May Not Get There With You: The True Martin Luther King, Jr.* (New York: The Free Press, 2000).

24. Talad Asad, *Formations of the Secular: Christianity, Islam, Modernity* (Stanford, CA: Stanford University Press, 2003), 15. See also Henry Goldschmidt and Elizabeth McAlister, eds., *Race, Nation, and Religion in the Americas* (New York: Oxford University Press, 2004).

18 *American Samson*

BIBLICAL READING
AND NATIONAL ORIGINS

LAURA E. DONALDSON

The popular 1991 film *Robin Hood: Prince of Thieves* opens with a panoramic sweep of Muslim Jerusalem in 1194, five years after Richard the Lionheart's failed Crusade to retake that city in the name of Christianity. Immediately following this scene, the film jump cuts to a dark prison in which a sword-wielding Arab guard amputates and then casually tosses aside the hand of a screaming white—and presumably British—man. Viewers soon discover that he was punished in this manner because he allegedly stole another inmate's loaf of bread. After another English prisoner denies stealing bread, the guard curtly gives the order to "cut off the infidel's hand." Through this visual dialogue, *Robin Hood* overtly demonizes Muslims as barbarically literal interpreters of the Bible[1]: from the Hebrew Testament, it recalls an eye for an eye and from the Gospel of Mark, "If your hand causes you to stumble, cut it off; it is better for you to enter life maimed than to have two hands and to go to hell, to the unquenchable fire" Mark 9:43, NRSV). In the wake of September 11, 2001, and the subsequent war on "Islamic terrorists," this stereotype of Muslims has escalated, but now it is articulated by more serious voices than those of characters in Hollywood action films. Consider, for example, the words of Patricia Chang, the academic director of a post-9/11 State Department program, the purpose of which is to bring Muslim scholars to the United States and expose them to American society's "pluralistic" nurturing of faith traditions: "Textual literalism is an important part of Islamic culture . . . [Muslims] learn Arabic by reading the Qur'an. This means that a traditional religious education provides no independent language skills with which to read the text critically. This makes issues of interpretation difficult, if not impossible, to discuss."[2] Like *Robin Hood*'s Muslim guards, Chang constructs Muslim readers of the Qur'an as both irrational and reductionist interpreters of their sacred text.

If the consequences of this distorted perception were not so dangerous, one could easily dismiss it as just more myopic thinking about religious and cultural "others." Those North Americans who espouse negative or fearful attitudes toward Islam because of its alleged literalism, however, would benefit from examining their continent's own history of biblical literalism—and particularly its literalist interpretation of the particular verses evoked by *Robin Hood*[3] and Chang. Most readers would view the biblical passage's insistence on preventive self-mutilation as a rhetorical hyperbole emphasizing the necessity of dealing with potential problems before they become actual ones[4]—unless, of course, you happened to be both American Indian and Christian in the seventeenth-century, North American colony of Massachusetts Bay. The experience of the Ninnimissinuok (in English, the Massachusett) who populated Natick, the first of John Eliot's "Praying Towns," reveals that a verbatim interpretation of Mark 9:43–48 (and its corollary in Matthew) was crucial both to the Puritan conversion of Turtle Island's Native peoples as well as the nascent ideology of America as a biblical nation.

"Come Over and Help Us"

Ironically, or perhaps symptomatically, the Puritan colony of Massachusetts Bay distanced itself from Native converts by adopting an analogical rather than literalist hermeneutic to encapsulate its project of nation building. At the heart of this imagined theological community was the plea of America's indigenous peoples to "come over and help us," which was forever immortalized in the 1629 Great Seal of Massachusetts Bay. The colony's seventeenth-century citizens would have certainly recognized the plea as a phrase from Acts 16:9–10, in which a Macedonian man appears in a vision to Paul. According to the Luke, Paul's companion on that journey, "when he had seen the vision, we immediately tried to cross over to Macedonia, being convinced that God had called us to proclaim the good news to them." Like Paul, the citizens of Massachusetts Bay would proclaim the Gospel to their colony's Indians. Unlike Paul, though, it would take Massachusetts Bay more than forty years to respond to their vision—a scandalous delay of what many considered the most important part of their mission. In this instance of traveling visions, if not traveling theory, the Puritan fathers established an interpretive asymmetry between their own analogical hermeneutics and Indian literalism that becomes crucial to the origin of the entity known as "the United States."

When they finally did "come over and help us," the colony's Puritan elders adopted an "affective model" of evangelism,[5] a process that John and Jean Comaroff more resonantly describe as "missionary mimesis." In their massive study of colonial evangelism in southern Africa, the Comaroffs define missionary mimesis as the conviction that adopting British customs and ways of life would subsequently lead Native peoples to embrace Christian beliefs.[6] It was his fervent belief in this process that moved John Eliot to petition the Massachusetts Bay government for funds to establish Natick, the first "town"—or in retrospect, a restrictive reservation—for Christian Indians. Located twenty-five miles outside Boston, Natick's nearly two thousand acres lay near the new Puritan settlement of Dedham and the old Massachusett town of Nonantum, the site of Eliot's initial missionary efforts. After Natick's establishment in 1651, Eliot at once imposed a form of biblical mimesis that influenced every aspect of town structure, including its political leadership. As a case in point, the model for Natick's governance mimicked Jethro's commandment to Moses in Exodus 18:25–26b to choose "able men from all Israel" and appoint them "as officers over thousands, hundreds, fifties, and tens." On

August 6, 1651, Eliot presumably stood in for Moses and supervised an election in which eligible Massachusett men voted to select one ruler of a hundred, two rulers of fifty, and ten rulers of ten.[7] In contrast to literary mimesis, however, where art supposedly reflects life, Eliot's mimesis inverted this relationship so that "life" (or more accurately, Natick's social order) mirrored the biblical text. This inversion also extended to the much more intimate realm of the Native body.

Like many of his Puritan counterparts, Eliot believed that Indians could not become true Christians until they had been "reduced" to civility (i.e., adopted the new social skin of anglicized dress as well as other Europeanized bodily disciplines):

> Not only did the early modern English believe that identity is created, or assumed, or assigned and communicated to the world through signs, but they also believed in the psychological power of donning a role. Once a role was taken up, and one's outward aspect tailored to the part, a person's actions were subtly molded to its demands. English writers describing colonial life constantly attested to their belief in the link between changes in clothing and in personality.[8]

Besides clothing, one of the most important masculine signs of a Christian Indian was closely cropped hair. As historian James Axtell has observed, a willingness to cut his long black hair indicated the male convert's desire to "kill the Indian in himself and to assume a new persona modeled upon the meek, submissive Christ of the white man's Black Book."[9] Although relatively little is known about the seventeenth-century tonsorial practices of the Massachusetts, one can glean some circumstantial hypotheses from closely related and more extensively documented Algonquian-speaking cultures. Among the Chesapeake Algonquians known as the Powhatan, for example, men who were not *pawwaws* (priests) wore their hair asymmetrically—very long on the left side and very short on the right—for both pragmatic and religious reasons. Practically, wearing short hair on the right prevented it from becoming tangled in bows when hunting or engaged in military conflicts;[10] spiritually, this asymmetry expressed men's relationship to Okeus, the Powhatans' most powerful and feared sacred being.

Uttamatomakkin, a Powhatan *pawwaw*, confirmed this to interviewer Samuel Purchas during a London sojourn with his famous sister-in-law, Pocahontas (then Mrs. Rebecca Rolfe). According to Uttamatomakkin, Okeus appeared to the Powhatan with a long left lock hanging down nearly to his foot,[11] and since that appearance, Powhatan men have adopted a similar style. Indeed, Uttamatomakkin even objected to Purchas that, in his eyes, Jesus lacked credibility because "he had not taught us [Christians] so to weare our haire."[12] William Wood's 1634 pamphlet *New England's Prospect* unwittingly noted a close connection between the Powhatan and the Massachusett when he described how Ninnimissinuok warriors usually wore their hair "long on one side, the other side being cut short like a screw."[13] The sacred symbolism of a long left lock constituted only one of the reasons that seventeenth-century Algonquian men, and American Indian peoples more generally, regarded hair as one of the most potent markers of age-related (and, I would add, gender-related) status and of passage from one status to another.[14] It was also why the regulation of Native men's hairstyles loomed so large in Eliot's Praying Towns. Although the Comaroffs address a different era (the nineteenth century) and a different area of the world (southern Africa), their insight that colonial evangelism made the Native body a crucial terrain on which the battle for Christianity would be fought—and on which personal identity would be "re-formed, re-placed, re-inhabited"[15]—seems equally appropriate to the earlier context of Puritan North America.

At its 1646 general session, the Massachusetts Bay General Court enacted two directives: first, that Eliot and his ecclesiastical partners secure a suitable land base for Christian Indians; and second, that they establish a legal and social code (the "Nonantum Code") for the benefit of their Native charges. Not surprisingly, the Nonantum Code's regulations focused most closely on issues of domestic relations and work habits, Native sexuality, and, finally, hairstyle.[16] It subjected Ninnimissinuok men who wore long hair, along with women who refused to restrain theirs, to fines of five shillings. Eliot condemned these hirsute lapses as not only transgressions of normative Euro-American gender identities, but also expressions of moral decadence.[17] Richard Cogley comments that Eliot manifested a widespread prejudice of the period when he associated Native men's long hair with two other objects of Puritan disdain—"lazy, self-indulgent Anglicans and unkempt, undisciplined frontiersmen."[18] If Eliot regarded longhaired Native men with contempt, those Massachusett who refused the barber's shears often ridiculed male members of their community who submitted: "Another [Ninnimissinuok man] complained of other *Indians* that did revile them, and call them Rogues and such like speeches for cutting off their Locks, and for cutting their Haire in a modest manner as the New-English generally doe; for since the word hath begun to worke upon their hearts, they have discerned the vanitie and pride which they placed in their haire, and have therefore of their owne accord (none speaking to them that we know of) cut it modestly."[19] The likelihood that masculine Algonquian hairstyles symbolized a sacred relationship persuasively contests this author's presumption of "vanitie and pride" as the primary motive for long hair; his supposition that Ninnimissinuok men cut their hair "of their owne accord," however, raises the vexed (and vast) issue of Native agency. This volitional account of Massachusett men's haircutting links to a more general view that discounts the powerful and seemingly inescapable influences of colonialism, race, and gender on Native peoples. Rather than offer an abstract deconstruction of this position, however, I will problematize it instead through the dramatic, and frequently moving, story of Monequassun, a Praying Indian who became the first schoolmaster of Natick.

"They Should Looke Onely into the Scriptures"

I have instructed them [the residents of Natick], that they should looke onely into the Scriptures, and out of the word of God fetch all their Wisedome,

Lawes, and Government, and so shall they bee the Lords People, and the Lord above shall Reigne over them, and governe them in all things by the word of his mouth. (John Eliot, "Strengthe out of Weakness")[20]

Monequasson was a Neponset Indian who moved to Natick from the village of Cohannet. In his confession of faith before Puritan leaders deciding whether the residents of Natick were ready to establish a "gathered" church (they weren't), Monequasson admitted that he initially scorned praying to the white man's God. Later, when the sachem Cutshmekin declared the village of Cohannet a "praying" one, Monequasson decided that he loved his ancestral home too much to leave: "I still hated praying, and I did think of running away, because I cared not for praying to God; but afterwards . . . I prayed not for the love of God, but for love of the place I lived in."[21] This statement implies that Monequasson originally became a Praying Indian so that he could retain his traditional Neponset relationship to the place of his ancestors—an immediate challenge to those who interpret conversion as the rejection of Native identity and acceptance of assimilation to Christianity. After making this decision, he decided to "learne the Catechisme on the lecture daies" and quickly became a "teacher" (i.e., an unlicensed preacher whom Eliot chose to exhort Natick's residents on biblical matters).[22] In *Tears of Repentance* (1653), the collection of Natick faith confessions that Eliot compiled to raise missionary funds, Monequasson's several testimonies raise crucial questions about biblical reading in Eliot's work among the Massachusett.

In the first confession, Monequasson emphasizes his struggle over staying at Cohannet, his lapses from Christian teaching, his search for wisdom, and his desire for repentance; nowhere, however, does he mention the status of his hair or the verses from Mark 9:43–48. The second, more lengthy, confession significantly revises the first; this testimony only mentions in passing the struggle over staying at Cohannet, and it includes new material concerning Monequasson's attempts to become literate in English as well as far more discourse and anxiety about sin. It also contains the following troubling anecdote:

> Afterward I heard that Word, That it is a shame for a man to wear long hair, and that there was no such custom in the Churches. At first I thought I loved not long hair, but I did, and found it very hard to cut it off; and then I prayed to God to pardon that sin also . . . Afterward I heard that word, *If thy right food offend thee, cut it off, or they right hand, or they right eye; its better to go to Heaven with one foot, or hand, or eye, than having both to go to Hell;* then I thought my hair had been a stumbling to me, therefore I cut it off, and grieved for this sin and prayed for pardon.[23]

According to Axtell, the major sin of long hair—whether Indian or English—was pride;[24] like John Eliot and the majority of Massachusetts Bay colonists, then, Axtell would blame Monequassun's reluctance to cut his hair on the character flaw of "vanitie." Monequasson's supposed hirsute vanity combined with Eliot's dictum to look only to the scriptures produced a literalist "hearing" of Jesus's words and an assimilative act of haircutting. In *Missionary Conquest* (1993), George Tinker identifies two destructive consequences of acts such as Monequasson's: they changed the self-identity and self-esteem of the converts, and they negatively affected the general cohesion and social organization of Indian peoples.[25] For Tinker, Eliot and other Christian missionaries were always collaborators in genocide who efficaciously "imposed" their values, beliefs, and theologies on Native cultures—or, to use Axtell's metaphor, who successfully staged Christianity's "invasion within." This focus on the violence underwriting colonial evangelism surely provides a necessary corrective to the triumphalist view of Christian missions that has so long dominated U.S. historical perspectives. Yet scholars have recently begun to challenge the interpretation of Native peoples as always only victims of missionary imperialism and have instead focused on American Indians' pragmatic appropriations of Christianity under the harsh conditions of colonization.

For example, some scholars have observed that the participation of the Massachusett in Eliot's Praying Towns provided a necessary step in maintaining a legal, social, and economic status as a Native American community.[26] Jean O'Brien (Kehoe) more particularly remarks that the public confessions of the Natick Indians articulated their hope that "the crucial nexus of personal relationships, kinship, community, and land could be preserved through English Calvinism. Coming to Natick would involve cultural compromises, but also offered attractive options in the context of aggressive English expansion."[27] Others have noted that much of Christianity's attraction was due to the massive disruptions triggered in early-seventeenth-century Massachusett society by diseases such as measles, typhus, dysentery, and even the common cold. Those who managed to survive these pandemics confronted an acute experiential crisis due to healing techniques that failed to work, the sudden disappearance of caregiving infrastructures, and the impossibility of proper burial for many victims.[28] In addition to Christianity's connection to European medical technologies, the besieged and decimated Ninnimissinuok likely perceived participation in Natick and other Praying Towns as a means of reconstituting their rapidly disintegrating communities. These revisionary perspectives might consequently interpret Monequasson's decision to become a "cuthair" as a regrettable but necessary step in the process of salvaging a compromised but still extant Neponset social, political, and cultural network. Nevertheless, the sign of Monequasson's short, or one might even say "amputated," hair continues to haunt me—and the images that I chose to evoke Monequasson's tonsorial dilemma yield important clues about why.

Figures 18.1 and 18.2 are not of Monequasson, but rather a young Navajo man named Tom Torlino, who matriculated at the Carlisle Indian School on October 21, 1882.[29] The first photo shows Tom on the day of his entrance into Carlisle, and the second, Tom after three years of subjection to Carlisle's pedagogical motto, "kill the Indian and save the man." Although this pictorial pair is perhaps the most widely circulated visual representation of government boarding schools and their culturecidal impact on Native students, very little is known of the human subject. According to the historical record, however, American Indians who arrived

Figure 18.1 Before: Tom Torlino, Navajo (1879). Courtesy of the National Anthropological Archives.

at Carlisle (and other boarding schools) did not do so voluntarily, and once they were students, they underwent a compulsory assimilation process that included the assignment of Euro-American names, the donning of Euro-American dress, the exclusive speaking of English, and the cutting of both girls' and boys' long hair. In this regard, the Torlino photographs might seem a strange choice to stand in for Monequasson—after all, unlike Tom Torlino, Monequasson made his own "choice" to become a "cuthair" and a Praying Indian. Or did he? As Talal Asad comments in *Genealogies of Religion* (1993), "even inmates of a concentration camp are able, in this sense, to live by their own cultural logic. But one may be forgiven for doubting that they are *therefore* making their own history."[30] To extend Asad's example, even in the displaced and detribalized context of a Praying Town, Monequasson discovered ways of assigning local meaning to forces beyond his control and making decisions about biblical meaning that were situated within a

Figure 18.2 After: Tom Torlino, Carlisle Indian School student (1879). Courtesy of the National Anthropological Archives.

larger traumatic history. But it is precisely this recognition of trauma that too often goes unremarked in the more positive revisions of Praying Indians' agency.

I would argue that Monequasson's haircutting connoted much more than Christian acculturation or a conscious act done "of his own accord": it is instead an ambivalent gesture connoting both agency and trauma—not only for the wife and child that Monequasson had recently lost to yet another "bloody flux," but also for a way of life rendered impossible by the coming of the whites. Edward Winslow reported in *Good Newes from New England* that when mourning, a Native father from the nearby colony of Plymouth would "cut his haire and disfigure him-selfe very much in token of sorrow."[31] Other sources indicate that for Algonquian cultures more generally, chopping off one's hair was also a sign of humiliation.[32] Archival evidence further suggests that Algonquian men regarded the loss of their long left lock as a form of emasculation. In his memoirs, Henry Spelman relates that before the Powhatan executed male criminals, they cut off their long lock—a custom that Helen Rountree declares punitively deprived "the men of their manhood."[33] Monequasson's conclusion that Mark 9:43–48 (and Matthew 8:8–9) required him to remove the stumbling (b)lock of his hair not only complicates any views of his haircutting as a simple expression of agency but also links him to the biblical Samson, another figure with problematic hair.

Thanks to Cecil B. DeMille's Hollywood epic *Samson and Delilah* (released in 1949 and starring Victor Mature and Hedy Lamarr), if not with the actual text of the Bible, most North Americans are familiar with the story of Samson, his hair, and Delilah. Although the narrative of Samson is lengthy, complex, and far beyond the scope of this short essay to explicate completely, its protagonist does illuminate the predicament of Monequasson as well as the meaning of my essay's title, "American Samson." Like Monequasson, Samson's long hair is the literal as well as metaphorical source of his strength. It is deeply connected to his masculinity and to his religious status as a Nazirite.[34] As Samson himself reveals, however, "if my head were shaved, then my strength would leave me; I would become weak, and be like anyone else" (Judges 16:17b, NRSV). In *Lethal Love: Feminist Literary Readings of Biblical Love Stories*, Mieke Bal draws a connection between the shaving of Samson's hair and Freud's classification of haircutting as a symbol of castration, the ultimate form of emasculation. One need not accept this psychoanalytic framework to understand the point that Samson's hair was an important source of his male identity and that the loss of it therefore meant the demise of his gendered status. It also meant losing his sacred status because Samson's hair marked him as devoted to the Nazirites, a religious order that required abstaining from alcohol and haircutting. Like the severed hair of Monequasson, then, the shaved tresses of the biblical Samson signifies a profound social as well as sacred disruption.

Although Samson's story parallels Tom Torlino's in the nonvoluntary nature of this disruption (Delilah calls a man to shave off the seven locks of his head), I hope I have suggested some significant ways in which the same can be said of Monequasson. Encouraged by John Eliot's literalist scriptural ethic, he reached a "voluntary" decision about how he must answer the urgent and disturbing exhortations of Mark's Jesus. It was a decision that was saturated with personal and historical trauma, however, and represented an agonizing dilemma for this conflicted and deeply emotional Neponset man. Unfortunately, after all was said and done, it did not ultimately shield him or his people from the larger realities of culturecide and genocide. It is for this reason that Monequasson (the figure whom I have named "American Samson") offers an important corrective—not only to those who move too quickly to assumptions of "Native agency" but also to those who have privileged Adam, rather than Samson, as the American icon of choice.

American Samson

Scriptural reading—and in particular, the Hebrew Testament's stories about men—remains one of the most significant sources for the mythology of America as a "biblical nation." While North America's Puritan fathers imagined themselves as Moses leading the Israelites into the promised land, later generations favored Adam as a more accurate icon for the newly formed United States. In his classic study *The American Adam* (1955), R.W.B. Lewis noted that in the eighteenth and nineteenth centuries, the figure of Adam before the Fall embodied that promise and possibility so crucial to architects of the nascent United States. Lewis argued that through this prelapsarian Adam, innocence rather than sinfulness became the hallmark of American character; he also conjured the nation as an individual emancipated from history and undefiled by the usual inheritances of ancestry and race.[35] Practitioners of the "new American Studies" have rightly questioned the appropriateness of Adam as the quintessential symbol of "Americanness." Among its many failings, the Edenic American Adam facilitates a profound imperialist nostalgia toward the Native peoples of Turtle Island: his innocence denies the nation's culpability for colonizing American Indians while it simultaneously laments the demise of indigenous cultures. Small wonder, then, that American Samson, rather than American Adam, seems a more suitable symbolization of North America. This is only one of many lessons that one can learn from the sign of Monequassun's hair. Others include the complex interaction of biblical and social texts, as well as the necessity of developing a richer theological and theoretical vocabulary to describe Native "agency." Most important, however, Monequasson—the American Samson— teaches us about the heartbreaking, and sometimes intolerably contradictory, acts of biblical reading that constitute American history.

NOTES

1. The updated story in which Robin of Loxley (Kevin Costner) is saved by and befriends Azim, a "Moorish" prisoner (Morgan Freeman), does not change this analysis. Azim is also a victim of Islamic law and his ethnicity as well as visual appearance suggests a significant difference from the Arab guards.

2. See Patricia M. Y. Chang, "Puzzled by Pluralism: Muslim Visitors Question the American Way" *Christian Century*, September 6, 2003, 8.

3. Matthew 5:29–30, 8:8–9, and Mark 9:43–48.

4. See for example, Mark Allan Powell, "Matthew," *The Harper Collins Bible Commentary*, ed. J. L. Mays (San Francisco: Harper, 2000), 876.

5. Michael P. Clark, ed., *The Eliot Tracts* (Westport, CT: Praeger, 2003), 25.

6. Jean and John Comaroff, *The Dialectics of Modernity on a South African Frontier*, vol. 2 of *Of Revelation and Revolution* (Chicago: The University of Chicago Press, 1997), 292–293.

7. In this election, Cutshamekin, the sachem of Nonantum, was elected the leader of the hundred; Waban, who had not been a sachem in Massachusett society, was elected one of two leaders of fifty; Thomas Speene and Peter were among the ten leaders of ten.

8. Karen Ordahl Kupperman, *Indians and English: Facing Off in Early America* (Ithaca, NY: Cornell University Press, 2000), 71.

9. James Axtell, *The Invasion Within: The Contest of Cultures in Colonial North America* (New York: Oxford University Press, 1985), 174.

10. Henry Spelman, a young hostage left among Powhatan's people by John Smith, reported that men wear their hair short on the right side so that "it might not hinder them by flapping about ther bow stringe, when they draw it to shoott." See Kupperman, *Indians and English*, 56.

11. Samuel Purchas, *Purchas His Pilgrimage, (or) Relations of the World and the Religion Observed in All Ages* (1613; repr., London: H. Fetherstone, 1614), 954; as cited in Kupperman, *Indians and English*, 56.

12. Ibid.

13. William Wood, *New England's Prospect*, ed. Alden Vaughn (1634; repr., Amherst: University of Massachusetts Press, 1977), 170.

14. Kathleen J. Bragdon, *Native People of Southern New England, 1500–1650* (Norman: University of Oklahoma Press, 1996), 170.

15. Comaroff, *The Dialectics of Modernity*, 220.

16. Richard W. Cogley, *John Eliot's Mission to the Indians Before King Philip's War* (Cambridge, MA.: Harvard University Press, 1999), 52–53.

17. Cogley, *John Eliot's Mission*, 54.

18. Ibid.

19. Anonymous, "The Day-Breaking, If Not the Sun-Rising of the Gospell with the Indians in New-England," in Clark, ed., *The Eliot Tracts*, 99.

20. In Clark, ed., *The Eliot Tracts*, 226.

21. John Eliot and Thomas Mayhew Jr., *Tears of Repentance Or A Further Narrative of the Progress of the Gospel Amongst the Indians in New England* (London: Peter Cole, 1653), 12.

22. It also involved some teaching of literacy so that converts could read the Bible for themselves—hence Monequasson was called the "schoolmaster" of Natick. Richard Cogley argues that Monequasson also probably assisted Eliot in the production of a Massachusett-language Bible (see Cogley, *John Eliot's Mission*, 119).

23. Eliot and Mayhew, *Tears*, 18–19.

24. Axtell, *The Invasion Within*, 177.

25. George E. Tinker, *Missionary Conquest: The Gospel and Native American Cultural Genocide* (Minneapolis: Fortress Press, 1993), 26.

26. Hilary E. Wyss, *Writing Indians: Literacy, Christianity, and Native Community in Early America* (Amherst: University of Massachusetts Press, 2000), 20.

27. Jean M. O'Brien, *Dispossession by Degrees: Indian Land and Identity in Natick, Massachusetts, 1650–1790* (Cambridge: Cambridge University Press, 1997), 52.

28. See Kupperman, *Indians and English*, 35–57.

29. Both Torlino photographs were taken by John Choate.

30. Talal Asad, *Genealogies of Religion: Discipline and Reasons of Power in Christianity and Islam* (Baltimore: The Johns Hopkins University Press, 1993), 4.

31. Edward Winslow, *Good Newes from New-England: or a True Relations of Things Very Remarkable at the Plantation of Plimoth in New-England*, William Bladen and John Bell 1624 [cited June 2004]; available from Early English Books Online http://gateway.proquest.com/openurl?ctx_ver=Z39.88-2003&res_id=xri:eebo&rft_val_fmt=&rft_id=xri:eebo:image:12033:1; 58.

32. Kupperman, *Indians and English*, 56

33. Helen Rountree, *The Powhatan Indians of Virginia: Their Traditional Culture* (Oklahoma City: University of Oklahoma Press, 1989), 116.

34. Mieke Bal, *Lethal Love: Feminist Literary Readings of Biblical Love Stories* (Bloomington: Indiana University Press, 1987), 55.

35. R.W.B. Lewis, *The American Adam: Innocence, Tragedy, and Tradition in the Nineteenth Century* (Chicago: University of Chicago Press, 1955), 5.

19   *Against Signifying*

PSYCHOSOCIAL NEEDS
AND NATURAL EVIL

LEONARD HARRIS

To "signify" is to modify texts by "riffing, woofing, scoring, getting loud on something or sometone."[1] Signifying refers to a wide-ranging critical mode of engagement with texts, not merely an exegesis or the search for the content-meaning of texts, including sacred ones. Signifying is also intended to capture the creation of symbols, meanings, and approaches that are unsettling and made by the social categories defined as subalterns, nondominant populations, minorities, populations on the margin of society, subordinated groups, the oppressed, and the exploited. I will refer to all of these social categories in the following as "subalterns" or "nondominant populations." Such social categories reform the canonical texts forced on them by dominating groups through signifying, thereby expressing different meanings, symbols, and values presumably beneficial to subalterns and nondominant populations. African Americans, the urban poor, and indigenous populations confronting missionaries are populations considered examples of subalterns using signifying to create discursive practices. Works such as Henry L. Gates Jr.'s *The Signifying Monkey*[2] and Mustpha Marrouchi's *Signifying with a Vengeance*[3] are examples of books that consider the importance of signifying as a way of inventing and creating symbols, meanings, and values that allow nondominant populations to express their experiences, offer critical commentary, and engage in self-authorship. "Signifying on scriptures" is intended to apply, study, evaluate, critique, and review the ways signifying occurs in relationship to the "scriptures" of religions.

I offer a skeptical voice, if not a comprehensive argument expressing doubt that signifying should be considered particularly beneficial to subalterns. Rather, I suggest a stance of agnosticism—namely, that we think of signifying as a tool that lacks evidence for its epistemic existence. In addition, I argue that signifying is not intrinsically beneficial to subalterns.

The Pathos of Signifying

All forms of signifying in relationship to sacred texts are modes of engagement with the core content of a faith. If white slave masters contended that the Bible justified racial slavery, for example, black slaves often reshaped that message. Nonetheless, the slaves maintained the Bible as scripture; the symbols slaves created were compatible with monotheism, the idea of personal salvation, redemption through the intervention of a personal savior, individual soul redemption, a creator God, and an afterlife consisting of individual souls. The dominant and the non-dominant populations often share the core of a faith. It is common for masters and slaves both to proclaim their faith in sacred texts, whether the text is the Qur'an, the Bible, Buddhist sacred writing, or shaman visions. Some family of meanings and symbolic implications differ between masters and slaves, but core contents and meanings remain. The core family of meanings stays as unmoved object. Riffing, consequently, must refer to a stable objective store of beliefs and texts, the same store that is used as the source of vile impressions of subalterns and creative meanings by subalterns.

Riffing is used by the marginalized to promote self-hatred as well as self-respect.[4] It is thereby, I suggest, a method, like all signifying methods, available for all and sundry purposes. The minstrel tradition is an example of an art form based on degrading blacks. Minstrelsy occurs only in relationship to blacks and whites in America: no population wants to be stereotyped in art as permanently inferior. Minstrels are whites purporting to emulate self-hating blacks, driven by illicit sexual passion, blacks pretending to be happy as subservient, sloppy, poor, and untrustworthy subjects. The minstrel tradition inscribes racist stereotypes by the use of riffing; contemporary decadent rap music does the same by using riffing to romanticize "niggers, bitches, whores, pimps, and prostitutes" and to promote the use of dangerous sexual behavior and illegal drugs. These significations are not just consumed by American audiences, who at best might interpret decadent rap or minstrelsy as the self-mutilations of the unjustly oppressed; but other populations outside America are forced to consume and endure such degrading images and think about what it is to be a "nigger." Americans, however, including poor black populations, are rarely forced to consider what it means to be a kiffer, kike, leather worker, immigrant, or refugee.

One way to think about why signifying may be the source of harm is to think about what it is to engage in self-injury. Signifying, in some instances, is analogous to a form of self-mutilation. "Paradoxically, self-injury is usually a life-sustaining act, a mechanism to cope with stress, relive inexpressible feelings, and gain attention. Most sufferers say it is a mechanism to stave off suicide or more serious forms of emotional disorganization; it is a 'life preserver' rather than an exit strategy."[5] When blacks are described as "whores, bitches, dogs, lazy, and niggers" in some rap and hip-hop music, this can be considered a form of self-injury.

Signifying is no sure route of escape. It offers no redemption. No one is saved. Signifying, at best, provides psychological solace, voice, and for some a sense of authentic self-authorship. At its worst, signifying is a useful method for voicing self-hatred and self-mutilation.

Signifying and Psychological Benefit

The meanings created by subalterns are arguably different from the meanings created by dominant populations. The meanings that are normally presented as examples of signifying show meanings that encourage perseverance in the face of hardship, hope in the face of interminable odds for success, and respect for persons often treated as unworthy of respect. No matter what meanings slaves created by signifying on sacred "scriptures," however, they more than likely lived and died as slaves—their survival was certainly financially beneficial to their masters. The same is true for contemporary subaltern populations.

Considering signifying beneficial to the subaltern as a practice and implicitly an epistemic intrinsically beneficial to subalterns is difficult because it fails to present the obvious: signifying requires affirming core beliefs of dominant texts; meanings created by signifying critical of dominant beliefs and texts inadvertently reaffirm the value of the core beliefs and texts of dominant traditions. The family of meanings defining core beliefs and texts remain unaltered by signifying. Cases in which signifying is a counter-discourse are cases that exist within the same sphere of imagination as texts central to the dominant culture. Signifying requires commenting on, and thereby affirming, if only satirically, the texts held sacred by subalterns as well as slave masters, racists, and exploiters. Signifying, for example, can at best function as if it were a patriotic antiwar protestor criticizing the military; the military and its actions, however, remain.

Even if antiwar protesting creates popular dissent and thereby forces the military to end some, if not all, of its actions, the existence of the military is likely to continue and antiwar protest remain a "reaction." Patriotic protesters never threaten the very entitlement for the military to exist, only what the military should do and what its actions may mean.

The reason signifying fails as a strategy by which the subaltern gains conceptual liberation is analogous to the issue about why propaganda often fails as a strategy for convincing a population to accept a set of beliefs. Signifying is trapped in constantly reproducing its own object of derision in the same way that propaganda reproduces the object it hopes to destroy. Propaganda, as the systematic attempt to propagate an idea using repetition, subterfuge, and stereotypical phrases, has been a popular missionary strategy used, for example, by Catholic missionaries, with the direction of such committees as the Congregation for the Propagation of the Faith, founded in 1622 at the Diocese of Seckau, Austria, and renamed the Congregation for the Evangelization of Peoples in 1967.[6] The goal of propaganda is characteristically to change the beliefs of persons considered infidels and in deep need of a true faith. The use of propaganda as a proselytizing tool is not unique to religious organizations. Diverse American antiracist political organizations in the 1920s—for example, the Communist Party, as well as the Universal Negro Improvement Association—used propaganda as a method to change the attitudes of racists and to encourage self-deprecators to become self-respecting despite the presence of demeaning racial stereotypes.[7] Antiracist groups often promoted images they considered respectful of subalterns. The images promoted were most often supportive of conservative cultural values, such as nuclear families as the only form of a healthy family. Novels often depicted the poor as persons motivated by benevolence, as those who love their neighbors and earn decent wages, while persons motivated by sordid avarice failed to live happy lives.

Propaganda, according to the philosopher Alain Locke, usually fails to change people's beliefs in a predictable way because it cannot reframe debates. Propaganda "speaks under the shadow of a dominant majority whom it harangues, cajoles, threatens, or supplicates." Antiracist propaganda has an invariant relation to its object and thus "perpetuates the position of group inferiority even in crying out against it."[8] Antiracist propaganda must use "race" as a category referring to a distinguishable population, even if the authors of antiracist propaganda know that race is a social construction of which its definition makes sense in one country but not another. Antiracist propaganda must use stereotypes, such as depicting all black people as members of a contiguous race, knowledgeable of lower-middle-class folk culture, faithful Christians, and honest entrepreneurs such that any deviation is an egregious effect of antiblack racism, while simultaneously hoping to end stereotypes. Propaganda is limited in its ability to make positive contributions to cognition because it cannot be a source of perceptions completely free of the object of its destruction. It offers no escape.

Analogously, signifying offers no conceptual escape. Signifying seems to work equally well for evil or good; it is a method readily available for the master and the abolitionist, the soldier and the antiwar protestor. It is quite common, for example, for slaves to share the religion of their masters. It is thus likely that if the slave master is Christian, the slave will be Christian—each will use the Bible as symbol of the embodiment of truth, source of solace, and verification of worthiness. It is arguable that slaves would be worse off if they did not have signifying as a method for creating modes of self-worth in the face of a system predicated on constantly encouraging self-loathing by the slave. It is trivially true, however, that life could always be worse under alternative descriptions; and it is trivially true that life could be better under alternative descriptions.

Sacred texts are neutral as a source of signifying because it is normal for people to engage in displacement. Displacement is the generation of meaning according to needs having nothing to do with the content or character of the source of meaning. An automobile, for example, can be used as a source of pride, but an automobile itself is a neutral object—nothing about it determines who may gain pride by virtue of its ownership. Analogously, for slave masters, God is on their side and the fact that they are able to enslave and elicit seemingly voluntary submission is objective evidence that an omnibenevolent and omnipotent God wills them to be masters; for the slave, God is on the side of the subjugated despite the obvious fact that it is the master who has material and military benefits. Signifying may benefit either group. No matter what sacred texts are popular, people will generate meanings using available texts according to their social needs as defined by their status as master, slave, subaltern, minority, and so on. The sacred texts and the signifying are just tools in a toolbox of cognitive strategies, a toolbox more or less full. One way to see this is by considering the causal force of gestures when used as evidence of virtues.

Evidence

It is common for outward behavior and ownerships to be considered important as expressions of inward virtues. Outward behavior is thereby considered as evidence of inward virtues. The "gesture is regarded as the outward (*fois*) physical expression of the inward (*intus*) soul. This conception of the expressivity of gesture (whether its referent is philosophical, religious or psychological), and the dual idea of the person that underlies it, are patterns constitutive of Western culture."[9] If we use Cicero as a guide, *scientia* (discerning truth), *beneficientia* (benevolence), *fortitudio* (strength), and *temperantia* (modesty, orderliness) are virtues made obvious by appropriate behavior. The body, if animated by agitation, expressiveness, excitement, and wild exuberance, is indicative of the lack of virtue. Greed "in Pomerius, fornication in Cassianus, pride in Gregory"[10] are also examples of outward behavior that indicate internal virtues.

I find little evidence to suggest that subalterns ever change their material condition—for example, their mortality rates, morbidity rates, ownership of houses and land, ownership of industries, employment rates, average income, or lower rates of incarceration as a function of signifying. It is certainly the case that some individuals find solace by signifying and that signifying creates a good deal of social criticism and alternative ways of symbolizing. Nothing suggests, however, that signifying is a salient casual variable influencing the overthrow of psychological hardship for more than some individuals or institutionally for any population.

Ownership of objective goods and the gestures and symbols accompanying them are inescapable features of social life helping to symbolize and convey the existence of intrinsic virtues. Certainly, members of an indigenous population who first encounter a Christian missionary purporting to offer them the truth may reform the missionary's message to fit their views. They may treat the Bible as evidence for the existence of many sacred and equally valuable windows into the holy. It is a far cry, however, from such significations to being able to stop the missionaries from using their overwhelming military power to subdue indigenous populations or sell them manufactured goods so that indigenous populations can express their views and symbols using paper, tape recorders, and computers manufactured in the modern West.

Although material conditions of the subalterns do not substantively change as a function of signifying, it would seem that gestures and symbols created by signifying may be nonetheless beneficial to help sustain the sort of psychological survival indicative of unhappy slaves—unhappy slaves may fight and achieve the abolition of slavery but generations of slaves have remained enchained by the core content and meanings of their master's sacred texts—and the freed slaves will almost certainly adhere to the faith of their former master. Even if agitation, expressiveness, excitement, and wild exuberance is indicative of subalterns creating alternative meanings rather than a lack of sublime virtues of modesty and orderliness, the benefit of those alternative meanings do not entail a force likely to change the life status of the subaltern. Signifying functions as a tool, a sort of cognitive servant used by persons in ways befitting their social status, needs, and opportunities whether unhappy slaves or happy slave masters.

Unequal Subalterns

Subalterns in different nations may share the conditions definable as nondominant, minority, populations on the margin of society, subordinated groups, oppressed and exploited. Considering why the Bible and Christianity are important to subalterns within America may shed light on why the significations of subalterns from dominant nations may be incompatible with the significations of subalterns in countries dominated by America capital, culture, and religion.

The reason that the majority of African Americans are Christians is because their ancestors were forced to become Christians through rape, torture, coercion; and the imposition of one form of manumission from slavery—manumission by conversion from traditional African religions or Islam to Christianity. After manumission by conversion was no longer allowed, it became "being a Negro" that defined a slave. Persons defined as a slave from birth are natally alienated.[11] That is, from the moment of birth they are slaves. At best, under conditions of racial slavery, even a "free" Negro was always potentially subject to be enslaved. African Americans were trapped by American race-based civil religion. The entrapment involved the following: if African Americans did not profess faith in Christianity they were terrorized; even if they professed Christianity, their social status could ascend no higher than a racially segregated "freedman." The children of the enslaved became servants for the propagation of the faith they inherited from their parents' masters. At present, African Americans, as a population in the modern West, are citizens of the most militarized postindustrial nation in the world and members of the world's dominant religious and cultural community. African American music, such as gospel, jazz, or rap, are all televised in other countries, but almost no other cultural music is heard on African American cultural media; the language of African American music, English, is imposed on its foreign listeners the same way that white rock music and white mid-Atlantic Protestant choirs impose their music on foreign listeners—communication industries. The riffing, scoring, and signifying of African Americans, including those forms from the most oppressed and isolated sections of the population, create meanings and symbols within a dominant cultural, material, and military matrix.

It is dubious whether the forms and content of signifying by members of the ruling world culture, even if they are among the most oppressed and isolated within that culture, are beneficial to populations outside the modern West. If, for example, gestures of aggressiveness (e.g., unbraiding, scoring, riffing, etc.) and immodesty (e.g., loud, frank, lewd speech) are beneficial as gestures encouraging the African American underclass to be assertive in pursuit of self-improvement, it is false that gestures of aggressiveness and immodesty elicit the same responses from the underclass of other cultures. When gestures are tied to the character of one's soul, that is, when outward appearances and movements are considered substantive indicators of the character of a person's moral quality, aggressiveness and immodesty may not encourage the underclass of many countries to be self-motivated nor may such gestures be considered morally worthy.[12]

Karl Marx was simply wrong to think that the consciousness of all and sundry proletariats would be enjoined with the same interest; Franz Fanon was simply wrong in *The Wretched of the Earth* to think that the colonized would develop a common response to the colonizer.[13] They were both trapped in the arrogance of theory in the sense that they assumed theoretical gathering terms, treated as ontological categories, such as "working class" or "the colonized," implied a uniting common interest, way of acting, and formation of commonly shared symbolic meanings. It is arrogant to think that generalities tell us about the practical realities of all persons across lines of nation, race, ethnicity, language, and heritage. It is at least reasonable to doubt that responses to signifying are ubiquitous across lines of nation, race, ethnicity, language, and heritage; and it is at least reasonable to doubt that the gestures, comportments, and values promoted by the wealthiest of the impoverished are beneficial to populations that have no way of imposing their music and language expressions on a world dominated by media of the modern West.

Signifying, as a strategy used by subalterns to resist subordination by dominant populations, is well used by dominant populations, too; signifying as a method entailing riffing and scoring to create alternative meanings is also well used by subalterns to create self-hating and self-mutilating meanings. Signifying is pathos. Signifying allows self-authorship by those enslaved to the core content of texts, sacred or otherwise, but offers no escape. In a world in which evidence of one's virtue is provided by material objects and bodily gestures, signifying is itself a neutral phenomenon akin to an automobile—of great benefit to humanity for ambulances and as well as for mounting guns. Signifying is a tool; it has no epistemic existence.

NOTES

1. Vincent L. Wimbush, introductory essay to this volume, 4.

2. Henry L. Gates Jr., *The Signifying Monkey: A Theory of Afro-American Literary Criticism* (New York: Oxford University Press, 1988).

3. Mustapha Marrouchi, *Signifying with a Vengeance: Theories, Literatures, Storytellers* (Albany: SUNY Press, 2002).

4. For the central importance of self-respect and honor to slaves and persons in general, see Leonard Harris, "Honor and Insurrection," in *Frederick Douglass*, ed. Bill E. Lawson (Malden, MA: Blackwell Publishing Company, 1999), 227–242; "Honor, Eunuchs, and the Postcolonial Subject," in *Postcolonial African Philosophy*, ed. Emmanuel C. Eze (Malden, MA.: Blackwell Publishing Company, 1997), 252–259.

5. Karen Conterio et al., *Bodily Harm: The Breakthrough Treatment Program for Self-Injurers* (New York: Hyperion, 1998), 29.

6. See J. Harold Ellens, ed., *Sacred Scriptures, Ideology, and Violence*, vol. 1 of *The Destructive Power of Religion*, 4 vols. (Westport, CT: Praeger, 2004).

7. See Abby Arthur Johnson and Ronald Maberry Johnson, *Propaganda and Aesthetics: The Literary Politics of Afro-American Magazines in the Twentieth Century* (Amherst: University of

Massachusetts Press, 1979); Nicholas J. Cull, David Culbert, and David Welch, eds., *Propaganda and Mass Persuasion: A Historical Encyclopedia* (Santa Barbara, CA: ABC-CLIO, 2003); Garth S. Jowett and Victoria O'Donnell, *Propaganda and Persuasion* (Newbury Park, CA: Sage, 1986).

8. Alain Locke, "Art or Propaganda?" *Harlem* 1 (November 1928): 12–13; see also "Freedom Through Art: Review of Negro Art, 1870–1938," *The Crisis* 45 (July 1938): 227–229.

9. Jean-Claude Schmitt, "The Ethics of Gesture," in *Zone*, ed. Michel Feher, Ramona Nadd-aff, and Nadia Tazi (New York: Zone, 1989), 129.

10. Ibid., 134.

11. See Orlando Patterson, *Slavery and Social Death* (Cambridge, MA: Harvard University Press, 1982).

12. See Schmitt, "The Ethics of Gesture," 129–147.

13. See Franz Fanon, *The Wretched of the Earth* (1963; repr., New York: Grove Press, 1965).

Orality, Memory, and Power

VEDIC SCRIPTURES AND
BRAHMANICAL HEGEMONY IN INDIA

PATRICK OLIVELLE

Over the past several decades we have seen a shift in the academic study of religion from phenomenological descriptions and analyses of beliefs and rituals to
the investigations of the social, political, and economic underpinnings and ramifications of religious practices and institutions. The new Institute for Signifying
Scriptures (ISS) at the Claremont Graduate University is directed at investigating
precisely such sociopolitical dimensions of "scriptures" cross-culturally. This essay
focuses on how social prestige and political power are related to the production,
transmission, and preservation of scriptures in India within the priestly class
of Brahmins. Although limited in scope, I hope some of the insights from this
necessarily brief inquiry will have cross-cultural applications, especially in such
scripture-dominated traditions as Judaism, Christianity, and Islam, where scholars
too often take "scriptures" as a given to be described rather than as a problem
requiring investigation.

William Graham, in his excellent article on "Scripture" in Mircea Eliade's
Encyclopedia of Religion, characterized scripture as a relational concept: "A text
becomes 'scripture' in living, subjective relationship to persons and to historical
tradition. No text . . . is sacred or authoritative in isolation from a community."[1]
We must imagine such a community as one that accepts the sacred and authoritative nature of its scriptures, and as one that reads, reflects on, and celebrates its
scriptures both privately and publicly. Such a definition is most easily applicable
to the Judeo-Christian traditions, although even there one may question this communitarian ideal of "scriptures." In the case of the central Hindu scriptures, the
Vedas, however, it is hard to imagine such a community, at least one that includes
all who are or who have been named "Hindu."[2] The Vedas were produced by a
small, elite, and exclusively male priestly group, the Brahmins. They were memorized and handed down orally within the male Brahmanical community.[3] For a
millennium or more they were not written down, and they were not divulged to
the broader "community" of Hindus, especially all women and also the males of
subaltern and marginalized groups, such as the Śūdras, which together comprised
perhaps 95 percent of all so-called Hindus at any given time in history. As Wimbush
has remarked,[4] to gain a fuller understanding of "scriptures" we have to go beyond

relationships and communities and look at the sociopolitical reality underlying the manufacture and transmission of these oral texts and their assumption of scriptural status.

Without a written text as an external object theoretically available to anyone who can buy or steal a copy, the only existence of the Vedas was within the memory of educated Brahmins, traditionally called *śiṣṭa*, a special cultural elite. With the transmission limited to students who are properly initiated, the Vedic scriptures were not a presence to the rest of the community except when they were ceremonially recited in public rituals. Even there the subalterns were excluded; one text calls for the pouring of molten lac in the ears of a Śūdra who dares to listen to the Veda when it is being recited.[5] The possession of this sacred and secret knowledge made the Brahmins a privileged community. This is a textbook example of "knowledge as power"; indeed the very term "Veda" and the term *vidyā*, also used as a synonym of Veda, simply means knowledge.

The exclusive possession of this knowledge-scripture was at the root of Brahmanical claims to power and prestige within society. The famous law book of Manu (circa second century CE), which is intent on guarding the privileges of Brahmins, uses this very argument for the superiority of this group over other segments of the population: "Because he arose from the loftiest part of the body, because he is the eldest, and because he retains the Veda, the Brahmin is by Law the lord of this whole creation" (Manu 1.93). A millennium or more before Manu, the cosmogonic hymn of the *Ṛg-veda* (10.90) had already presented the social structure of caste as a natural phenomenon origination from the very nature of the creative process. The Brahmin arose from the mouth, that is, "the loftiest part," of the primeval cosmic being, whereas the royalty arose from the arms, the commoners from the loins, and the servile classes, the subalterns, from the feet. The mouth is here clearly associated with sacred speech contained in the Vedas. Not only is the Brahmin connected to sacred speech in his very origin, he is also the eternal repository of that sacred speech, because he carries the Veda in his mind and memory. These are the two reasons Manu singles out for the preeminent position he occupies in society. The Veda personified is presented as coming to the Brahmin and asking him to protect her: Vidyā (Vedic knowledge) came up to the Brahmin and said, "I am your treasure. Guard me!" (Manu 2.114). The ideology that placed the Brahmin at the zenith of society is well articulated by Manu (11.85): "By his very origin, a Brahmin is a deity even for the gods and the authoritative source of knowledge for the world; the Veda clearly is the reason for this."

Manu draws clear conclusions from the Brahmin's preeminence as a result of his connection to the Veda: "This whole world—whatever there is on earth—is the property of the Brahmin. Because of his eminence and high birth, the Brahmin has a clear right to this whole world. The Brahmin eats only what belongs to him, wears what belongs to him, and gives what belongs to him; it is by the kindness of the Brahmin that other people eat" (Manu 1.100–101). This conclusion may be more ideology than social reality; nevertheless, it is clear that Brahmanical privileges are here theologically anchored in the Brahmin's special relation to the Veda. These privileges included exemption from taxes, from corporal and capital punishment, and from the confiscation of property.

Beyond orality, there was also the hegemony of language. The Vedas were composed in an early form of Sanskrit. By at least the middle of the first millennium BCE, Sanskrit was no longer a "natural" language spoken at home and the market place. It was a learned language of the educated elite. Only Brahmins and a small segment of other upper-class groups had access to it. Clearly the marginal communities, and even Brahmin women, were excluded from this language. In ancient Sanskrit plays, only Brahmins, kings, and other upper-class individuals speak in Sanskrit; most women and all lower-class men speak in a variety of vernaculars, collectively called Prakrit. The use of Sanskrit divided the ancient Indian population. Sanskrit was the prestige language, and, with few exceptions, the Brahmins were the guardians not only of the sacred Veda but also the sacred language, Sanskrit. The language of the Veda by itself, therefore, limited access to it on the part of the "Hindu" community; clearly this was not a community that read, reflected on, and celebrated the Vedic scriptures.

Within the "Hindu" scriptures, then, there are fault lines crisscrossing the Indian population in terms of both gender and class. How were the Vedas appropriated and interpreted by the non-Brahmanical and marginalized communities and by women? Did they acknowledge the Vedas as "scriptures" even when they could not recite or understand them and were deliberately excluded from access to them? Did they ignore, were they ignorant of, or reject the Vedas? One can only speculate on these issues; we do not have the sources to draw firm conclusions. There may indeed have been multiple responses from different groups in different regions and at different period of time. We do have, however, parallel sacred texts produced in India that removed some of the barriers to access and were open, at least in theory, to women, lower classes, and marginal groups. We have the early examples of Buddhism and Jainism. The adherents of these new religions rejected the authority and the scriptural nature of the Vedas, producing a parallel set of scriptural texts composed not in Sanskrit but in middle Indo-Aryan languages known as Prakrit, which were probably the spoken languages of the time. Their monastic orders accepted both women and members of lower classes. Significantly, it was Buddhism that was able to transcend the ethnic boundaries of India and spread its message to north and east Asian countries; Buddhist scriptures were the first Indian texts to be translated into a non-Indian language (Chinese).

In the medieval period we have the rise of devotional Hinduism called *bhakti* with numerous sects. One of these, the Vīraśaivas, explicitly rejected the Vedas and heaped scorn on established religion. The Vīraśaiva saints produced instead heartfelt songs (*vacana*) in the vernacular language Kannada, songs that became Vīraśaiva scriptures. As A. K. Ramanujan notes: "The *vacana* saints reject not only the 'great' tradition of Vedic religion, but the 'little' local traditions as well. They not only scorn the effectiveness of the Vedas as scripture; they reject the little legends of local gods and goddesses."

See-saw watermills bow their heads,
So what?
Do they get to be devotees
to the Master?

The tongs join hands.
So what?
Can they be humble in service
to the Lord?

Parrots recite.
So what?
Can they reach the Lord?[6]

Note the parody on recitation. The reference is to the loud recitation of the Vedas by Brahmin priests, who are compared to parrots. Neither the Brahmins nor the parrots reach God through their meaningless recitations.

Perhaps no one was as acerbic in his condemnation of both Brahmins and Muslim leaders as the fifteenth-century weaver from Benares, Kabir.

Pundit, how can you be so dumb?
Veda, Puranas—why read them?
It's like loading an ass with sandalwood!
Hey Qazi,
what's that book you're preaching from?
And reading, reading—how many days?
Still you haven't mastered one word.[7]

We will never know the full extent of the reactions down the centuries on the part of subaltern communities throughout the subcontinent to the Vedas as scripture over which the Brahmins exercised a monopoly. Nevertheless the social status of Brahmins could not have been what it was had there not been a co-opting of Brahmanical "knowledge" by the ruling powers of India. Sheldon Pollockhas called this "deep orientalism."[8] He notes the claims of some scholars[9] involved in the critique of "orientalism" that it was the colonial construction of knowledge that accepted Brahmanical formulations of social structures, elevating the Brahmin to the apex of society. This is only partly true. Brahmanical discourse down the centuries would not have survived until the arrival of colonial powers had there not been similar co-opting of Brahmanical formulations by political and economic powers in precolonial India.

The Vedas themselves became a focus of literary activities under the last major "Hindu" empire of Vijayanagara in the fourteenth century. Under the patronage of the early Vijayanagara kings, we have the writing of the first extensive commentaries on most Vedic texts by a Brahmin minister named Sāyaṇa. Although there is no direct evidence, some form of imperial sponsorship of this enormous and unprecedented literary task appears likely, possibly with an eye to further strengthening its legitimacy. A millennium or more before Sāyaṇa, a Brahmin under the pseud-onym Kauṭilya wrote the only existing manual on statecraft, political science, and government: the *Arthaśāstra*. This text explicitly recommends that the chief minis-ter of any king be a Brahmin. Though themselves not exercising political power,[10] Brahmins made close alliances with the ruling authorities. Indeed, even ancient Vedic texts state that success is assured only when the priestly and the royal powers (*brahma* and *kṣatra*) are united. The legal text of Manu (9.322) reiterates this posi-tion: "The Kṣatriya does not flourish without the Brahmin, and the Brahmin does not prosper without the Kṣatriya; but when Brahmin and Kṣatriya are united, they prosper here and in the hereafter." The chief minister and the influential chaplain (*purohita*) were expected to be Brahmins. The judiciary was, for the most part, entrusted to Brahmins: "When the king does not try a case personally, however, he should appoint a learned Brahmin to do so" (Manu 8.9). Members of the lower classes were explicitly barred from exercising judicial functions: "Let a king, if he so wishes, get someone who is a Brahmin only by name to interpret the Law, or even someone who simply uses his birth to make a living, but under no circum-stances a Śūdra. When a Śūdra interprets the Law for a king, his realm sinks like a cow in mud, as he looks on helplessly" (Manu 8.20–21). The Brahmanical view of the lower classes of society is nicely illustrated in the food metaphor common in the Vedas: Brahmins and Kṣatriyas (king and nobles) are the eaters, the lower classes of society are their food.[11]

It is well known that the Brahmins produced texts containing sacred knowledge that were classified into two categories: the Veda or *śruti*, and the *smṛti*. Both can be classified as "scriptures." The latter class of texts contains an open-ended list of tra-ditional documents, some of the most significant of which are the *Dharmaśāstras*, the treatises on sacred law that also contained sections on the duties of kings, criminal, civil and personal law, and legal procedure. With this class of "scriptures," the Brahmins co-opted a broad range of "knowledge" that affected the running of government and civil society. As Pollock has shown, a large body of literature based on the *Dharmaśāstras*, including commentaries and legal digests, was created between the eleventh and the eighteenth centuries CE under royal patronage. Such patronage both legitimized the royal authority of the patrons and affirmed the social standing of the community that produced such knowledge, the Brahmins.

One could go a step further than Pollock and see the very production of the ancient *Dharmaśāstras* (circa first to fifth centuries CE) as part of the patronage system that consolidated the power at the apex of society represented by the two highest classes (*varṇa*), the Kṣatriya and the Brahmins. We do not have the kinds of evidence for that early period as we do for medieval times, but it is difficult to envisage how these complex texts could have been produced and could have reached authoritative status without some kind of intervention by the political-economic powers. A similar assumption can be made for the much larger texts, the epics *Mahābhārata* and the *Rāmāyaṇa*.

This has been necessarily a brief and cursory look at the manufacture and transmission of "scriptures" within India. It is significant, however, that power (in the sense of political and economic power, as well as social prestige) was at the heart of knowledge production and transmission that created the so-called Hindu scriptures. Relationship to a broader community, no doubt, exists, but often as a relationship of power rather than of community.

NOTES

1. William Graham, "Scripture," in *The Encyclopedia of Religions*, ed. Mircea Eliade, 13 (New York: Macmillan, 1987), 134.

2. The category of "Hindu" is deeply problematic. It derives partly from Muslim and partly from colonial reflections on the religious landscape of India. The category became a label of self-identification only in the nineteenth and twentieth centuries. The Vedas are better identified as the Brahmanical scriptures, because they were more or less the exclusive property of the Brahmin community. Besides the Vedas, there are other sacred texts that can claim scriptural authority. These non-Vedic sacred texts are broadly referred to as *smṛti*.

3. The transmission and, to some degree, the production of the vedic texts were carried out by hereditary Brahmanical schools called *śākhā* ("branch"). It was later, probably toward the last centuries of the first millennium BCE, that the entire Veda was considered as authoritative and the property of all Brahmins and twice-born individuals.

4. See Wimbush, introductory essay to this volume.

5. *Gutama Dharmasūtra* 12.4.

6. A. K. Ramanujan, *Speaking of Śiva* (Baltimore: Penguin, 1973), 25.

7. J. S. Hawley and M. Juergensmeyer, *Songs of the Saints of India* (New York: Oxford University Press, 1988).

8. Sheldon Pollock, "Deep Orientalism? Notes on Sanskrit and Power Beyond the Raj," in *Orientalism and the Postcolonial Predicament: Perspectives on South Asia*, ed. Carol A. Breckenridge and Peter van der Veer (Philadelphia: University of Pennsylvania Press, 1993), 76–133.

9. G. G. Rajeha, "India: Caste, Kingship, and Dominance Reconsidered," *Annual Review of Anthropology* 17 (1988): 497–523; N. B. Dirks, *The Hollow Crown: Ethnohistory of an Indian Kingdom* (Cambridge: Cambridge University Press, 1987).

10. At least in theory, although Brahmin dynasties are well-known in history, such as that of the *Sātavāhanas* during the closing centuries of the first millennium BCE.

11. See Brian K. Smith, "Eaters, Food, and Social Hierarchy in Ancient India: A Dietary Guide to a Revolution in Values," *Journal of the American Academy of Religion* 58 (1990): 177–205.

21   *Reading Places / Reading Scriptures*

WESLEY A. KORT

The principal point of this essay is that places are textual and can be read. As texts, places can be treated under textual categories, including the category of "scripture." I give primary attention in this paper to what I call "personal space." I do this not because I think that it is the most important kind of place in any theory of human spatiality but because it is the least valued these days and the most difficult to clarify. It is the least valued because spatial theory is primarily oriented to and by socially, politically, or economically constructed and determined space. It is the most difficult to clarify because, by definition, it is the most improvised and particular kind of space. Before turning to texts of personal space and their potential as scripture, however, some foundational assumptions need to be clarified.

The first of these assumptions concerns modernity. I argue, in *"Take, Read": Scripture, Textuality and Cultural Practice*, that Western modernity can, at least in part, be understood as the exchange of reading the Bible as scripture for reading other "texts" as scripture, namely, nature, history, and literature. At first these other texts, biblically warranted, complemented reading the Bible as scripture; gradually they largely displaced the Bible in priority, and they continue to complement, rival, or displace reading the Bible as scripture. In my opinion, reading in modernity, as a particular cultural practice, remained, despite these exchanges, fairly constant. What changed were the texts that were culturally read as scripture, as central.[1]

    The second assumption concerns "scripture" as a category in textual theory. By "scripture" I mean that location on the textual field that both orients persons and groups and provides them with resources for direction, identity, and reconstitution. "Scripture" stands, in textual theory, then, between the contrary categories of "writing," which levels the textual field, and "canon," which abstracts particular texts from it.[2] I take these three categories of textuality—writing, scripture, and canon—as designating not so much something about texts as something about the way texts are read or regarded. Furthermore, because I take people generally to be neither lost on the textual field (writing) nor abstracted from it (canon) but located or able to be located on the textual field (scripture), I tie recognizing one's scripture as basic to an ordinary way of being in the world.

    The third assumption concerns postmodernity. Along with whatever else it is, postmodernity is marked by a shift from the primacy of reading history as scripture to the primacy of reading place and space as scripture. I agree with Fredric Jameson when he says, "I think it is at least empirically arguable that our daily life, our psychic experience, our cultural languages, are today dominated by categories of space rather than by categories of time, as in the preceding period of high modernism proper."[3] The major scriptural texts of postmodernity are spatial: architectural, urban, economic-political, and the like. It should also be said that postmodernity differs from its cultural predecessor in that the spatial texts of postmodernity's scriptures are not warranted biblically or involved in dynamics of negative and positive relations to biblical texts. The consequence is that spatial texts, while functioning as scripture, are also not recognized as playing that role. This situation either creates or exacerbates the general disarray or incoherence of current spatial theory.

The fourth assumption concerns narrative. Narrative tends to be undervalued in recent, spatially oriented cultural theory and criticism because narrative is largely defined in terms of temporality. By defining narrative in this way, narrative theories inadvertently contribute to the diminishing cultural importance of narrative. That is, when defined in terms of human temporality or history or both, narrative becomes increasingly irrelevant to the dominantly spatial texts that constitute postmodern scriptures. I contend that this is unfortunate and unnecessary because the language of space and place is actually or potentially as important for narrative as are any of its other languages, including its language of action and event. The stabilization needed for spatial theories can, I think, be secured by realigning spatial theory with narrative discourse. It should be possible, in my opinion, to allow narrative discourses to assume for human space and place the kind of role that they have played, especially for what Jameson calls the period of high modernism proper, for our understanding of and relation to human temporality and history. The narrativization of place and place-relations will allow at least some theorists to relate narratives in which the language of place and space is dominant to biblical texts, thereby giving a kind of coherence and weight to theories of place and place-relations that they now lack. This would encourage the emergence of clearer, more consistent, and more widely shared norms for identifying and evaluating places and place-relations than currently exist.

Finally, it is necessary to locate personal space, to which attention will be drawn in this essay, in a larger theory of human spatiality and place-relations, one that I develop in my recent book *Place and Space in Modern Fiction*.[4] In this book I examine the fiction of six modern writers and extrapolate from their narratives the implicit theory of the positive place-relations that are narrated or implied by them. I argue that all of these writers are responding to a history of dislocation and spatial disorientation that is the fruit of many changes in modern culture, beginning especially in the early nineteenth century. They respond by narrating or implying alternative, more positive human places and place-relations, those, that is, that contribute to rather than undermine human moral and spiritual well-being. I extrapolate from their fictional narratives the outlines of a basic, adequate theory. That theory has three parts. The first concerns the kinds of place-relations that constitute the repertoire of human spatiality. In these narratives there are, I conclude, three kinds of places or place-relations that need to be distinguished from, and clarified in their differential relations to, one another. There is, first of all, comprehensive or cosmic space; second, there is social or political space; and, third, there is personal or intimate space.[5] While all three kinds of place-relations are necessary to a fully realized spatial orientation, people can differ, as do the six writers, as to which kind of place-relation is dominant or central for them. The second part of the theory of human spatiality extracted from the narratives is that human place-relations have two sides, a physical and a spiritual side.[6] While both sides need to be present for positive place-relations, one side can be for some people more important than the other. The third part of the theory concerns the norm for evaluating place-relations, and I denote that norm with the term "accommodating." I include under this term the following characteristics of positive place-relations: they are marked by a mutual adjustment between person and place, by a commodious quality that allows contrary human interests to be brought into relation with one another, by having both a restoring and a freeing effect, and by exhibiting gratuitous, gift-like qualities.[7]

Having clarified the basic assumptions for reading places as texts and as scripture, I want now to turn to some instances of personal space in the Gospel of Luke. This choice is not arbitrary; the language of place and space is prominent in Luke. Indeed, it would be interesting to bring the theory of spatiality and human place-relations indicated above fully into contact with the whole of the Gospel of Luke in order to determine its "geography." This kind of study would complement all the attention that has been given to the organization of the actions and events of Luke, its plot. It also would be good to do that for Luke's related text, Acts, which is also a narrative whose "geography" is prominent. But I shall limit myself to Luke and, even more, to personal spaces in Luke. And even among the many instances of personal space in the Gospel I shall refer to only a few. To repeat, I have chosen instances of personal space because personal space is a kind of place-relation that is very difficult to substantiate in our culture primarily because social space tends to swamp personal spaces.

I focus my interest in the personal spaces of Luke's narrative on his fondness for the adversative particles, *de* and *plen*: "but," "however," or "nevertheless." These uses in the narrative indicate points of exchange from a location within the determinations of social space to a less certain but in all respects more beneficial location in personal space. I select three striking instances. First, in 5:4–5, Peter, told by Jesus to put the boat out into the deep and to let down the nets, protests that they have toiled all night and caught nothing. Nevertheless, *de*, he says, he'll let down the nets. We find another instance in 13:38 in Jesus's response to the news that Herod wants to kill him. Irritated but undaunted, Jesus inserts his "nevertheless," *plen*. He will continue with his work and pursue his goal despite political intimidation. The third is this well-known use of *plen* by Jesus in 22:42: "Nevertheless, not my will, but thine, be done."

These three instances of "nevertheless," of taking exception, taken together, form quite an inclusive repertoire: turning from the force of logic and empirical evidence and toward the possible; defying political intimidation to pursue an agenda of truth and reconciliation; and putting aside the will toward personal well-being for the sake of a higher destiny. In each instance, "nevertheless" locates the speaker at a transition from social space to a space that is exceptional. I read these textual markers as exits to spaces that, I think, can have the force and meaning of "scripture" even in our own culture. Let's name that exit "nevertheless," and let's look at some examples of it in more recent texts, various additional signs, that is, of exit from social to personal space.

I call first on Muriel Spark, the Edinburgh-born novelist, and the attention she draws to what she calls the "nevertheless principle." She attributes a great deal to it. Indeed, she relates her literary vocation and her decision to become Roman Catholic to the "nevertheless principle." She finds a graphic metaphor for this principle in the space between the new and old towns in Edinburgh created by the abrupt intrusion or exception of Castle Rock. This rock, she says, is a "statement of an unmitigated fact preceded by 'nevertheless.'"[8] Spark not only associates the "nevertheless" principle with her religious and vocational identities; she also employs it in her novels. Most of her principal characters are in search of places free from the coercions of late- or postmodernist social space, and some find them. They are compelled in this search by the need and desire for a space where personal integrity and value can be nurtured, and they often are helped, as Harvey Gotham is helped in *The Only Problem*, by the biblical book of Job, by texts that narrate the move from social to personal space. Highly motivated and textually aided, some of her characters locate exits from pervasive social conformities, exits to places of personal exception. The places they enter, because the culture is a culture of certainty, necessarily cause them to be less certain about themselves and puzzles to others.

A second example of the "nevertheless" principle as indicating an entrance to personal space is found, I think, in Virginia Woolf's *A Room of One's Own*. Woolf points out that women have not had places of their own, places undetermined by men, both because women are undervalued and because making their work vulnerable to interruption confirms its unimportance.[9] Being valued or having value has everything to do with a place of one's own, that is, with taking exception. Creativity depends not only on having value but, as she points out, on being valued, because creative people are more sensitive to acts of personal devaluation than are others. Women have been denied personal space in order to keep them from developing a sense of self-worth and of doing creative work that would confirm their value. The result is an eventual atrophy of the ability to take exception, to disclose personal space through the exit signed "nevertheless."

E. M. Forster, to turn to another example, based his construction and affirmation of personal spaces, I think, on his admiration for the Thornton family, with which he had personal connection through his great-aunt Marianne. Henry Thornton was a major player in the Clapham sect, which met at his home on Battersea Rise. The Clapham sect was a small group of devout and socially concerned people who met regularly during a period roughly from 1790 to 1830 to strategize against social evils, most notably slavery. Forster was, consequently, keenly aware of the moral force that can be generated by like-minded people who take exception to dominant social patterns and their oppressive and corrupting results in order to deploy morally and spiritually sponsored alternatives. The emphasis in his fiction on personal space and on taking exception was motivated not only by his desire to establish homosexual identity as a positive human possibility, although it was also that. He wanted, as well or perhaps even more, to affirm that social space finds its correctives and directives in those places secured by people in order to take moral exception to social patterns and coercions. Rather than determined and colonized by social and political space, personal spaces can challenge and alter social spaces, because it is in personal space that creativity and moral integrity are nurtured.[10]

We find another instance of the "nevertheless" principle in the work of the enigmatic and influential Jewish theorist and literary artist Maurice Blanchot. Blanchot analyzes modernity, among other ways, in terms of its need for answers, its need for certainty. For him, answers suppress questions and conceal their primacy. He says, in *The Infinite Conversation*, that "the answer is the question's misfortune, its adversity."[11] Answers are so highly valued in modernity because they resemble commodities and appeal to the culture's desire to possess and control. Answers are abstracted from the questions that give rise to them as commodities are abstracted from the conditions that produce them. This modernist thirst for answers conceals a latent violence. The notion that something or someone must yield up its secrets and conform to the general scheme of things is consistent with the practice of torture. As moderns we are suspicious of exceptions and question persons who take them. Blanchot implies that Jewish homes constituted an exception to the cultural drive toward clarity, uniformity, and certainty. The Holocaust can be seen, he suggests, then, as a horrible intensification of the modern impatience for distinctive, nonconforming practices and for the personal spaces, such as Jewish homes, in which exceptions reside and are acted out. The question posed by people who take exception requires an answer, a "final solution." The concentration camp is the logical modern response to the question created by personal spaces and the "nevertheless" principle.

One more example, if I may. It's given to us in bell hooks's autobiographical essay "Homeplace: A Site of Resistance." She describes the walk that, as a little girl, she took through white neighborhoods to reach the home of her grandmother. The walk was scary, and arrival meant a homecoming, a restored sense of worth and assurance. Moving from this experience hooks defines what she means by "homeplace." It's "the one site where one could freely confront the issue of humanization, where one could resist."[12] "Homeplace" is the kind of place where people can become "subjects" instead of "objects." In "homeplace" people can affirm one another and, by so doing, heal many of the wounds inflicted by racism. It is an exceptional space, a site, she says, of "resistance and liberation." Afflicted people need places of restoration, places "where one could resist." She values "homeplaces," and we are, she thinks, too easily lured into discounting them. They are counter-sites where identity, self-worth, and personal relations can be nurtured. While her advocacy of "homeplaces" arises out of her experience of racism, I do not think that we injure her work when we say that people more generally need places where personal integrity and personal relations, especially when damaged or discounted in social space, can develop and be strengthened.

When such textual instances as these of exits from the determinations of social space into personal space are encountered, readers in their need and desire for personal spaces of their own can allow such texts to become scripture, to become their own sign of location on the textual field. This location encourages and enables them to be alert to the possibility of clarifying personal spaces of their own by taking exception, when necessary, to social space, by deploying the "nevertheless" principle. Contemporary texts, texts in the tradition, and biblical texts can mark exits from dominant and coercive social, cultural, and political patterns and can form a scripture, a center in the textual field.

A scriptural location is important also because not all attempts to take exception lead to personal space. There are ways of taking exception that reveal self-aggrandizement, the thirst for being socially exceptional. In a culture of self-promotion and narcissism, people may readily want to be exceptional, to be treated as a cut above or as unlike others. In a crowded world people feel compelled to insist on being treated in an exceptional way or as being exceptions.

We also should not confuse personal spaces with moral indifference. While entering personal space may at times require crossing moral boundaries, we may also, when that occurs, be determined by the cultural identification of creativity and individuality with amorality and self-indulgence. We tend to think in our culture that the moral life is one of restrictions and conformities incompatible with creativity and personal particularity. But morality is not contrary to a creative and particularized location, and taking exception more likely means crossing thresholds than crossing boundaries. While it is at times difficult to distinguish a threshold from a boundary, we need very much to sharpen our ability to do so, and one of the ways of sharpening that ability is by means of a textual center of morally and spiritually truthful exits to personal space.

Finally, we should not confuse personal space with ownership, with *private* space. Private space, while not necessarily contrary to personal space, subjects it to social space. Private space is determined by the structure of boundaries and the laws that constitute the principal, especially economic, characteristics of social space.

By reading narratives that point out exits from the controls, conformities, certainties, and comforts of modernity and whatever we should call what we now are in, the possibility for securing the nurture of creative and moral challenges and healings in and by personal spaces can be revealed. Those texts, by providing a scriptural location and reading, become guides and warrants for our own acts of locating personal space by taking exception. In this way the nature and role of scriptures are opened up. Texts can alert and lure us to the potentials of those narrow spaces where, to return to the Gospel of Luke, the possible can trump the logical and empirical, the mission of truth and reconciliation can spurn political threats, and one's own well-being can defer to something more important.

NOTES

1. See Wesley A. Kort, *"Take, Read": Scripture, Textuality and Cultural Practice* (University Park: Pennsylvania State University Press, 1996), 37–67.

2. See Wesley A. Kort, *Story, Text and Scripture: Literary Interests in Biblical Narrative* (University Park: Pennsylvania State University Press, 1989), 119–124.

3. Fredric Jameson, "Postmodernism and the Cultural Logic of Late Capitalism," *New Left Review* 146 (1984): 64.

4. See Wesley A. Kort, *Place and Space in Modern Fiction* (Gainesville: University of Florida Press, 2004), 149–206.

5. Ibid., 149–172.

6. Ibid., 173–189.

7. Ibid., 190–206.

8. Muriel Spark, "Edinburgh-born," *Critical Essays on Muriel Spark,* ed. Joseph Hynes (New York: G. K. Hull and Co., 1992), 22.

9. Virginia Woolf, *A Room of One's Own,* forward by Mary Gordon (1929; repr., San Diego: Harcourt Brace and Company, 1981), esp. 35 and 108.

10. Kort, *Place,* 66–85.

11. Maurice Blanchot, *The Infinite Conversation,* trans. Susan Hanson (Minneapolis: University of Minnesota Press, 1993), 13.

12. bell hooks, "Homeplace: A Site of Resistance," in *Yearning: Race, Gender, and Cultural Politics* (Boston: South End Press, 1990), 42.

22   *Taniwha and Serpent*

A TRANS-TASMAN RIFF

JO DIAMOND

Ma o matau atua e manaaki, e tiaki—may our deities bless and keep us.

This essay is the written form of a verbal presentation containing a two-part riff inspired by Vincent Wimbush's introductory essay to this volume. Not attempting to own the knowledge, practical familiarity, let alone complexities, of riff production by any means, I hope to contribute to the spirit of this conference from a Trans-Tasman (Aotearoa New Zealand and Australia) perspective. It occurs to me that the concept of a riff is particularly suited to this perspective given that indigenous peoples in Aotearoa New Zealand and Australia have oral, not written, traditions. Writing came with a "Western" colonizer early in the eighteenth century. It could be said that a considerable amount of scriptural "riffing" has occurred throughout history to turn Maori and indigenous Australian cultures into the written forms they take today.

My riff in this essay therefore leads toward and signifies the theme that such Trans-Tasman perspectives, marginalized in some circles though they are, may have important and ongoing contribution to make to the new Institute for Signifying Scriptures (ISS) in Claremont. This riff includes references to snakes in written and non-written religious "scriptures." It comprises two parts that pertain first to times and spaces before the arrival of Europeans in Aotearoa New Zealand and Australia, and second to the effect of the Christian Bible in this Trans-Tasman context. It ends with some brief references to Trans-Tasman indigenous dialogues that may contribute to the new Institute.

A Riff—Part One

In the beginning of our southerly migration, there were no land snakes. Sea snakes, however, accompanied our *waka*, our huge seafaring outrigger vessels that "flew" over southern oceans toward our new home. That home is made of three main islands, representing the waka of our deified ancestor *Maui* (the South Island), its anchor (Stewart Island), and the large *ika* (fish) that Maui raised from the sea (North Island) with the aid of a magical fishing line and hook. This new home was first seen as a cloud-covered archipelago that more than challenged our adventurous ancestors with snow, sleet, and a new meaning for "cold." Traditional Maori narratives that would eventually be appropriated by non-Maori peoples called this land Aotearoa (long, white cloud).

Since time immemorial, we had also known that *taniwha* (guardian spirits) could seal our eventual fate with twists and turns of fortune depending largely on the effectiveness of our *tohunga* (priests) and our *karakia* (incantations). Taniwha shape themselves into sea snakes, eels, wind and water turbulence, and various other forms either killing our people or protecting them, depending on the quality of our spiritual relationship with them. They are part of a pre-Christian Maori pantheon, replete with associated epic journeys and superhuman feats, not to mention a multidimensional cosmology.[1]

Then one day at the dawning of colonial time, land snakes came to us within the form of a book called the "Bible." Here, on a new technology called the written page, we saw and heard for the first time the power of the word that gave the *minita* (church minister) a direct line to a new god. From the minita and the book, good and evil also came, approximating (though not closely enough) the ideas of positive and negative energy that we had always known. Good and evil were new and foreign concepts to us. We did not have the same notions of heaven or the wrath of hell fire and brimstone. The need for self-sacrifice in order to attain life after death was not so much of an "either/or" equation to us. Rather, life and death were an inevitable cycle that promoted human wisdom and luck in lived experiences, including the use of the necessary precautions and incantations to bring favorable guardianship from spiritual entities such as taniwha. It encouraged respect for elders and ancestors as well as deities.

The Bible turned our attention away from the taniwha and other pre-Christian spiritualities. It held new revelations, according to its priesthood, including the notion that land snakes are different, from taniwha. This book that came to be known as the *paipera tapu* (holy Bible) "said" that these land snakes are only evil. They are, so the scriptures tell us, in league not with God but with a devil that could only be harmful, never kind.[2] It was the "good god" who inspired his servants, via the missionaries, to save us from our sins and the harmful works of the devil, including his snakes. The devil's work also extended to people, and some people are more prone to evil than others. So we were told.

The new god, however, was contradictory. Sometimes his minita called us "primitive innocents" who needed to be shown the "light" of Christian revelations contained in the Gospels. Other times we were called dark "savages," obsessed with war, allied with the devil, and beyond redemption. The contradictory word of this new god and his minita was powerful, ever more so when our people began to die from strange illnesses originating from faraway lands.

The clergy that spread this word apparently knew all the remedies, presuming their superiority over our technologies (including those medicinal), languages, and spiritual beliefs, in the name of Jesus Christ. Our land, our culture, our beliefs in our gods, ancestors, and taniwha began to disappear as a price for Christian salvation.[3] Some of us resented this loss and fought against it. Precolonial inter-tribal warfare was replaced by insurgence against the British soldier, politician, businessman, and priest (or minita), but also brought new grievances among us. Pragmatism joined political ambition, and our people (now collectively called Maori in order to distinguish ourselves from the non-Maori new settlers) were not always adverse to alliances with foreign guests.[4] New firearm technology was eventually adopted, for example, that tipped the scales of inter-*iwi* (tribal) war in favor of those with guns. Our weapons technology became obsolete and large-scale massacres became more common.

A notable feature of mid- and late-nineteenth-century Maori wars was, nevertheless, the struggle against a non-Maori system that progressively and unfairly deprived Maori of land and other resources. This struggle continues today, though more and more of us are beginning to use our brains in educational and governmental institutions rather than our brawn in physical combat.[5]

We are a culturally diverse people: some defying the power of colonialism, including its Bible and minita, some accommodating and exploiting it (and each other), many unaware of its various obfuscations. Our collective spirit may still respect the power of that Bible, but many of us have lost faith in this Christian god's messages and messengers. Some of us are instead reclaiming our taniwha as part of a bid to reclaim our sense of Maori identity and culture. Many of us still hate snakes, though the only snakes we may see are on the TV, in the zoo, and in our imaginations—perhaps a biblically based hangover or nightmare. Our postcolonial struggles continue and our spirits are far from free.

The Second Part of This Riff

Let's now "talk" about Australia. According to some Christianized Maori elders, Australia is an "evil" place because it is full of snakes.[6] Nonetheless, many elders recognize Australia as the place that takes their young ones away for work and a better life than Aotearoa New Zealand can offer them. Australia is now a quick flight across the Tasman Sea. Yet, for many Maori migrants, and the elders they leave behind, it is a long way from home. Australia can signify, therefore, a good country that has alleviated the stresses of disadvantage that so many Maori people experience in their home country today. But for some, it is also too full of snakes and therefore unable to shake its associations with biblical evil.

Maori migration across the Tasman Sea in fact began over two hundred years ago. The colonial sailing ships progressively replaced our waka as modes of oceanic travel. Yet the history books are sanitized in their recollections of history. Only snippets tell of relationships with indigenous Australians and Maori.[7] Such recollections are largely produced by nonindigenous scholars and can therefore be likened to holy scriptures that we who identify as indigenous to Australia or Aotearoa New Zealand did not write, and yet are expected to believe and emulate.

Perhaps if more people knew about the Rainbow Serpent, things would be different. Only relatively recently (notably from the 1960s and 1970s) has the religiosity of indigenous Australians been anthropologically recognized.[8] The highly successful commercial market in indigenous Australian art has also helped to convey the diversity of indigenous Australian experience, transcending the monolithic and racist stereotypes often assigned to them by "white" Australian society. The Rainbow Serpent appears in many examples of indigenous Australian art and culture and numerous nonindigenous Australian scholars have written "his" stories. Western "progress" has, however, often been ignorant of "his" existence and power that continues to prevail, despite the ravages of colonial time.

For this country we now called Australia is in fact made of many aboriginal countries, with distinct languages and ceremonial protocols, perhaps totaling two hundred according to one well-respected authority, Howard Morphy.[9] It is clear that many indigenous Australians retain access to an indigenous kinship and religious belief system, one that has not necessarily bowed to a Christian god. Nor can their adherence to non-European cultures been seen as antiquated and degenerative. As Morphy notes, "[Australian] Aboriginal engagement with history has not been backward looking . . . rather it has be designed to influence the course of future events while at the same time acknowledging change."[10] There has been, for example, a two-way dialogue with colonialism, including Christianity, by indigenous Australians where their non-Christian spirituality has often remained intact and is demonstrated in their art, song, and other cultural forms.

How easy then, is it to see similarities between Rainbow Serpent and taniwha through visual art? Known by various names, the Rainbow Serpent is a magnanimous creator, an ancestral being often male but with other related manifestations such as the female Eingana, who carries dilly bags full of life-giving provisions. The Rainbow Serpent brings life and in doing so knows death full well. Pre-Bible Maori spirituality can converse with this serpent from a land replete with its indigenous land snakes and other creatures that Aotearoa New Zealand has never known. This need not be a devilish pursuit. Yet it is one that acknowledges the scope for comparisons between two spiritual beings from at least two distinct cultural groups, Maori and indigenous Australian.

I therefore ask the following questions. Has the scripture of the Bible brought so much to these Trans-Tasman countries (and others) as to ultimately lead to the negation of a thirst for knowledge and its exchange? Although the history of colonization and Christianization of Australia and Aotearoa New Zealand has included the presumptions and arrogance of British colonialism it need not dismiss indigenous conversations and contributions any longer. In fact their inclusion may enhance the spirituality of all peoples. Other questions can be asked of Christianity: does it not contain a ceremonial rationale within its scriptures that always respected indigenous inhabitants, in peace as well as war, approximating the idea of the commandment "love thy neighbor"?

In terms of the ideal uniformity of Christian belief placing one god above all others, must the Bible, by very definition, Christianize the idea of yin-yang balance and condemn to hell nonbelievers through a stereotyping fear of difference? Does the Bible actually help to save the heathen savage from his or her devilish inclinations? Or can such "devilish inclinations" actually reflect the paranoia of Christian "do-gooders"? Such questions may be disturbing for many "believers" of the Bible, and it takes far more theological expertise than I can currently lay claim to in order to provide definitive answers. I would, however, recommend their pursuit in any tertiary-level institution of learning.

At least one more question remains: can a snake and a taniwha actually teach (or at least converse with) a Christian god, his minita, and other holy brethren (not to mention representatives of other spiritual faiths) on equal terms?

As unfashionable and erroneous as it might seem to some indigenous revivalist movements, I do not condemn the Bible or any other written "scripture," and I have had a lifelong love affair with books. I know enough of books to know by now, though, that they cannot tell us everything. For if they did, why would we continue to write new ones? I believe that many of us in the human race do not like "change" in what we interpret of the world as "reality," whether this interpretation is religious or not. Equally, most of us appreciate stories such as those found in the Bible. Many of us can be both fascinated and repulsed by gory details. I know that my own spirituality lies deep within many stories, some of which have not reached a published page. I know that in this, I am not alone.

Many cultural syntheses as well as appropriations have occurred in our relentless search for meaning and belonging. Some of us clutch tightly to fundamentalist interpretations of a spiritual world. Some of us brought death and destruction because of arrogant social Darwinism, depicting and supporting ourselves as superior to others. Those "others" in this oh-so-human scenario now wait for balance to be regained, if not for redress and reprisals. Still others cause their own kind of damage. Driven by understandable anger and impatience, and carrying wounds of the past that cannot heal, they undertake extremist measures, bringing more death and destruction.

The Rainbow Serpent and the taniwha endure as the focus of further intellectual enquiry. With more study we may see how "scriptures" in written form have thus far excluded them to our detriment. For many people would equate their survival with all forms of ecological health and sustainability, not only that of one group. Paying them adequate attention may be part of the paving of a road toward a brighter, safer world for our children.

So, in ending this short presentation as a lone representative of the Antipodeans, I fancy myself as an emissary, bringing a drop of the ocean I know as home. It is a home that is now known as the South Pacific, Aotearoa New Zealand, and Australia. It is a home, rich in diversity and very familiar with colonialist power that came only a few hundred years ago from Europe. It is a home that knows many adventurous spirits, strong systems of spirituality, both indigenous and nonindigenous, as well as many sociopolitical struggles. It knocks on the doors of those familiar with it, those who have been alienated from it, those who want to deny it, and those who would warmly welcome it. I remain extremely grateful to Vincent Wimbush and his staff for opening the door to it and to what I hope will be a continuing relationship with our part of this world. Maybe here is where this riff ends . . . for the time being, at least.

NOTES

1. Antony Alpers, *Maori Myths and Tribal Legends* (Auckland: Longman Paul, 1964); M. King, ed., *Te ao hurihuri: Aspects of Maoritinga* (Auckland: Reed, 1992); and others.

2. I refer here to various popular interpretations of the Bible based largely on Genesis 3.

3. Donald Denoon, Philippa Mein-Smith, and Marivic Wyndham, *A History of Australia, New Zealand and the Pacific* (Malden, MA: Blackwell, 2000), 74. Note, for example, that Christian missionary schools, between 1840 and 1874, "with tuberculosis [they] were probably more lethal than plantations, as they assembled pupils as boarders. The perverse result is that [the presence of tuberculosis] is an index of Christianity."

4. See A. S. Atkinson, "What Is Tangata?" *Journal of the Polynesian Society* 1 (1892): 133–136; and R. H. Paora, "Notes on Mr. A. S. Atkinson's Paper 'What Is Tangata Maori?'" *Journal of the Polynesian Society* 2 (1893): 116–118, for early debate over the name Maori as applied to peoples identifiably indigenous to Aotearoa New Zealand.

5. Numbers of Maori people participating in tertiary education have increased in the late twentieth and early twenty-first centuries, though still lag markedly behind non-Maori participation in Aotearoa New Zealand.

6. I have witnessed this opinion being voiced among some sections of the Christian Maori population in Aotearoa New Zealand.

7. See Denoon, Smith, and Wyndham, *A History of Australia*.

8. R. M. Berndt and C. H Berndt, *The World of the First Australians* (Sydney: Ure Smith, 1964), 227–335.

9. Along with describing the kinship system and its role in establishing relationships with "people, land and sacred property," Morphy notes in his seminal work on aboriginal art that Australia's aboriginal people "are continually trying to insert, as precedents for action, values and beliefs about the world that have their genesis in pre-colonial times . . . [they] speak over two hundred languages and each language often contains a number of different dialects." See H. Morphy, *Aboriginal Art* (London: Phaidon, 1998), 4, 6. This view supports my opinion of the indispensability (and generosity) of indigenous Australian cultures to other cultures around the world.

10. Morphy, *Aboriginal Art*, 4.

23

Scriptures Without Letters, Subversions of Pictography, Signifyin(g) Alphabetical Writing

JOSÉ RABASA

I define myself as a Mexican atheist. With such identification I seek to underscore a long history of atheism in Mexico (particularly pertinent to the magistrate), which in my case I trace to a filiation with an anarcho-communist tradition that includes the names of Ricardo Flores Magón, Antonio Gramsci, Walter Benjamin, Antonio Negri, and Alain Badiou. This legacy leaves room for maneuvering outside the narrow antireligious vein that has dominated anarchism and communism.

I seek to respond to—or better, expand—on a certain critique of subaltern studies.[1] Instead of working with assumptions that subalterns embody a revolutionary consciousness, subalterns are most often, at least in Gramsci, not the ideal subjects that subalternist theoreticians assume. I raise the specter of subalterns persecuting, banishing, and murdering other subalterns for religious reasons. If Gramsci would have solved the problem by insisting on a solid dose of science, we may find such a solution naïve today. My affiliation with atheism is perhaps more methodological than a statement of belief.

Whereas I entertain questions of messianicity as posed by Walter Benjamin and Jacques Derrida, and welcome Alain Badiou's reflections on Saint Paul, I have no sentimental attachments to universal understandings of God that would absorb all expressions of spirituality as partaking of one and the same ultimate supernatural reality (read: the Greco-Abrahamic tradition and the phenomenon of globalatinization, which flattens out cultural differences in the application of such concepts as the sacred, ritual, sacrifice, religion, God, etc.).[2] Given that my work concerns itself with Amerindian cultures, in particular with the Nahuas of central Mexico, the suspension of belief in God will keep me from imposing or even assuming a particular understanding of the supernatural as universal—let alone the no-less violent reduction of all Mesoamerican culture to idolatry. I will return to the question of idolatry at the end of this essay. In what follows, I want to suggest lines of research on Mesoamerican encounters with Christianity and the written word that could be illuminated by and carried out under Vincent Wimbush's proposal for the Institute for Signifying Scriptures (ISS).

The Franciscan friar Bernardino de Sahagún wrote the following assessment of pictographic writing in one of his prologues to the *Historia General de las Cosas de la Nueva España*:

> This people did not have letters or any characters. They communicated with one another by means of representations and paintings. And all their ancient customs and books they had about them were painted with figures and representations in such a way that they knew and had records of the things their ancestors had done and had left more than a thousand years ago, before the Spaniards had come to this land. Most of these books and writings were burned when the other idolatrous things were destroyed. But many remained hidden, for we have seen them. And, even now, they are kept; through them we have understood their ancient customs.[3]

This passage lends itself to at least two possible readings. One can put the emphasis on the negation that Amerindians had any form of writing and thus see Sahagún as exercising power by denying them writing. The arguments that Native Americans were people without writing lent support to the view that they were less human, much in the same way that the eighteenth century drew the distinction between peoples with and without history. But I am not sure the analogy works. There is no indication that the Nahuas of Central Mexico internalized the denial of writing. I will return to this question later. For now I would like to give more weight to the second part of the passage, where Sahagún states that the Nahuas had writings. The term he uses in Spanish is *escrituras*. I propose that we must understand how power was exercised in the sixteenth century not in the denial that Nahuas had writing, but rather in the implicit recognition that the Nahuas did have a system of writing. Let us first attend to what is meant by escrituras in the sixteenth century.

In the *Tesoro de la lengua castellana o española*, the first dictionary of the Spanish language published in Madrid in 1611, Sebastián de Covarrubias provides three definitions under "escritura": 1) in the most general sense, escritura stands for "that which is written"; 2) *escritura pública* is done in the presence of a legal *escribano* with its "solemnidades y fuerza" [solemnities and force]; 3) by antonomasia one uses *Escritura Sagrada* for the Bible. I would argue that Sahagún's use of the term *escritura* participates of the three definitions; obviously, native *escrituras* were not the Bible, but that he understood that certain genre of pictographic writing had a similar authority among the Nahuas.[4]

For Sahagún and other sixteenth-century friars and lay officials, the so-called religious books fulfilled a function not unlike that of the Bible. The Nahuas not only had writing but very powerful forms of inscribing the supernatural, rituals, and initiation ceremonies. It is not a coincidence that with the exception of three books, the precolonial pictographic writings that have survived were perceived as strictly historical, in spite of the explicit agency of the gods in such texts. As to the second definition, Sahagún and Spanish bureaucrats generally also recognized pictographic texts as fulfilling a legal function with its own "solemnities and force," to borrow Covarrubias' terms.

Sahagún was also aware that Mesoamerican escrituras written with solemnity and force constituted the sacred. He constantly laments that the whole of native culture was considered to practice superstitions. Missionaries and lay officials isolated the mystical foundation of polities from the cartographic descriptions of territories and historical narratives. Spaniards referred to the mystical foundation in historical texts as *hablillas* (tales) and *fábulas* (fables), terms that resonate with oral discourse, but these terms also served to differentiate the stories they told from the stories contained in the Bible. Missionaries burned the religious books, not because they were not considered forms of writing, but rather because as signifying systems they were perceived as expressions of the devil. This would explain the scarcity of religious books among those that survived the conquest or were produced during the colonial period. Some colonial texts reproduced the religious pictographs, but these were mainly intended for Spanish consumption and to facilitate the identification of religious practices that remained inscribed in the social body well after the ancient books were destroyed at the beginning of the conquest.

If there was a denial of writing, it seems to me, at least from within the parameters and objectives of the ISS, that we should study complex forms of exercising power. As I have already pointed out, there was such a denial of writing, but it was hardly relevant to the exercise of power over Indians in the daily affairs of the colony. If there is scant evidence that Amerindians internalized the denial, we do find Spanish appropriations and subversions of pictographic writing. What would constitute more convincing proof of the fairness of the *encomienda* system as a natural continuation of the ancient order than a Nahua pictorial text that documented precolonial forms of tribute? Or of the suitable appropriation of communal fields by Spaniards than a native map using pictographic conventions that identified wastelands?[5] This rhetoric builds authority on the use of pictographic signifiers.

But by the same token, we must also trace forms of resistance in pictographic writing during the colonial period. If the oppositional practice of signifyin(g) as defined by Henry Louis Gates Jr. and Vincent Wimbush could be appropriated by those in power, the adoption of signifiers pertaining to an oppressed culture also entails the continuity of these forms within a historical horizon of readings that build on the memory recorded by missionaries and lay officials. The identification of superstitions and idolatries in Sahagún's *Historia General de las Cosas de la Nueva España*—intended for the suppression of signs and signifying practices that invested daily life with meaning—constitutes a place of memory for future Indian generations. This ambivalence did not escape church officials when they confiscated Sahagún's writings in the 1570s.

If one can signify for repressive purposes, the logic of signifyin(g) entails the creation of a place in which, to borrow Michel de Certeau's terms, "memory does its work in a locus which is not its own."[6] Signifyin(g), then, involves an open-ended process of signification and exappropriation that cannot be held for long by those seeking to retain power. I derive the term exappropriation from Derrida: "What is a stake here, and it obeys another 'logic,' is rather a 'choice' between multiple configurations of mastery without mastery (what I have proposed to call 'exappropriation'). But it also takes the phenomenal form of a war, a conflictual tension between multiple forces of appropriation, between multiple strategies of control."[7] As such, signifyin(g) illustrates the paradoxical notion that resistance precedes power, but by the same token the ever-present will to appropriate and control oppositional practices. Power, because it aims to control and to conserve, lacks the creativity of cultural practices that can never be fully anticipated.

In fact, we find a proliferation of pictographic signifiers that were produced to represent the Spanish order of things. Native painters, the *tlacuilo* of colonial pictographic books, developed a pictorial vocabulary that depicted the new objects, ceremonies of authority, evangelical differences, forms of torture, and European signifiers that the colonial order introduced in Mesoamerica. We tend to forget that the tlacuilo and other Indian intellectuals were often trilingual, who spoke and wrote in Nahuatl, Spanish, and Latin, and were well acquainted with Christian theology, grammar, and Greco-Roman literature.

Thus, the tlacuilo of the sixteenth-century *Codex Telleriano-Remensis* developed a vocabulary out of the precolonial systems of signification to represent the difference between the theological traditions that informed the evangelical and ethnographic practices of missionaries belonging to the Franciscan and Dominican orders.[8] The tlacuilo not only uses a baptismal font, scapulars, habits, and a confessional manual to identify the evangelical practices of the two orders, but also perspective in frontal representations of Franciscan friars that conveys their preference for the sacrament of the penance and their participation in inquisitorial investigations. The depiction of a Franciscan missionary holding a confessional manual, facing us and looking out (one of two frontal representations in *Codex Telleriano-Remensis*; the other depicts the first bishop of Mexico, Fray Juan de Zumárraga, who had inquisitorial powers), reveals a symbolic use of Renaissance perspective, rather than the usual function to represent individual features realistically. At once, it represents the inquisitorial gaze and signifies the production and articulation of a new vocabulary. Beyond the gaze of the friar we sense the smiling eyes of the tlacuilo looking back, who seeks to underscore the brilliance of her use of perspective for symbolic purposes. In other documents, we find the adoption of perspective to represent the clash of cultures beyond the depiction of military battles. Again, perspective functions as a signifier that locates resistance in terms of an ongoing struggle beyond the military defeat of Tenochtitlan in 1521.[9] Thus the epistemic power of perspective is recognized but not used exclusively for a representation of reality. The emphasis is on the signifier rather than on the capacity to signify the real, indeed, in the understanding of perspective as a system of representation and a symbolic regime.

Let us now consider another commonplace that establishes a binary opposition between oral and literate cultures. Here once more I am not interested in expanding the commonplace that examines how alphabetical writing embalms oral discourse in a single version of stories that could otherwise be told in endless forms. One could add that writing also erases the bodies that perform the stories.

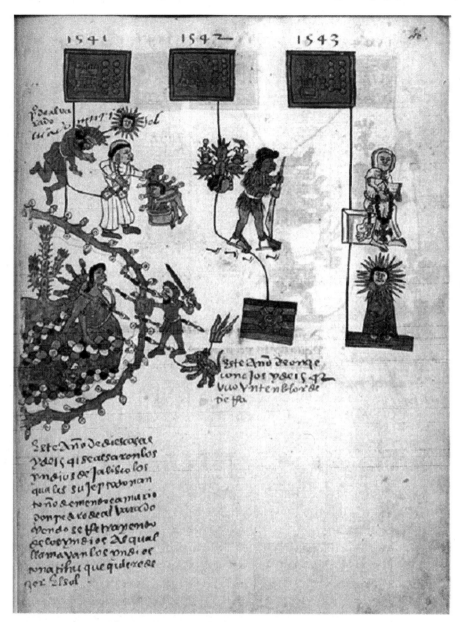

Figure 23.1 *Codex Telleriano-Remensis*, fol. 46r. Courtesy of the Bibliothèque nationale de France.

These observations obviously function on the premise that alphabetical writings will be read in silence and in private. Writing also tends to be identified with a particular grammar and syntax, as if the mere act of using the alphabet entailed a linear logical regime rather than the record of the temporal flow of speech. But the alphabetical recording of oral discourse aspires to record voice rather than to impose a narrative pattern and a specific syntax. This could very well happen in the process of translation, but not necessarily in the use of a phonetic system for the recording and transcription of voice. I would as part of the translation process presume an able stenographer in the colonial period or in today's technology a good audio or, even better, a video recorder and the eventual transcription. I insist on the transcription because the recording or the video would privilege the single occasion over reading as performance even more than an alphabetical version.[10] The capacity of the alphabet to record voice fascinated Indians in the sixteenth century. By embalming oral discourse, writing lends itself to an invocation of ghosts that would be brought to life through reading and oral performance. All the elements that are supposedly lost by writing down verbal performances only make sense if the writings are not intended for a performance that bring to life the rich texture that seemingly would be lost by alphabetical inscription. Writing as a register of voice understands phonetic representation as a system of signifiers that record sound, rather than as a grammar for producing particular meanings. Consider the opening lines from song 20 of the *Cantares Mexicanos*, that wonderful collection of sixteenth-century songs that were intended to invoke the ghosts of the dead leaders of olden times:

Xiahuilompehua xiahuiloncuican ticuicanitl *huiya* ma xonahuiacany,
    onelquixtilon ypalnemobuani *yyeo ayahuui ohuaya* etc.
(Strike up in pleasure, singer! Sing in pleasure. May you all be pleasured.
    Life Giver is entertained.)[11]

The words underlined in Nahuatl, first "*huiya,*" and then the sequence "*yyeo ayahuui ohuaya,*" followed by the "etc.," indicate the loud cries that the chanting would include, which, because of their lack of a meaning beyond sound were left untranslated. These songs obviously were recorded for performance and not for silent reading.

We need to make the distinction between an alphabetical record of voice as in the verbal performance of a pictorial codex and writing as the inscription of internal voice and thought on a blank page, which can actually be equally haunting, if not more. The *Historia Tolteca-Chichimeca*, which consists of pictorial representations of the origins and foundation of the town of Cuauhtinchan and alphabetical recordings of the speeches, songs, and other aspects of a verbal performance, best exemplifies writing as the record of external voice. As for the inscription of internal voice, several Nahuatl texts exemplify the practice of writing as the act of composing directly on the page. I am thinking, in particular, of the Indian historian don Domingo de San Antón Muñón Chimalpahin Quauhtlehuantzin (1593–1621).

Chimalpahin, who was from the town of Chalco, worked as copyist in Mexico City. We can identify a wide range of texts as penned by Chimalpahin: histories of his own, histories written by other native intellectuals, transcribed letters, a diary, Mesoamerican year counts with the corresponding European equivalences, and an *Ejercicio quotidiano* (daily exercise).[12] The *Ejercicio quotidiano*, which consists of a series of meditations for each day of the week, is perhaps the least-related text to those records of verbal performances that Chimalpahin and other Nahua historians diligently transcribed into the alphabet. Take for instance Fernando de Alva Ixtlixo-chitl who writes in the *Cronica Mexicayotl*: "I listened to the rulers don Diego de Alvarado Huanitzin, my parent, don Pedro Tlacahuepan, my uncle, don Diego de San Francisco Tehuetzquititzin, and other highborn noblemen who indeed rightly understood the ancient one's accounts. Here I took their statement."[13] Elsewhere in the *Cronica Mexicayotl*, Tezozomoc states: "Here ends the account of old Alonso Franco, whose home was here in the *altepetl* and city of Mexico Tenochtitlan and who died in the year of 1602. He was a 'mestizo.'"[14] The identification of the sources does not mean that they were conceived as authors, nor in fact that the native historian viewed himself as an author, but that their stories would remain as a collective voice. We can actually envision the verbal accounts of the pictorial *in tlili in tlapalli*, "the red, the black," given by Tezozomoc's father, his uncle, and other highborn (including the explicitly mentioned mestizo, Alonso Franco), as a collective performance. Their voices are recorded but not necessarily individu-ally. Observe that the only copy we have of Tezozomoc's *Cronica Mexicayotl* was penned by Chimalpahin and that he often introduces observations and corrections of factual information, especially when it concerns his native Chalco: "But I who here tell my name, Domingo de San Antón Muñón Chimalpahin, have investigated and considered the year-count book of the Chalca as to the time when the Mexica were beseiged in Chapultepec. It was in the year Two Reed, 1299."[15] Just as verbal performances where collective affairs, Chimalpahin's voice becomes one more author-ity.

On the other hand, the *Ejercicio quotidiano* records a voice that speaks to the inner self and engenders an internal meditation, a voice that constitutes the sin-gular subject. As such, it manifests the genius of Christianity—the call to make its truth one's own. More precisely, the *Ejercicio* entails the exappropriation of the transformation baptism brings about: "Listen, whoever you are who have been baptized. By being baptized you already belong to God; you are already a Christian."[16] In a marginal note, dutifully recorded by Chimalpahin, Bernardino de Sahagún identifies himself as responsible for the corrected version and expresses wonder at finding the exercise among Indians: "I found this exercise among the Indians. I do not know who produced it, nor who gave it to them. It had many errors and incongruities. But in truth it may be said that it was done anew rather than that it was corrected. In this year of 1574, Bernardino de Sahagún."[17] One can-not but find irony in that the *Ejercicio* found among the Indians was rediscovered at the Newberry Library in Chicago among the papers of another Indian, who by all accounts would have been able to produce the *Ejercicio*, even if, perhaps, not free of incongruities. Indeed, the absence of incongruities, whatever these might have been, does not mean that the reading, the meditations it would provoke, would not entail an exappropriation of the scriptural passages drawn from the Gospel that provide the motifs for the daily exercises. The passages are first given in Latin and then translated to Nahuatl, with the exception of the citation of Luke 22:15–20, which also includes a Spanish version.[18] In their introduction to *Codex Chimalpa-hin*, Arthur Anderson and Susan Schroeder have pointed out that the *Ejercicio* is untypical of Sahagún's writings and that it reveals, at least on the level of orthography, possible changes by Chimalpahin.[19] I will argue that the writing and reading of the *Ejercicio* exemplifies the practice that Henry Louis Gates Jr. defines as "making the white written text speak with a black voice is the initial mode of inscription of the metaphor of the doubled voice."[20]

Closer to Thomas à Kempis's *Of the Imitation of Christ* than to Ignacio de Loyola's *Spiritual Exercises*, Chimalpahin's *Ejercicio* speaks to the reader's most intimate self. Whereas Loyola classifies forms of meditation, provides the framework for the visualization of passages from the gospels, and outlines an abstract program of exercises, Chimalpahin's voice leads the reader through concrete exercises that seek to develop a *habitus* that will enable the soul to recognize the gifts of the Lord. This is not a text to be performed or read out loud, as in the case of Chimalpahin's historical works. The *Ejercicio* is designed for silent reading, for the interiorization and exappropriation of truth. It presupposes a subject that has consciously accepted baptism and is fully aware of the spiritual event that baptism brings about. The central tenet prescribes love of God, neighbor, and self, and then defines the "Ten Commandments of the only Deity, God, and the Five Commandments of our mother the holy Church" as rules of conduct.[21] As in Thomas à Kempis's *Imitatio*, the pleasures of the flesh must be avoided, but the specifics are left to the singular subject's meditations. Thus, the *Ejercicio* speaks Christianity in Nahuatl; the interior voice it produces is a voice that makes the passages from the Gospel and its commentaries, "the white book," speak with an Indian voice.

The *Ejercicio* denounces idolatry, in very general terms, with no specific reference to the Mesoamerican pantheon, and one cannot but wonder if the rigor with which it defines *latria* (service, worship, from *latron*, pay, hire) could not turn into an indigenous mode of critical thought. We may entertain the thought that Chimalpahin and other sixteenth- and seventeenth-century Nahua interrogated the imposition of the insistence on one deity only. The text does not say this. But the reduction of all possible names for the ultimate deity to the Christian Dios would have been aberrant to someone reflecting on latria and its dangerous supplement, *eidolon* (phantom, image, from *eidos*, that which is seen, form, shape, figure). In the *Ejercicio* every mention of Dios is paired by Nahuatl terms such as *tloque nahuaque*, "the near, the close," a particularly gorgeous way of speaking of the simultaneous presence of then immanent and the transcendent, and *ypalnemoani*, the life giver, that by means of which life is sustained. Here we find the option of reading these forms through the term God, and thereby translating them as speaking of one entity, or of interrogating the supposed universality of the term God to speak of tloque nahuaque and ypalnemonai.

As a record of internal and external voices, alphabetical writing lends itself particularly well to idolatry when one forgets that the voices we bring forth in silent reading and performance are phantoms, specters, revenants that we invoke and bring to life. Over the last two centuries, the alphabetical transcriptions of sixteenth- and seventeenth-century verbal performances of pictographic writings were reified by historian who reduced them to depositories of facts. As for the Christian texts, the most devastating specter in scriptural studies corresponds to fundamentalist reading practices that presume that their interpretations are univocal and exclusive of others. Signifyin(g) as articulated by Gates and Wimbush suggests forms of reading that are open-ended and dialogical. We may even assume that the practice of signifyin(g) is integral to Christianity in so far as it claims to be universal and translatable into all idioms—that is, that its truth depends on its exappropriation. Deep down, Christianity might amount, in its call for love, to the differentiation between latria and *idolo-latria*, but also to the invocation of specters and the vigilance over their haunting.

The project for a Mesoamerican component in the Institute for Signifying Scriptures would now consist of identifying the particular types of Nahuatl that emerges out of the practice of alphabetical writing. Of particular interest would be the study of the mediations and the kinds of voice that writing induces. Even in cases such as the *Ejercicio quotidiano*, a text designed to create an internal voice, hence read in silence, native discourses retain Nahuatl grammar. Remember that Sahagún taught Latin to native collegians to discuss the properties of Nahuatl grammar. Note that the Indian historians who wrote in Nahuatl in the sixteenth and seventeenth centuries did not aspire to reproduce the histories and meanings of Spanish historiography, but rather to record readings of pictographic texts and the voices of elders. Nowhere do we find an urgency to prove that Nahuatl was an appropriate vehicle for the writing of history according to European standards. Nor were Spaniards particularly interested in denying Nahuatl the ability to elaborate a historical narrative like those of Spanish vintage. Nor was the suitability of Nahuatl for Christianity questioned. Early missionaries were particularly interested in the exappropriation of Nahuatl rhetoric, poetics, and syntax for writing sermons, confessionals, and catechisms.

Writing clearly embalms voice and life, but this is only half a story that must also include reading practices, both in verbal performances and silent meditations. There certainly were sixteenth-century Spaniards who denied writing to Mesoamerican cultures. One must, however, complement this exercise of power with studies of how missionaries and lay officials subverted pictographic writings, but also of how Indians created pictographic signifiers to represent the colonial order in ways that Spanish missionaries could not even begin to anticipate. By representing the apparently irreconcilable differences between the Franciscan and the Dominican evangelical practices, the tlacuilo of *Codex Telleriano-Remensis* conveyed a truth that made manifest the relativism implied in the friars' different ways of world making. The logic of the signifier suggests a way to understand the dictum "resistance precedes power" that I find imbedded in Gates's and Wimbush's understanding of signifyin(g). The *Ejercicio quotidiano* suggests that colonial Indians could have used the call for love as an indigenous form of critical thought that would have interrogated the exclusivity, hence idolatrous nature, of the term "Dios."

NOTES

1. See Ranu Samantrai's essay in this volume.

2. I can only allude to these authors here. Derrida elaborates the concept of messianicity without messianism. See Jacques Derrida, *Specters of Marx: The State of the Debt, The Work of Mourning, and the New International*, trans. Peggy Kamuf (New York: Routledge, 1994). I have also benefited from Derrida's discussion of globalatinization. See "Faith and Knowledge" in *Acts of Religion*, ed. Gil Anidjar and trans. Samuel Weber (New York: Routledge, 2002), 42–101. For Walter Benjamin, see his "Theses on the Philosophy of History," in *Illuminations* (New York: Schocken, 1969), 253–264. As to Alain Badiou and Saint Paul, see *St. Paul: La fondation de l'universalisme* (Paris: PUF, 1997).

3. Bernardino de Sahagun, *General History of the Things of New Spain. Florentine Codex*, 13 vols. (Santa Fe: The School of American Research and Museum of New Mexico, and the University of Utah, 1950–1982), 1:82.

4. In passing, let me mention that for practical purposes we classify as religious books Mesoamerican writings that contain what looks to us as representations of gods and the supernatural. Not unlike the Spaniards of the sixteenth century, we distinguish religious and historical books. As good humanists, who follow the steps of Sahagún and the defenders of the Amerindians from classifications that minimized or excluded Indians from a full humanity (Juan Ginés de Sepulveda's term was homunculi, little men), we readily ascribe religion and history to Mesoamerican life-forms that we don't quite understand. See Juan Ginés de Sepúlveda, *Democrates Alter/Tratado sobre las causas Justas de la Guerra contra los indios*, Latin/Spanish ed., trans. Marcelino y Mendez y Pelayo (Mexico City: Fondo de Cultura Ecoonomica, 1941), 110. This benevolent act of love that reduces the corpus of Mesoamerican writings to these two antithetical Western terms exerts epistemic violence by erasing particular understandings of historicality, the supernatural, and their blending in forms that render their separation arbitrary. I am questioning the transparency and universal applicability of history and religion, and for that matter of the term God.

5. For a reading of the rhetorical use of pictography to justify the encomienda in Codex Mendoza, see "Pre-Columbian Pasts and Indian Presents in Mexican History," special issue on *Subaltern Studies in the Americas*, ed. José Rabasa, Javier Sanjinés, and Robert Carr, *Dispositio/n* 46 (1996): 245–270. In *The Mapping of New Spain*, Barbara Mundy ([Chicago: University of Chicago Press, 1996], 181–211) studies *mercedes* and land-grant maps in which native painters use indigenous conventions to authenticate the representation of vacant lands.

6. See Michel de Certeau, "On the Oppositional Practices of Everyday Life," *Social Text* 3 (Fall 1980): 40.

7. Jacques Derrida, "Faith and Reason," in *Acts of Religion*, ed. Gil Anidjar and trans. Samuel Weber (New York: Routledge, 2002), 37.

8. I elaborate these ideas in detail in "Franciscans and Dominicans under the Gaze of a Tlacuilo: Plural-World Dwelling in an Indian Pictorial Codex," lecture from Morrison Inaugural Lecture Series (Berkeley, CA: Doe Library, 1998). For an edition of *Codex Telleriano-Remensis*, see E. Quiñones Keber, *Codex Telleriano-Remensis: Ritual, Divination, and History in a Pictorial Aztec Manuscript* (Austin: University of Texas Press, 1995).

9. See my discussion in *Inventing America: Spanish Historiography and the Formation of Eurocentrism* (Norman: University of Oklahoma Press, 1993), 110–116, of the pictorial component of book 12 of Sahagún's *Historia de las cosas de la Nueva España*.

10. On issues pertaining to technology, voice, and testimony, see Jacques Derrida and Bernard Stiegler, *Echographies of Television*, trans. Jennifer Bajorek (Oxford: Polity Press, 2002).

11. John Bierhost, ed. and trans., *Cantares Mexicanos: Songs of the Aztecs* (Stanford, CA: Stanford University Press, 1985), 183.

12. Arthur J. O. Anderson and Susan Schroeder, ed. and trans., *Codex Chimalpahin*, 2 vols. (Norman: University of Oklahoma Press, 1997).

13. Ibid., 1:65.

14. Ibid., 1:75.

15. Ibid., 1:91.

16. Ibid., 2:131.

17. Ibid., 2:183.

18. Ibid., 2:172.

19. Ibid., 2:7–9.

20. Henry Louis Gates Jr., *The Signifying Monkey: A Theory of African-American Literary Criticism* (New York: Oxford University Press, 1988), 131.

21. Anderson and Schroeder, ed. and trans., *Codex Chimalpahin*, 2:131.

Talking Back

Yes, yes, the social psychology, the power issues and dynamics—how could these matters not be considered as part of the probing of "scriptures"? These are matters having to do not with the one-time explosive moment in which the originary impulse behind the invention of scriptures is revealed. No, what has been addressed in the foregoing essays are some of the ongoing historical and new and widely varied social-psychological needs and power dynamics and issues that focus on peoples' situations.

The pointed question is this—do we need scriptures? If so, why? What offices or functions do we make them provide for us? Is it the need for center-ing? Is it the creation and maintenance of a discursive cultural field within which one come to know where one is, who one is?[1] No exhaustive evidence was provided here, nor was such intended. But the probing here seems to suggest that given a chance human beings tend to create scriptures—as center forces, as canons, as cultural fields. Even before those complex moments and situations in history in which the writing and the textual were invented, there is evidence that human beings invented and had experiences with some things that worked for them in ways that approximate texts as scriptures. We must continue to probe whether this is the case or what it might mean—for human shaping and striving, survival and thriving—if this were the case.

—ed.

NOTES

1. Pierre Bourdieu, *Outline of a Theory of Practice* (Cambridge, UK: Cambridge University Press, 1977); Wesley A. Kort, *"Take, Read": Scripture, Textuality, and Cultural Practice* (University Park: Pennsylvania State University Press, 1996).

PART V

SIGNIFYING
ON THE QUESTIONS

24   *In Hoc Signum Vincent*

A MIDRASHIST REPLIES

BURTON L. VISOTZKY

In an attempt to offer an intellectual patrimony to the literary mode of signifying, and to associate it with an older, sister community that historically experienced oppression, I respond to Vincent Wimbush's essay[1] from the vantage point of rabbinic interpretation of "scriptures" or Midrash. In the spirit of friendship, however, allow me to call this response not "critique" but rather, to use Wimbush's vocabulary, a bit of "riffing, woofing," perhaps even signifying on his essay.

"There Was a (Wim)Bush All Aflame, Yet the (Wim)Bush Was Not Consumed" (Exodus 2:2)

Text and canon are the identifiers around which certain communities form and around which a communal identity is shaped by readings of "scriptures." This is not only true of modern or postmodern societies; indeed the lengthy history of rabbinic interpretation of scriptures is that of what Wimbush calls a "historically dominated . . . peoples."[2] Further, Hebrew scriptures themselves (namely the Tanakh as opposed to the Old Testament) are the very canon of a "historically subaltern people," and the literature is that of a "relatively powerless group." I will return to the significance of these initial statements.

I assume that the "phenomena" referred to as "scriptures" include rabbinic interpretations. Jewish-rabbinic interpretations of scripture typically take place in two loci: 1) synagogue—there as a religious-didactic exercise of ongoing interpretation of the Torah to and for the covenantal people who accept it as binding them within a community of auditors; and 2) the study house—where rabbinic disciples learn the intricacies of interpreting that covenantal document.

I concentrate on classical rabbinic literature that in some way reflects the Jewish community, and if not precisely that community, then certainly the "loose canon" of the Jewish community of the distant past. This assumes that the past intersects with the present, but I shall in this essay privilege the past over the present. I do not wish to write about the synagogues and study halls of metropolitan New York, nor Los Angeles, nor even Claremont. Rather the settings of my observations are drawn primarily from the rabbinic community of occupied Roman Palestine of the second through sixth centuries and its sister rabbinic community in Sassanian Babylonia. In other words, I will be commenting on rabbinic Palestinian and Babylonian *literature* from what Jews call the Talmudic period.[3]

The mode of rabbinic approach to the biblical canon during this period is called Midrash. It is not my place here to define Midrash or even contextualize it historically;[4] for the purposes of this essay I take those as more or less given. Rather I speak of Midrash as a Jewish mode of the interpretation of "scriptures" and focus on what we may learn from this phenomenon for the practice of signifying "scriptures" in the twenty-first century. In particular, it is important to note that the phenomenon of Midrash took place under the political hegemony of the Roman or Sassanian imperium. Thus Midrash approaches "scriptures" as a mode of subaltern expression in reaction to hegemony.[5] I will return below to the problems manifest when comparing Midrash and signifying "scriptures" as subaltern reactions to hegemony. For now I wish to focus on the ways in which Midrash anticipated signifying as a means of reacting to a canonical text. I do so primarily by turning to Henry Louis Gates Jr.'s *The Signifying Monkey*[6] and commenting on intersections between Gate's descriptions of signifying and Midrashic approaches to "scriptures."

"Open for Me the Righteous Gates" (Psalms 118:19)

There are remarkable congruities between themes in *The Signifying Monkey* and Midrash. I list some here as fuel for debate. On the one hand I challenge Gates's and Wimbush's arguments for the uniqueness of Signifying, while on the other I provide signifying with a potential literary ancestry. Gates writes, "to revise the received sign (quotient) literally accounted for in the relation represented by *signified/signifier* at its most apparently denotative level is to critique the nature of (white) meaning itself, to challenge through a literal critique of the sign the meaning of meaning."[7] This too is the fundamental trope of Midrash which approaches "scriptures" as apparently having a surface contextual meaning. The later rabbis referred to it as *peshat*. The rabbis critique the meaning of that text through their own operations of Midrash, yielding a new meaning for their own time and community. As Gates puts it, "Signifyin(g), in other words, is the figurative difference between the literal and the metaphorical, between surface and latent meaning."[8] This definition almost perfectly inscribes the distinction between what the rabbis characterize as peshat and *derash*.

Gates is even thoughtful enough to graph and describe the relationship of the "(white) text to its Signified reply" or, if you will, the peshat to its derash. "Whereas signification operates and can be represented on a syntagmatic or horizontal axis, Signifyin(g) operates and can be represented on a paradigmatic or vertical axis."[9] Gates's characterization is as emphatically true of rabbinic literature and its distinctions of peshat and derash, the "paradigmatic" most notably evident when derash is represented in its narrative forms of *Aggada*.

Gates notes that this move is not as simple as I have characterized it: "It is not sufficient merely to reveal that black people colonized a white sign."[10] The implications of Gates's astute recognition of the complex social interaction will be explored below regarding the rabbinic community and its dual reaction to both the canonical text of their own community and how their interpretations of that scripture embodied their reactions to the varied hegemonies under which they lived.

Yet even as the scriptural canon receives a new interpretative reading, Gates points out that "it would be erroneous even to suggest that a concept can be erased from its relation to its signifier."[11] In fact, this observation was made long ago within the Babylonian (read: Iraqi) rabbinic community, which struggled over the replacement of the contextual meaning of scripture (what contemporary church fathers referred to as *theoria* or *historia*) by the allegorizing methods of interpretation that ran the risk of obliterating the peshat in favor of its new interpretation (derash). The great Babylonian teacher Mar said, "Scripture cannot lose its literal or contextual sense."[12]

The borders between these senses of "scriptures," whether characterized by Gates as literal and figurative or by the rabbis as peshat and derash, are more fluid and porous than some scholars might prefer. The interpretative senses are on a continuum, and one community's "literal" might be another community's "figurative." As Gates writes, "it is this relationship between the literal and the figurative, and the dire consequences of their confusion, which is the most striking repeated element of these tales."[13] These consequences are best observed within the rabbinic community of interpretation when the mystic approaches scripture; for it is the mystic interpreter's penchant to read the figurative as the literal, the metaphoric as the concrete. The "dire consequences" will be immediately apparent to those who characterize Jewish theology as an iconic and particularly eschewing physical (incarnational) descriptions of the deity.

In fifth century Roman Palestine, the following Midrash circulated:

> God said, "Let there be light" (Gen. 1:3). Rabbi Shimeon ber' Yehotzadak asked Rabbi Shmuel bar Nahman, "I have heard that you are a master of *Aggadah* (rabbinic [esoteric?] lore). From where was light created?"
>
> He replied, "The Blessed Holy One wrapped Himself in light, as in a garment and shined forth the radiance of His beauty from one end of the universe to the other." He said this in a whisper [as a sign of its esoteric content].
>
> He said, "It is explicitly Scripture, 'Wrapped in light as a garment' (Psalm 104:2), why do you whisper?"
>
> He replied, "Just as I heard it in a whisper, so I transmit it in a whisper."[14]

Switching between figurative and literal is but one of many tropes of both Midrash and signifying. Gates writes of another, "repetition, with a signal difference, is fundamental to the nature of Signifyin(g)."[15] This use of repetition with a difference as a mode of signifying is typical in Midrash, whether in its Aramaic garb as Targum or in its medieval garb as the Retold Bible.[16]

These broader principles are enumerated by Gates:

> Signifyin(g) is a trope in which are subsumed several other rhetorical tropes, including metaphor, metonymy, synecdoche, and irony (the master tropes), and also hyperbole, litotes, and metalepsis . . . to this list we could easily add aporia, chiasmus, and catechresis, all of which are used in the ritual of Signifyin(g) . . . The black rhetorical trope, subsumed under Signifyin(g), would include

marking, loud-talking, testifying, calling out (of one's name), sounding, rapping, playing the dozens, and so on.[17]

Gates turns to earlier authorities for his various enumerations of the tropes of signifying. But neither he nor they are the first to articulate lists of hermeneutic methods of interpretation. So, in the introduction to the early-third-century rabbinic commentary to Leviticus, we preserve a text that teaches, "Rabbi Yishmael says there are thirteen tropes of [rabbinic] Midrash on the Torah."[18]

It is no great discovery to find the listing of modes of exegesis cross-culturally. Midrash and Signifying also cross-culturally share the performative aspects of "oral literature." As Gates describes signifying, "its self-consciously open rhetorical status, then, functions as a kind of writing, wherein rhetoric is the writing of speech, of oral discourse." This is a subtle and decidedly abstract approach to capturing the phenomenon. But the "talking book" phenomenon has been much explored by rabbinic scholars of late, both from a semiotic perspective[19] and from the viewpoint of those who map oral performance.[20] It is sufficient for our purposes here to note that rabbinic *literature* is referred to as *Torah Shebe'al peh*, oral Torah, which ostensibly functions as commentary on *Torah shebeketav*, namely the "written" canon of the Hebrew Bible.

Acknowledging the performative aspects of signifying requires a return to situation or location. Of signifying, Gates writes, "The Monkey tales generally have been recorded from male poets, in predominantly male settings such as barrooms, pool halls, and street corners."[21] While the rabbis do not usually locate their stories in barrooms and certainly not pool halls (no rabbis in River City), they do transmit and perform Midrash in the primarily male domains of the study house and the synagogue. Like signifying, classical Midrash (as opposed to largely feminist modern Midrash) is primarily a male phenomenon, performed by the men for men.

Within that male culture a certain narrative fantasy world obtains. Gates characterizes this as "the Daydream of the Black Other, chiastic fantasies of reversal of power relationships."[22] Rabbinic texts are dotted with stories of how the rabbis either outwit the hegemon,[23] wisely advise the hegemon (as in the tales of Rabbi Judah, presumptive patriarch of Jewish Palestine in the early third century, and the Emperor Antoninus [B.AZ 10a–b]), or ultimately convert The Man (e.g., B. Gittin 56a, where the Emperor Nero converts to Judaism).

On a narrower syntactic level, Gates notes that during signifying "the speaker and his audience realize that 'Signifying is occurring and that the dictionary-syntactical meaning of the utterance is to be ignored.' . . . 'it is the cleverness used in directing the attention of the hearer and audience to this shared knowledge upon which a speaker's artistic talent is judged.' Signifyin(g), in other words, depends on the success of the signifier at invoking an absent meaning ambiguously 'present' in a carefully wrought statement."[24]

There is a piquant version of this phenomenon of coded speech in the Babylonian Talmud (Eruvin 53b). A conversation is imagined between the above-mentioned Rabbi Judah and his maid. He is hosting a dinner party when "she asked him, 'The ladle strikes against the jar, shall the eagles fly to their nests?'" By which she meant: "the wine vat is empty. Are the guests leaving soon?" The Talmud continues, "When she wished them to remain at table she asked him, 'Will the crown of her friend be removed so that the ladle will float in the jar like a ship that sails in the sea.'" As we might say it more directly, "Is it time to open another wine-cask?"

I alluded above to Midrashic tales in which a rabbinic character outwits a Roman. In a classic example, a famous Rabbi is arrested and gains release by apparently flattering the pagan judge. The flattery, however, is fueled by the misprision of the judge whose ego makes him misconstrue the rabbi's remarks. As Gates writes of the Signifying Monkey, "first, the Monkey 'tropes-a-dope' the Lion, by representing a figurative statement as a literal statement, depending on the Lion's thickness to misread the difference."[25]

Rabbi Eliezer was once arrested for heresy-Christianity (*minut*). He was brought up to the tribunal (*bema*) for judgment. That governor (*hegemon*) said to him, "Does an elder like you occupy himself with such idle things?" He replied, "I put my faith in the judge."

That governor thought that Rabbi Eliezer was referring to him, while Eliezer only had his father in heaven in mind. The judge said, "Since you have put your faith in me, so I opine: Is it possible that these gray hairs would err in such idle matters? *Dimissus*, behold you are released."[26]

In case you missed it, the rabbinic story, told in Hebrew, takes the trouble to transliterate the term "hegemon." I promise more on the problem of the rabbinic subaltern reacting to hegemony.

But before I close the righteous Gates, allow me one more specific example from his *Signifying Monkey* and a few comparative comments. Gates recounts one of the premiere locutions of signifying: "Your mama."[27] There is a veritable catalogue of "your mama" insults, counted in "the dozens," if not actually thousands. While I stipulate "your mama" is a trope particular to black signifying, I would be derelict not to mention an adorable Aramaic fantasy from fifth-century Roman Palestine in which the rabbinic fabulist speculates on the luxury enjoyed by the generation of Noah's flood. How luxurious was it? It was so luxurious that women gave birth only three days after conceiving, and their babies were so precocious that their mothers could send them to find a flint to cut their umbilical cords. Once, a tot on such a mission ran into Asmodeus, prince of demons. They wrestled until dawn, when Asmodeus could no longer prevail. That demon said to the tot, "*Zil glog le'imach*" ("Go boast to your mama, that the cock crowed, otherwise I would have killed you"). The baby replied, "Go tell *your* mama that if my umbilical cord had been cut, I would have killed you!"[28] I grant you the diss here is to the demon and not to Asmodeus's mama or, worse, his grandmother. But no matter what language or era, your mama is your mama.

In the realm of global comparisons between Midrash and signifying, I note with pleasure that Gates titles a section of his work "Intertextuality."[29] In my field the concept of intertextuality has been brilliantly explored by our colleague

Daniel Boyarin in his highly influential book *Intertextuality and the Reading of Midrash*.[30]

Gates insists that "Signifyin(g) is so fundamentally black."[31] Yet so much of what Gates describes in *The Signifying Monkey* is equally true of Midrash as a mode of interpretation, of discourse, and repositioning of the community with its own canon. One might contend that every culture must have its own signification of its canon, otherwise that canon would lose significance as the community evolved. So this is the case of Midrash for the Jews, "typology, historia and theoria" for the church fathers of Asia Minor, and so forth.[32]

Gates gets to what is at the very heart of signifying, a notion that Wimbush also addresses in his comment about "the (re)bleaching of Scriptures."[33] Gates contends, "the manipulation of these classic black figures of Signification—[allows] the black person to move freely between these two discursive universes. This is an excellent example of what I call linguistic masking, the verbal sign of the mask of blackness that demarcates the boundary between the white linguistic realm and the black."[34]

Spoken within the hegemony of the white community, black signifying is a subversive mode of subaltern discourse. *When applied to "scriptures," however, signifying ceases to be subversive and potentially becomes religiously revelatory*—but only, I believe, if the community of readers ceases to see the canon as a white man's book and reclaims it instead as an African document; not just an African/American narrative but an African/Jewish narrative.

"Stranger in a Strange Land" (Exodus 2:22)

It is precisely here that the comparison between Midrash and signifying falters. Hegemony and subaltern signifying are unquestionably common to both Midrash and signifying. Both Gates and Wimbush contend that signifying is done by the African American community on the (white) canon. Because the Bible was introduced to the African American (slave) community as the white man's canon, it is understandable that signifying undermines the meaning of the "scriptures" and subverts it by remaking it as something new for the black community.

This was never the case with Midrash. Although the rabbis were constantly engaged in reinterpretation of "scriptures" through the vehicle of Midrash, and although the literature was unquestionably that of Jewish subalterns toward the Roman or Christian hegemony, nevertheless the scripture signified on was always a *Jewish* canon (even as the church colonized it). The rabbis did Midrash on the Tanakh—the Jewish Bible. It was not an alien (white) culture they sought to subvert, but their own patrimony with which they were in dialogue. Midrashic reading of scripture, however subversive it may in fact have been, was simultaneously deeply traditional. It sought to establish links of continuity and faith rather than emphasizing discontinuity and lack of faith with the hegemonic Other. Midrash did react toward the Other—be it Rome, Christianity, or, later, Islam. But the scripture it interpreted was quintessentially Jewish, never Other.

This deep divide between Midrash and signifying is important in considering the problems of Midrash as a paradigm for the Institute for Signifying Scriptures. An alternate approach to "scriptures" and Midrash that might be taken by the ISS could be that of recent feminist studies as a subaltern approach to "scriptures."[35] In popular works, Jewish feminists have found modern Midrash to be a very fruitful means of (re)entering "scriptures." In these writings and tellings, the voices of biblical women are newly heard, recaptured, and imagined. Academic Jewish feminist criticism has made immense strides in approaching the patriarchal biblical Other and in some ways repossessing scripture as belonging to the community of women.

"I Am Black and Beautiful" (Song of Songs 1:5)

This last point is one I wish to elaborate on. When we speak of "signifying scriptures," we must ask: *whose "scriptures"?* Wimbush thinks of the Old and New Testaments as a WASP (white Anglo-Saxon Protestant) canon. "Signifying," as Gates defines it, also seems to imply this. But neither the Tanakh nor the New Testament is, in point of fact, a white book. True, each has a long tradition of white colonization—but that does not make them white texts.

The Torah, or at least the book of Exodus, purports to be an African document. Whether we follow the chronology of Genesis or Exodus, the Jews spent two hundred to four hundred years in Africa—as slaves. When Moses slew the Egyptian and fled, his future wife mistook him for an Egyptian. One imagines her saying: funny, you don't look Jewish. But it is equally likely that at that moment, Tzippora looked at this African man of color and thought he *did* look Jewish. And let us not forget that Moses married an Ethiopian woman.[36] I have no wish to recapitulate the *Black Athena*[37] debate here, merely to point out that for the African American community, it is possible to view "scriptures" through the lens of ownership, and not just through the hermeneutic of identification with the slave narratives while capitulating the canon to white hegemony.

There are then two Jewish paradigms to reclaim the biblical canon for the African American community. The first, as I just indicated, is to view the Tanakh as an African document (African-Israelite/African-American). It is most certainly not a WASP (white) document. The second paradigm is that of Midrash and "signifying scriptures" (I also harbor no wish to recapitulate the Handelman, *Slayers of Moses*,[38] debate by implying that signifying has actual Jewish roots). There are many affinities between Midrash and signifying. I believe it is the challenge of this institute to signify "scriptures" in the ways in which the rabbis, mutatis mutandis, did Midrash: by establishing the canon as an African document and keeping the faith.

The Institute for Signifying Scriptures is off to an auspicious start, (re)colorizing "scriptures." This work is essential and yet difficult; for if "scriptures" are not a black book, a "talking book" as Gates describes it, then the risk remains of abetting the "bleaching" of "scriptures." For people of color, hegemonic white scriptures still run the risk of being read, as that which the most canonical of Dead White

Male authors tells it, as "a tale told by an idiot, full of sound and fury, Signifying nothing."[39]

In conclusion I return to one of Wimbush's opening questions: *where* does it happen? My answer, from Deuteronomy 30:12, 14, "It is not in heaven . . . no, the phenomenon is very close to you, it is in your mouth and in your heart; do it."

NOTES

1. See Vincent L. Wimbush's introductory essay to the current volume, 13.

2. Ibid.

3. Burton L. Visotzky, "The Literature of the Rabbis," in *From Mesopotamia to Modernity: 10 Introductions to Jewish History and Literature*, ed. Burton L. Visotzky and David E. Fishman (Boulder, CO: Westview Press, 1999), 71–102.

4. See, for example, Visotzky, *Mesopotamia*.

5. See Hayim Lapin, "Hegemony and its Discontents: Rabbis as a Late Antique Provincial Population," in *Jewish Culture and Society Under the Christian Roman Empire*, eds. Richard Kalmin and Seth Schwartz (Leuven: Peeters, 2003), 319–347; Joshua Levinson, "'Tragedies Naturally Performed': Fatal Charades, Parodia Sacra, and the Death of Titus," in *Jewish Culture and Society Under the Christian Roman Empire*, eds. Richard Kalmin and Seth Schwartz (Leuven: Peeters, 2003), 349–382; Homi K. Bhabha, "Of Mimicry and Man: The Ambivalence of Colonial Discourse," *The Location of Culture* (London: Routledge, 1994), 85–92; R. Guha, *Dominance Without Hegemony* (Cambridge, MA: Harvard University Press, 1997); J. F. Scott, *Domination and the Arts of Resistance: Hidden Transcripts* (New Haven, CT: Yale University Press, 1991).

6. Henry Louis Gates Jr., *The Signifying Monkey: A Theory of African-American Literary Criticism* (New York: Oxford University Press, 1988).

7. Ibid., 47.

8. Ibid., 82.

9. Ibid., 49.

10. Ibid., 47.

11. Ibid., 48.

12. Shab 63a; cf. Burton L. Visotzky, "Jots and Tittles: On Scriptural Interpretation in Rabbinic and Patristic Literatures," in *Fathers of the World: Essays in Rabbinic and Patristic Literatures* (Tübingen: Mohr/Siebeck, 1995), 28–40.

13. Gates, *The Signifying Monkey*, 55.

14. Genesis Rabbah 3:4, cf. Pirke de-Rabbi Eliezer (PRE) 3 and G. Scholem, *Gnosticism, Merkabah Mysticism, and the Talmudic Tradition* (New York: JTSA, 1965).

15. Gates, *The Signifying Monkey*, 51.

16. Gesa Vermes, *Scripture and Tradition in Judaism*, 2nd ed. (Leiden: Brill, 1973).

17. Gates, *The Signifying Monkey*, 52.

18. See Saul Lieberman, "Rabbinic Interpretation of Scripture," in *Hellenism in Jewish Palestine* (New York: JTSA, 1950), 47–82.

19. Jose Faur, *Golden Doves with Silver Dots: Semiotics and Textuality in Rabbinic Tradition* (Bloomington: Indiana University Press, 1986).

20. Martin Jaffee, "The Oral-Cultural Context of the Talmud Yerushalmi" in *The Talmud Yerushalmi and Graeco-Roman Culture I*, ed. Peter Schäfer (Tübingen: Mohr/Siebeck,1998), 27–61.

21. Gates, *The Signifying Monkey*, 54.

22. Ibid., 59.

23. T. Hullin 2:24.

24. Claudia Mitchell-Kernan quoted in Gates, *The Signifying Monkey*, 86.

25. Gates, *The Signifying Monkey*, 63.

26. T. Hullin 2:24, and see Burton L. Visotzky, "Methodological Considerations in the Study of John's Interaction with First-Century Judaism," in *Life in Abundance: Studies in the Gospel of John in Tribute to Raymond E. Brown*, ed. John Donahue (Collegeville, MN: Liturgical Press, 2005), 91–107.

27. Gates, *The Signifying Monkey*, 66.

28. Genesis Rabbah 36:1, cf. Leviticus Rabbah 5:1, where the baby's reply is, "Go tell your mama's mama."

29. Gates, *The Signifying Monkey*, 60.

30. Daniel Boyarin, *Intertextuality and the Reading of Midrash* (Bloomington: Indiana University Press, 1990).

31. Gates, *The Signifying Monkey*, 64.

32. Cf. Visotzky, "Jots and Tittles."

33. See Wimbush's introductory essay in this volume, 11.

34. Gates, *The Signifying Monkey*, 75.

35. For example, Phyllis Trible, *God and the Rhetoric of Sexuality* (Philadelphia: Fortress Press, 1978); Phyllis Trible, *Texts of Terror: Literary-Feminist Readings of Biblical Narratives* (Philadelphia: Fortress Press, 1984); Judith Plaskow, *Standing Again at Sinai: Judaism from a Feminist Perspective* (San Francisco: Harper, 1990); Elisabeth Schüssler Fiorenza, "The Ethics of Interpretation: De-Centering Biblical Scholarship," *Journal of Biblical Literature* 107 (1988): 3–17; Elisabeth Schüssler Fiorenza, *Wisdom Ways: Introducing Feminist Biblical Interpretation* (Maryknoll, NY: Orbis Books, 2001).

36. Burton L. Visotzky, "Stranger and Stranger in a Strange Land," *CommonQuest* 3 (Winter 1998): 4–6.

37. Martin Bernal, *Black Athena: The Afro-Asiatic Roots of Classical Culture* (New Brunswick, NJ: Rutgers University Press, 1989).

38. Susan Handelman, *The Slayers of Moses: The Re-emergence of Rabbinic Interpretation in Modern Literary Theory* (Albany: SUNY Press, 1982). Cf. David Stern's reply to Handleman: David Stern, "Moses-cide, Midrash and Contemporary Literary Criticism," *Prooftexts* 4 (1984): 193–204.

39. Shakespeare, *Macbeth*, act V, scene 5.

25 *Powerful Words*

THE SOCIAL-INTELLECTUAL LOCATION OF THE INTERNATIONAL SIGNIFYING SCRIPTURES PROJECT

ELISABETH SCHÜSSLER FIORENZA

The inauguration of the Institute for Signifying Scriptures (ISS), which has been initiated by Professor Wimbush, is a historic event that calls for celebration and critical reflection. This international institute is historic because it programmatically intends to study the signifying of scriptures by subaltern peoples rather than to focus on the biblical text and its ancient contexts. At the same time this event calls for critical reflection because the ISS intends to do so within the disciplinary parameters and interdisciplinary opportunities of the university. It will not come as a surprise that I engage in such a critical reflection on questions of method and institutional location from a critical feminist perspective,[1] which is in tension with a phenomenology of religion approach.[2]

Theoretical Frameworks

I began work on this panel's topic, "Settings/Situations/Practices," with a rather impressionistic inventory of the social locations and sites where "signifying scriptures" takes place and then compared my own rather unscientific list of the phenomenon with the ethnographic inventory detailed in the prior project, *African Americans and the Bible.* This inventory, which was developed by student researchers in collaboration with sociologists and ethnographers for charting the sites of the study of and engagement with the Bible, has utilized four major heuristic categories for sorting its findings: institutions/organizations, socialization contexts, cultural contexts and expressions, and political/economic contexts.[3]

Such an inventory lacks, however, a critical edge insofar as it cannot tell us much about *who* is engaging the Bible in, for example, barbershops, universities, political movements, education of children, films, the White House, or nursing homes, and *to what ends* they are doing so. Are those who are engaging the Bible evangelical or Catholic wo/men,[4] are they fundamentalist or liberal men, highly educated or illiterate people? Is the political rally where scripture is used or appealed to as an icon an antigay or a wo/men's reproductive rights rally? Is scripture engaged by a community of feminist or fundamentalist theologians?

It might have been unnecessary to spell out social location, subjects, goals, and function of scriptural interpretation in the preceding project, which focused on one specific group of signifiers, African Americans, although it did not elaborate the perspective of African American women and womanist interpretation. To separate settings/situations and practices from the "practitioners" and agents of signifying as well as from psychosocial needs and consequences seems neither advisable nor possible in this present undertaking. Rather it is necessary to focus on the practices of inquiry into power relations, structural functions, and ideological goals for engaging the scriptures. Because the present Signifying Scriptures project does not presuppose a single, unified subject of signifying or claim to speak from a particular social location within a specific community of marginalized people, an ethics of interpretation[5] (i.e., a second order critical reflection on the method and ethos of the envisioned ISS) is called for. This is especially necessary if one approaches the "phenomenon" of signifying scriptures with a critical feminist perspective, which insists that wo/men of all races, classes, colors, and religions must become visible and audible subjects of interpretation. Hence it is crucial to scrutinize the phenomenological method of the Signifying Scriptures project, which is taken over from the *academic* comparative religions or history of religions approach.

First, Vincent Wimbush's discussion paper for this conference seems to work with this phenomenological method, although he clearly states that he does not find this approach quite satisfactory:

> I threaded the question not through the dominant world religions and the investigative and rhetorical categories they provoke, but through some of the experiences of the historically and persistently subaltern, usually darker peoples of the world.[6]

Yet, in order to articulate such a subaltern interpretation, one must critically ask whether the phenomenological method is helpful or counterproductive to this intent. The phenomenological approach involves not only synchronic or cross-cultural comparisons and the search for universal essences, patterns, or types,[7] often called comparative religion, "but also historical study of religions with an emphasis on philology and text."[8] Because the envisioned ISS does not emphasize the historical study of scripture, it is part of the comparative religion direction, which looks for cross-cultural and cross-religious comparisons and describes as the center of such comparisons the phenomenon "of signifying sacred scriptures," thereby understanding sacred scripture as an essence or type.

The phenomenological method is characterized by empiricism, subjectivism, idealism, and hermeneutics. It seeks to "discover underlying types, models, themes, and structures in the overwhelming mass of religious 'data,'" a search that was instantiated by the descriptive thematic of the conference panels. It understands itself as "rigorously nonparochial, scientific and neutral," disassociating itself from any one tradition, point of view, or claim to truth "in order to distinguish itself from Christian theology and history."[9]

Since this method calls for the suspension or bracketing (*epoché*) of judgment and evaluation "in order to describe rather than explain the phenomenon as it appears," it cannot reflect on the social location of the interpreter, nor grasp the historically and politically situated character of a phenomenon such as "signifying sacred scriptures," nor evaluate "the thing in itself" as a "product of its own production, reproducing its producer's positionality, particularity and contingency."[10] In short, the phenomenological method is essentializing, dehistoricizing, homogenizing, and ideologizing, obfuscating and dissimulating a phenomenon's particular embeddedness in power relations. Hence one must ask whether it serves the research interests of the ISS with its commitment to the subalterns and the voices on the margins of the academy and biblical studies.

Second, as the program of this international conference indicates and the inauguration of the Institute for Signifying Scriptures as an institute of Claremont Graduate University makes clear, this project intends to speak from the social location of "marginal" scholars within the interdisciplinary academic study of religion and proposes to research the practices of signifying on scriptures by marginal and subaltern peoples. The university and the academic study of religion, its power relations, its practices of knowledge production and socialization are the institutional setting of the ISS. *This institutional location*, I suggest, signifies both ISS's historical possibilities and its potential cooptation. Hence it is necessary to focus critical reflection on the social location of the Signifying Scriptures project in the academy in general and in biblical studies and its practices of meaning making in particular. The academy and not the religious community or social movements for change is the *institutional* site where signifying scripture discourses are articulated and engaged.

Third, if one focuses on the academic setting of this project rather than on discussing a range of situations where the phenomenon of signifying scriptures is sited, it is necessary to locate "the phenomenon" within religious studies in general and biblical studies in particular, as well as to question the definition of scripture "as true, authoritative, and sacred" in relation to scripturalizing communities. Such a critical problematization does not seek to stifle comparative practices but to make them critically aware of power relations.

In her article "Beyond the Guild: Liberating Biblical Studies,"[11] the historian of religion Barbara Holdrege[12] has argued that the ISS approach to scripture like the previous project, *African Americans and the Bible*, and Wimbush's discussion paper, takes over the definition of the Harvard school of comparative religions.[13] She claims that this comparative religion approach introduces "a new paradigm of biblical studies that is above all relational—and thereby scriptural—in its approach."[14] This Harvard comparative religions approach uses scripture as a cross-cultural and relational category, which according to Holdrege "refers not simply to a text" but to a text "in relationship to a religious community for whom it is sacred and authoritative."[15] Holdrege chides biblical scholars for focusing too much on their own individual readings of texts rather than on the communal practices that valorize texts as holy scripture. She does not, however, problematize "relations" in terms of power structures and ask which kind of relations are engaged or which members of religious communities articulate authoritative interpretations. In a similar way, Miriam Levering also defines scripture as "a special class of true and powerful words, a class formed by the ways in which these particular words are received by persons and communities in their common life."[16]

This emphasis on an approach "that is above all relational—and thereby scriptural"[17] opens up for Holdrege the possibility of comparing the Bible with the Vedas in terms of canonical authority, social location, and modes of transmission and reception. Holdrege assumes a difference in social location of interpreters and concludes that the interpretation of the Vedas belonged to the elite, while biblical criticism was open to a greater range of interpreters. The general populace in India, who were barred from interpreting the sacred scriptures, created new forms of literature such as epic poems and stories of the gods in order to embody their own visions. Therefore she concludes that the category of sacred scripture is different in the two cultures and religions.

Coming from a cultural Catholic context, however, this comparative construction of difference becomes questionable. In Catholic Christianity and culture we find the same division between the official and popular interpretation of scripture. The authoritative interpretation of sacred scriptures, like the interpretation of the Vedas, has been in the hands of a caste of elite, educated clergymen. Until shortly before Vatican II, common people in many countries were still barred from reading scripture. Hence popular religion has elaborated biblical stories in legends, arts, poetry, and rituals. This popular elaboration, however, has not always been critical of structures of domination but has often been in line with the dominant cultural and political-religious ethos. Like scholarly interpretation it also has functioned to inculcate culturally established norms and normalized social prejudices with the help of authoritative sacred scripture. Consequently the "sacredness" and "authority" of scripture and its use in marginalized communities may not simply be presupposed but must be critically investigated. Hence it is necessary to recognize that the Signifying Scriptures project is rooted in the prevalent discourses of academic biblical studies, which have decisively shaped the relation between scriptures and religious communities. This situatedness needs to be critically analyzed.

Tracing Paradigms of Interpretation

Paradigm criticism can help us to locate the ISS in biblical studies and to critically assess the different and manifold ways of scripture interpretation. Paradigm construction has developed a typology of shifting practices that shape and determine both the discipline of biblical studies and popular biblical interpretation. Such paradigms or exemplary instances of theoretical framework and method can exist alongside each other, or they can be overlapping or exclusive of each other. They can utilize each other's methodological approaches and can work in corrective interaction with each other.

Fernando Segovia charts four paradigms in biblical studies in terms of *modern* academic biblical criticism rather than in terms of the overall history of biblical interpretation. Like Wimbush, he is concerned with debunking historicist criticism, but his focus is still on both the understanding of biblical texts and the function of scripture in the ongoing life of "actual flesh-and-blood religious communities":

Historical criticism (1), which uses the text as *means*, was according to him the dominant paradigm through the 1970s. Literary criticism (2), which dislodged historical criticism in the 1980s, analyzes the text as *medium*. Cultural criticism (3), an umbrella term that encompasses lines of inquiry such as socioeconomic and ideological, Neo-Marxist, and various forms of sociological analysis, understands the text as *medium and means*. Finally, cultural studies or postcolonial criticism (4) takes account of the influx of marginal voices and locates the meaning of the text in the encounter between the text and the flesh-and-blood reader.

At this point it might be helpful to look at my own somewhat different paradigm construction, which considers not just the academy but also communities of faith in their relation to scripture. If one recognizes such theological interpretation, the genealogy of biblical criticism reads somewhat differently. The four basic paradigms that I have articulated in *Bread Not Stone*[18] and refined and renamed again and again take this theological paradigm of interpretation into account. Then the four paradigms of biblical interpretation are: the theological-canonical paradigm (1), the scientific-positivist paradigm (2), the cultural-hermeneutical paradigm (3), and the rhetorical-emancipatory paradigm (4). Such a paradigm construction is not only able to comprehend the struggle between the first and second paradigms but also to underscore the affinities among the first, third, and fourth paradigms of interpretation.

For centuries the prevalent paradigm of Christian biblical interpretation has been the first theological-canonical paradigm, which understands the biblical record as sacred scripture and revealed authoritative Word of G*d.[19] This paradigm of biblical interpretation is at home in communities of faith but has been practiced by a class of elite, educated clergymen from which women and other marginal people were excluded.

The ancient and medieval Christian method of interpretation sought to establish a fourfold sense of scripture: the literal (historical), the tropological (moral), the allegorical, and the anagogical (future-oriented) meaning of a text. Beginning with humanism and the time of the Reformation, this open-ended dynamic mode of medieval interpretation controlled by church authority changed. The Reformation taught that "scripture alone" (*sola scriptura*) is the foundation of faith, that it is self-interpreting and can be understood by everyone. The orthodox successors of the Reformers, however, soon introduced the dogma of "verbal inspiration" and the principle of biblical infallibility to control the interpretation of scripture, a theological move that is still defining scriptural interpretation in Christian communities. Literalist fundamentalism insists that the biblical message proclaims universal moral values and revealed truth. Like modern science, it claims that this truth can be positively established and proven. Its emphasis on verbal inerrancy asserts that the Bible transcends ideology and particularity. This view obscures the power relations and interests at work in all biblical texts and interpretations. It thereby shares in the second modernist paradigm of interpretation.

The second scientific-positivist paradigm of knowledge gives primary import to evidence, data, and empirical inquiry—that is, to the "logic of facts." This scientific-positivist paradigm of historical factual and formalist literary biblical studies was developed in the context of the European Enlightenment over and against the dogmatic control and authority of the churches. Its social institutional location is the modern university. This positivistic ethos of scientific biblical criticism, however, is not just at home in the academy but has become popularized by literalist fundamentalism. Hence it is important to explore critically to what degree religious communities have internalized the presuppositions of this modern scientific-positivistic academic paradigm.

Just as other academic discipline in the humanities sought to prove themselves as objective sciences in analogy to the natural sciences, so also did biblical studies. Scientific biblical interpretation claimed to establish "facts" and "data" objectively, free from philosophical considerations or political interests. The mandate to abstract from social location and normative concepts in the immediate encounter with the text allegedly functioned to ensure that the resulting historical or literary accounts would be accurate and free from any ideology.

Because biblical scholarship in the United States developed in the political context of several heresy trials at the turn of the twentieth century,[20] its rhetoric of disinterested objectivity tends to reject all overt religious or theological engagement as ideological and therefore "unscientific." The aspiration to "scientific" status in the academy, and the claim to universal, unbiased modes of inquiry, denies the hermeneutical-rhetorical character and masks the sociohistorical location and sociopolitical interests of biblical interpretation. The phenomenological comparative and history of religions approaches to scripture can be situated either in this second or in the following third paradigm, depending on whether they stress objectivism and value neutrality or hermeneutic empathy and meaning.

The third, hermeneutic-cultural paradigm, underscores the rhetorical character of biblical knowledge and acknowledges the symbolic, multidimensional power of biblical texts and artifacts. It understands scripture as cultural icon and ascribes personified status to the text in order to construe it as a dialogue partner or divining agent. Alternatively, it sees the sacred text as a multicolored tapestry and texture of meaning. This third paradigm likens the reading of the Bible to the reading of the classics of Western culture, whose greatness does not consist in their accuracy as records of facts, but depends chiefly on their symbolic power to transfigure human experience and symbolic systems of meaning.

The hermeneutic-cultural paradigm seeks to *understand* sacred texts and their function in the life of peoples and sees texts as perspectival discourses constructing a range of meanings. Because alternative symbolic universes engender competing definitions of the world, they cannot be reduced to one single, definitive meaning. Therefore competing interpretations are not simply either right or wrong. Rather they constitute different ways of reading and of constructing historical and religious meaning.

Like the modern scientific paradigm of biblical criticism, the hermeneutic-cultural approach to biblical interpretation is also located in the university and other cultural institutions. Whereas two decades ago the historical-positivist and literary-formalist paradigms of scientific biblical interpretation reigned in the Anglo-American academy, today hermeneutical and postmodern epistemological discussions abound, discussions that are critical of both the canonical-theological and the positivist-scientific ethos of biblical studies. Feminist, postcolonial, and liberation theological interpretations have played a great part in the postmodern hermeneutical transformation of academic biblical scholarship. Postmodern hermeneutic-cultural and critical feminist-postcolonial analyses of power relations meet in their critique of modernity, because its achievements have been bought at the price of misogyny, racism, colonialism, and slavery. Insofar as these approaches have insisted on critical evaluation and transformation of scripture by the marginalized subjects of interpretation and refused to relinquish overarching stories of meaning, they have inaugurated the fourth, rhetorical-emancipatory, paradigm.

This paradigm of biblical interpretation is not new but has a long history in political-religious struggles for emancipation and radical democracy. It is not so much interested in dogmatic proof, spiritual edification, scientific facts, or cultural sublimation. Rather it investigates the ways in which scriptural texts and icons exercise influence and power in cultural, social, and religious life. Its commitment to change structures of domination and practices of dehumanization compels it to explore how biblical texts function in specific social locations and religious contexts. Working within this paradigm, one investigates how scripture is used to inculcate interpretive practices that condition people to accept and internalize violence and prejudice. One also searches for visions of equality, freedom, and well-being for all of creation that are also inscribed in scriptures but have been historically unrealized possibilities.

This fourth emerging paradigm seeks to redefine the self-understanding of biblical interpretation in ethical, rhetorical, political, and emancipatory terms. In contrast to postmodern criticism, the voices from the margins of biblical studies insist that the subjugated others cannot afford to abandon either the notion of being historical subjects and agents or the possibility of knowing the world and the divine differently. Rather the critical voices from the margins of religious communities and the academy maintain that we who are the "subordinated and silenced others" must engage in a political and theoretical process of constituting ourselves as subjects of knowledge, history, and interpretation.

Situating the International Signifying Scriptures Project

Studying the genealogy of biblical studies from the perspective of emancipatory movements helps one to realize that scriptural "meaning making" has been practiced for the most part not only by elite, Western, educated clergymen but also for the benefit of Western cultural and capitalist interests. A Western doctrinal, fundamentalist, or scientific approach declares its own culturally particular readings as universal divine revelation or scientific data that may not be questioned. Scripture is understood either as an absolute and true oracle of the will of G*d that cannot be challenged but must be obeyed or it becomes a storehouse of antiquity or a cultural classic. Either scripture reveals timeless truth and universal principles and gives definite answers to modern-day problems and questions, or it elaborates hegemonic cultures. The form of biblical interpretation most closely associated with colonialism is manifested not only in otherworldly evangelicalism and literalist fundamentalism, which are oriented toward the salvation of the soul, but also in scientific, objectivist, Eurocentric biblical scholarship.

Whenever minority communities read/hear/interpret scripture or any other text, they read/hear/interpret it by engaging one or more of these paradigms of interpretation. But whereas the three hegemonic malestream paradigms of interpretation do not enable a critical process of reading that indicts the dehumanizing power of scriptural texts, the fourth, critical-emancipatory-political paradigm does so by making explicit the critical hermeneutical lenses and goals with which it approaches the scriptures. While the other three paradigms obfuscate the fact that they also have sociopolitical and cultural religious interests and goals, the rhetorical emancipatory paradigm openly confesses that it engages in biblical interpretation for the sake of conscientization and well-being.

The phenomenological comparative religion approach, which seems to be at work in the grounding discussion paper for ISS and the organization of this conference, not only tends to locate the Signifying Scriptures project within the third hermeneutical-cultural paradigm but also seeks to surpass this paradigm insofar as it is consciously articulating its social location and positionality in subaltern communities. If this reading is correct, it is necessary to discuss the methodological-interpretational differences of the third and fourth paradigms. Whereas the hermeneutical paradigm approaches scriptures with empathy, the emancipatory paradigm starts with critically reflected experience. Whereas the third paradigm appreciates historicity and contextuality, the fourth paradigm insists on systemic analysis of historical dominations. Whereas the third paradigm stresses linguisticality and values tradition, the fourth paradigm insists on a hermeneutics of suspicion and evaluation of text and traditions in terms of an ethics of interpretation. Whereas the third paradigm insists on pre-understanding, the fourth paradigm insists on imagination. Whereas the third paradigm appreciates scripture as a cultural and religious classic and studies its history of interpretation, the fourth paradigm scrutinizes the *Wirkungsgeschichte* of scripture and engages in critical historical reconstruction and ideological re-visioning. Finally, whereas the hermeneutical paradigm seeks a fusion of horizons, the emancipatory paradigm seeks change and transformation.

In short, the fourth paradigm stresses experience, social location, relations of power and interested perspectives of interpreters, and the rhetoricality of text and interpretation as well as the institutional locations that determine all four paradigms of biblical interpretation. It seeks to research and lift into consciousness the legitimizing, dissimulating, and reifying or normalizing functions of ideology at work in signifying scriptures. Hence it is important to locate the hermeneutics of the signifying scriptures project within this fourth paradigm. Yet in order to do so the ISS would have to relinquish the phenomenological approach, because this method calls for the suspension or bracketing (epoché) of judgment and evaluation. It therefore cannot reflect on the social location of the interpreter, nor grasp the historically and politically situated character of scripture

Moving from Phenomenology to Critical Theory

All four paradigms can be illuminated and tested by critical theory as to what kind of knowledge they produce. Jürgen Habermas delineates three types of knowledge about the world: the empirical-analytical, which seeks to control both religious-spiritual and social-cultural realities, corresponds to the second scientiftic-positivist and the first literalist-fundamentalist paradigms; the hermeneutical-historical-poetic, which seeks to qualitatively understand reality, is embodied in the four-dimensional model of the first paradigm and at home in the third paradigm; and finally, the critical-emancipatory-political, which seeks to transform individual and collective consciousness and reality, governs the fourth emancipatory paradigm of biblical studies.[21]

At this point it becomes clear why the kind of phenomenological definition of scripture of the Harvard comparative religions school as authoritative, revelatory sacred text threatens to mute and take away the critical edge[22] of the Signifying Scriptures project. Scriptures have not only been defined, selected, codified, and interpreted for the most part by a class of elite, educated men, but also made taboo and protected from the critical scrutiny of those people who have been prohibited by custom and law to engage in codifying and signifying scripturalizing practices.

For instance, depending on its definition of scripture, the Signifying Scriptures project could be located either within the first *authoritative-dogmatic-ecclesial paradigm*, or it could be situated within the *hermeneutical-cultural aesthetic paradigm*, or it could be positioned within the last, the *rhetorical-emancipatory-political paradigm*. If one accepts the history of religions understanding of scripture as a "text in relationship to a religious community for whom it is sacred and authoritative," then one has to situate the Signifying Scriptures project in the first paradigm. If one pays attention to its institutional location within the university, one could easily understand its work in line with the second paradigm if it only sets out to accumulate knowledge about the scripturalizing and signifying of "the others."

If one in turn appreciates the phenomenon of scripture as a culturally embodied sacred icon that is celebrated in ritual, song, and dance, then one positions the Signifying Scriptures project in the third paradigm. If one stresses the agency of marginalized and excluded persons and communities who seek to change structures of domination and try to deconstruct or make meaning out of scripture for such emancipatory ends, then this project belongs to the fourth paradigm of biblical studies. Its work, however, can contribute to the emancipatory-political paradigm only if it both eschews the academic value-detachment of the second paradigm and also abandons the notion of scripture of the first paradigm as sacred, true, authoritative word or that of the third paradigm as authoritative classic. If the project of ISS were to be located within the first or third paradigms, then the history of religions conceptualization of scripture as sacred and authoritative would be appropriate. If it were to be situated within the fourth paradigm, then scripture would be appropriately defined as "powerful and potent" scriptural signs, icons, and words, words *that are always enmeshed in power relations* that are historically concrete and ideologically conditioned.

Furthermore, anyone aware of the debate between Gadamer[23] and Habermas[24] or of Michel Foucault's analysis of knowledge-power[25] will want to modify the definition of scripture as a special class of "true and powerful" or "sacred and authoritative" words that receive their authority from their reception by a community. For instance, the arguments against wo/men's ordination, reproductive rights, and same-sex marriage have shown that the authority and tradition of religious and other communities has been and still is kyriarchal, in other words, defined by elite male power and domination. If reception makes words sacred and true (i.e. scripture), then marginalized people must be wary of such a definition because it sanctions the words of the dominant culture and religion.

Moreover, it must not be overlooked that marginalized and marginal people also have internalized the dominant cultural and religious values of alienation and domination and therefore receive the icons and words of scripture as "true and authoritative" divinely sanctioned words, even if they inculcate domination and submission. For instance, wo/men may continue to stay in violent abusive marriage relationships because they have internalized that sacred scripture teaches that they have to subordinate themselves to their husbands.

As the study of religious and cultural canons shows, scriptures that are accepted by the community as "true and powerful sacred words" both inspire and energize and marginalize and exclude those who are second-class citizens within a community. That is, they are *powerful and potent* but not necessarily true or sacred. After all, scripture has not only been engaged by white, elite, Western, heterosexual men as "authority" to exclude. It also has been engaged by subaltern men or elite white wo/men to exclude, silence, control, and dehumanize the "other," wo/men, gay, lesbian, bisexual, and transgendered people, as well as "others" who do not conform to the ethos and self-understanding of the minority or majority community.

If the ISS research project would consider relinquishing the comparative religions definition of scripture, which itself is deeply shaped by the first, the dogmatic-communal-ecclesial, paradigm of biblical studies, and consider situating itself explicitly in the fourth rhetorical-emancipatory paradigm, it could moreover give up its polemic against "text study" or historical criticism and become bifocal: the Signifying Scriptures project could focus on the meaning-making practices of individuals and communities with respect to scriptures as "powerful potent" words and their functions and ends not only in the academy but also in religion, society, and culture, and not only in the present but also in the past. It could pay equal attention to biblical and other sacred texts or icons of diverse religions, critically analyze them, name their marginalizing and dehumanizing *Wirkungsgeschichte*. It also could cultivate the as-yet unfulfilled powerful visions of justice and well-being also inscribed in scriptures.

In both instances, the ISS would not only need to analyze scriptures as powerful rhetorical discourses that can inculcate and foster domination or religious visions of hope and well-being. It also would need to scrutinize scripturalizing and signifying individuals and communities and their practices of exclusion and dehumanization. Such a research project would need to question the academic disciplinary and interdisciplinary structures that it engages, the presuppositions and implications of its methods of study, and the academic ethos of objectification, value-detachment, and competition. Most important, it would need to be translated into interdisciplinary educational practices that foster the critical-emancipatory development of biblical scholars of religion and theology as well as of scriptural-religious communities able to name and transform global unjust structures of subordination and oppression.

NOTES

1. The misunderstanding of feminism as *hatred of men* is widespread not only in the United States but also in other countries. See, for instance, Maitrey Chatterjee, "The Feminist Movement in West Bengal From the 1980s to the 1990s," in *Faces of the Feminine in Ancient, Medieval, and Modern India,* ed. Mandakranta Bose (New York: Oxford University Press, 2000), 322–334: "The term 'feminist' creates a block in West Bengal. The image of a feminist is not one that many women would like to have. Feminism has been variously associated with aggressiveness, sexual permissiveness, immodesty, lack of womanly virtues and antimotherhood and antifamily attitudes. In fact, it is a cocky counter to the 'ideal woman,' who is selfless, obedient and home loving" (322). My understanding of feminism is best expressed in a bumper-sticker definition that says: "feminism is the radical notion that women are people." Anyone who works to change the second-class citizenship of *every wo/man and all wo/men* in religion and society, therefore, is a feminist. Moreover, it must not be forgotten that according to Alice Walker, a "*womanist*" is a "feminist of color." For the theoretical elaboration of such a feminist perspective see my books *But She Said, Sharing Her Word, Jesus and the Politics of Interpretation,* and *Wisdom Ways,* as well as my article "Method in Women's Studies in Religion: A Critical Feminist Hermeneutics," in *Methodology in Religious Studies: The Interface with Women's Studies,* ed. Arvind Sharma (Albany: SUNY Press, 2002), 207–242.

2. David Kinsley, "Women's Studies and the History of Religions," in *Methodology in Religious Studies,* ed. Arvind Sharma, 1–15.

3. Cf. Velma Love, "The Bible and Contemporary African American Culture I: Hermeneutical Forays, Observations and Impressions," in *African Americans and the Bible,* ed. Vincent L. Wimbush (New York: Continuum, 2000), 49–65; and J. M. Shopshire, I. Rousseau Mukenge, V. Erickson, and H. A Baer, "The Bible in Contemporary African American Culture II: Report on a Preliminary Ethnographic Project," in ibid., 66–82.

4. This writing of "wo/men" has a double communicative function: it seeks to startle readers into recognition by ironically reversing the use of *man* and *he* as inclusive of *woman* and *she* in kyriocentric languages and instead using *wo/men* as the generic term, which is inclusive of marginalized men. It also seeks to communicate that "wo/men" is a fragmented political name that points to the differences among and within wo/men, and asserts that wo/men as a socially constructed group do not have a defining essence in common.

5. See my book *Rhetoric and Ethic: The Politics of Biblical Studies* (Minneapolis: Fortress, 2000), and my article "Defending the Center, Trivializing the Margins," in *Reading the Bible in the Global Village: Helsinki* ed. Heikki Räisänen et al. (Atlanta: SBL, 2000), 29–48.

6. See Vincent L. Wimbush's introductory essay in this volume, 11.

7. See my article problematizing the methodological approach to "apocalypticism," Elisabeth Schüssler Fiorenza, "The Phenomenon of Early Christian Apocalyptic: Some Reflections

on Method," in *Apocalypticism in the Mediterranean World and the Near East Proceedings of the International Colloquium on Apocalypticism, Uppsala, August 12–17, 1979*, ed. David Hellholm, 2nd ed. (Tübingen: J.C.B. Mohr, 1989), 295–316.

8. Katherine K. Young, "From the Phenomenology of Religion to Feminism and Women's Studies," in *Methodology in Religious Studies*, 18.

9. Kinsley, "Women's Studies," 2.

10. Karen L. King, *What Is Gnosticism?* (Cambridge, MA: Harvard University Press, 2003), 225.

11. Barbara Holdrege, "Beyond the Guild: Liberating Biblical Studies," in *African Americans and the Bible*, ed. Vincent L. Wimbush, 138–142.

12. I want to thank Barbara Holdrege for a clarifying and engaging sustained discussion of my proposal after my presentation at the conference.

13. Cf. Wimbush's introductory essay in this volume and its references to the grounding work of W. C. Smith, *What Is Scripture? A Comparative Approach* (Minneapolis: Fortress, 1993), as well as to the work of Barbara Holdrege, William Graham, and Miriam Levering.

14. Holdrege, "Beyond the Guild," 141.

15. Ibid., 140.

16. Miriam Levering, "The Study of Religion and the Study of the Biblie," in *Rethinking Scriptures: Essays from a Comparative Perspective*, ed. Mariam Levering (Albany: SUNY Press, 1989), 2.

17. Holdrege, "Beyond the Guild," 141.

18. See Elisabeth Schüssler Fiorenza, *Bread Not Stone: The Challenge of Feminist Biblical Interpretation* (Boston: Beacon Press, 1984), 23–42, which is a revised form of my article "For the Sake of Our Salvation: Biblical Interpretation and the Community of Faith," in *Sin, Salvation and the Spirit*, ed. D. Durken (Collegeville, MN: Liturgical Press, 1979), 21–39.

19. In order to mark the inadequacy of our language for speaking about the divine, I write G*d in such a broken form. For discussion of the term "God," see Francis Schüssler Fiorenza and Gordon Kaufman, "God," in *Critical Terms for Religious Studies*, ed. Mark C. Taylor (Chicago: University of Chicago Press, 1998), 136–159.

20. See, for instance, the heresy trials of David Swing in 1874, Charles A. Briggs in 1891, and Arthur Cushman McGiffert in 1900

21. See Raymond A. Morrow with David D. Baron, *Critical Theory and Methodology* (Thousand Oaks, CA: Sage Publications, 1994), 130–149.

22. See, e.g., Patricia Hill Collins, *Fighting Words: Black Women and the Search for Justice* (Minneapolis: University of Minnesota Press, 1998); Rosemary Hennessy, *Materialist Feminism and the Politics of Discourse* (New York: Routledge, 1993); and Marsha Aileen Hewitt, *Critical Theory of Religion: A Feminist Analysis* (Minneapolis: Fortress Press, 1995).

23. See Hans Georg Gadamer, *Truth and Method and Philosophical Hermeneutics* (Berkeley: University of California Press, 1976); Richard Bernstein, "What Is the Difference That Makes a Difference? Gadamer, Habermas, and Rorty," in *Hermeneutics and Modern Philosophy*, ed. Brice R. Wachterhauser (Albany, NY: SUNY Press, 1986), 343–376; and Paul Ricoeur, *Hermeneutics and the Human Sciences*, ed. and trans. John B. Thompson (Cambridge: Cambridge University Press, 1981), 197–221. Ricoeur's theory of interpretation has argued that action may be regarded as a text. If an action like a text is a meaningful entity, then the "paradigm of reading" can also be applied to socioreligious practices.

24. Jürgen Habermas, "Ideology," in *Modern Interpretations of Marx*, ed. Tom Bottomore (Oxford: Blackwell, 1981), 166. Cf. John B. Thompson, *Studies in the Theory of Ideology* (Cambridge: Polity Press, 1984).

25. See Michèlle Barrett, *The Politics of Truth: From Marx to Foucault* (Stanford, CA: Stanford University Press, 1991).

26 Racial and Colonial Politics of the Modern Object of Knowledge

CAUTIONARY NOTES ON "SCRIPTURE"

JOSEPH PARKER

How might we reconsider the topic of "scriptures" in the midst of what the African historian Steven Feierman has called the "general epistemological crisis affecting all the social sciences and humanities"?[1] We find ourselves at sea in this crisis every time we write, not just when explicitly describing the other, and can only navigate its politics successfully if we recognize the dangers of what Emmanuel Levinas termed an ontological imperialism where otherness vanishes as part of the same of modernity.[2]

For Feierman this crisis has centered on the gradual dissolution of unilinear narratives of world history as the spread of modernity out of Europe; historians have confronted their accountability to the Others of Europe both within Europe and beyond in colonial territories.[3] In the case of modern conceptions of "scriptures," a similar crisis centers on the dissolving of modern notions of sacred text deriving from the biblical tradition, particularly that of Christianity, as it is entangled in direct colonization and the more pervasive process of ontological imperialism. The object of knowledge known as "scripture" may be reconstituted in ways that refuse appropriation into this unfortunate heritage as an ethics and politics of accountability to the Others of modernity. In this essay I explore a few signs that may be useful while at sea on the voyage to accountability for the academy, accountability to the populations whose perspectives are erased every time seemingly neutral knowledge claims to universal truths and categories are made.

For my first sign I turn to Gayatri Chakravorty Spivak on "marginalia" to think through the epistemological crisis as it applies to "scripture." Spivak asks us to give attention to the way in which any explanation presupposes an explainable universe and an explaining subject, and thereby excludes "the possibility of the radically heterogeneous." If our objects of knowledge, such as "scriptures," are not naturally given to us, we have to call them into coherence, cathect them as we distinguish them from what they are not, and thereby always already stake out a political position. Spivak terms these exclusions the "prohibited margin" and indicates that as a political event and a productive event, each particular explanation specifies a particular politics.[4] Through our attempts to theorize and understand "scriptures," then, we already engage in a highly politicized act of exclusion, an exclusion of heterogeneity even if our object of knowledge is precisely that of the heterogeneous excluded margin. Spivak's project is one of persistently attempting to renegotiate the prohibited margin of the object of knowledge to practice an ethics and a politics of feminism, anti-class exploitation, and decolonization within limits, a project we may pursue with regard to "scriptures" and their Others.

At stake is more than the ethical and political status of our objects of knowledge: if we are not careful our specific politics will also reinforce the marginalization of our work as good liberal humanists in the academy. The specific politics through which humanists are marginalized that Spivak calls our attention to is what she calls "advanced capitalist [and masculinist] technocracy." As academic custodians of culture, Spivak suggests that our traditional role is "to produce and be produced by *official* explanations in terms of the powers that police the entire society."[5] As we are thereby being written into the text of capitalist and masculinist technocracy, we also constitute that very text as collaborators in its inscription who have agency and yet are without full control over the text.

This is a second sign, a warning or omen: unless the work of studying "scriptures" addresses issues of advanced capitalist and masculinist technocracy, we run the risk of supporting through an unacknowledged complicity the powers that police the entire society by excluding these policing powers from the objects of our study. The category of "scriptures" may perhaps seem to be as far as one can get from the powers that police society, and this suggests the need to profoundly reshape the limits of the object known as "religion." Religion is often understood within the truth regime of modernity as something other than science and technology, medicine, legal enforcement systems, psychology, literature, philosophy, economics, or politics. These are the notorious disciplinary boundaries into which we are being constituted even as are also always co-constituting them in our work through our agency, the grid of intelligibility and its disciplinary politics that Michel Foucault critiqued in his early work on the history of the modern human sciences.[6]

It is through the enforcement mechanisms of these meticulous distinctions and exclusions that the prohibited margin is produced, focusing our attention on "religion" or "scripture" as constituted outside of the workings of "advanced capitalist and masculinist technocracy" that police and by which we ourselves police our entire society. We know full well that the enforcement mechanisms of our own day are quite brutal when they come into play. We would see them in action if we were to begin hearing the voices of God, as did Muhammad and Elijah, or if we were to overturn the tables in the marketplace, as did Jesus, or if we were to heal suffering based on the Popul Vuh or Buddhist scriptures rather than Eurocentric medicine, or if we redirected the flows of our own King George's tax revenues. We would then be locked up and put away. The politics of these limits have high stakes, so we would best be cautious as we talk so freely of renegotiating and riffing on them, as if our signifying on its own can reshape or even bring down the dark walls that hold those who have been put away. Yet I would suggest that it is precisely at the moment when these categorical distinctions are problematized, when we approach the edge of incoherence, that we may meet with the radical heterogeneity and the prohibited margin that excludes the subaltern and keeps us marginalized as academic humanists, good citizens in preserving the bloody social "order" of our day.

The politics of these seemingly arcane distinctions must be clear by now. The construction of our object of knowledge and its limits is a profoundly politicized moment, a turning point where we may constitute objects known as "scriptures" within the terms of the power-knowledge limits of academic humanism or in terms Other to these limits. The objective of this work is not to produce some more "complete" or "true" or "authentic" object of knowledge as determined by an essentialized Other to humanist, Eurocentric biblical studies. Rather this work may come to produce the always already present prohibited margins whose politics do something other than support the epistemic violence of ontological imperialism and the literal violence of the "brutal ironies" of advanced capitalist and masculinist technocracy.[7]

To reconsider the tradition of interpreting "scriptures" as if they exist some-how outside of racialized and colonial relations, I turn to two complementary examples of what might be termed the Other of modernity through which we might reconsider the epistemological limits and racialized and colonizing politics of "scriptures" as objects of knowledge. The first is an encounter with racialized texts, which I approach through the work of Henry Louis Gates Jr. Gates has developed signifyin(g) as an approach to these texts in an effort to undermine their essentialized rendering under Eurocentric racialized representations.[8] By turning to a loosely deconstructionist approach to difference in reading major African American texts, Gates demonstrates a certain limited type of freedom of African American authors in their relation to the social and economic conditions of their day. He rejects essentialist renderings of African American texts as determined by context. This step of rejecting essentialist renderings of the Other in the eyes of the colonizer erodes the grip of fixed social positionings that make domination possible and is an important part of any critical enterprise.

Yet Gates's references to "black tradition" or "blackness" as coherent and uni-fied erases the considerable heterogeneity of the category in terms of gender, class, sexual orientation, generation, immigration status, and other factors. As some African Americans begin to rise to positions of suburban success and considerable institutional authority, including in the academy, this comes at the expense of their solidarity with the common folk of the African diaspora. Gates does not address these questions in his analysis of texts, moving glibly from slave narratives to texts by Zora Neale Hurston and Alice Walker that are now established as canonical without carefully examining class and gender differences. In subjecting himself and his readers to the modern need for coherence, difference and the Other are erased and obscured.

While Gates's rendering of "text" is still largely limited to the written text, his deployment of the vernacular and the oral tradition introduce the vocally outspoken and bodily unruly African American tradition of riffing, woofing, and getting loud.[9] That is the notion of signifyin(g) as something colloquial and locatable within a particular racialized social or cultural setting always determined and yet never successfully totalized by the power-knowledge regime of modernity. These behaviors do more than bring the African American colloquial and "street" attitudes into the academy, for they dislocate what Michel Foucault termed the meticulous rituals of power[10] and potentially take "scriptures" outside of what Robert Young has called the "truth protocols of modernity."[11]

This approach to signifyin(g) is potentially profoundly unsettling to biblical studies, to "scriptures," to the academy, and perhaps even to world social relations. These practices invite certain unruly modes of engaging and disagreeing and signifyin(g) and physical behavior and certain failures of bodily docility and certain bodily distributions into arenas where they are not generally welcome: the classroom, dissertation, academic publications, faculty appointments, church pulpits, and social-change movement organizing. If we are to problematize the origins of the object of knowledge, it is precisely such "meticulous rituals of power" and docile protocols of truth that need to reconfigured. Gates's emphasis on the vernacular opens the door to less-docile bodies and to uses of language that do not follow the protocols of middle-class politeness that maim and kill so many diverse views and that erase attempts to acknowledge the history of violent domination. This emphasis asks us how the docile body of modernity, seen most readily in the rigid arrogance of white masculine bodies, might come to be decolonized.[12] Constructive encounters with this and other oral and vernacular traditions helps us to decolonize not only the bodies of our objects of knowledge but also the academic body, perhaps unlearning some of the docility that was the price of our privilege in the academy, maybe learning a new politics of the body in signifyin(g) with an attitude not just in theory but embodied, not just textually but physically.

Yet Gates grounds his reading of texts in the second half of the book in a binary contrast of "the Western tradition" and "the black vernacular," asserting that African American authors turn to the black vernacular to ground their textual practice "outside the Western tradition."[13] Gates's objective in this argument is to affirm the importance of vernacular texts and the interpretive strategies of signifyin(g) as comparable in importance to the intertextual heritage of Western literature and as making possible a critical tradition of reading and writing. Yet this frame reproduces the binary logic of West/Africa or white/black and reinscribes Gates's project back into the logic of colonial domination and master/slave relations. By working uncritically with the categories of the colonizer, such as the category of blackness, the Other is subjected to the terms provided by the ontological imperialism of Eurocentric modernity, claiming subject status in the terms already established by the imperial ontology. This is one of the problems that must be avoided in reconstituting "scripture" beyond the logic of modernity and the imperial ontology, another warning sign on the voyage to accountability.

One of the ways to avoid such domestication into the imperial logic of modernity is to displace the binarisms and differences by which modernity works.[14] Jack

Forbes takes a different approach to the systems implementing and enforcing race, slavery, and racism in his study of relations of Native Americans and those of the African diaspora in the Americas.[15] By examining a vast profusion of empirical evidence of confusion in the terminology of racist categorization, Forbes's book ultimately mocks the workings of the institutional structures that attempt to enforce claims to "rational" categorization. Forbes demonstrates how the vocabulary of slavery and racism is constituted through juridical practices as the apparatuses for enforced subjection, providing a historical concreteness and link to political, social, and legal history that is missing from Gates.

Rather than attempting to claim parity through difference of black with white or African American with Western, Forbes stages a displacement of the very grounds and terms on which such comparative claims could be made. Forbes uses modern methods to document the disappearance of the indigenous populations, not through the traditional argument that they succumbed to disease and warfare but through showing how the racial classification system incorporated them into other categories again and again. Rather than adopting the vocabulary and categories of the colonizer and the slave master, Forbes demonstrates the erasures, aporias, and violence of that system. This critique practices an accountability to the radical alterity of the Other commonly erased by academic work that claims to represent difference without critiquing the terms of the modern. Moreover, such a critique does not require postmodern theory for its development, only deep wariness of claims to the politically neutral status of the "factual" by social systems that enforce modern forms of inequality and exploitation.[16]

Through tracking the traces of subaltern group members "cunningly obliterated in the interest of dominant history," Gayatri Spivak has argued that Forbes's work belongs with the work of subalternist historians.[17] Yet Spivak cautions against the move to a generalized use of the term "subaltern," if it is to retain some of its political force and learn from the work of the subaltern studies group of historians and theorists. This term itself has a complex and highly contested history, but for the present purposes we might think briefly of two different conceptions. Antonio Gramsci took the term to mean something like the subproletariat, those below the working class in a Marxist class analysis. With the intervention of Spivak in the work of the subaltern studies group, we were asked to consider, first, how the subaltern was gendered and, second, how problematic was the relationship of the subaltern to language.

The relation of the subaltern to language and intelligibility was summarized in Spivak's provocative article title, "Can the Subaltern Speak?"[18] While Spivak has over the years revised her thinking on this last problem,[19] I would suggest that for today we might reductionistically consider her example of the subaltern as an illiterate farming woman from the Third World. Many African Americans and other members of racially marginalized groups in the United States and others in the Third World academy do not seem very compatible with the Gramscian subaltern, a kind of subproletariat below the working class, or the illiterate rural farming woman that Spivak sees as typical. We need only consider the remarkable uniformity of those of us in the academy in terms of high literacy levels and proficiency in the language(s) of the colonizer(s) and our at the least middle-class socioeconomic status to see how application of the category of subaltern to those of us in the academy would be profoundly misleading.

It is useful in examining the politics of this object of knowledge to ask what range of relations do those of African, Asian, or others in the Third World have to the category of subaltern? Clearly there would be some sectors in the United States, say rural and even urban men and women, certainly of the nineteenth century and even of our own decade, that might closely fit with Gramsci's and even Spivak's conceptions. Other sectors of the Third World diaspora community, however, might have much more distant relations to the status of the subaltern, whether we think of a Henry Louis Gates or a Gayatri Spivak, a Toussaint L'Overture or a Rigoberta Menchú.[20] Many of these individuals carry considerable economic privilege well above anything resembling a subproletariat, are highly literate, are mostly men and mostly urban in affiliation if not in their origins, and in this regard cannot be termed subaltern. Preserving the political force of the category "subaltern" would require working actively with the heterogeneity of these groups across lines of difference of class, gender, literacy level, nomad/sedentary, and urban/rural.

The politics of representation are perhaps always an invitation to appropriation and consolidation into the ontological imperialism of modernity, that network of institutions that set the limits that exclude what Spivak termed the "prohibited margin." The possibility of appropriation can be seen very directly in my own participation in discussions of the Other, as a Northern European heterosexual literate male holding forth on the status of subalterns and African Americans in a settler colony, where my people have colonized and still colonize the indigenous peoples and have enslaved and still subordinate African Americans in myriad ways. As I construct a coherent object of signification and produce my own subjectivity and the legitimacy of my object of knowledge, there are obvious dangers of appropriation. Yet while these dangers are certainly racialized and gendered in my own particular location politics, their limits are also set by the linguistic structures of modernity. These limits pressure us toward ready-made appropriations and consolidations into the structures of modernity: the nation-state, urban centers and depopulated rural areas, the Eurocentric academy, gendered late capitalism, neocolonialism and settler colonies, mass education and literacy/illiteracy boundaries, and so forth. Spivak's work suggests that we must be very wary of the limits to this otherness and of the politics of those limits.

The risks of appropriation have direct implications for a return to the topic of "scripture" marked in the present volume, with its profoundly troubled history of canonization and domination. While these issues are most obvious and straightforward in the case of biblical studies and particularly the role of Christianity in European imperialism, my own field of Buddhist studies also struggles with issues of colonization. Colonization is an ongoing problem for Buddhists, as in the case of the deployment of Buddhist missionaries in Japanese colonization of the continent during the Pacific War.[21] Yet the more general problem of Eurocentric ontological imperialism is illustrated in the usefulness of the emphasis on text for British imperialist domination India,[22] and the subtle way in which such an emphasis inserts Protestant Christian presuppositions into the academic project.[23]

Finding the value for "scripture" in developing representations of the Other that are accountable to radical alterity is a double-edged project, one that can open new doors but one that is founded on the quicksand of appropriation. By turning to canonical scriptures, revisionist significations and even "woofing" on these texts has considerable power to reach a broad audience, to persuade funding agencies to support research, and even to build a mass movement precisely because the text is already well-known with considerable legitimacy. Yet this same strength is also its primary weakness, because an entrenched, highly constricted arena of meanings is thereby chosen for the site for the struggle of re-signification. This means that the central project of the center, focusing on "scriptures," is primed and poised for appropriation and consolidation into the terms of the truth regime of the society and episteme in which it has been made canonical. This is another auspice on the road to accountability for the research into "scriptures."

I offer two countermeasures to address these problems. The first is to broaden the term "scripture" as has already been done in certain sectors of the poststructuralist project with the term "text," namely reconfigure it to a broader meaning more closely approximating the phrase "social text." Such a project has been admirably accomplished by the journal of that same name and by many other groups and individuals in the academy and beyond. A similar direction has been taken by Foucauldians in rewriting the notion of "discourse" to mean something quite other to the limits of language or of "written text."[24] Broadening the term "scripture" in this way would be important, as it might imply such phrases as "discursive regime" and "truth regime." The term "regime" is much harder to domesticate into something innocuous term like "signifyin(g)" that can be riffed on in some sort of putatively free play.

The second countermeasure is to actively and consciously redefine who it is that makes decisions about which "scriptures" are considered as central to the phenomena. In this way Gates's and Feierman's turn to the vernacular and the oral is important. Also, African historians have adopted multiple methods to resist the entrenched Eurocentrism and unilinear narratives of historical writing to reach the underclasses generally left out of academic histories, including oral histories, historical archaeology, historical linguistics, historical anthropology, and anti-dynastic histories.[25] Feierman draws on these methods through the work of Marcia Wright to develop an analysis of a woman, Narwimba, living in Africa under the shadow of slavery to reject Eurocentric analyses that see European international trade as the driving force of history.[26] Instead Feierman suggests that local practices of kinship, production, sacrifice, and rights and duties profoundly shaped very large scale processes, such as overseas trade and the colonial economy—how the local forms the transnational not through univocal and universalized histories but through multiple local narratives.[27]

Students of "scripture" would need to adopt similar measures to begin to answer questions about what subaltern illiterate rural women consider to be sacred text and how they interpret it. Such an approach might build comparative analyses of canonical "scriptures" with those of the indigenous colonized and formerly enslaved peoples of North America in insurgent work. These comparative analyses would be important in displacing the hegemonic determinism in the United States of "scriptures" in terms defined by the "white Bible"[28] or the "colonizer's Bible"[29] or the "masculine Bible"[30] and other racialized and colonizing ways that continue to be enforced in academic and community practices.

To this end we may work with the illiterate subaltern who produces the scriptural text, from the First World African American to the Third World rural illiterate subaltern woman to the suited academic body—male and female. If the subaltern is seen reductively as an illiterate rural woman from the Third World, and a "scripture" is seen narrowly as a text the presumes literacy, then how might we ever understand the phrase "subaltern scripture"? How does the domestic U.S. First World context of "African American" be brought to crisis in a fruitful way by the transnational Third World emphasis of "subaltern"? The relation of the "subaltern scripture" to urban African American gendered youthful "woofing" or "getting loud" is no simple one either. While the African American experience has been interpreted as an "internal colony,"[31] its history as part of the First World leads in many but not all cases to considerable privilege compared to rural illiterate third world women. And the relation of "subaltern scripture" to our own writings and teaching as highly literate academics is even more problematic. Spivak suggests that it is only through an ethics enacted consistently through a crisis that opens up the limits of the grid of intelligibility and rewrites the prohibited margins of the object of power-knowledge that we may begin to earn "the right to be heard and trusted by the subaltern."[32]

Knowing that the representations we produce are always already misnamings allows us to construct a critical distance from our own truth claims. It also produces a profound critical awareness that our power-knowledge regime severely constricts key aspects of the objects of knowledge that we construct. If used effectively, this critical distance may provide a wedge to begin to open space up for the radical heterogeneity that we exclude in the prohibited margins of our own coherence as we signify within the limits of the Eurocentric academy, racialized and gendered colonialism and power-knowledge regime of modernity, and of one of the languages of domination, English, the language of this essay.

NOTES

Subsequent revisions to this essay were made possible by a sabbatical from teaching funded by Pitzer College.

1. Steven Feierman, "African Histories and the Dissolution of World History," in *Africa and the Disciplines: The Contribution of Research in Africa to the Social Sciences and the Humanities*, ed. Robert H. Bates, V. Y. Mudimbe, and Jean O'Barr (Chicago: University of Chicago Press, 1993), 184. I am grateful to Dan Segal for introducing me to Feierman's work.

2. Feierman, "African Histories," 185, citing Robert Young, *White Mythologies: Writing History and the West* (New York: Routledge, 1990), 12–16.

3. Feierman, "African Histories," 167–171, 172, 198, and 201n15.

4. Gayatri Chakravorty Spivak, "Explanation and Culture: Marginalia," in *The Spivak Reader: Selected Works of Gayatri Chakravorty Spivak*, ed. Donna Landry and Gerald MacLean, (1979; repr., New York: Routledge, 1996), 33.

5. Spivak, "Explanation and Culture," 35. Spivak uses the phrase "advanced capitalist technocracy," which she then links to what she calls "masculism" (35, 47–48nn8–9).

6. Michel Foucault, *The Order of Things: An Archaeology of the Human Sciences* (1966; repr., New York: Vintage Books, 1994).

7. Spivak, "Explanation and Culture," 38. For Spivak's notion of epistemic violence, which diverges somewhat from Levinas on ontological imperialism, see her "Subaltern Studies: Deconstructing Historiography," in *The Spivak Reader*, 219; trenchant application of her concerns with epistemic violence to the field of religious studies may be found in Laura Donaldson, "The Breasts of Columbus," in *Postcolonialism, Feminism, and Religious Discourse*, ed. Laura E. Donaldson and Kwok Pui-lan (New York: Routledge, 2002), 48–55.

8. Henry Louis Gates Jr., *The Signifying Monkey: A Theory of African-American Literary Criticism* (New York: Oxford University Press, 1988).

9. An application of these notions to religious scripture may be found in Vincent L. Wimbush introductory essay to this volume.

10. Michel Foucault, *Discipline and Punish: The Birth of the Prison*, trans. Alan Sheridan (1975; repr., New York: Vintage Books, 1995).

11. Robert Young, *Postcolonialism: An Historical Introduction* (Malden, MA: Blackwell Publishing, 2001), 70.

12. An analysis of the racialized and gendered body that explores the failure of modern docility may be found in Elaine Kim, "Bad Women: Asian American Visual Artists Hanh Thi Pham, Hung Liu, and Tong Soon Min," in *Making More Waves: New Writing by Asian American Women*, ed. Elaine H. Kim, Lillia V. Villanueva, and Asian Women United of California (New York: Beacon Press, 1997), 184–194; for an analysis of the body under slavery that decolonizes the modern gaze, see Saidiya V. Hartman, *Scenes of Subjection: Terror, Slavery, and Self-Making in Nineteenth-Century America* (New York: Oxford University Press, 1997). I am grateful for Leila Neti and Lindon Barrett for suggesting the latter reference.

13. Gates, *The Signifying Monkey*, xxii.

14. The work of deconstruction may be characterized in terms of a reversal of social and textual hierarchies of meaning and power, when the binary terms of the hierarchy are then displaced. See Gayatri Chakravorty Spivak, "Translator's Preface," in Jacques Derrida, *Of Grammatology* (Baltimore: Johns Hopkins University Press, 1976).

15. Jack Forbes, *Africans and Native Americans: The Language of Race and the Evolution of Red-Black Peoples*, 2nd ed. (1988; repr., Urbana: University of Illinois Press, 1993).

16. Spivak, "Race Before Racism: The Disappearance of the American, *boundary 2* 25 (1998): 38–39.

17. Ibid., 46.

18. Gayatri Chakrovorty Spivak, "Can the Subaltern Speak?" in *Marxism and the Interpretation of Culture*, ed. Gary Nelson and Lawrence Grossberg (London: Macmillan, 1988).

19. See her reconsiderations in "Subaltern Talk," in *The Spivak Reader*, 287–308, and Spivak, *A Critique of Postcolonial Reason: Toward a History of the Vanishing Present* (Cambridge, MA: Harvard University Press, 1999), 269–273.

20. A thoughtful analysis of the appropriations of Rigoberta Menchú by academics may be found in Caren Kaplan, "The Politics of Location as a Transnational Feminist Critical Practice," in *Scattered Hegemonies: Postmodernity and Transnational Feminist Practices*, ed. Inderpal Grewal and Caren Kaplan (Minneapolis: University of Minnesota Press, 1994), 146–148.

21. Brian (Daizen) Victoria, *Zen at War* (Tokyo: Weatherhill, 1997).

22. Philip C. Almond, *The British Discovery of Buddhism* (New York: Cambridge University Press, 1988).

23. Gregory Schopen, "Archaeology and Protestant Presuppositions in the Study of Indian Buddhism," *History of Religions* 31 (1991): 1–23.

24. Foucault, *Discipline and Punish*.

25. Feierman, "African Histories," 183–184, 197–198.

26. Marcia Wright, *Strategies of Slaves and Women: Life-stories from East Central Africa* (New York: L. Barber Press, 1993).

27. Feierman, "African Histories," 186–197.

28. Critiques of racialization in biblical interpretation are by now well established by a significant scholarship. For important examples see Charles Long, *Significations* (Philadelphia: Fortress Press, 1986), and Vincent L. Wimbush, ed., *African Americans and the Bible: Sacred Texts and Social Textures* (New York: Continuum, 2001); for the implications of racialization in the growth of North American Buddhism, see Joe Parker, "The Subtle Presence of Race in Buddhism: A White Perspective," *Turning Wheel* (Fall 2000): 36.

29. The movement away from notions of scripture and religion deriving directly from Christian missionaries and colonization and indirectly from more subtle processes is a long one. For important work on the more subtle modes of colonization see Brian K. Smith, "Exorcising the Transcendent: Strategies for Defining Hinduism and Religion," *History of Religions* 27 (1987): 32–55; Aijaz Ahmad, "Between Orientalism and Historicism: Anthropological Knowledge of India," *Studies in History* 7 (1991): 135–163; Talal Asad, *Genealogies of Religion: Discipline and Reasons of Power in Christianity and Islam* (Baltimore: The John Hopkins Press, 1993); and Musa Dube, *Postcolonial Feminist Interpretation of the Bible* (St. Louis: Chalice Press, 2000).

30. The vast scholarship, theology, and feminist social movement literature re-visioning scripture beyond androcentrism is well-known; early foundational work would include Mary Daly, *Beyond God the Father: Toward a Philosophy of Women's Liberation* (Boston: Beacon Press, 1973), and Audre Lorde, "An Open Letter to Mary Daly," in *Sister Outsider: Essays and Speeches by Audre Lorde* (Freedom, CA: The Crossing Press, 1984), 66–71, among many others. For English language critiques of this problem in considering Buddhist scriptures, see the work of Rita Gross, *Buddhism After Patriarchy: A Feminist History, Analysis, and Reconstruction of Buddhism* (Albany, NY: SUNY Press, 1993), and Miranda Shaw, *Passionate Enlightenment: Women in Tantric Buddhism* (Princeton, NJ: Princeton University Press, 1994), among a growing body of writing.

31. Robert Blauner, *Racial Oppression in America* (New York: Harper and Row, 1972).

32. Spivak, "More on Power/Knowledge," in *Outside in the Teaching Machine,* (New York: Routledge) 1993), 51.

27   *Who Needs the Subaltern?*

RANU SAMANTRAI

To the ordinary man.

    *To a common hero, an ubiquitous character, walk-
ing in countless thousands on the streets. In invoking
here at the outset of my narratives the absent figure
who provides both their beginning and their necessity,
I inquire into the desire whose impossible object he
represents. What are we asking this oracle whose voice
is almost indistinguishable from the rumble of history
to license us, to authorize us to say, when we dedicate
to him the writing that we formerly offered in praise of
the gods or the inspiring muses?*

                         —Michel de Certeau[1]

I read the call for an Institute for Signifying Scriptures primarily as a methodological statement, one that resonates well with my own research affiliations and
inclinations. Vincent Wimbush proposes an approach to "scriptures" that shifts
attention from the correct interpretation of canonical texts to the use of scriptural
material in practice. Understood as phenomena, "scriptures" derives their meaning not from authorial intent but from their activation in everyday life in often
unintended and surprising uses. Shifting from *"what 'scriptures' mean"* to *"how
'scriptures' mean,"* Wimbush also directs our attention to the range of scriptural
materials evident in the meaning-making, or signifying, practices of ordinary people.[2] Too often ignored or devalued in scriptural scholarship, vernacular and oral
traditions that fall outside the major religions are particularly rich resources for
the disenfranchised peoples who concern Wimbush. He suggests that here, outside
the official interpretations of the dominant religions, we find a wealth of ways in
which "scriptures" signify and are significant.

    In short, Wimbush proposes that we change both the objects and the meth-
ods of our analysis. But taken together, the two alterations necessitate a further
rethinking: they call into question the role of the investigating agent and his or her
relationship to the objects of analysis. Running throughout the proposal before us
is the implication that our knowledge production has very real consequences, not
least because our recognition contributes to the conditions of enfranchisement.

To become self-conscious about crafting or selecting the objects and methods of our analysis is to acknowledge responsibility for the consequences of our scholarly choices. It is to cease to believe ourselves to be innocent observers of objective phenomena and to begin to understand our implicatedness in the power-knowledge nexus. The model of scriptural study as canon interpretation valorizes interpreters (priests, intellectuals) as privileged readers whose authority resides in their position as gatekeepers and mediators. By contrast, the model of "scriptures" as social phenomenon positions interpreters, in Clifford Geertz's famous formulation, as "straining to read over the shoulders of those to whom [the phenomena] properly belong."[3]

I offer, then, a friendly amendment to the proposal before us. To grapple with all three elements in our methodological model—investigator, investigated, and tools of investigation—let us add a further set of issues to the categories already proffered for our consideration: the role of the scholar, and the relationship between the student and the studied.[4] What does it mean to be responsible for our scholarly choices and self-conscious regarding our desires in that relationship?

Although I am not a scholar of "scriptures," from Wimbush's proposal I derive a generally applicable method for the analysis of cultural practices including, but not limited to, scriptural practices. It is a model that resonates in my fields, postcolonial and cultural studies. I am, therefore, delighted to find an emphasis on everyday and lived engagements with received meanings that, in the process of incorporation, reshape those meanings in unpredictable and often subversive ways. Cultural studies especially takes as its methodological foundation that texts or discourses do not control their meanings. They come into being as they are received and practiced, in a complex dialectic of culture and consciousness, of being made and in turn remaking the world. It advocates a shift from text to reading, or more generally from production to consumption, and so from the elite who presume to make the world to the masses who put the made products they receive to unintended uses. That creative consumption in turn becomes a new production, setting in motion the generation, or signification, of new meanings. In postcolonial studies this gesture has taken the form of the turn to the subaltern, a term that signifies forms of agency that do not and perhaps cannot appear in either official or revisionist historical records.

In both cultural and postcolonial studies, then, there has been a shift away from conceptualizing oppositional politics as reacting against a monolithic, suffocatingly stable dominant discourse imposed on the oppressed; there has been a move toward the model of culture as a hybridized discourse that results from the mutual engagement of the powerful and the disenfranchised. From the point of view of signifying practices, mutual production indicates not harmony, but contention—the unpredictable signification that wrests meanings away from the intentions of their original makers. The shift also questions the "speaking truth to power" model of resistance, and with it the possibility that dominant discourse can be usurped by a simple externalization and rejection. We are left with the much more difficult proposition of a common, albeit contentious, discourse that encompasses both the powerful and the disenfranchised as its producers. Because it is in many ways better rooted in the everyday, it is much more difficult to dislodge. We attend to discourses in which of course there are privileged and marginalized actors, but no agent or site of agency is left unnamed. Nor can a given discourse exhaust the possibilities of the agents it names. In postcolonial studies this has led us to the sometimes uncomfortable and at other times romanticized acknowledgement that even dominant discourse is an interrupted discourse of mutuality, a discourse that cannot control its own terms. It is both site and stake of struggle; it also provides the resources for engagement. In such terrain externalization and rejection are inadequate strategies of resistance.

Hence I am uneasy when we seek the marginalized as though they remain unrepresented or invisible in official discourse. It is not so; they play a crucial role, even if that role is to be the content of the category of the invisible or the unnamed. In that category they are particularly important to and even ubiquitous in revisionist, critical scholarship. The question for me is not why are certain subjects invisible, but what is gained, and by whom, when we say that they are invisible?

There is no doubt the impulse behind the search for the disenfranchised is well-intentioned. Surely the speech of dominant actors, no matter how interrupted, cannot substitute for what might be said independently by the disenfranchised. Cultural studies has embraced the figure of the dispossessed, the consumer rather than the producer, and from that perspective has insisted on the world-shaping importance of hitherto overlooked meaning-making practices. But it has also had to confront the danger of romanticizing that figure by, for instance, attributing to it the oppositional positions that we wish it to take. We already know what the dispossessed want to say, and they will always say what we want to hear. The colonized always resist the colonizer and long for independence; people of color are by definition antiracist; women instinctively join the global sisterhood; and workers of course want to replace capitalism with socialism. The marginalized may even be able to criticize us in our positions of privilege—in which case we would have the opportunity of humbly, nobly accepting their truth spoken to our power. We can count on the dispossessed to speak truth to power; else what is the point of encouraging them to emerge from obscurity?

But if we already know what they are going to say, then why do we need them to say it? Who does it benefit, when they speak the words we want to hear? One interesting side effect of the speech of the disenfranchised is the gain in authority for the agent who enables or fosters that speaking, or who claims attention for it from those in power. That would be us: oppositional intellectuals whose careers are built on and whose authority is legitimated by that elusive category variously known as the people, the marginalized, the dispossessed, the subaltern, and so forth. We describe ourselves equally variously: our job is to act on behalf of, or to claim attention for, or to make space for, or to get out of the way of the disenfranchised. But all these projections of ourselves end in one outcome: we are the hinge between official discourse and its undoing. We have returned to our familiar position of gatekeeper and mediator between authority and the aggrieved. On us rests the burden of history.

Meanwhile the disenfranchised play a predictable role in our humanistic drama. The second benefit of our successful search for the agency of the subaltern again accrues to us as intellectuals: confirmation of the Enlightenment principles that undergird both our scholarship and our political narratives of oppression and liberation. Having found the agency of the dispossessed we can say that we know it exists because we have found it. And hence our tools for locating it, the tools of humanistic inquiry, including our critique of power imbalances, are proven valid. Alone among all other peoples, the figure of the dispossessed is transparent to itself: it knows its own interests, which are noncontradictory, and is able to articulate them. In short, it is the people, the revolutionary class—the only class that does not suffer from false consciousness. This is what we demand when we desire the speech of the subaltern: the truth that guarantees our own understanding of the world.

It is precisely this suffocating circularity that the subaltern scholars tried to crack with their iconoclastic readings of insurgencies on the Indian subcontinent.[5] Both colonial and nationalist historical narratives assigned a predetermined role to those who participated in insurgency: for the former insurgents were savages resisting civilization; for the latter they were an incipient and instinctive nation, acting in a revolutionary manner throughout colonial history to free themselves of the oppressor's yoke. The subaltern scholars argued that the content and effect of insurrection is neither predetermined nor consistent from one event to the next; still less can it be used as predictive template. Neither dominant nor revisionist historiography allows for the possibility of genuine alterity, the possibility that there may be subjects whose speech cannot appear as coherent in the familiar Enlightenment drama of oppression and emancipation, especially when those terms are framed by the nation. Hence they went searching for effects, not actors, and for practices, not archived texts. And whatever speech they found in insurgency, they insisted that it could not be reduced to predictable historical agency complete with the enlightened consciousness of the revolutionary, sovereign subject-agent.

Some argue that the subaltern scholars failed, as perhaps they were bound to do, for in the quest for the as-yet undiscovered site and source of agency there is no blueprint for an alternative to humanism; there is only the skill with which one dissents.[6] Perhaps the best-known articulation of this position is Gayatri Spivak's now infamous essay "Can the Subaltern Speak?" As you know, her answer to that question is "no."[7] I teach this essay frequently and am always distressed to find that despite my strenuous efforts to the contrary, most students persist in reading Spivak as saying that actual individual human beings are incapable of agency, in general, and of oppositional speech, in particular. In addition to being wrong, such a reading remains bound within the liberal humanism that Spivak scathingly criticizes. Her essay is about the desire of radical, even antihumanist intellectuals whose intellectual and political projects paradoxically depend on the existence of the oppressed, authentic subject-agent. She addresses precisely the resurgence of that humanist subject and interrogates not its lack, but our intense longing for its appearance. Whatever the effects may be of subaltern practices, that speech is drowned out by our incessant demand for it. No wonder then that it can only say what we already know it wants to say.

Finally, if the authority gained by the speech of the dispossessed is primarily ours, what does it authorize us to do? To return to some ideal place or time? To recapture something lost? Return to or recapture what? And who among us can be the expert who knows what someone else's proper disposition or orientation should be? Again, we must consider our place in this familiar story: we intellectuals who want to help people are the unnamed presence, the behind-the-scenes subject. Radical intellectuals are valorized by having found the authentic subaltern and heard its speech. As a result we know what it should say. On that basis we can undertake the task of teaching the inauthentic about their authenticity, thereby helping them return to their proper state. With the dispossessed playing their predictable role as the revolutionary subject of history, we intellectuals can return to our familiar position in the vanguard. And with that move our desire is satisfied and our authority is complete.

If we have already identified the space in which the speech/agency of the dispossessed must exist, then all that is left is for us to find that speech, repeatedly. The details may change, the specific names, dates, and places still have to be filled in, but there is nothing truly new left for us to learn. Or is it possible that the subaltern stands for the limits of our knowledge, and that we do not already know what, if anything, it wants to say?[8] If genuine alterity exists, it will not present itself to us in familiar terms. Indeed, it may not appear in terms to which we have access at all. I, for one, wish to hold on to the hope that the world is not already fully described. So, who needs the subaltern? Well, we do.

NOTES

1. Michel de Certeau, dedication, *The Practice of Everyday Life* (Berkeley: University of California Press, 1984).

2. Wimbush, introductory essay to this volume, 15.

3. Clifford Geertz, "Notes on the Balinese Cockfight," in *The Interpretation of Cultures: Selected Essays* (New York: Basic Books, 1973), 452–453.

4. Of course this immediately raises the possibility that the intellectual and the practitioner are one and the same, which in turn quickly leads on to the question of insider and outsider knowledge, and so on. The question of the scholar's status is a particularly productive line of inquiry for those interested in the practices of everyday life.

5. Volumes of *Subaltern Studies: Writings on South Asian History and Society* (Oxford: Oxford University Press) began appearing in Delhi in 1982. The subaltern studies scholars came to prominence in the United States in 1988 with the publication of Ranajit Guha and Gayatri Chakravorty Spivak, eds., *Selected Subaltern Studies* (New York: Oxford University Press, 1988). In that volume Ranajit Guha's "The Prose of Counter-Insurgency" (45–84) is a particularly useful articulation of the argument delineated above.

6. My language is borrowed from Rosalind O'Hanlon's superb critique of the subaltern project: "Recovering the Subject: Subaltern Studies and Histories of Resistance in Colonial South Asia," in *Mapping Subaltern Studies and the Postcolonial*, ed. Vinayak Chaturvedi (New York: Verso, 2000), 72–115.

7. Gayatri Chakravorty Spivak, "Can the Subaltern Speak?" in *Marxism and the Interpretation of Culture*, ed. Cary Nelson and Lawrence Grossberg (Urbana: University of Illinois Press, 1988), 271–313.

8. In his essay in this volume, José Rabasa points out that for Gramsci the subaltern was a liminal and problematic category, for actual people often refuse to behave as the revolutionary class ought to do. In the terms of this essay, they will not play their assigned roles in our drama of oppression and liberation. Rabasa is absolutely correct that we lose a crucial quality of the subaltern if we use the term as a synonym for various victimized, substantive social identities (e.g., "the oppressed," "the marginalized," "the nondominant"). The term serves us best if it names the limit of our knowledge. To the extent that I allow slippage here, I follow the lead of the essay to which I respond. Nevertheless, my aim is to demonstrate the dangers of eliminating the liminality of the subaltern in favor of the knowability, through their own speech/acts, of autonomous subject-agents. In the process I hope it is clear that I do not recommend taking "the subaltern" as another name for the autonomous, albeit disenfranchised, subject-agent.

Talking Back

Ah, yes, the flipping of the question . . . about the questions, about the questioner(s), about the project. This question flipping, this signifying on the signifying and on the signifiers, is most important and welcome. No fear of such here!

Phenomenology? The basic approach? Yes and no: I want once more to try to be as clear as possible in asserting that the "phenomenon" of focus is *not* text, but "scriptures." The latter is shorthand—for social textures, dynamics, behaviors, orientations, power dynamics. The focus is not upon texts per se. And so the phenomenon focused upon is not the focus of an older phenomenology. (This phenomenon-ology is not that of my teacher or my teachers' teachers.) That is the point of making the focus the subaltern—or at least those whose experiences and creative orientations have not been considered worth critical consideration. The shift in focus does not represent straight-laced political sensitivity or correctness. The subaltern and their tradents represent an actual heuristic-intellectual challenge. They force questions and issues that are not usually offered up on the table of discussion, in this case, regarding "scriptures."[1]

The point of the orientation modeled in this project is that the experiences of the subaltern in relationships to scriptures can teach us much—about who the subaltern are, about who the rest of us are, about the phenomenon of scriptures, and about human shaping and striving. No apologetics here . . . nothing mystifying . . . no special pleading . . . there is no need here to discover scripturalizing and signifying as antidote to all that has ailed the world or the oppressed in the world. There is need only to understand more clearly and more deeply that aspect of human behavior, orientation, and politics that can be subsumed under the poignant short-hand "scriptures." If we can crack open what has been occluded, rendered off-limits and made mystifying in "scriptures," all questions—including all questions about the questioners' agenda—are up for grabs, no, very much welcomed.

The questioning represented here, with the subaltern as special but not exclusive, fetishizing focus, has not been done; it needs to be done. There has not been a history of sustained disciplined probing; mostly, there has been only generalities made, impressionistic statements offered regarding such peoples' dynamics, including their play with scriptures. The potential here to discover something new or a different slant on the familiar is great. Recognition of such potential is not the same thing as ignoring the potential pitfalls associated with the venture. What is refused is paralysis in the face of the possibility of pitfalls, missteps, and mistakes.

We must make it clear that notwithstanding the wide-ranging, different, some-times conflicting arguments found in this collection of essays, what is asserted and modeled by the collection is that the study of scriptures should not be confused with any one particular discipline or field, that it is not the province of Western theology or religious studies, that it is not to be limited to any one religious tradition or cultural complex—it is not only about the Jewish-Christian Bible!—that it is not about texts per se, but about us, about human collectivities, human practices, human dynamics. It is about what and how we communicate with one another regarding that which we say centers and focuses us, regarding that which we claim matters most to us.

This collection as a whole suggests but leaves wide open the range and type of questions and issues and problems to be engaged as part of the project of excavating—signifying (on)—scriptures. And not so much in spite of but precisely because of the intensifications of scriptural fundamentalisms and their screeching apologetics and coarsening politics around the world, this collection—not through any one essayist's arguments but simply by virtue of the orientation to and modeling of the signifying (on) scriptures project—strongly suggests the senescence of the Enlightenment-inspired, modern-era, text-exegetical practices with their self-masking, self-obfuscating politics. We must free ourselves to raise and pursue deeper, more poignant questions and issues about ourselves insofar as scriptures have shaped us and as we persist in scripturalizing. Scriptures can no longer be the projected obfuscating and occluding force, protecting, preventing us from a self-knowing; they must now be one of the sharpest and most powerful analytical wedges for the pursuit of such knowledge. The excavation is on. It cannot be hindered.

—ed.

NOTES

1. Cf. Satya P. Mohanty regarding "epistemic status of cultural identity in his *Literary Theory and the Claims of History: Postmodernism, Objectivity, Multicultural Politics* (Ithaca, NY: Cornell University Press, 1997).

Bibliography

Note: In order to facilitate conversation struck by the essays in this volume, the following listing of sources deliberately transgresses disciplinary boundaries.

Abrahams, Roger D. *Deep Down in the Jungle: Negro Narrative Folklore from the Streets of Philadelphia*. Hatboro, PA: Folklore Associates, 1964.

———. *Talking Black*. Rowley, MA: Newbury House Publishers, 1976.

Adorno, Rolena. *Guaman Poma: Writing and Resistance in Colonial Peru*. Austin: University of Texas Press, 1986.

Althusser, Louis. "Ideological State Apparatuses (Notes toward an Investigation)." In *Essays on Ideology*, 1–60. New York: Verso, 1984.

Andrews, William L. *To Tell a Free Story: The First Century of Afro-American Autobiography, 1760–1865*. Urbana: University of Illinois Press, 1986.

Anzaldúa, Gloria. *Borderlands/La Frontera: The New Mestiza*. San Francisco: Spinsters/ Aunt Late, 1987.

Asad, Talal. *Formations of the Secular: Christianity, Islam, Modernity*. Stanford, CA: Stanford University Press, 2003.

———. *Genealogies of Religion: Discipline and Reasons of Power in Christianity and Islam*. Baltimore: Johns Hopkins University Press, 1993.

Austin, Allan D. *African Muslims in Antebellum America: Transatlantic Stories and Spiritual Struggles*. New York: Routledge, 1997.

Axtell, James. *The Invasion Within: The Contest of Cultures in Colonial North America* New York: Oxford University Press, 1985.

Badiou, Alain. *Saint Paul: La fondation de l'universalisme*. Paris: Presses Universitaires de France, 1997.

Bailey, Randall C. "The Danger of Ignoring One's Own Cultural Bias in Interpreting the Text." In *The Postcolonial Bible*, edited by R. S. Sugirtharajah, 66–90. Sheffield: Sheffield Academic Press, 1998.

———, ed. *Yet With a Steady Beat: Contemporary U.S. Afrocentric Biblical Interpretation*. Atlanta: Society of Biblical Literature, 2003.

Baker, James N. "The Presence of the Name: Reading Scripture in an Indonesian Village." In *The Ethnography of Reading*, edited by Jonathan Boyarin, 98–138. Berkeley: University of California Press, 1993.

Bakhtin, M. M. *Speech Genres and Other Late Essays*. Austin: University of Texas Press, 1986.

Barlow, Philip L. *Mormons and the Bible: The Place of the Latter-Day Saints in American Religion*. New York: Oxford University Press, 1991.

Barth, Fredrik. *Ethnic Groups and Boundaries: The Social Organization of Cultural Difference*. Prospect Heights, IL: Waveland Press, 1969.

Bell, Catherine. "'A Precious Raft to Save the World': The Interaction of Scriptural Traditions and Printing in a Chinese Morality Book." *Late Imperial China* 17 (June 1996): 158–200.

———. "Printing and Religion in China: Some Evidence from the Taishang Ganying Pian." *Journal of Chinese Religions* 20 (Fall 1992): 173–186.

Bellah, Robert N. *The Broken Covenant: American Civil Religion in Time of Trial*. Chicago: University of Chicago Press, 1975.

Bhabha, Homi K. *The Location of Culture*. London: Routledge, 1994.

Boyarin, Daniel. *Intertextuality and the Reading of Midrash*. Bloomington: Indiana University Press, 1990.

Bravmann, René A. *African Islam*. Washington DC: Smithsonian Institution Press, 1983.

Canfield, Joseph M. *The Incredible Scofield and His Book*. Vallecito, CA: Ross House Books, 1988.

Certeau, Michel de. *The Practice of Everyday Life*, translated by Steven Rendall. Berkeley: University of California Press, 1984.

———. "On the Oppositional Practices of Everyday Life." *Social Text* 3 (Fall 1980): 3–43.

Chang, K. C. *Arts, Myth, and Ritual: The Path to Political Authority in Ancient China*. Cambridge, MA: Harvard University Press, 1983.

Chevillard-Maubuisson, Anne, and Alain Marchadour. "Caïn et Abel: Lecture et relectures." In *Le Temps de la lecture: Exégèse biblique et sémiotique: Recueil d'hommages pour Jean Delorme*, edited by Louis Panier, 267–288. Paris: Les Éditions du cerf, 1993.

Chireau, Yvonne. *Black Magic: African American Religion and the Conjuring Tradition*. Berkeley: University of California Press, 2003.

———. "The Uses of the Supernatural: Towards a History of Black Women's Magical Practices." In *A Mighty Baptism: Race, Gender, and the Creation of American Protestantism*, edited by Susan Juster, 171–188. Ithaca, NY: Cornell University Press, 1996.

———. "Varieties of Spiritual Experience: Magic, Occultism, and Alternative Supernatural Traditions Among African Americans in the Cities, 1915–1939." In *The Black Urban Community: From Dusk Till Dawn*, edited by Gayle Tate and Lewis A. Randolph. New York, NY: Palgrave Macmillan, 2006.

Clarke, Sathianathan. *Dalits and Christianity: Subaltern Religion and Liberation Theology in India*. New Delhi: Oxford University Press, 1998.

———. "Viewing the Bible Through the Eyes and Ears of Subalterns in India." *Biblical Interpretations* 10 (2002): 245–266.

Comaroff, Jean, and John Comaroff. *Of Revelation and Revolution*, vol. 2 of *The Dialectics of Modernity on a South African Frontier*. Chicago: The University of Chicago Press, 1997.

Cone, James H. *The Spirituals and the Blues: An Interpretation*. New York: The Seabury Press, 1972.

Dening, Greg. *Performances*. Chicago: University of Chicago Press, 1996.

Denzin, Norman K. *Performance Ethnography: Critical Pedagogy and the Politics of Culture*. Thousand Oaks, CA: Sage, 2003.

Deol, Jeewan Singh. "Illustration and Illumination in Sikh Scriptural Manuscripts." In *New Insights into Sikh Art*, edited by Kavita Singh, 50–67. Mumbai: Marg, 2003.

Derrida, Jacques. "Faith and Reason." In *Acts of Religion*, edited by Gil Anidjar and translated by Samuel Weber. New York: Routledge, 2002.

———. "Force of Law: The Mystical Foundation of the Law." In *Deconstruction and the Possibility of Justice*, edited by Drucilla Cornell, Michael Rosenfeld, and David Gray Nelson, 3–67. New York: Routledge, 1992.

Derrida, Jacques, and Bernard Stiegler. *Echographies of Television*, translated by Jennifer Bajorek. Cambridge: Polity Press, 2002.

Díaz-Stevens, Ana María. "In the Image and Likeness of God: Literature as Theological Reflection." In *Hispanic/Latino Theology: Challenge and Promise*, edited by Ada María Isasi-Díaz and Fernando F. Segovia, 86–103. Minneapolis: Fortress Press, 1996.

Díaz-Stevens, Ana Maria, and Anthony M. Stevens-Arroyo. *Recognizing the Latino Resurgence in U.S. Religion: The Emmaus Paradigm*. Boulder, CO: Westview Press, 1998.

Douglas, Mary. *Natural Symbols: Explorations in Cosmology*. London: Barrie and Rockliff, 1970.

———. *Purity and Danger*. London: ARK Paperbacks, 1966.

Dube, Musa, ed. *Other Ways of Reading: African Women and the Bible*. Atlanta: Society of Biblical Literature, 2001.

Eliot, John, and Thomas Mayhew Jr. *Tears of Repentance Or A Further Narrative of the Progress of the Gospel Amongst the Indians in New England*. London: Peter Cole, 1653.

Ellens, J. Harold, ed. *The Destructive Power of Religion: Violence in Judaism, Christianity, and Islam*. Westport, CT: Praeger, 2004.

Enwall, Joakim. "The Bible Translations into Miao: Chinese Influence Versus Linguistic Autonomy." In *Bible in Modern China: The Literary and Intellectual Impact*, edited by I. Eber et al., 199–234. Sankt Augustin: Institut Monumenta Serica, 1999.

Esack, Farid. *The Qur'an: A Short Introduction*. Oxford: OneWorld, 2002.

Fabre, Geneviève, and Robert O'Meally, eds. *History and Memory in African American Culture*. New York: Oxford University Press, 1994.

Fanon, Franz. *The Wretched of the Earth*. 1963. Reprint, New York, Grove Press, 1965.

Faur, Jose. *Golden Doves with Silver Dots: Semiotics and Textuality in Rabbinic Tradition*. Bloomington: Indiana University Press, 1986.

Felder, Cain H., ed. *Stony the Road We Trod: African American Biblical Interpretation*. Minneapolis: Fortress Press, 1991.

Feldman, Allen. *Formations of Violence*. Chicago: University of Chicago Press, 1991.

Fernández Armesto, Felipe, and Derek Wilson. *Reformations: A Radical Interpretation of Christianity and the World (1500–2000)*. New York: Scribners, 1996.

Finke, Roger, and Rodney Stark. *The Churching of America, 1776–1990*. New Brunswick, NJ: Rutgers University Press, 1992.

Foucault, Michel. *Archaeology of Knowledge*, translated by A. M. Sheridan Smith. 1969. Reprint, New York: Pantheon Books, 1972.

Freud, Sigmund. *Civilization and Its Discontents*, edited and translated by James Strachey. 1930. Reprint, New York: W. W. Norton, 1961.

Gadamer, Hans Georg. *Truth and Method and Philosophical Hermeneutics*. Berkeley: University of California Press, 1976.

Gaither, Joan E. *Choice, Identity, and Layers of Meaning*. Baltimore: Maryland Institute College of Art, Pinkard Gallery, 2004.

Gates, Henry Louis, Jr. "Blackness of Blackness: A Critique of the Sign and the Signifying Monkey." In *Figures in Black: Words, Signs, and the "Racial" Self*, 235–276. New York: Oxford University Press, 1987.

———. "Canon-Formation, Literary History, and the Afro-American Tradition: From the Seen to the Told." In *Afro-American Literary Study in the 1990s*, edited by Houston A. Baker Jr. and Patricia Redmond, 14–38. Chicago: University of Chicago Press, 1989.

———. *The Signifying Monkey: A Theory of African-American Literary Criticism*. New York: Oxford University Press, 1988.

Gilmont, Jean-François. "Protestant Reformations and Reading." In *A History of Reading in the West*, edited by G. Cavallo and R. Chartier, 213–237. Oxford: Polity Press, 1999.

Givens, Terryl. *By the Hand of Mormon: The American Scripture That Launched a New World Religion*. New York: Oxford University Press, 2002.

Golden, Mark, and Peter Toohey, eds. *Inventing Ancient Culture: Historicism, Periodization, and the Ancient World*. New York: Routledge, 1997.

Goldschmidt, Henry, and Elizabeth McAlister, eds. *Race, Nation, and Religion in the Americas*. New York: Oxford University Press, 2004.

Goody, Jack. *The Interface Between the Written and the Oral*. New York: Cambridge University Press, 1987.

———. *The Logic of Writing and the Organization of Society*. New York: Cambridge University Press, 1986.

Goody, Jack, and Ian Watt. "The Consequences of Literacy." In *Literacy in Traditional Societies*, edited by Jack Goody, 27–68. Cambridge: Cambridge University Press, 1968.

Graham, William A. *Beyond the Written Word: Oral Aspects of Scripture in the History of Religion*. Cambridge: Cambridge University Press, 1987.

———. "Scripture." In *The Encyclopedia of Religions*, vol. 13, edited by Mircea Eliade. New York: Macmillan, 1987.

Gruzinski, Serge. "La occidentalización y los vestigios de las imágenes maravillosas." In *Barrocos y Modernos: Nuevos caminos en la investigación del Barroco iberoamericano*, edited by Petra Schumm, 355–370. Frankfurt: Vervuert, 1998.

Guha, Ranajit. *Dominance Without Hegemony*. Cambridge, MA: Harvard University Press, 1997.

Guha, Ranajit, and Gayatri Chakravorty Spivak, eds. *Selected Subaltern Studies*. New York: Oxford University Press, 1988.

Gundaker, Grey. *Signs of Diaspora/Diaspora of Signs: Literacies, Creolization, and Vernacular Practice in African America*. New York: Oxford University Press, 1998.

Gutjahr, Paul C. *An American Bible: A History of the Good Book in the United States, 1777–1880*. Stanford, CA: Stanford University Press, 1999.

Habermas, Jürgen. "Ideology." In *Modern Interpretations of Marx*, edited by Tom Bottomore, 155–170. Oxford: Blackwell, 1981.

Handelman, Susan. *The Slayers of Moses: The Re-emergence of Rabbinic Interpretation in Modern Literary Theory*. Albany: SUNY Press, 1982.

Harding, Susan F. *The Book of Jerry Falwell: Fundamentalist Language and Politics*. Princeton, NJ: Princeton University Press, 2000.

Harris, Leonard. "Honor and Insurrection." In *Frederick Douglass*, edited by Bill E. Lawson, 227–242. Oxford: Blackwell Publishing Company, 1999.

———. "Honor, Eunuchs, and the Postcolonial Subject." In *Postcolonial African Philosophy*, edited by Emmanuel C. Eze, 252–259. Oxford: Blackwell Publishing Company, 1997.

Harris, Roy. *Signs of Writing*. New York: Routledge, 1995.

Harrison, Nick. "Sacred Texts: It's Still the Good Book." *Publishers Weekly* (October 13, 1997): 32–40.

Havelock, Eric A. *Origins of Western Literacy*. Toronto: Ontario Institute for Studies in Education, 1976.

Hawley, J. S., and M. Juergensmeyer, eds. *Songs of the Saints of India*. New York: Oxford University Press, 1988.

Hewitt, Marsha Aileen. *Critical Theory of Religion: A Feminist Analysis*. Minneapolis: Fortress Press, 1995.

Hills, Margaret. *The English Bible in America*. New York: American Bible Society, 1962.

Hobsbawm, Eric, and Terence Ranger, eds. *The Invention of Tradition*. Cambridge: Cambridge University Press, 1983.

Holdrege, Barbara. *Veda and Torah: Transcending the Textuality of Scripture*. Albany: SUNY Press, 1996.

Hughes, Langston, and Zora Neale Hurston. *Mule Bone: A Comedy of Negro Life*. New York: HarperCollins, 1991.

Hurston, Zora Neale. *The Complete Stories*. New York: HarperCollins, 1995.

———. *Folklore, Memoirs, and Other Writings*. New York: Library of America, 1995.

———. "Hoodoo in America." *Journal of American Folklore* 44 (October–December, 1931): 317–417.

———. *Novels and Stories*. New York: Library of America, 1995.

———. *The Sanctified Church*. Berkeley, CA: Turtle Island, 1983.

———. *Voodoo Gods: An Inquiry into Native Myths and Magic in Jamaica and Haiti*. London: J. M. Dent, 1939.

Jaffee, Martin. "The Oral-Cultural Context of the Talmud Yerushalmi." In *The Talmud Yerushalmi and Graeco-Roman Culture I*, edited by Peter Schäfer, 27–61. Tübingen: Mohr/ Siebeck, 1998.

Jameson, Fredric. *The Political Unconscious: Narrative as a Socially Symbolic Act*. Ithaca, NY: Cornell University Press, 1981.

———. "Postmodernism and the Cultural Logic of Late Capitalism." *New Left Review* 146 (1984): 53–92.

Jowett, Garth S., and Victoria O'Donnell. *Propaganda and Persuasion*. Newbury Park, CA: Sage, 1986.

Kent, Eliza F. "Tamil Bible Women and the Zenana Missions of Colonial South India." *History of Religions* 39 (November 1999): 117–149.

Kohli, Surinder Singh. *A Critical Study of the Adi Granth*. Delhi: Motilal Banarasidass, 1961.

Kooij, A. van der, and K. van der Toorn, eds., with an annotated bibliography compiled by J.A.M. Snoek. *Canonization and Decanonization: Papers Presented to the International Conference of the Leiden Institute for the Study of Religions (Lisor), Held at Leiden 9–10 January 1997*. Leiden: Brill, 1998.

Kort, Wesley A. *Place and Space in Modern Fiction*. Gainesville, FL: University of Florida Press, 2004.

———. *Story, Text and Scripture: Literary Interests in Biblical Narrative*. University Park: Pennsylvania State University Press, 1989.

———. *"Take, Read": Scripture, Textuality and Cultural Practice*. University Park: Pennsylvania State University Press, 1996.

Lafaye, Jacques. *Quetzalcoatl and Guadalupe: The Formation of Mexican National Consciousness, 1531–1813*, translated by Benjamin Keen. 1974. Reprint, Chicago: University of Chicago Press, 1976.

Levering, Miriam, ed. *Rethinking Scripture: Essays from a Comparative Perspective*. Albany: SUNY Press, 1989.

Lieberman, Saul. "Rabbinic Interpretation of Scripture." In *Hellenism in Jewish Palestine*, 47–82. New York: JTSA, 1950.

Liew, Tat-siong Benny, ed. *The Bible in Asian America*. Atlanta: Society of Biblical Literature, 2002.

Locke, Alain. "Freedom Through Art: Review of Negro Art, 1870–1938." *The Crisis* 45 (July 1938): 227–229.

Logan, Robert K. *The Alphabet Effect: The Impact of the Phonetic Alphabet on the Development of Western Civilization*. New York: St. Martins Press, 1986.

Long, Charles H. *Significations: Signs, Symbols, and Images in the Interpretation of Religion*. Minneapolis: Fortress Press, 1986.

Lounsbury, Floyd G. "The Ancient Writing of Middle America." In *The Origins of Writing*, edited by Wayne M. Senner, 203–238. Lincoln: University of Nebraska Press, 1989.

Madigan, Daniel. *The Qur'an's Self-Image: Writing and Authority in Islam's Scripture*. Princeton, NJ: Princeton University Press, 2001.

Maduro, Otto A. *Religion and Social Conflicts*. Maryknoll, NY: Orbis Books. 1982.

Maier, Gerhard, ed. *Der Kanon der Bibel*. Giessen: Brunnen Verlag, 1990.

Mann, Barbara. "The Fire at Onondaga: Wampum as Proto-writing." *Akwesasne Notes: A Journal of Native and Natural Peoples*, 26th Anniversary Issue 1 (Spring 1995): 40–48.

Mann, Gurinder Singh. *The Making of Sikh Scripture*. New York: Oxford University Press, 2001.

———. *Sikhism*. Upper Saddle River, NJ: Prentice Hall, 2004.

Maravall, José Antonio. *Culture of the Baroque: Analysis of a Historical Structure*, translated by Terry Cochran. 1975. Reprint, Minneapolis: University of Minnesota Press, 1986.

Marrouchi, Mustapha. *Signifying with a Vengeance: Theories, Literatures, Storytellers*. Albany: SUNY Press, 2002.

Martin, Henri-Jean. *The History and Power of Writing*. Chicago: University of Chicago Press, 1994.

McDannell, Colleen. *Material Christianity: Religion and Popular Culture in America*. New Haven, CT: Yale University Press, 1995.

McWillie, Judith. "Writing in an Unknown Tongue." In *Cultural Perspectives on the American South*, edited by Charles Reagan Wilson, 103–117. New York: Gordon and Breach, 1991.

Mignolo, Walter D. "Signs and Their Transmission: The Question of the Book in the New World." In *Writing Without Words: Alternative Literacies in Mesoamerica and the Andes*, edited by Elizabeth Hill Boone and Walter D. Mignolo, 220–270. Durham, NC: Duke University Press, 1996.

Miller, Keith. *The Voice of Deliverance: The Language of Martin Luther King, Jr. and Its Sources*. New York: The Free Press, 1992.

Mitchell, W.J.T., ed. *Iconology: Image, Text, Ideology*. Chicago: University of Chicago Press, 1987.

Mitchell-Kernan, Claudia. "Signifying." In *Mother Wit from the Laughing Barrel: Readings in the Interpretation of Afro-American Folklore*, edited by Alan Dundes, 310–328. Englewood Cliffs, NJ: Prentice Hall, 1973.

Mohanty, Satya P. *Literary Theory and the Claims of History: Postmodernism, Objectivity, Multicultural Politics.* Ithaca, NY: Cornell University Press, 1997.

Monier-Williams, M. *The Holy Bible and the Sacred Books of the East: Four Addresses to Which Added a Fifth Address on Zenana Mission.* London: Seeley and Co., 1887.

———. *Modern India and Indians.* London: Trübner and Co., 1889.

Morrison, Toni. *Playing in the Dark: Whiteness and the Literary Imagination.* Cambridge, MA: Harvard University Press, 1992.

Moses, Wilson Jeremiah. *Afrotopia: The Roots of African American Popular History.* Cambridge: Cambridge University Press, 1998.

Moziani, Eliyahi, Jr. *Torah of the Alphabet, Or, How the Art of Writing Was Taught Under the Judges of Israel (1441–1025).* Herborn: Baalschem Press, 1984.

Ong, Walter J. *Orality and Literacy: The Technologizing of the Word.* New York: Methuen, 1982.

Page, Hugh R., Jr. "Ethnological Criticism: An Apologia and Application." In *Exploring New Paradigms in Biblical and Cognate Studies*, edited by H. R. Page Jr. Lewiston: Mellen Biblical Press, 1996.

Persuitte, David. *Joseph Smith and the Origins of the Book of Mormon.* Jefferson, NC: McFarland, 2000.

Polk, Patrick A. "Other Books, Other Powers: the Sixth and Seventh Books of Moses in Afro-Atlantic Folk Belief." *Southern Folklore* 56 (1999): 115–133.

Pollock, S. "Deep Orientalism? Notes on Sanskrit and Power Beyond the Raj." In *Orientalism and the Postcolonial Predicament: Perspectives on South Asia*, edited by Carol A. Breckenridge and Peter van der Veer. Philadelphia: University of Pennsylvania Press, 1993.

Quiñones Keber, Eloise, ed. *Codex Telleriano-Remensis: Ritual, Divination, and History in a Pictorial Aztec Manuscript.* Austin: University of Texas Press, 1995.

Quintero Rivera, Angel A., ed. *Virgenes, Magos y Escapularios: Imaginería, Etnicidad y Religiosidad Popular en Puerto Rico.* San Juan: Centro de Investigaciones Sociales, Universidad de Puerto Rico, 1998.

Rabasa, José. "Franciscans and Dominicans under the Gaze of a Tlacuilo: Plural-World Dwelling in an Indian Pictorial Codex." Morrison Library Inaugural Lecture Series 14. Berkeley: Doe Library, 1998.

———. *Inventing America: Spanish Historiography and the Formation of Eurocentrism.* Norman: University of Oklahoma Press, 1993.

———. "Pre-Colombian Pasts and Indian Presents in Mexican History." In *Subaltern Studies in the Americas*, edited by José Rabasa et al. Special issue, *Dispositio/n* 46 (1996): 245–270.

Ramsey, Guthrie P., Jr. *Race Music: Black Cultures from Bebop to Hip-Hop.* Berkeley: University of California Press, 2003.

Rawick, George P., ed. *The American Slave: A Composite Autobiography*, supplement, series 2. vol. 2 of *Texas Narratives*, edited by Jan Hillegas and Ken Lawrence. Westport, CT: Greenwood Press, 1979.

Ricoeur, Paul. *Hermeneutics and the Human Sciences*, edited and translated by John B. Thompson. Cambridge: Cambridge University Press, 1981.

Rivera Pagán, Luis N. *Evangelización y Violencia: La Conquista de América*. San Juan: Ediciones Cemi. Translated by Luis Rivera as *A Violent Evangelism: The Political and Religious Conquest of the Americas*. 1991. Reprint, Louisville, KY: Westminster/John Knox Press, 1992.

Runions, Erin. *Changing Subjects: Gender, Nation, and Future in Micah*. New York: Sheffield Academic Press, 2001.

Sakai, Tadao. "Confucianism and Popular Education Works." In *Self and Society in Ming Thought*, edited by Wm. Theodore de Barry and the Conference on Ming Thought. New York: Columbia University Press, 1970.

Schmid, Alex P., and Janny de Graf. *Violence as Communication: Insurgent Terrorism and the Western News Media*. London: Sage, 1982.

Schüssler Fiorenza, Elisabeth. *Bread Not Stone: The Challenge of Feminist Biblical Interpretation*. Boston: Beacon Press, 1984.

———. "The Contribution of Catholic Orthodoxy to Caribbean Syncretism: The Case of La Virgen de la Caridad del Cobre in Cuba." *Archives de Sciences Sociales des Religions* 117 (2002): 37–57.

———. "Defending the Center, Trivializing the Margins." In *Reading the Bible in the Global Village*, edited by Heikki Räisänen, 29–48. Atlanta: SBL, 2000.

———. "Earth Religions and Book Religions: Baroque Catholicism as Openness to Earth Religions." *Comparative Civilizations Review* 49 (Fall 2003): 54–75.

———. "Earth Religions and Book Religions: The Religious Door to Civilizational Encounter." *Comparative Civilizations Review* 48 (Spring 2003): 65–82.

———. "The Emergence of a Social Identity Among Latino Catholics: An Appraisal." In *Hispanic Catholic Culture in the U.S.: Issues and Concerns*, edited by Jay Dolan and Allan Figueroa Deck, 77–130. Notre Dame, IN: University of Notre Dame Press, 1994.

———. *An Enduring Flame: Studies in Latino Popular Religiosity*. New York: Bildner Center Books, 1994.

———. "The Ethics of Interpretation: De-Centering Biblical Scholarship." *Journal of Biblical Literature* 107 (1988): 3–17.

———. "The Evolution of Marian Devotionalism Within Christianity and the Ibero-Mediterranean Polity." *Journal for the Scientific Study of Religion* 37 (1998): 50–73.

———. "For the Sake of Our Salvation: Biblical Interpretation and the Community of Faith." In *Sin, Salvation and the Spirit*, edited by D. Durken, 21–39. Collegeville, MN: Liturgical Press, 1979.

———. "The Phenomenon of Early Christian Apocalyptic: Some Reflections on Method." In *Apocalypticism in the Mediterranean World and the Near East Proceedings of the International Colloquium on Apocalypticism, Uppsala, August 12–17, 1979*, 2nd ed, edited by David Hellholm, 295–316. Tübingen: J.C.B. Mohr, 1989.

———. *Rhetoric and Ethic: The Politics of Biblical Studies*. Minneapolis: Fortress Press, 2000.

———. *Wisdom Ways: Introducing Feminist Biblical Interpretation*. Maryknoll, NY: Orbis Books, 2001.

Schüssler Fiorenza, Elisabeth, and Ana María Díaz-Stevens. "Religious Faith and Institutions in the Forging of Latino Identities." In *Handbook for Hispanic Cultures in the United States*, edited by Felix Padilla, 257–291. Houston: Arte Publico Press, 1993.

Schüssler Fiorenza, Elisabeth, and Andrés I. Pérez y Mena, eds. *Enigmatic Powers: Syncretism with African and Indigenous Peoples' Religions Among Latinos*. New York: Bildner Center Books, 1995.

Scott, James C. *Domination and the Arts of Resistance: Hidden Transcripts*. New Haven, CT: Yale University Press, 1990.

———. "Protest and Profanation." *Theory and Society* 4 (1977): 1–38.

———. *Weapons of the Weak: Everyday Forms of Peasant Resistance*. New Haven, CT: Yale University Press, 1985.

Segovia, Fernando. *Decolonizing Biblical Studies*. Maryknoll, NY: Orbis Books, 2000.

Simian, Lü. *Introduction to Pre-Qin Thought*. Shanghai: Chinese Encyclopedia Publishing House, 1985.

———. "The Similarities and Differences Between the Musician and the Historiographer Tradition and Their Implications." In *The Musician and the Historiographer: Collected Papers on Traditional Chinese Political Culture and Political Institutions*. Beijing: Sanlian Shudian, 2001.

Singh, Harbhajan. *Gurbanhi Sampadan Nirnai*. Chandigarh: Satinam Prakashan, 1989.

Singh, Pashaura. *The Guru Granth Sahib*. New Delhi: Oxford University Press, 2000.

Smith, Jonathan Riley. "Religious Authority." In *The Future of the Past: Big Questions in History*, edited by Peter Martland, 1–15. London: Pimlico, 2002.

Smith, Theophus H. *Conjuring Culture: Biblical Formations of Black America*. New York: Oxford University Press, 1994.

Smith, W. C. *What Is Scripture? A Comparative Approach*. Minneapolis: Fortress Press, 1993.

Smitherman, Geneva. *Talkin' That Talk: Language, Culture, and Education in African America*. 1999. Reprint, New York: Routledge, 2001.

Stevens-Arroyo, Anthony M. "The Inter-Atlantic Paradigm: The Failure of Spanish Medieval Colonialism of the Canary and Caribbean Islands." *Comparative Studies in Society and History* 35 (July 1993): 515–543.

Stock, Brian. *Listening for the Text: On the Uses of the Past*. Baltimore: Johns Hopkins University Press, 1990.

Street, Brian V. *Literacy in Theory and Practice*. New York: Cambridge University Press, 1984.

Sugirtharajah, R. S., ed. *Asian Biblical Hermeneutics and Postcolonialism*. Maryknoll, NY: Orbis Books 1999.

——, ed. *The Bible and The Third World: Precolonial, Colonial, and Postcolonial Encounters*. New York: Cambridge University Press, 2001.

Sundquist, Eric. *To Wake the Nations*. Cambridge, MA: Harvard University Press, 1993.

Taji-Farouki, Suha, ed. *Modern Muslim Intellectuals and the Qur'an*. Oxford: Oxford University Press, 2004.

Thompson, John B. *Studies in the Theory of Ideology*. Cambridge: Polity Press, 1984.

Tinker, George E. *Missionary Conquest: The Gospel and Native American Cultural Genocide*. Minneapolis: Fortress Press, 1993.

Trible, Phyllis. *Texts of Terror: Literary-Feminist Readings of Biblical Narratives*. Philadelphia: Fortress Press, 1984.

Tweed, Thomas A. *Our Lady of the Exile: Diasporic Religion at a Cuban Catholic Shrine in Miami*. New York: Oxford University Press, 1997.

Vermes, Geza. *Scripture and Tradition in Judaism*, 2nd ed. Leiden: Brill, 1973.

Visotzky, Burton L. "Jots and Tittles: On Scriptural Interpretation in Rabbinic and Patristic Literatures." In *Fathers of the World: Essays in Rabbinic and Patristic Literatures*, 28–40. Tübingen: Mohr/Siebeck, 1995.

——. "The Literature of the Rabbis." In *From Mesopotamia to Modernity: Ten Introductions to Jewish History and Literature*, edited by Burton L. Visotzky and David E. Fishman, 71–102. Boulder, CO: Westview Press, 1999.

——. "Stranger and Stranger in a Strange Land." *CommonQuest* 3 (Winter 1998): 4–6.

Vovelle, Michel. *Ideologies and Mentalities*. Chicago: University of Chicago Press, 1990.

Walls, Neal. *Desire, Discord, and Death: Approaches to Ancient Near Eastern Myth*. Boston: American Schools of Oriental Research, 2001.

Wan, Sze-kar. "Allegorical Interpretation East and West: A Methodological Enquiry into Comparative Hermeneutics." In *Text and Experience: Towards a Cultural Exegesis of the Bible*, edited by Daniel Smith-Christopher, 154–179. Sheffield: Sheffield Academic Press, 1995.

Weber, Max. *The Protestant Ethic and the Spirit of Capitalism*. 1904. Reprint, London: Routledge, 1930.

Webster, Edward. *Print Unchained: Fifty Years of Digital Printing, 1950–2000 and Beyond—A Saga of Invention and Enterprise*. New Castle, DE: Oak Knoll Press 2000.

Williams, Rhys H. "Religion as Political Resource: Culture or Ideology?" *Journal for the Scientific Study of Religion* 35 (1996): 368–378.

Wimbush, Vincent L. *The Bible and African Americans: A Brief History*. Minneapolis: Fortress Press, 2003.

———. *The Bible and the American Myth: A Symposium on the Bible and the Construction of Meaning*. Macon, GA: Mercer University Press, 1999.

———, ed., with the assistance of Rosamond C. Rodman. *African Americans and the Bible: Sacred Texts and Social Textures*. 2000. Reprint, New York: Continuum, 2001.

Wink, Andre. *The Making of the Indo-Islamic World*. New York: Oxford University Press, 1997.

Wright, Jeremiah A. "Music as Cultural Expression in Black Church Theology and Worship." *The Journal of Black Sacred Music* 3 (Spring 1989): 1–5.

Wyatt, N., ed. *Religious Texts from Ugarit: The Words of Ilimilku and His Colleagues*. Sheffield: Sheffield Academic Press, 1998.

Wyss, Hilary E. *Writing Indians: Literacy, Christianity, and Native Community in Early America*. Boston: University of Massachusetts Press, 2000.

Žižek, Slavoj. *Mapping Ideology*. London: Verso, 1994.

———. *The Sublime Object of Ideology*. Phronesis. London: Verso, 1989.

Notes on Contributors

WILLIAM L. ANDREWS is the E. Maynard Adams Professor of English at the University of North Carolina, Chapel Hill. His publications include *To Tell a Free Story: The First Century of African American Autobiography, 1760–1865* (Urbana: University of Illinois Press, 1986). His edited volumes include *Classic African American Women's Narratives* (New York: Oxford University Press, 2002).

CATHERINE BELL is the Bernard J. Hanley Professor of Religious Studies at Santa Clara University. Her publications include *Ritual: Dimensions and Perspectives* (New York: Oxford University Press, 1997) and *Ritual Theory, Ritual Practice* (New York: Oxford University Press, 1992).

YVONNE P. CHIREAU is associate professor of religion at Swarthmore College. Her publications include *Dimensions of the Supernatural in African American Religion* (Berkeley: University of California Press, 2006) and *Black Magic: Religion and the African American Conjuring Tradition* (Berkeley: University of California Press, 2003).

SATHIANATHAN CLARKE is professor of theology, culture, and mission at Wesley Theological Seminary. His publications include *Dalits and Christianity: Subaltern Religion and Liberation Theology in India* (New Delhi: Oxford University Press, 1998) and "Dalit Religion as Resourceful Symbolic Domain," *Religion and Society* 49, nos. 2, 3 (2004): 30–48.

JO DIAMOND is lecturer in the School of Fine Arts at the University of Canterbury, Christchurch, New Zealand. Her publications include "Royn Kahukiwa: Nurturing Mäori Identity," *Art AsiaPacific Quarterly* 23 (2002): 76–81, and "Hine-Titama: Mäori Contributions to Feminist Discourses and Identity Politics," *Australian Journal of Social Issues* 34, no. 4 (1999): 310–317.

JACQUELINE COGDELL DJEDJE is professor of ethnomusicology as well as chair and director of the ethnomusicology archive at the University of California, Los Angeles. Her publications include *American Black Spiritual and Gospel Songs from Southeast Georgia: A Comparative Study* (Los Angeles: UCLA Center for Afro-American Studies, 1978). Her edited volumes include *California Soul: Music of African Americans in the West*, with Eddie S. Meadows (Berkeley: University of California Press, 1998).

LAURA E. DONALDSON is associate professor of English at Cornell University. Her publications include *Decolonizing Feminisms: Race, Gender, and Empire-Building*

(Chapel Hill: University of North Carolina Press, 1992). Her edited volumes include *Postcolonialism, Feminism and Religious Discourse*, with Kwok Pui-Lan (New York: Routledge, 2001).

GREY GUNDAKER is associate professor of anthropology and director of the American studies program at the College of William and Mary. Her publications include *No Space Hidden: The Spirit of African American Yardwork*, with Judith McWillie (Knoxville: University of Tennessee Press, 2004) and *Signs of Diaspora/Diaspora of Signs: Creolization, Literacy, and Vernacular Practice in African America* (New York: Oxford University Press, 1998).

SUSAN F. HARDING is professor of anthropology at the University of California, Santa Cruz. Her publications include *The Book of Jerry Falwell: Fundamentalist Language and Politics* (Princeton, N.J.: Princeton University Press, 2002). Her edited volumes include *Histories of the Future*, with Daniel Rosenberg (Durham, N.C.: Duke University Press, 2005).

LEONARD HARRIS is professor of philosophy at Purdue University. His edited volumes include *Racism* (New York: Humanity Press, 1999) and *Exploitation and Exclusion: Race and Class in Contemporary U.S. Society*, with Abebe Zegeye and Julia Maxted (London: Hans Zell Publishing Co., 1991).

TAZIM R. KASSAM is associate professor of religion and director of graduate studies at Syracuse University. Her publications include *Songs of Wisdom and Circles of Dance: Hymns of the Satpanth Ismaili Saint, Pir Shams* (Albany, NY: SUNY Press, 1995) and "Balancing Acts: Negotiating the Ethics of Scholarship and Identity," in *Identity and the Politics of Scholarship in the Study of Religion*, ed. Sheila Devaney and José Cabezón (New York: Routledge, 2004), 133–162.

LESLIE KING-HAMMOND is the graduate dean at the Maryland Institute College of Art. Her publications include *Amalia Amaki: Boxes, Buttons, and the Blues*, with Andrea D. Barnwell and Gloria Wade Gayles (Seattle: University of Washington Press, 2005) and *Casting Shadows: Images from a New South Africa*, with Edward West (Ann Arbor: University of Michigan Museum of Art, 2001).

WESLEY A. KORT is professor in and chair of the department of religion at Duke University. His publications include *"Take, Read": Scripture, Textuality and Cultural Practice* (University Park: Pennsylvania State University Press, 1996) and *Story, Text, and Scripture: Literary Interests in Biblical Narrative* (University Park: Pennsylvania State University Press, 1988).

GURINDER SINGH MANN is professor of global studies and religious studies at the University of California, Santa Barbara. His publications include *The Making of Sikh Scripture* (New York: Oxford University Press, 2001) and *Buddhists, Hindus, and Sikhs in America*, with Paul David Numrich and Raymond Brady Williams (New York: Oxford University Press, 2001).

COLLEEN MCDANNELL is the Sterling McMurrin Professor of religious studies and professor of history at the University of Utah. Her publications include *Picturing Faith: Religious America in Government Photography, 1935–1943* (New Haven, CT: Yale University Press, 2004) and *Material Christianity: Religion and Popular Culture in America* (New Haven, CT: Yale University Press, 1995).

OYERONKE OLAJUBU is senior lecturer of comparative religion at the University of Ilorin, Nigeria. Her publications include *Women in the Yoruba Religious Sphere* (Albany, NY: SUNY Press, 2003) and "Seeing through a Woman's Eye: Yoruba Religious Tradition and Gender Relations," *Journal of Feminist Studies in Religion* 20, no. 1 (2004): 41–60.

PATRICK OLIVELLE is professor of sanskrit and Indian religions and chair of the department of Asian studies at the University of Texas, Austin. His publications include *The Āśrama System: History and Hermeneutics of a Religious Institution* (New York: Oxford University Press, 1993). His edited volumes include *Dharma: Studies in Its Semantic, Cultural, and Religious History*, special double issue of *Journal of Indian Philosophy* 32 (2004): 421–873.

HUGH R. PAGE JR. is dean of first year of studies at the University of Notre Dame. His publications include *The Myth of Cosmic Rebellion: A Study of Its Reflexes in Ugaritic and Biblical Literature*, supplements to *Vetus Testamentum* 65 (Leiden: E. J. Brill, 1996). His edited volumes include *Exploring New Paradigms in Biblical and Cognate Studies* (Macon, GA: Mellen Biblical Press, 1996).

JOSEPH PARKER is associate professor of international and intercultural studies at Pitzer College. His publications include *Zen Buddhist Landscape Arts of Early Muromachi Japan (1336–1578)* (Albany, NY: SUNY Press, 1999) and "Contested Orthodoxies in Five Mountains Zen Buddhism," in *Religions of Japan in Practice*, ed. George Tanabe Jr. (Princeton, N.J.: Princeton University Press, 1999), 423–434.

JOSÉ RABASA is chair of and professor in the department of Spanish and Portuguese at the University of California, Berkeley. His publications include *Writing Violence on the Northern Frontier* (Durham, N.C.: Duke University Press, 2000) and *Inventing America: Spanish Historiography and the Formation of Eurocentrism* (Norman: University of Oklahoma Press, 1993).

ERIN RUNIONS is assistant professor of religious studies at Pomona College. Her publications include *How Hysterical: Identification and Resistance in the Bible and Film* (New York: Palgrave, 2003) and *Changing Subjects: Gender, Nation and Future in Micah* (London: Sheffield Academic Press, 2001).

RANU SAMANTRAI is director of graduate studies and professor in the English department at Indiana University. Her publications include *AlterNatives: Black Feminism in the Postimperial Nation* (Stanford, CA: Stanford University Press, 2002) and "Weapons of Culture: Collective Identity and Cultural Production," *REAL: Yearbook of Research in English and American Literature* 14 (1998): 131–148.

ELISABETH SCHÜSSLER FIORENZA is the Krister Stendhal Professor of Divinity at Harvard Divinity School. Her publications include *Wisdom Ways: Introducing Feminist Biblical Interpretation* (Maryknoll, NY: Orbis Books, 2001) and *In Memory of Her: A Feminist Theological Reconstruction of Christian Origins* (New York: Crossroad, 1983).

R. S. SUGIRTHARAJAH is professor of biblical hermeneutics at the University of Birmingham, United Kingdom. His publications include *Postcolonial Criticism and Biblical Interpretation* (New York: Oxford University Press, 2002) and *The Bible and the Third World: Precolonial, Colonial and Postcolonial Encounters* (Cambridge: Cambridge University Press, 2002).

BURTON L. VISOTZKY is the Nathan and Janet Appleman Professor of Midrash and Interreligious Studies at the Jewish Theological Seminary of America. His publications include *Fathers of the World: Essays in Rabbinic and Patristic Literature* (Tübingen: Mohr/Siebeck, 1995). His edited volumes include *From Mesopotamia to Modernity: Ten Introductions to Jewish History and Literature*, with David Fishman (Boulder, CO: Westview Press, 1999).

SZE-KAR WAN is the John Norris Professor of New Testament Interpretation at Andover Newton Theological School. His publications include *Power in Weakness: Conflict and Rhetorics in Paul's Second Letter to the Corinthians* (Valley Forge, PA: Trinity Press International, 2000). His edited volumes include *The Bible in Modern China: The Literary and Intellectual Impact*, with I. Eber and K. Walf (Sankt Augustin: Monumenta Serica, 1999).

VINCENT L. WIMBUSH is professor of religion and director of the Institute for Signifying Scriptures at Claremont Graduate University. His publications include *The Bible and African Americans: A Brief History* (Minneapolis: Fortress Press, 2003). His edited volumes include *African Americans and the Bible: Sacred Texts and Social Textures*, with the assistance of Rosamond C. Rodman (New York: Continuum, 2000).

YAN SHOUCHENG is professor of Asian languages and cultures at the National Institute of Education, Nanyang Technological University, Singapore. His publications include *Intellectual Continuity and Change in Recent China* (Taipei: National Institute for Compilation and Translation, 2003) and "Syncretism versus Synthesis: Han Yu and Liu Zongyuan in Regard to Buddhism," in *Tang Literature and Religion*, ed. Liu Chuhua (Hong Kong: Chung Hwa Book Company, 2004), 113–143.

Index